THE POLITICS OF PRAYER

THE POLITICS OF PRAYER

*Feminist Language and
The Worship of God*

Edited by
Helen Hull Hitchcock

IGNATIUS PRESS   SAN FRANCISCO

Cover art by Christopher J. Pelicano
Cover design by Roxanne Mei Lum

© 1992 Ignatius Press, San Francisco
ISBN 0–89870–418–9 (SB)
ISBN 0–89870–425–1 (HB)
Library of Congress catalogue number 92–73724
Printed in the United States of America

For my parents, Downer Lee Hull and Thelma Kelly Hull, who taught me (and countless others) to speak, read, and esteem the English language — and through whose example I learned to love the Word of God.

"And the whole earth was of one language and of one speech ... And they said: Go, let us build us a city and a tower whose top may reach unto heaven; and let us make us a name, lest we be scattered abroad upon the face of the whole earth.

"And the Lord came down to see the city and the tower, which the children of men built. And the Lord said, Behold, the people is one, and they have all one language; and this they begin to do: and now nothing will be restrained from them, which they have imagined to do.

"Let us go down and there confound their language that they may not understand one another's speech. So the Lord scattered them abroad from thence upon the face of all the earth: and they left off building the city.

"Therefore is the name of it called Babel—confusion; because the Lord did there confound the language of all the earth: and from thence did the Lord scatter them abroad upon the face of all the earth."

Genesis 11:1:4–9

"He hath scattered the proud in the imagination of their hearts."

Luke 1:51b

CONTENTS

CONTRIBUTORS

Joseph C. Beaver
Joseph C. Beaver is professor emeritus of linguistics, Northeastern Illinois University. He has published scholarly articles on linguistics and is the author of a monograph, *The Prosody of John Donne*. Professor Beaver also holds a master's degree in theology and is a licensed lay preacher in the Episcopal Church. The essay included herein appeared in 1988 in the theological journal *Dialog*.

Deborah Belonick
Deborah Malacky Belonick is a lay theologian who holds a master of divinity degree from St. Vladimir's Orthodox Theological Seminary. She is the author of *Feminism in Christianity: An Orthodox Christian Perspective* and is a member of the Orthodox Theological Society of America. Her essay in this collection first appeared in *Pastoral Renewal* in April 1986.

Peter and Brigitte Berger
Peter Berger, a sociologist, Lutheran lay theologian, and author of many books and essays on the sociology of religion and other related topics, is a university professor at the Institute for the Study of Economic Culture, Boston University. Among his best known books are *A Rumor of Angels* and *The Heretical Imperative*. Brigitte Berger, also a sociologist, is his wife and collaborator in several scholarly works, including *The War over the Family*, from which the essay included here is excerpted. She is a professor of sociology at Boston University.

Donald G. Bloesch
Dr. Bloesch, an ordained minister of the United Church of Christ, is professor of theology at the University of Dubuque Theologi-

cal Seminary and author of many scholarly books and articles. A
chapter from his 1985 book *The Battle for the Trinity* is included here.

The Rev. Lawrence C. Brennan, C.M.

Father Brennan, a Vincentian priest, is academic dean and profes-
sor of systematic theology at Kenrick-Glennon Seminary in St.
Louis. He is a representative of the National Council of Catholic
Bishops to the Commission on Faith and Order of the National
Council of Churches and a consultor to the Vatican's Pontifical
Council for Dialogue with Non-Believers.

Brother Chrysostom Castel, O.C.S.O.

Brother Chrysostom is a Cistercian monk of Gethsemani Abbey in
Trappist, Kentucky. A native of New Orleans, Brother Chrysostom
entered Gethsemani in 1961. He has served on the Abbey's Council and vocation team and is head cantor and electrician for the
monastery. The article included in this collection was first published in the *Homiletic and Pastoral Review* in April 1990.

Donald De Marco

Dr. De Marco teaches philosophy at St. Jerome's College in
Kitchener, Ontario, Canada, and has written extensively on human
sexuality. He is author of *Biotechnology and the Assault on Parenthood* (Ignatius Press, 1991). This article was first published in 1989
as a pamphlet entitled "God He/She? Inclusive Language and Its
Consequences" by Life Ethics Centre.

Roland Mushat Frye

Dr. Frye is a noted literary critic and emeritus professor of English
at the University of Pennsylvania who has served as secretary of
the American Philosophical Society and president of the Renaissance Society of America and the Milton Society of America. He
is chairman of the Center of Theological Inquiry in Princeton.
His monograph "Language for God and Feminist Language: Problems and Principles" (1988; available from the Center) has been
reprinted in the United Kingdom and United States, and a revised
version appears in *Speaking the Christian God*, edited by Alvin
Kimel, Jr. (Eerdmans, July 1992). The article here first appeared in
the *Anglican Theological Review* in 1992.

Helen Hull Hitchcock

Mrs. Hitchcock, who is director of Women for Faith and Family, writes and lectures on issues involving the Catholic Faith, women, and the family. She is married to historian James Hitchcock and is the mother of four daughters. The Hitchcocks live in St. Louis.

Jon D. Levenson

Professor Levenson is the Albert A. List Professor of Jewish Studies at Harvard Divinity School and the author, most recently, of *Creation and the Persistence of Evil: The Jewish Drama of Divine Omnipotence* (Harper). The article included here appeared in *The Christian Century,* February 5–12, 1992.

Michael Levin

Dr. Levin is professor of philosophy at New York City College, CCNY. His research interests include ethics and the mind, and he is the author of *Metaphysics and the Mind: Body Problems.* The essay in this collection is from his 1987 book, *Feminism and Freedom.*

Joyce A. Little

Dr. Little teaches theology at the University of St. Thomas, Houston, Texas, has written extensively on feminism, and is currently working on a catechism. The essay included in this collection was originally given as an address to the Women for Faith and Family annual conference in 1990 and was published (edited version) in *Crisis* in January 1992.

The Rev. Paul V. Mankowski, S.J.

Father Mankowski, a Jesuit priest, is a specialist in ancient Semitic languages and Scripture who has written and lectured extensively on contemporary Church issues and has been active in antiabortion "rescues". He holds master's degrees from Oxford and Weston School of Theology and is a doctoral candidate at Harvard University.

The Rev. Paul M. Quay, S.J.

Father Quay is a priest of the Society of Jesus and research professor of philosophy at Loyola University of Chicago. After serving in World War II, he received his doctorate in theoretical physics from M.I.T., and he also holds degrees in classics, philosophy, and theology. Father Quay has both taught and published widely in the areas of physics, philosophy, and theology. His current research includes the theology of the spiritual life, medical moral theology, the philosophy of science, and thermodynamics. He is the author of *The Christian Meaning of Human Sexuality* (Ignatius, 1988).

Suzanne R. Scorsone

Dr. Scorsone, who received her doctorate in social anthropology from the University of Toronto in 1979, is the director of the Office of Catholic Family Life for the Archdiocese of Toronto and commissioner of the Royal Commission on New Reproductive Technologies. She is an author, lecturer, wife, and mother of five. The essay that appears in this collection was first published in *Communio,* Spring 1989.

The Most Rev. John R. Sheets, S.J.

Bishop Sheets, a former professor of theology at Creighton University in Nebraska and founding member of the editorial board of the theological journal *Communio,* is auxiliary bishop of Fort Wayne–South Bend. The article in this collection appeared in *The Priest* in 1985.

Kenneth D. Whitehead

K. D. Whitehead is the translator of seventeen books from German, French, and Italian. He is also author of four books and coauthor of another as well as the author of dozens of published articles, mostly on subjects of Catholic interest.

Juli Loesch Wiley

Mrs. Wiley, a veteran activist in prolife and antiwar issues, was a founder of JustLife and a member of Feminists for Life, for whom she coauthored *Pro-Life Feminism, Different Voices.* She lives in Johnson City, Tennessee, with her husband and young son. The essay included in this collection was originally an address to the Women for Faith and Family annual conference in 1990.

The Rev. Ralph Wright, O.S.B.
Father Ralph, a Benedictine monk and published poet, has also
been a consultant for the International Commission on English in
the Liturgy (ICEL). A native of England, Fr. Ralph teaches
English and religion at the Priory school in St. Louis.

ACKNOWLEDGMENTS

Grateful acknowledgment is extended to the following for permission to reprint previously published material that appears in this compendium.

"Inclusive Language Re-examined", by Joseph C. Beaver, is reprinted with the permission of *Dialog,* 2481 Como Avenue, St. Paul, Minn. 95108, USA.

"Father, Son, and Spirit—So What's in a Name?" by Deborah Belonick (The Alliance for Faith Renewal, 1986). Reprinted with permission from *Faith and Renewal* (formerly *Pastoral Renewal*), P.O. Box 8617, Ann Arbor, Mich. 48107, USA.

"Femspeak and the Battle of Language", by Peter L. Berger and Brigitte Berger, originally appeared as a part of a chapter in their book *The War over the Family* (Doubleday Anchor, 1983) © 1983 by Brigitte and Peter L. Berger and is reprinted with permission of Doubleday, a division of Bantam Doubleday Dell Publishing Group, Inc.

"Authority and the Language of the Bible", by Donald G. Bloesch, originally appeared in *The Battle for the Trinity* (Ann Arbor, Mich.: Servant, 1985), chapter 5, "The Problem of Authority", and is reprinted with the permission of the author.

"A Feminist Psalter?" by Brother Chrysostom Castel, O.C.S.O. (April 1990), is reprinted with the permission of *Homiletic and Pastoral Review,* 86 Riverside Drive, New York, N.Y. 10024, USA.

"Iconology: Revising God", by Donald De Marco (original title, "Inclusive Language in an Exclusive World" published in 1989), is newly revised by the author and reprinted with permission from Life Ethics Centre, The Rev. Alphonse de Valk, C.S.B., publisher, 53 Dundas St., E., Ste. 308, Toronto, Ontario, M5B 1C6, Canada.

"On Praying 'Our Father': The Challenge of Radical Feminist Language for God", by Roland Frye. © 1991, *Anglican Theological Review* (vol. 73, Feb. 1991). Reprinted with permission.

"Theological Liberalism Aborting Itself", by Jon D. Levenson, is reprinted with permission of *The Christian Century,* 407 South Dearborn, Chicago, Ill. 60605, USA.

"Feminism, Freedom, and Language", originally Chapter 12, "Language", in *Feminism and Freedom,* by Michael Levin, is reprinted with the permission of Transactions, Rutgers University, New Brunswick, N.J. 08903, USA.

"Words, Words Everywhere — and Not a Thought to Think", by Joyce A. Little, originally an address to the Women for Faith and Family annual conference in 1989, is reprinted with permission of *Crisis* magazine (January 1992), Box 1006, Notre Dame, Ind. 46556, USA.

"In the Image of God: Male, Female, and the Language of the Liturgy", by Suzanne R. Scorsone, is reprinted with permission of *Communio* (no. 17 [Spring 1989]: 139–51), P.O. Box 1046, Notre Dame, Ind. 46556, USA.

" 'Sexist Language': The Problem behind the Problem", by Bishop John R. Sheets, S.J. was published in *The Priest* (February 1986) and is reprinted with the author's permission.

"Criteria for the Evaluation of Inclusive Language" is reprinted with the permission of the United States Catholic Conference, 3211 4th Street NE, Washington, D.C. 20017, USA.

"Statement on Feminism, Language, and Liturgy". © 1989 by Women for Faith and Family. P.O. Box 8326, St. Louis, Mo., 63132. Reprinted with permission.

"Generic Man Revisited", by Ralph Wright, O.S.B., was published in an edited version by Catholic Answers under the title *Is the Word 'Man' Sexist?*, Sept. 1990.

INTRODUCTION

WORDS ON THE WINDS OF CHANGE

The subject of this book is not a dispute over contemporary versus traditional religious idiom used to express the same religious truth. It is not about a struggle between uneducated reactionaries fearful of change and modern biblical scholars whose insights enhance understanding of revealed religious truth. It is not simply a critical response to the style of biblical translations and corresponding liturgical innovations, or a dispute over matters of preference or taste (although these are hardly unimportant).

The subject of this book is, essentially, the conflict over objective religious truth. The matter which concerns the contributors to this volume is the retranslation of the biblical and liturgical texts—both the source and the means of communicating that truth—and the effect of the continuing (and currently intensified) politicization of those translations which has relativized that truth. The project of retranslation has progressed unimpeded (and virtually without critical comment) for nearly thirty years. This introductory chapter, focusing on the recent history of the retranslation project in the Catholic Church, and its consequences in liturgical "reform", may help to give historical and social context to the current manifestation of this quite ancient conflict about the communication of religious truth which now affects all Western worship of God.

I

There are two ways to achieve power over others: by coercion and by persuasion or seduction. These may, in fact, be combined. Hubert Humphrey, asked by a reporter why politicians are so often womanizers, is said to have made a similar observation: a good politician, he opined, is one whose stock-in-trade is persuasion—convincing others to act or respond in a way consistent with the politician's wishes. Successful seduction provides both assessment and confirmation of one's power. Personal power is validated by the ability to seduce or convince another to conform to one's own will.

The Church is in danger of being seduced by ideological dialectic of feminism based on power. In the matter of liturgical language, it is of central importance to feminists that they control every utterance in the Church. In the Catholic Church, this can be accomplished only with the collaboration of the hierarchy, who alone can mandate liturgical language. Therefore the hierarchy itself must be co-opted in order that it can be used to accomplish its own demolition. It is essential that some members of the hierarchy, those nearest the center of power—within the structure of the bishops' conferences in particular—first be convinced to embrace the feminist world view.

In the primal "myth" of Judaism and Christianity, the Fall of Man was accomplished by seduction, not coercion. The Serpent did not force Eve to sample the forbidden fruit. Eve did not coerce Adam to take a bite of it. The Serpent convinced Eve that she would be foolish (appeal to vanity) not to eat so desirable a fruit which would make her wise "as gods, knowing good and evil" (appeal to pride) simply out of fear of transgressing God's command. The Serpent's seductive lie convinced Eve that she should decide for herself rather than remain in her "ignorant" obedience to God. Adam was not unwilling to disobey. Not only did he not admonish Eve for her disobedience, he joined in her action willingly, without resistance. Then Adam, confronted by God with his disobedience, blamed Eve for tempting him, as Eve blamed the Serpent.

In order to seduce someone, you must first appeal to the potential victim's vanity and pride (or "self-image", in contemporary psychobabble). You must make the target of your seduction believe that he (or she) would be (or appear) foolish not to submit to the action you desire. In order for a seduction to take place, it is essential that the one who is seduced *choose* to change his mind — to comply *voluntarily* with the wishes of the seducer — in fact, not merely to submit to the desire of the seducer but to participate actively in the *desire* itself as well as in the action. Thus the challenge for the seducer is to overcome resistance not only to the action the seducer desires but to the *desire* for the action as well. For the seducer, the action to which he wishes his victim to submit is of secondary importance to the confirmation of power he exerts over the other person. Power over the very will of the seduced is what the seducer requires, and this power is proved only by the willing (voluntary) submission of the victim.

The use of lies is nearly always essential to suborn the will of the other person, the object of seduction. The classic example is the man who tells a woman he loves her in order to overcome her resistance to his sexual advances. She *wants* to believe him, especially if she loves him or is dependent on him — even if she may suspect he is lying. The complicity of the seduced is essential in order for a seduction to be complete. Don Juan did not love women. In fact, he despised his victims and abandoned them at the moment he overcame them. He was not even motivated primarily by his sexual urges but by his insatiable desire to control. His "conquests" were necessary to prove his power, yet, their very submission made them unfit objects of pursuit; hence the endless repetition of seductions, conquests, abandonments.

What does Don Juan have to do with the matter at hand?

Feminists (of both sexes) hate the Church, because she represents, or in fact personifies, for them, everything which impinges on or limits their "liberty" to do as they wish. The Church's moral teaching constrains them, accuses them of sin. In effect, they must make the Church *become* "sin". For the ultimate sin, for them, is to impose limitations on their "autonomy"—their unchecked personal liberty and power.[1]

So long as the Church stands, the Church's moral law "oppresses" them—makes them feel powerless. It should be no surprise that the priesthood is the focus of utter abhorrence for the feminist/liberationist. First of all because it claims authority—in fact, *Divine* authority, *super*natural authority which transcends human experience and comes, not "from within", but from outside the self. Second (and at least equally), because the priesthood is utterly and unchangeably male. For feminists of both sexes, resentment against, if not hatred of, the male sex is the filter through which all existing institutions—especially religion, and certainly including the language of worship—must be strained.

For many feminists the determination to exact justice for their oppression by "patriarchal religion" dominates virtually every other concern.[2] Deep and ineradicable resentment underlies the feminist attack on the authority of the priesthood as well as the demand that the exclusively male priesthood be abolished. (It is clear, of course, that the destruction of both the authority and the masculinity of the Catholic priesthood cannot be achieved without the complicity of clergy, who have the most authority and power within the Church.)[3]

Clergy who collaborate in this self-destructive project seem to fall into two main categories: (1) those who have been "converted"

[1] It is not irrelevant, surely, that the party of feminist reform rejects, also, the traditional metaphor of Church as "Mother". Although resentment is overtly directed at "the patriarchy", the Church is also neutered by feminists—is not called "she" or "Mother". Karl Stern has examined the rejection of the feminine in his classic work, *The Flight from Woman*.

[2] This resentment is essentially inaccessible to logic (in fact, logic itself is, according to feminists, a "male" mode of thinking which women need not—should not—observe). In a "listening session" held at St. Louis University in the fall of 1984, a nun in her sixties ended her impassioned call for "justice" by stating, "Absolute power corrupts absolutely. Men have always had absolute power. It is time that women had their turn to have power."

[3] Several bishops have written their own pastoral letters on "women's issues" during the past two decades. In her book *Mind Your Metaphors: A Critique of*

to feminism, have themselves become feminists;[4] and (2) those who, convinced by feminist rhetoric, believe themselves to be sinful and sexist and wish to appear "sensitive" to the demands of women (that is to say, of *feminist* women). There are some in authority, also, who seem to favor capitulating to feminist demands out of a misplaced sense of chivalry. Still others evidently fear badgering, harassment and "guilt trips" imposed on them by feminist women who work for them, and they worry about the smooth functioning of the diocese if these women are not appeased. Most bishops seem only now to have begun to be aware that the office of bishop—and priestly ordination itself—is under grave threat by feminism, and to entertain critical thoughts about the feminist movement.

Meanwhile, the feminists' thirst for power, combined with deep resentment of the Church (which, for them, looms as the most insuperable obstacle to their achievement of "freedom" and exercise of power), gives rise to their overwhelming desire—and apparently equally overwhelming energy—to destroy her at her

---

the Language in the Bishops' Pastoral Letters on the Role of Women (New York: Paulist Press, 1991), Sr. Maureen Aggeler, R.S.C.J., analyzes thirteen bishops' pastorals written from 1974 to 1987 as they reflect a change in language in response to feminist "concerns". Sr. Maureen attempts to show how "the bishops' metaphorical constructions actually serve as paradigms" which may "help us envision a paradigm of church [sic] which will accommodate our new understanding of personhood, equality, and mutuality" (p. 16).

[4] Bishop Matthew Clark, in his keynote address November 29, 1990, to the "Wisdom of Women Symposium" sponsored by the NCCB/USCC Committees on Women in Arlington, Virginia, told delegates from about eighty dioceses of his "conversion" to feminism after he became bishop of Rochester (NY) in 1979. Bishop Clark, who heads the NCCB Committee on Women in Society and in the Church and is a member of the Writing Committee for the controversial "women's pastoral", also told participants that "the church is most alive when she is expansive and inclusive, when she stands in dialogue with the time and culture in which she is infleshed, . . . when she expresses fully the truth she bears in language which speaks to the people of the age." He also called for dialogue on the "complex issues" of abortion, birth control, celibacy, women's ordination, and for selection of bishops by the people they will serve. Bishop Clark's address was published in *Origins,* December 20, 1990, vol. 20, no 28, pp. 445–52.

very foundation: the Word of God — the Scripture, and rites and prayers based on and acknowledging that Divine authority.

In case this seems exaggerated, one has but to open nearly any book of theology written by a feminist. Some feminist writers are, of course, more extreme and more radical than others. Mary Daly, who still teaches at the Jesuit's Boston College, is by common consent of "religious feminists" themselves the most extreme. She candidly calls herself "post-christian" and has invented a language of her own in which to express her anger at men and religion. We will read some samples from Sister Mary Collins below, detailing her own involvement with the liturgical and linguistic renovations of the International Commission on English in the Liturgy (ICEL).

There are, in fact, many radical feminist women in positions of considerable influence in the Catholic Church, none more so than Sister Sandra Schneiders, although she may be less well known, in some circles, than Rosemary Ruether or Elisabeth Schüssler-Fiorenza. She is important for two reasons: (1) because she is a member-in-good-standing of a religious order (Sister Servants of the Immaculate Heart of Mary); and (2) she is actively engaged in the education and formation of future priests (as professor of New Testament and spirituality at the Jesuit School of Theology at the Graduate Theological Union in Berkeley, California). Her views, therefore, are of more than passing interest to anyone concerned about the future of the Catholic Church, or who tries to understand why some women demand that the language in which all worship of God is expressed be made to conform to their desires, or who still may hope that feminism and the Catholic Faith can somehow be reconciled.

Sister Sandra's most recent book (1991) is called *Beyond Patching*, an allusion to the scriptural metaphor about sewing new patches to old garments. In her view, she explains, it is the Catholic Church which is decayed "beyond patching". She writes,

> Consciousness raising, the critical appropriation of personal experi-
> ence as systemic oppression, has been encapsulated in a phrase
> that some have called the analytical nerve of feminism, namely,
> "the personal is political".

What this phrase means, she tells us, is that what women have been taught to experience as "personal problems" are actually generated by the social systems, which must be transformed through "personal transformation". "Consciousness-raising" and "accessing one's personal power" are necessary to achieve personal transformation; and the "process of personal transformation has come to be called feminist spirituality."[5]

"Radical feminism", says Sister Sandra, "is the branch of the movement that is most concerned with religion, both religion's role in the subordination of women and religion's potential for liberation. Feminist spirituality . . . is predominantly located within the precincts of radical feminism . . . [including] . . . women's support groups in universities, seminaries, parishes, and other male-dominated institutions, feminist prayer and liturgy groups. . . . "[6]

"There is no question", according to this seminary professor, "that Mary Daly saw, before most Catholic feminists did, that the Catholic Church was a major participant in the oppression of women and that this was not an accidental historical development but a major systemic problem with Catholicism itself."[7]

In a chapter entitled "Scripture: Tool of Patriarchy or Resource for Transformation", we are by now not surprised to read,

As feminist biblical scholarship has progressed during the past two decades . . . it is no longer possible to deny that the *text itself* is not only androcentric, i.e., a male-centered account of male experience for male purposes with women relegated to the margins of salvation history, but also patriarchal in its assumptions and often in its explicit teaching, and at times deeply sexist, i.e., anti-woman. Its God language and imagery are overwhelmingly male. When the official church invokes scripture to justify its discriminatory treatment of women it does not have to resort to fundamentalist prooftexting or to

[5] Sandra Schneiders, S.S.I.H.M., *Beyond Patching* (New York: Paulist Press, 1991), pp. 17, 18.
[6] Ibid., p. 30.
[7] Ibid., p. 31.

questionable exegetical methods. In other words, *the problem is in the text.*[8]

Throughout this book Sister Sandra maintains a consistently high level of animosity toward the Church, Scripture, and, of course, men (non-feminist women apparently are beneath contempt).

In an earlier work, a monograph called *Women and the Word,* focused on the usual theme of patriarchal subordination of women throughout the history of Christianity (in Scripture in particular), we find this very sharply honed passage:

> If the demonic influence of patriarchy on the religious imagina-
> tion is to be exorcised, if the neurotic repression of the feminine
> dimension of divinity is to be overcome, the imagination must
> be healed. *It is absolutely imperative that language, which appeals to
> the imagination through metaphor . . . be purified of patriarchal overtones,
> male exclusive references to God, and the presentation of male religious
> experience as normative.* We must learn to speak to and about God
> in the feminine; we must learn to image God in female metaphors;
> we must learn to present the religious experience of women as
> *autonomously valid.*[9]

Sister Sandra sets up an either/or alternative for women whose consciousness has been raised: either women can choose to accept inferiority and spiritual dependence on men, "or they can aban-don Christianity as a hopelessly patriarchal religion and seek their spiritual home in a religious tradition in which women and women's experience are central and valued". Women who are "educated and aware" will find it difficult to find a future in Christianity, according to this vowed religious woman who holds a prestigious post in the seminary of a male religious order.

Given the views expressed by Sister Sandra, the response of John L. Page, executive secretary of ICEL, to an interviewer's

[8] Ibid., p. 38 (emphasis added).
[9] Sandra Schneiders, S.S.I.H.M., *Women and the Word* (New York: Paulist Press, 1986), p. 70. This monograph was presented as the 1986 Madeleva Lecture in Spirituality at the Center for Spirituality of St. Mary's College, Notre Dame.

question about "intellectual pressure" on bishops to adopt "more radical inclusive language" seems almost disingenuous:

> ... it is true that in some communities, where there is a *higher degree of education,* and in the various theological faculties and in Catholic universities, things are being discussed by a certain group of people—who, *because they are experts* in liturgy, or Latin, or Biblical studies, do *influence the work the Church does.* Many of them are taking these opinions—not the Goddess, I don't think anyone involved with ICEL would go that far.... We certainly don't use language like "Goddess" or referring to God as She. Some people want to refer to the Holy Spirit as "She".[10]

The project of destroying the power of the Church through deconstructing Scripture is not limited to the techniques of modernist and post-modernist Scripture scholarship, which views the Sacred text as the culturally determined writings of an oppressed minority of Hebrews (OT) or Jewish Christians (NT) (though this project emphatically continues); for, although this undermines the authority of the Scripture, the destruction cannot be complete so long as the liturgy of the Church remains intact. This is because most believers are not Scripture scholars or theologians and are, therefore, unlikely to read these works or to be particularly sensitive to the collapse such scholarship intends to effect (and does accomplish) through defective catechesis. Thus the deformation of the liturgy is at least an equally important objective, and this can most quickly be accomplished by retranslating the texts. Resistance to such changes, because they destroy familiar modes of worship and the language of prayer used collectively by millions of Catholics, will naturally be greater than to even quite radical theological innovations.

The current situation is one of great peril to the future of the Catholic Church—and to all authentic worship of God. In the Catholic Church, the bishops alone have the ultimate authority to effect these changes—or to stop the demolition of the Word and the

[10] Robert J. Hutchinson, "Whether 'Tis Nobler in the Mind ... " (interview with John L. Page), *The Catholic World Report,* August 1992; vol. 2, no. 8, p. 37 (emphasis added).

sacraments. Without their courageous defense, the war for the Word will be lost.

It will not be easy to resist the powerful forces for demolition of the language of worship. It will be difficult to resist the temptation to abandon the field. Among the recurring arguments which will have to be resisted are:

1. *To resist the new language is to resist change.* Assumption: all change is good. Metaphors of "growth", "mature faith appropriation", "progressive", etc., are common rhetorical weapons used to vaporize opposition to new language by implying that standard usage, the norm, is retrograde, ignorant, unenlightened, bad.

2. *To resist new "inclusive" translations is to show oneself ignorant of the most current thinking of an elite group of individuals who have special knowledge* (e.g., revisionist Scripture scholars and theologians).

(Both of the above could be called the "Emperor's New Clothes" technique—enlisting the *pride* of the target of seduction.)

3. *Women feel excluded and offended by normal (standard) usage.* It is extremely common for a feminist woman to claim she suffers great pain and anguish when she hears standard English. Ordinary men do not want to make women feel bad. Neither do they want to give grounds for accusations of being an oppressor or a "male chauvinist". Most women, however, have to be *convinced* they feel bad when standard English is used.

Techniques used to produce this effect on women include story-telling, sharing feelings, consciousness-raising, mythmaking, etc., which put one in a relationship of trust/dependence with another person. Men must prove their sensitivity to women collectively, by responding to demands of a small but articulate and influential special-interest group of women (usually religious professionals) who claim to speak for all women. But these techniques of "feminization" actually discriminate against the majority of women (and men and children), who do not belong to the group demanding the change.

If compliance by these means is not achieved, there is another method: coercion and threats. Examples of this technique include the following:

1. *Change is inevitable: those who persist in resisting change cannot succeed; furthermore, they will be ground to a powder.* Your future effectiveness will depend on your compliance.

2. *The majority want—nay, demand—"inclusive" language in worship.* If you persist in resisting, *you* are divisive and disruptive. Furthermore, you are alone. No one will support you. You will be ridiculed—left to twist slowly in the wind.

What is now at stake in the decades-long project to re-create the words of worship is, quite simply, the Faith itself—its history, its tradition, and its communication to future generations.

II

"The way to respect the original words [of God] is to retranslate them as our understanding changes."

—Letty M. Russell, professor of theology, Yale University

It has now been three decades since the Second Vatican Council's Decree on the Sacred Liturgy permitted translation of liturgical texts into the vernacular. It is probably safe to say that at least half of all Catholics have no vivid memory of the old Latin Mass and did not experience the confusion which ensued because of radical changes in the worship of the Church. For Catholics under age thirty-five—and all converts entering the Church since the Council—"liturgical renewal" is old hat, and continual change is all they have ever known.

For millions of English-speaking Catholics, the chief effect of the Second Vatican Council was the almost immediate translation of the Latin liturgical texts into contemporary English. The project of retranslation of the Bible into the contemporary usages, however, antedated the Council and had received cautious encouragement from several twentieth-century Popes, notably Pius XII in his *Divino Afflante Spiritu.*

The massive undertaking of "renewal" of liturgical texts during the sixties was accomplished by committees of experts—Scripture scholars, theologians, liturgists—presumably for the sake of speed in implementing the Council's permission for liturgical use of the vernacular. Catholic Scripture scholars, linguists, and liturgists who could not have expected to see their works used liturgically in the Catholic Church before the Council were hastily employed.

The International Commission on English in the Liturgy (ICEL) was established in 1963 to produce and oversee these translations, in order to assure uniform English texts. Eleven bishops representing all the English-speaking national conferences of the Catholic Church form its Administrative Committee, and fifteen others (where English is a second language) are associate members. Archbishop Daniel Pilarczyk, of Cincinnati, is the Administrative Committee's current chairman. A long-time member of ICEL's Administrative Committee, he is also current president of the National Conference of Catholic Bishops (NCCB).

A parallel Protestant body, the International Consultation on English Texts (ICET), now called the English Language Liturgical Consultation (ELLC), was organized under the auspices of the National Council of Churches (NCC) at about the same time as ICEL for the same purpose: updating Scripture translations and liturgical texts. The two groups have collaborated closely from the outset.

A multitude of translation projects were undertaken in the wake of the Council. It eventually became apparent that these efforts were not merely confined to straightforward translation but contained an "updated" ideological component. And despite the "ecumenical spirit" which then prevailed, newly empowered Catholic liturgists virtually ignored the large body of traditional English-language sacred music accumulated by the Protestant Churches since the time of the Reformation. The opportunity to translate traditional Latin liturgical music into English was missed as well. New music in a then-contemporary popular musical style and theological idiom was hurriedly composed, universally employed, and strenuously promoted. The "new vision" of the Church is still accompanied by this dated, aging music of the sixties. In fact, ecumenical efforts of theological and liturgical experts have been almost uniformly directed toward reduction of the "shared faith" to the lowest possible common denominator in both theology and ritual. Mainline Protestant churches have pursued a parallel "renewal".

Liturgical experimentation flourished in the years following the Council. The prevailing winds of change blew through the "open windows" of every Catholic parish; and since every change was (and continues to be) presented as the will of the bishops—of Rome—sweeping changes in Catholic liturgical practice were accomplished, in many cases quite literally overnight. It evidently rarely occurred to anyone to question the motives of the individuals who engineered these changes. This may have been in part because of the confusing and distracting profusion of new material, but also because the full authority of the Church was invoked in their promulgation.[11] People had been convinced that obedience to the highest Church authority required their acceptance of any and all liturgical innovations.

Jacques Maritain, the great French Catholic philosopher, wrote in a letter to Pope Paul VI in March 1965, "In reality the first duty of a translator, who is not a traitor, is *always,* ... but especially when one is dealing with an inspired text or a liturgical text, to respect the word that was chosen by the author ... and to use the exact equivalent to it, even at the price of obscurity: an inevitable obscurity, a blessed obscurity, because it is the shadow borne, upon our human language, of the grandeur of things divine."[12] And historian James Hitchcock observed that "innovating religious commentators may employ the traditional vocabulary, but

---

[11] Invocation of Roman authority for changes continues. In July 1992, the pastor of a small country parish in Kansas thus explained the newly mandated retranslation of *Dei Verbum,* changed from "This is the Word of the Lord" to "The Word of the Lord". Actually, the change, proposed by ICEL, was introduced at the November 1991 NCCB meeting and approved by a majority of bishops, and only subsequently by the Vatican at the request of the NCCB. Although virtually no worshipper is aware of it, this apparently inconsequential revision presaged massive changes which will ensue when the newly approved Lectionary and revised Sacramentary (now in final stages of preparation) are introduced.

[12] Jacques Maritain, letter quoted in "World Watch", *The Catholic World Report,* August 1992, p. 11.

it is often evident that they have altered the meanings of the words without acknowledgement. . . . At a minimum those who would promote such departures and such redefinitions have an obligation to make clear what they are doing, to offer fair warning of the fullest implications of their work."[13]

Fully six years after ICEL had begun rapidly producing vernacular liturgical texts, in 1969, the Vatican issued an *Instruction on the Translation of Liturgical Texts* to provide guidelines for the new translation projects.

Among the earliest of the Scripture translations to appear after the Council was the Jerusalem Bible (so called because it was the pioneering work of the School of Biblical Studies in Jerusalem), first published in 1966.[14]

The New American Bible [NAB] is the English translation by the Catholic Biblical Association, done at the request of the Bishops' Confraternity on Christian Doctrine. This is the translation which appears in parish missalettes. The original English NAB took more than a quarter of a century to produce. It was published in 1970, although its earliest copyrights had been granted in 1953. Translation into vernacular English of *The Roman Missal,* comprised of Lectionary (Scripture readings) and Sacramentary (Order of Mass, eucharistic prayers, creeds and other liturgical material), was complete by 1973.

Revised translations of these revised translations were begun almost as soon as these were finished, however. By 1975, ICEL's translators had adopted the principle of feminist language, to which all subsequent alterations in the language of the liturgy would conform. More updating was considered necessary princi-

---

[13] James Hitchcock, *Recovery of the Sacred* (New York: Seabury Press, 1974), preface, x.

[14] The English translation of the Jerusalem Bible was based on the famous French translation, newly compared with original texts in Hebrew and Greek. A note on Psalms first appeared in a one-volume edition in 1961 in French, by Père Roland de Vaux, O.P. Principal collaborators in the English version were 20–25 people, including Anthony Kenny, Edward Sackville-West, J. R. R. Tolkien. The Rev. Alexander Jones, Lecturer in Divinity at Christ College, Liverpool, was its general editor. Other scholars on the committee were from the Gregorian and the Biblicum in Rome and L'Ecole Biblique in Jerusalem.

pally in order to incorporate feminist language, and some changes
were introduced immediately, bypassing even the approval of the
national bishops' conferences.[15] The project of ICEL's retranslation
of the English texts of Scripture used in the liturgy (Lectionary)
was formally initiated in 1978 with the Psalms (Psalter). This
portion of the massive new feminist language retranslation of *The
Roman Missal* was approved by the NCCB in July 1992.[16] A
revised translation of the Sacramentary portion of the Missal,
formally begun in October 1982, is now in its final stages of
preparation, and the entire two-volume work is scheduled for
issuance to the bishops' conferences in June 1994.[17] The introduction
to the final progress report states that

> throughout the revision process ICEL has been attentive to the
> question of inclusive language. Since 1975 ICEL has pledged
> itself to the use of "horizontal" inclusive language (referring to
> the assembly) in all of the texts prepared under its auspices.
> Unfortunately this decision came too late for many of the major
> texts issued in the first six or seven years of ICEL's work. These
> included the texts of *The Roman Missal. Inclusive language on the
> horizontal level is used throughout the present revision of the Missal.*
> Over the course of the 1980s, ICEL also studied the question of
> masculine language used of God. In the revisions an effort has
> been made to keep the title "Father" in most instances wherever
> the Latin has *Pater,* but to remove what many have criticized
> as the gratuitous introduction of the title "Father" into many of
> the translated prayers found in *The Roman Missal* of 1973. Where
> doctrinal or linguistic considerations allowed, *the revisions have*

[15] Probably the best known of these changes is the original 1973 ICEL translation of *pro multis* (literally "for many"), originally "for all men". The change to
"for all" was incorporated into the official text more than a decade ago.

[16] A mail ballot was taken after the June 1992 NCCB meeting. According
to published reports, results were 219 in favor; 27 opposed.

[17] The *Third Progress Report on the Revision of the Roman Missal* (International
Commission on English in the Liturgy, Inc. [ICEL], Washington, D.C., 1992),
was received by the US bishops in May 1992. Their comments were to be
transmitted to ICEL's Episcopal Board by June 1. The report "deals with a
fairly small section of the Missal . . . that is at the very core of the eucharistic
celebration", p. 7.

avoided the use of masculine pronouns to refer to the First and Third Persons of the Trinity. In *both the translated and original prayers* an effort has been made to use a *larger variety of titles and images for God* in order to open up a greater sense of the mystery and majesty of the Godhead [emphasis added].[18]

"Most of all, there would hardly be a need for another translation of the psalms today that did not use inclusive language", according to Father Lawrence Boadt, C.S.P., a member of ICEL's committee, writing on the new revision of the Psalter.[19] He also observes with evident satisfaction that

One of the ironies for those who criticize the ICEL version on these grounds is that the editorial committees of the older English translations (to which these critics point so proudly) are scrambling to develop inclusive language modifications of their own, namely, the New American Bible (1986), the New Jerusalem Bible (1985) and the New Revised Standard Version.[20]

Father Boadt discusses the principles of "inclusive language" employed by the ICEL Committee:

From its beginning in 1978, the ICEL Liturgical Psalter project has been committed to the principle of achieving an English translation that employs inclusive language as far as possible. In particular this has meant that where the Hebrew uses a masculine singular pronoun to express a truth about all humans ... a gender-neutral vocabulary has been employed in English. ... Masculine singular pronominal forms for God are also translated by gender-neutral alternatives.

ICEL has considered this question carefully on many separate occasions because there has always been a *small but consistent opposition to this usage* among those who have reviewed and

[18] Ibid., p. 10.

[19] Lawrence Boadt, C.S.P., "Problems in the Translation of Scripture as Illustrated by ICEL's Project on the Liturgical Psalter", in *Shaping English Liturgy,* ed. Peter C. Finn and James Schellman (Washington, DC: Pastoral Press, 1990), pp. 405–29.

[20] NCC's New Revised Standard Version was accepted by the NCCB in 1991 and speedily approved (1992) by the Vatican for liturgical use in American churches.

critiqued the completed psalm translations. The psalter subcommittee has been persuaded to take its present position, however,
by *numerous studies that point to the androcentric character of English
usage as a reflection of the androcentric nature of a society in which
women have been treated less than equally as a rule* [emphasis added].

Father Boadt cites works of radical feminist theologians to substantiate his claim. One of these is Lutheran Gail Ramshaw-Schmidt's
essay, "The Gender of God",[21] in which she says,

> It is incumbent upon us to eliminate altogether in American
> English the expository use of pronouns referring to God. . . .
> Sentences must be recast. The adjective "divine" is helpful in
> possessive constructions. "Godself" works well as a reflexive. . . . As
> a result of the Black Power movement, educated Americans
> removed from their active vocabularies the word "Negro". Such
> alterations are quite possible if the motivation is present. *What is
> required is not only the will to change one's vocabulary, but a renewed
> perception of God.* . . . Change of speech is a willing task if it
> follows a conversion of mind. . . . Contemporarily accurate trans-
> lation of theological works will rid the study of Christianity of
> much of its overwhelming male overtone.[22]

To substantiate further his claim that "numerous studies" show the
necessity for feminist language, Father Boadt cites feminist Patricia
Martin Doyle.[23] He also notes that the chairman of ICEL's committee for translating the Psalter is Sister Mary Collins, O.S.B.
Her article "Glorious Praise: The ICEL Liturgical Psalter"[24]
appeared only a few weeks after the bishops had their first look at
ICEL's current revision of the Sacramentary.

Sister Mary Collins is a Benedictine who chairs the department
of religion and religious education at The Catholic University of

[21] Gail Ramshaw-Schmidt, "The Gender of God", in *Feminist Theology—A
Reader,* ed. Ann Loades (Louisville, KY: Westminster/John Knox Press, 1990),
pp. 168–80.
[22] Ibid., pp. 178–79 (emphasis added).
[23] Patricia M. Doyle, in *Religion and Sexism,* ed. Rosemary Ruether (New
York: Simon and Schuster, 1974), pp. 15–40.
[24] Mary Collins, "Glorious Praise: The ICEL Liturgical Psalter", in *Worship,*
July 1992, pp. 290–310.

America [CUA]. She is advisor on feminist theology to *Concilium,* past president of the North American Academy of Liturgy, and a long-time associate of the extremist feminist group, Women's Alliance for Theology, Ethics and Ritual [WATER], headed by Mary Hunt. She was also a presenter at a NCCB/USCC sponsored catechetical symposium in September 1991.[25] Her article "reflects my own involvement in the project from 1978 to the present, including collaboration in the research that gave it its shape". The new Psalter, Sister Mary states alliteratively, "would have as its larger purpose exposing the power of the psalter as a primer for prayer". Applying the principle of "dynamic equivalence" honoring "the idiom of the receptor language" would yield contemporary English poetry, she writes; and the new Psalter would be further distinguished by "attention both to *emerging English gender usage and contemporary theological discussions about inclusive language*".

> This consideration included first of all a commitment to overcome lapses in earlier translations into what has been called "translator's bias", the unexamined preference for male pronouns and male-centered images and metaphors even when these were not warranted by the original text.... Once this commitment was made to be alert to the inclusive language question (a confirmation of the broader ICEL commitment to inclusive language made during this period), *language would have to be carefully crafted to honor it.*[26]
>
> ICEL style also took shape under the influence of contemporary discussions about linguistic gender among literary theorists, biblical interpreters and theologians.... The *issue was never whether the matter of gender would receive attention in this translation for use in the praying Church, only how it was to be approached critically.* Who could deny the impression of many translations that the poetry of the psalms gives overt voice to male devotees interacting with a putatively male God?[27]

---

[25] This "forum for discussion of catechetical issues" was funded by the Lilly Foundation and publishers Benzinger, Silver Burdett/Ginn, and Sadlier, according to the report of the Committee on Education, Division of Catechesis/Religious Education in the NCCB's November 1991 Agenda—Committee Reports, pp. 149, 150.

[26] Collins, p. 295 (emphasis added).

[27] Ibid., pp. 300–301 (emphasis added).

She states that, throughout its ten years of Psalm translation, the ICEL editorial committee had employed strategies reflecting a "typology for *refashioning English speech* about personal and social reality" which describes feminist usages:

> Non-sexist usage avoids gender-specific terms; inclusive language balances gender references; emancipatory language reshapes and transforms language to challenge stereotypical gender references.[28]

J. Frank Henderson, also a participant in the ICEL's language project from 1977 to 1987, writes with remarkable candor of the progressive influence of feminism on this powerful, if mostly anonymous, body.[29] He draws on the minutes of meetings of the Advisory Committee [AC], the subcommittee on "discriminatory language" (as it was then called), and other ICEL publications and reports.

Henderson unhesitatingly describes the feminist perspective forming ICEL's "primary focus and priority", and he quotes its "proposal concerning discriminatory language" adopted in November 1977:

> The discriminatory language under consideration has to do with sex, race, color, culture, religion (e.g., anti-semitism), state in life (clericalism), and related matters, and the problem must be seen in the context of more general problems of social, legal, and economic discrimination against minority or underprivileged groups. Under this broad scope, the AC considers the issues of sexist, racial, and anti-semitic discrimination to be of particular urgency.[30]

But ICEL had already employed the principles of inclusive language in all new translations from 1975 on, Henderson writes, despite the results of its survey of the eleven English-speaking bishops' conferences which revealed general opposition to ICEL's offer of "immediate, interim relief" from discriminatory language

[28] Ibid., p. 302.
[29] J. Frank Henderson, "ICEL and Inclusive Language", in *Shaping English Liturgy*, pp. 257–78.
[30] Ibid., p. 262.

suggested by then chairman of ICEL's board, Archbishop Denis Hurley of South Africa. (Archbishop Hurley held this position from 1975 until May 4, 1991, when Archbishop Daniel Pilarczyk of the US was elected to succeed him.)

In 1987, the Secretariat of the Bishops' Committee on the Liturgy (NCCB) published a book called *Thirty Years of Liturgical Renewal,* edited with commentary by Monsignor Frederick R. McManus.[31] The book contains extracts from statements issued by the Commission on the Liturgical Apostolate and the NCCB Liturgy Committee since 1963. It also contains the revealing editorial comments of Msgr. McManus, a member of the Advisory Committee and sometime officer of ICEL, a professor of canon law at CUA since 1958, editor since 1959 of the highly influential publication of the Canon Law Society of America, *The Jurist,* and a member of the Board of Directors of the Association of Catholic Colleges and Universities. Msgr. McManus also was a consultant to the Pontifical Preparatory Commission on the Sacred Liturgy for the Second Vatican Council (and a *peritus* to the Council from 1962 to 1965), was director of the Secretariat of the Bishops' Committee on the Liturgy from 1965 until 1975, at which time he was appointed permanent staff consultant. Msgr. McManus was a consultant to the *Consilium* for the Implementation of the Constitution on the Liturgy after the Council and to the Pontifical Commission for the Revision of the Code of Canon Law (1967 to 1983).

Msgr. McManus also contributed an article on the aims of the ICEL liturgical Psalter project.[32] Although Msgr. McManus' name has not become a Catholic household word, unlike those of some theologians, he ranks high on a very short list of the most powerful priests in America on matters of both liturgy and canon law.

In his comments accompanying the 1985 statement of Arch-

---

[31] Other members of the Liturgy committee's Secretariat are Fr. Ronald F. Krisman, Executive Director; Msgr. Alan F. Detscher, Assoc. Dir., Sister Linda Gaupin, C.D.P., Assoc. Dir. and C. Rena Hinnant, Administrative Secretary. Msgr. McManus is listed as "consultant" to the committee in the Fall 1991 NCCB Agenda/Documentation: Committee Reports, p. 26.

[32] "ICEL: 1963–1965", in *Shaping English Liturgy.*

bishop Pilarczyk (then chairman of the NCCB Liturgy Committee) "clarifying" the position of the Committee after the revised Grail Psalter (which "had as its distinctive feature the elimination of consciously exclusive language, that is, language discriminating on the basis of gender")[33] had failed to secure the approval of the bishops, Msgr. McManus notes that although "minor adjustments and corrections" made by editors and proprietors of the liturgical texts had been done routinely, in the case of the Grail revision, as well as all ICEL revisions, there is one issue to be considered, and that is "inclusive" language. His remarks merit careful attention:

> The broader issue at stake is that of inclusive language in general. There has been a gradual realization, coincidental with the liturgical renewal of the past thirty years, that changes in the meanings of words in the English language, as well as the perception of those meanings, have to be taken seriously. The notion of exclusive language, whether it works to the exclusion of women or is a discriminatory allusion to some group or race or people, has to be attended to. Any generic references must now be carefully scrutinized, even though they may well be unintentionally exclusive or may have been appropriately understood as generic a generation ago.
>
> The liturgical texts in English produced by ICEL in the years prior to the mid-1970s illustrate . . . an evident effort to embrace the total community of the Church or of humankind. . . . In other texts, the much more common use of "man" or "men" and the masculine pronouns to refer to both women and men *survived and now grates on the ear.* This is true not only in North America . . . but increasingly throughout the English-speaking world. . . .
>
> Beginning in the early 1970s, with a *greatly raised consciousness* concerning the question, the ICEL texts—and thus the texts approved by the American conference of bishops at the recommendation of its episcopal committee—were translated or composed with a *careful avoidance of exclusive language. Often this fact is not even noticed,* but it becomes an issue when an existing English text is revised to expunge exclusive or sexist language.

[33] Frederick R. McManus, editor, *Thirty Years of Liturgical Renewal—Statements of the Bishops' Committee on the Liturgy* (Washington, DC: Secretariat, Bishops' Committee on the Liturgy, NCCB, July 1987), p. 247.

The first formal recognition of the problem by [ICEL] is worth noting: it dates from August 1975: *"The Advisory Committee recognizes the necessity in all future translations and revisions to avoid words that ignore the place of women in the Christian community altogether or that seem to relegate women to a secondary role."* Since enlarged and refined, the principle has been applied to new translations and revisions and to original liturgical texts submitted by ICEL to the conferences of bishops in the English-speaking world. In the case of the eucharistic prayers, slightly revised in 1980 to reflect this concern, the American conference of bishops quickly approved the revision. . . .

[The proposed Grail Psalter] gave the Bishops' Committee on the Liturgy the chance to affirm strongly, through its chairman, support for the principle of inclusive language.[34]

Archbishop Pilarczyk's statement says that the Committee "looks favorably upon the revised version of the psalter" and emphatically affirms the Liturgy Committee's commitment to the revised Grail Psalter and to new liturgical language:

The [NCCB] has favored the use of inclusive language in liturgical texts and has approved such language since 1978. . . . Nonauthorization of the revised Grail Psalter at this time should not be construed as insensitivity to the question. . . .

The [Committee] maintains its commitment to those plans and projects of the [ICEL] in which liturgical texts are revised or translated with inclusive language in mind.

The [Committee] applauds and commends the work of The Grail in this . . . carefully revised inclusive-language version of the psalter . . . [and] looks forward to [its] publication. . . .

Finally, the [Committee] wishes to make it known that the question of inclusive language is a matter that deserves attention in the Church because of the cultural development of the English language. . . . The [Committee] intends to commission a scholarly review of the elements inherent in the inclusive language issue. The [Committee] does not understand the matter of inclusive language as a "women's issue" only. . . . Rather, the [Committee] understands inclusive language to be a question of the cultural development of the English language and therefore

[34] Ibid., p. 249.

important to all worshiping members of the Church. It is the hope of the [Committee] . . . that an inclusive language version of the psalter be authorized for liturgical use in the dioceses of the United States.[35]

Although approval of the Grail Psalter was delayed for the time being, the Liturgy Committee report at the November 1991 NCCB meeting says they "agreed to reexamine the revised Grail Psalter (Inclusive Language Version) and will establish a mechanism to recommend to the publisher changes required by the *Criteria for the Evaluation of Inclusive Language Translations*", and that "once all the problems have been satisfactorily resolved, the Committee will recommend that the NCCB authorize this version of the psalter for liturgical use."[36]

Sooner or later nearly all revisions and retranslations proposed have met with approval when submitted to the bishops' conference for vote. This phenomenon has persisted to the present.

At the November 1990 NCCB meeting, at the recommendation of the Liturgy Committee, now chaired by Chicago Auxiliary Bishop Wilton Gregory, the US bishops adopted *Criteria for the Use of Inclusive Language in Scripture Translations* —fifteen years after ICEL's commitment to employ feminist language as a guiding principle for all liturgical translations.

The retranslation of the New American Bible (NAB) Lectionary, prepared explicitly to incorporate "gender inclusive language", has also been accepted by the bishops.[37] At the November

[35] Ibid., p. 250.

[36] *Agenda Report,* November 1991, report of the NCCB Committee on the Liturgy, p. 27.

[37] This and numerous other new retranslation projects, major and minor, approved by the bishops or in progress, and principles governing the process, are described in the *Agenda Report, Documentation for General Meeting of the NCCB,* November 11–14, 1991; *Action Items* 2–4, reports by the Liturgy Committee (pp. 1–11, 228–34; 238–40), and in *Information Items,* p. 33. Also in the *Agenda Report* (*Action Items,* pp. 252–56) is the report of the Committee on Pastoral Practices on granting of *imprimaturs* in the name of the NCCB by a small internal committee. Other less sweeping revisions are planned as part of the "inculturation" process for "Native Americans" and other minority groups.

1991 meeting, in a special statement to the bishops on the NAB Psalter revision policy by the "Revisers and Steering Committee", the *Criteria* adopted by the NCCB in 1990 is referenced;[38] and the anonymous writers say that changing the text can be "legitimate, for it gives the sense and does not violate our sensibilities".

> When Hebrew uses the third person masculine in generalized contexts, it is used as it formerly was used in English, i.e., in an inclusive sense. But since in English it no longer has that inclusive sense, to render it as third person masculine would not be a literal translation (i.e., one which gives the true meaning of the text) but a mistranslation.
>
> In the case of horizontal language, our revision of the Psalter avoids exclusive language by various means; most often this is by resorting to the plural....
>
> The case of vertical language is more difficult. The Bible depicts God in predominantly masculine terms, and no attempt is made to change the imagery of king, warrior, shepherd, etc. The use of the masculine pronoun is somewhat different. The revision committee proceeded on the conviction that the Bishops would agree that *urgent pastoral needs override the demand for strict literalism.* To that end we *eliminate the use of the masculine pronoun for God* where it can be done gracefully....
>
> Taking into account the primary concern of presenting a Psalter for use in the liturgy, *noting the Bishops' grave pastoral concern, and intending to make this revision respond to the needs of our day, we believe the means we have used to make the language of this revision inclusive* are legitimate.[39]

It seems evident that the members of ICEL and the NCCB Liturgy Committee were of one mind regarding the principal objectives of renovation of liturgical texts. Their view seems compatible, also, with that expressed by Letty Russell, an Episcopalian priest who teaches feminist theology at Yale Divinity School, when she said, "The way to respect the original words [of God] is to retranslate them as our understanding changes."

---

[38] For the complete text of *Criteria* and brief critical comments, see Appendix B.
[39] *Agenda Report,* pp. 233, 234 (emphasis added).

Also at their Fall 1991 meeting, the bishops officially approved a laughably inept American Bible Society translation of a Lectionary for Masses with Children (it was actually the subject of an editorial cartoon), including its introduction, which states:

> Upon publication, the Lectionary for Masses with Children will be the *only approved lectionary* for use at Masses with children in the dioceses of the United States of America.[40]

The Liturgy Committee proposed granting permission for the creation of a new Lectionary based on the National Council of Churches (NCC) New Revised Standard Version (NRSV), stating, "Since the recently revised versions of these biblical translations *use inclusive language,* the Secretariat has received several requests that they now be authorized for liturgical use."[41] The NCCB Administrative Committee had already granted its *imprimatur* to the NRSV translation in September 1991; so the bishops were in the awkward position of being asked to vote on a translation already given this form of approval. The NRSV handily secured the required two-thirds majority of the voting members of the conference; and it was almost instantly approved for liturgical use by Rome.

A new NAB-based Lectionary, created principally for the purpose of rendering its "outdated" English usage acceptable to feminists,[42] was introduced at the June 1992 meeting. Twenty minutes was scheduled on the agenda for discussion and vote on this translation, which will deeply affect the future of the

---

[40] *Agenda Report—Action Items,* p. 11. During the NCCB meeting, the Lectionary for Masses with Children became known in the press-room as the "Sesame Street Bible", or the "Away-in-a-Feedbox" translation, referring in particular to the translation of "manger" as "feedbox". Despite the energetic defense of "feedbox" by the chairmen of the bishops' committees on liturgy and pastoral practices, the bishops voted to change the word back to "manger". This was the only emendation the bishops sought before granting their approval to the entire text.

[41] Ibid., p. 238.

[42] See above references to Sr. Mary Collins, O.S.B., J. Frank Henderson, Lawrence Boadt, et al., in *Shaping English Liturgy.*

liturgy. Ballots were mailed, and the outcome of the bishops' voting was announced six weeks later: 219 in favor; 27 opposed. The lopsided voting is not surprising, however. Again, the bishops could hardly be expected to reject a translation which had already officially received their collective *imprimatur* nd *nihil obstat* through their own Administrative Committee and the newly created ad hoc Committee for Approval of Revised Scripture Translations.

By the time these "theologically correct" translations reach the floor of the bishops' meeting, they are already, in effect, a "done deal". The bishops are expected to rubber-stamp the work of anonymous committees. The remarkable candor of those involved in the retranslation project, who no longer bother to conceal their feminist agenda, is doubtless attributable to their confidence that formal approval by the bishops and the Vatican will be automatically forthcoming. When the "will of the bishops" in America is conveyed to the appropriate Vatican officials, they customarily accede to the expressed desire of the national conference. Thus Archbishop Pilarczyk, in his report on ICEL to the NCCB at the November 1991 meeting, expressed confidence that the depleted financial resources of ICEL will be replenished when the new liturgical books are ready for distribution in about 1997.[43]

---

[43] *Agenda Report—Information Items,* p. 113. "ICEL's income is from the liturgical texts that it prepares and licenses publishers to produce after the authorization of the conferences. Present indications are that ICEL's financial condition will be difficult over the next few years, beginning particularly in 1993. This situation results from the high costs of the Missal revision project, which will have taken twelve years from the initial consultation phase to the presentation to the conferences, and from a decline in overall revenues from the earlier liturgical books prepared by ICEL. More recent books, such as the *Order of Christian Funerals,* the *Rite of Christian Initiation of Adults,* the *Book of Blessings,* and the *Ceremonial of Bishops,* while providing some revenue, have brought only a small infusion of funds. In some cases the monies spent in preparing these texts have yet to be recouped and realistically may never be, given the many costs involved in preparing liturgical books. The declining financial situation will likely continue until the beginning of 1997, when new income is expected from the revised Missal."

The history of the ICEL liturgical renewal project, as documented by its own members, reveals: (1) that commitment to "inclusive" language has been a guiding principle for about twenty years; (2) that ICEL's decisions regarding all English translations of Scripture and prayers used in public worship have with very rare and minor exceptions been accepted, virtually without question, by the bishops' conferences; (3) that ICEL's committees have been and continue to be heavily influenced by radical feminist theology and Scripture scholarship; (4) that only eleven English-speaking bishops on ICEL's Episcopal Board approve the work of an even smaller number of people who actually produce these translations; and (5) that ICEL's commitment to "change", to a revisionist theological and ecclesial position, has been imposed on millions of English-speaking Catholic worshippers by gradual incorporation of feminist-language texts throughout the English-speaking Church. Documents of ICEL's sister-organization, now called the English Language Liturgical Consultation (ELLC), would undoubtedly reveal parallel development throughout the Protestant members of the NCC. And if the active politicization of the prayer of the Church has encountered negligible resistance from Catholic bishops, the feminist reform of other religious bodies has evidently met with none at all. Most mainline denominations now have multiple "alternative" Creeds, and, although technically they may be optional, they bear the official approbation of the governing body of the church, and appear in the official books of worship, hymnals, etc.

As in the Catholic Church, it is apparent that the liturgical reform in other mainline religious groups has usually been accomplished through the work of a very small, self-perpetuating group of experts rigorously committed to a limited and highly revisionist view of the nature of faith and the purpose of prayer. A distinction of potential importance, however, may be that the polity of most non-Catholic religious bodies, generally representative or "democratic" in structure, gives some control over liturgical and doctrinal innovations to worshippers—at least in theory. Conceivably, then, the party of reform could be defeated at some future legislative synod or convention.

In the Catholic Church, of course, only the bishops bear final responsibility for shaping the English liturgy. Bishops who persist in defending the Scripture and liturgy of the Church from ideological assault have been unable, so far, to mount effective opposition to the liturgical reform projects. Bishops who are outspoken critics of the politicization of the doctrine and liturgy of the Church risk being stereotyped as reactionaries, fundamentalists, "traditionalists", cranks, or simply disdained as "amateur". Perhaps even more damaging than these appellations within the bishops' conference itself is the charge of being "controversial". So far there has been little evidence that the members of the bishops' conference will mount any effective opposition to or control over the system of "liturgical renewal" in the Catholic Church, a system which has worked infallibly for the past thirty years. To date, its success has encountered no resistance worth bothering about.

III

"The life of the liturgy", Cardinal Joseph Ratzinger has said, "does not consist in 'pleasant' surprises and attractive 'ideas' but in solemn repetitions. It cannot be an expression of what is current and transitory, for it expresses the mystery of the holy.... In the liturgy there is a power, an energy at work which not even the Church as a whole can generate.... The liturgy, for the Catholic, is his common homeland, the source of his identity.... It must be something 'given' and 'constant' [because] by means of the ritual, it manifests the holiness of God."[44]

This view of the liturgy expressed by the Prefect of the Congregation for the Doctrine of the Faith probably has less in common with the understanding of the liturgy operative in the ICEL retranslating teams than with many Catholics far less capable of articulating their convictions.

But there exists a substantial distinction, also, between liberal and radical ideological perspectives on the liturgy. The liberal view

---

[44] Joseph Cardinal Ratzinger, *The Ratzinger Report,* ed. Vittorio Messori (San Francisco: Ignatius Press, 1985), p. 126.

leans toward "reconciliationism", universalism, cultural homogenization; while radicals (including most religious feminists) advocate radical reform, uprooting of traditions (whether "ethnic", cultural, or religious)—actual revolution, transformation, and destruction, if necessary to substitute a new religious "structure" for that deemed defective.

Common to both views, however, is a concept of truth as subject to the particular experiences—of an individual or of the culture: i.e., deliberately ignoring history. This denial or, in fact, rejection of the past, of history, is also a rejection of authority outside the self. If one is isolated from one's own history, this has consequences for language, also, since one of the principal functions of a language is to transmit culture from one generation to another. Rejection of the past, of one's rootedness in a culture, entails the rejection of the language which gives it expression. The function of spoken language in the formation and transmission of culture is, of course, related to the broader question of "inculturation". It was quite common in immigrant families, for example, for the foreign-born parents to refuse to teach the "mother tongue" to their children, whom they hoped to Americanize thoroughly. It was also effective.

An example of an attempt to improve relations among peoples through the use of language was the effort to promote use of Esperanto as a universal language. Esperanto was a deliberately manufactured language; a "reconciliation" or homogenization of disparate languages. Predictably, its creator and its promoters failed, in spite of the apparent superiority and logic of the homogenized language. Probably many things account for this failure. But surely two principal reasons must be that there was no mandate from the people to create such a language; and no coercion from governments enforced its use. It died the natural death of many ideas which look good on paper but cannot thrive. But there is an additional factor. A living language cannot be invented. It must develop organically, much as any other living thing. Into the mix, of course, must go constituent elements almost too subtle, too complex, too deeply ingrained and intertwined, to submit readily to definition. Like culture, or religion, it must grow genuinely and at its own, not a legislated, pace. For it is commonly held understandings of basic underlying truths—and a shared language in which to express them—that make a people, a true community. Anything that disrupts this fertile field of organic growth does violence not only to the language but to the beliefs which help to create a common tongue—and the spirit of a people. Applying this principle to the language of worship of God, it follows that continually changing the words symbolically destroys the Word—the common language, the common understanding—which makes it possible to speak of a "people of God".

An illustration of the disintegrative effect on a communion of believers when violence is done to their primary means of expressing commonly held understandings, and the role of language in both unifying and perpetuating a religious body, can be seen in the experience of the Anglican Communion, who "contemporized" and "optionalized" the language of liturgy in the 1970s. The denomination has suffered continuous hemorrhage ever since— not only in dramatic loss of membership but in repeated schisms. Quite possibly the only thing that all Anglicans truly had in common, by the 1970s, was the language of the Book of Common Prayer. Essentially unchanged since it had been composed by Thomas Cranmer in 1549, soon after Henry VIII declared his autonomy from the Catholic Church and named himself head of the Church of England, the Book of Common Prayer had been the single most potent factor which allowed the world-wide Anglican Communion to come into being. It had made it possible for Anglicans to transcend doctrinal disputes and liturgical styles for a period of more than four hundred years.

Since the first "Services for Trial Use" appeared in the mid-seventies (called the "Green Book", it offered alternatives in traditional and contemporary language), there have been several different Books of Common Prayer.[45] None of these versions has truly

[45] See Alvin Kimel, Jr., "A New Language for God? A Critique of Supplemental Liturgical Texts", Prayer Book Studies 30 (pamphlet), Shaker Heights, OH: Episcopalians United, 1990, p. 2. The Reverend Kimel, an Episcopalian priest, has also edited a collection of articles critical of feminist language, called *Speaking the Christian God: The Holy Trinity and the Challenge of Feminism* (Grand Rapids: Eerdmans, 1992).

been *common* prayer, of course. None has been around long enough to achieve anything approaching commonality. During the seventies, the Episcopal Church in the USA also led the process of disintegration of Anglicanism (and decimation of its active membership) by its unilateral action in other important matters central to the radical feminist agenda: chiefly the ordination of women to the "priesthood", advocacy of abortion "rights", and a policy of tolerance bordering on encouragement of other serious moral and doctrinal aberrations even among its bishops.

The Anglicans are not alone among Protestants in their active collaboration with the *Zeitgeist,* however. Nearly every Protestant body has rushed to update its worship and its beliefs to accommodate a particular view of modernity. The new Methodist Book of Worship, for example, employs feminist principles exclusively to its several "alternate" creeds (God is addressed as "mother" in one, and footnotes in the traditional creeds retained provide further alternative choices).

The problem of feminist liturgical language is not confined to Christian churches. Editors of a prayer book, *Vetaher Libenu* (Purify Our Hearts) published by Congregation Beth El in Sudbury, in Massachusetts, wrote in the *Wall Street Journal* letters column in May 1992:

> Since publication [in 1980] of the first egalitarian prayer book in the Jewish community . . . our Prayer book has been reviewed, cited, studied, copied and used by thousands of theologians, journalists and laypeople . . . and we are particularly pleased that nearly 20% of our orders have come from Christian[s].
>
> It should not be so surprising that more and more worshippers of all denominations "have come to believe", as our Ritual Committee declared . . . , "that the exclusive use of masculine imagery to describe God invites idolatry and that imagery too easily becomes reality."
>
> They may be inspired, as we were, by the oldest description of God in the Torah: "And God created humankind in God's image; male and female did God create them" (Genesis 1:27).[46]

[46] Nancy Lee Gossels, Joan S. Kaye, C. Peter R. Gossels, editors of *Vetaher Libenu* (Sudbury, Mass.: Congregation Beth El, 1980) in *The Wall Street Journal,* May 27, 1992, "Letters to the Editor", p. A15.

All four drafts of the US bishops' "Pastoral Response to Women's Concerns" have explicitly advised that feminist language be employed in the Church's worship. "Inclusive language" requirements are found in seminary handbooks, and official and unofficial "guidelines" have been produced for use in Catholic hospitals, publications, etc.

In late July 1992, Bishop Edward D. Head, of Buffalo, New York, released a pastoral letter, *Guidelines for Inclusive Language, Diocese of Buffalo,* explicitly mandating use of feminist language throughout the Church in his jurisdiction and outlining liturgical "reforms". The document was "written collaboratively" by the diocesan Commission on Women in Church and Society, the Office of Worship, the Office of Church Ministry, the Office of the Vicar for Religious and the Commission on Peace and Justice. In an interview in his diocesan newspaper (before the *Guidelines* appeared) conducted by Sr. Barbara Riter, S.S.M.N., of his "women's commission", Bishop Head asks rhetorically, "If our 'forefathers' who wrote ['all men are created equal'] understood 'men' to be inclusive of women, why did it require a Constitutional Amendment for women to vote?" He assures readers that "within the liturgical setting, there are some sections which presently we may adapt and some which await the approval of the [NCCB], the [ICEL] and the Holy See."[47] Bishop Head's list of "Documents Which Substantiate Adapting Liturgical Texts" includes the second draft of the "women's pastoral" ("One in Christ Jesus", March 1990); and the recommended resources listed include works by radical feminists Elisabeth Schüssler-Fiorenza, Fr. Thomas Groome, Rosalie Maggio, Gail Ramshaw-Schmidt, Casey Miller, and Kate Swift.[48]

[47] Sister Barbara Riter. "Bishop Promulgates Inclusive Language Guidelines", in *The Western New York Catholic Visitor,* June 8, 1992.

[48] Bishop Edward D. Head, *Guidelines for Inclusive Language Diocese of Buffalo,* July 26, 1992.

IV

"Death to the old in order to give birth to the new."

Rosemary Ruether, in *Sexism & God Talk*

On reading the contemporary Scripture translations, one might be tempted to think that translators and liturgists have tried to create a sort of liturgical Esperanto; or that they simply had tin ears, and new scholarship, new knowledge of the ancient languages have made the task of rendering the original text in good contemporary English (the "receptor language") too difficult to worry much about how it sounds. But that would be to mistake the actual aims of the committees of experts (virtually always anonymous) who have spent nearly three decades at uglification of the biblical text and banalization of the liturgy. One cannot help sensing deliberate vandalism by people who have problems with their own faith and want to diminish it in others, or at least to make it as difficult as possible to retain by removing from the language of worship a sense of the sacred, of the transcendent—of that which is greater than man, beyond the limitations of time and unconditioned by the particularity of culture: in other words, Divine Inspiration. "Openness to change" has been rigidly and coercively enjoined on worshippers—in the name of creativity and freedom, literary quality, musical adaptability, *and,* most of all, "justice" to women who "feel excluded" by the patriarchal religion of Judaism and Christianity.

Justifying their bias in favor of translations which will be "dynamically equivalent", rather than "formally equivalent", the translating teams have deliberately rejected the influence of earlier translations in favor of a new "horizontal" language, more compatible with their own ecclesial opinions of the nature of the Church. But sensitizing people to the issue of liturgical language—involving gender matters in particular—has the jarring and distracting effect of forcing everyone who uses language (new or old) to become acutely conscious of the new "correct" words. Feminist liturgical language, by forcing unnatural and awkward constructions, circumlocutions, and other linguistic gymnastics in order to make the words convey a particular political message, also destroys music, poetry, rhythms, distorts and confuses meanings, eliminates nuance, and impoverishes symbol. For example, when "Son" is replaced by "Child", since the meanings of the words are not identical and each has a variety of meanings, entirely separate, violence is done to the understanding drawn from the text. It muddles rather than clarifies the meaning. This is hardly accidental, of course. Clearly it is also consciously political.

Fundamental questions about the project of translation, to which Cardinal Ratzinger alludes, remain: Is the original biblical and liturgical language entirely conditioned by the culture at the time it was written, or does it transcend limitations of culture, time? Those who regard the biblical texts as authentic revelation, as divinely inspired, hence authoritative, will, of course, think of these questions quite differently from those who regard biblical texts as reflective of the attempt by a particular people of a particular time to compile a common myth in order to render their universe intelligible. Myth can be true, of course; but truth is not a myth.

A myth is a powerful story that shapes reality through its own set of symbols. Feminists talk a lot about myths—and about de-mythologizing and re-mythologizing. Feminist consciousness-raising always includes "telling stories" in an attempt to create a new mythology which will enhance the project of feminization of religion. Telling personal "stories" in a consciousness-raising group also serves to break down resistance to change through forming new relationships of "mutual trust" and friendship with other group participants—and especially its leaders—whose ideas, no matter how radical, one thus becomes disposed to accept. This technique developed by secular feminism has been seamlessly incorporated into the very fabric of religious life in America during the years following the Second Vatican Council. The process of radical transformation of the entire belief system of Catholic women religious has been described very recently and candidly by two former heads of the Leadership Conference of Women Religious [LCWR], Lora Ann Quiñonez, C.D.P., and Mary Daniel Turner, S.N.D.deN., in their revealing book, *The Transformation of American Catholic Sisters.*[49]

A particular danger arising from the massive projects of retranslation of the words of worship is the overwhelming temptation for the translators to substitute their own view of reality for the one which is actually conveyed by the original texts. Translators have immense power to impose their own culturally conditioned and limited view of reality on others by infusing their translations with ideology alien to the original texts. They do, after all, control the words which will be spoken in worship. Translators actually have the power to cause worshippers to speak *their* words; to cause the Church to express *their* beliefs.

"Control of language is an immensely powerful force in any society", Cardinal Joseph Bernardin of Chicago told participants in the National Workshop on Christian-Jewish Relations on November 7, 1990. "We must honestly ask whether this immensely powerful vehicle is not now becoming increasingly a source of the degradation of human persons, especially in certain areas of the communications arts."[50] He was speaking about dehumanizing language used to neutralize immoral actions such as abortion and racial genocide. But the Cardinal's words apply equally well to the project of feminization of the Church's liturgical language.

Words have no power if people have no words. It is possible to prevent people from learning words (and the ideas or beliefs they contain) by constantly changing them. Nearly everyone by now has had the experience of attempting to sing a hymn, familiar since childhood, and finding that the words have been changed. Disposable missalettes and hymn books help keep the liturgy in flux. People may experience a vague sense of discomfort with the unfamiliar words, but since the books are replaced every few weeks, there is no "authentic text" with which compare them. Some liturgists now urge that worshippers be given no books at

---

[49] Lora Ann Quiñonez, C.D.P., and Mary Daniel Turner, S.N.D.deN., *The Transformation of American Catholic Sisters* (Philadelphia: Temple University Press, 1992).

[50] *Origins,* Washington, DC: Catholic News Service, vol. 20: no. 26, December 6, 1990, p. 428.

all. Their argument is that people should be listening, not reading, in order to participate fully in the communal action of worship. But an unspoken reason, surely, is to allow the "presider" at a worship service maximum control with minimum resistance from the pews. Lacking a reliable text, "informed dissent" from liturgical innovations is less likely.

If there is an impulse to destroy, where does it come from? The source of the destructive anger may be in the assertion of absolute personal autonomy and the self-affirming desire to control. There is a perverse desire to destroy what cannot be controlled—and to control the destruction as well. One time-honored way of retaining control of a situation, whether personal or institutional, is by keeping everyone off balance, uncomfortable, uncertain, insecure. The effectiveness of this psychological manipulation can be observed on playgrounds, in boardrooms and chancery offices, and on fields of battle.

But another aspect of the destructive impulse is turned inward. For when one rejects all reality outside the self, denies authenticity to any person or any idea which does not have its origin in one's own individual consciousness (or "lived experience"), no matter how high that consciousness may have been raised, it will still be radically isolated—alone with its own subjective feelings— and unable to receive affirmation from a source truly exterior to itself. (Consciousness-raising groups and "listening sessions" actually function more as mirrors reflecting one's own emotions and ideas than as real interaction.) Thus the ultimate end of the declaration of one's radical personal autonomy, or rejection of reality outside one's self (i.e., objective truth), is not liberating, after all, but profoundly restricting, isolating. Therefore, it tends to lead, finally, to a rejection of the self—to self-destruction, disintegration. In order to preserve the self from total disintegration, then, some kind of order must be imposed by the self on the universe—the world "out there". The existence of anything exterior to the self, along with the genuine integrity of the self, and of one's own person in relation to others, becomes problematical with the rejection of exterior reality—of objective truth.

The rejection of the transcendent dimension of reality—of that which exists outside and independent of one's self, gives rise also to an imitation of a religious reality, based on individual feelings, experiences, emotions. The next step, then, is the divinization of self, the religion of the immanent (the popular epithet "navel-gazing" fits well here). When there is no recognition of power or authority or reality exterior to one's own imagination or self-consciousness, the self may attempt to prove itself to itself (affirm itself) through the exercise of power. In other words, the self confirms its own "divinity" only through its exercise of power over others. In the religion of the immanent, in the denial of the transcendent, immutable, absolute, and unconditionable God, then, it would follow that everything, including religion, must be seen by the "self-divinized" person in terms of power. Or, as Sister Sandra Schneiders described it, personal transformation through consciousness-raising and "accessing one's power" *is* feminist spirituality.[51]

Creation of a new reality-shaping myth is necessary, also, in order to avoid personal chaos and psychological disintegration. It is essential, too, that the new myth be expressed in a new language free from the assumptions of the old myth. It is necessary, in order to destroy the old oppressive myth, to deconstruct the assumptions and the language which gave it—and continues to give it—life. New meanings must be given to old words, new connotations imparted to them, and new words concocted. Otherwise the words themselves may inhibit and restrict the development of the new myth—the revised story upon which the new vision of reality must be based.

The will to destroy the word—the language in which the old myth has been clothed, and which, like clothes, expresses its meaning or significance—inheres in the will to reject, in fact, to nullify the power of the old myth (i.e., objective truth) to influence the newly divinized, radically autonomous self. To complete the overpowering of the "oppressive" truth (and those who are formed by it, defend it, or cling to it), it must be made speechless—

[51] See above, note 4.

something like cutting out the tongue of the messenger who brings bad news. So long as words capable of expressing this truth can still be spoken, the birth of the new myth—and the restructuring of reality—can never take place.

Our contemporary version of the Tower of Babel is the attempt to construct a "new structure"—one which is liberated from the limitations and "oppression" of the past—whereby man attempts to assert his power over everything which inhibits him from becoming "as gods". Such a structure is destined to fall, just as the original did, in an incomprehensible confusion of sounds. Our task—the task of religious believers—is to listen ever more attentively to the only abidingly intelligible speech—God's Word.

All that will live godly in Christ Jesus shall suffer persecution. But evil men and seducers shall wax worse and worse, deceiving, and being deceived. But continue thou in the things which thou hast learned and hast been assured of, knowing of whom thou hast learned them; and that from a child thou hast known the holy scriptures, which are able to make thee wise unto salvation through faith which is in Christ Jesus.

All scripture is given by inspiration of God, and is profitable for doctrine, for reproof, for correction, for instruction in righteousness; that the man of God may be perfect, perfected unto all good works [2 Timothy 3:13–17].

Helen Hull Hitchcock
Feast of the Assumption
August 15, 1992

I

THE POLITICS OF LANGUAGE

WORDS, WORDS EVERYWHERE—
AND NOT A THOUGHT TO THINK

Joyce A. Little

A recent issue of *Boston College Magazine* contained an article entitled "Writing Catholic", in which several Catholic writers were asked to describe how their Faith affects their work. One of the respondents, a woman named Mary Helen Washington, noted toward the end of her contribution that, some years ago, an essay she had written for a magazine was returned to her by one of the editors, with this remark: "Say something about your sex life or your readers will think you're weird." Ms. Washington responded to this as follows:

> I thought about my mother, about my high school teachers, my college teachers, confession, the sixth commandment; and I wrote these cryptic and evasive lines: "I'd like an alliance with a man who could be a comrade and a kindred spirit, and I've had such alliances in the past; even with the hassles they were *enriching* and *enjoyable* experiences." For anyone interested in the phenomenon of religious linguistics, that, I assure you, is truly a Catholic sentence.[1]

These comments raise at least three interesting and important questions for us. First, is there such a thing as a "Catholic" sentence? Second, if so, just what elements would be required to make a sentence Catholic? Third, does Ms. Washington's sentence contain these elements?

Before attempting to answer any of these questions, however, I

[1] Mary Helen Washington, "Writing Catholic", *Boston College Magazine* 48 (Summer 1989): 31.

3

would like to consider, first, why language is important enough to talk about at all, and, second, what sort of use we have been making of the English language in modern American society.

THE IMPORTANCE OF LANGUAGE

Although there are many reasons why language is important, two in particular deserve our special attention. The first of these is the relationship between language and reality. One expert in the field of communication maintains that "communication creates what we call reality",[2] and language guidelines now in use in some universities in this country begin with the remark, "Language reflects, reinforces and creates reality."[3] While not everyone would agree that language alone creates reality, most people would grant that language does express and influence the way we perceive reality. Not for nothing do we say that the "pen is mightier than the sword".

Second, language is important because language is by its very nature communal. There is no such thing as a private language, any more than there is a private solar system. In the words of Catholic priest and theologian Romano Guardini, "Speech is not something added to a complete human existence. We exist in the word, in conversation, hence in relation to others and by the universal communality of life."[4] For this reason, the American journalist Edwin Newman is quite right when he insists that "the language belongs to all of us. We have no more valuable possession."[5]

[2] Paul Watzlawick, *How Real Is Real?* (New York: Random House Vintage Books, 1976), p. xi.

[3] Guidelines adapted from "Guidelines for Equal Treatment of the Sexes in McGraw-Hill Book Company Publications" and "Linguistic Sexism", *Journal of Ecumenical Studies* 11.

[4] Romano Guardini, *The Focus of Freedom,* trans. Gregory Roettger (Baltimore and Dublin: Helicon, 1966), p. 37.

[5] Edwin Newman, *A Civil Tongue* (Indianapolis and New York: Bobbs-Merrill, 1975).

MODERN AMERICAN USE OF ENGLISH

What use have we Americans been making of this precious possession of ours? The word that best characterizes how we use words
today is, I think, "abstraction". According to *Webster's New
Universal Unabridged Dictionary,* the three primary definitions of
the adjective "abstract" are "(1) thought of apart from any particular instances or material objects; not concrete. (2) expressing
a quality thought of apart from any particular or material object;
as, beauty is an *abstract* word. (3) not easy to understand, ab-
struse". Abstraction, in other words, has the effect of removing
from consideration the specific, the particular, and, perhaps most
importantly, the material elements of anything about which we
might be thinking. Abstraction therefore tends to eliminate from
our thinking the limits, the boundaries that confront us in everyday experience. The beautiful sunset upon which we are gazing
embodies beauty in a concrete, specific, material way. The word
"beauty", in contrast, floats free of any such specificity, any such
limits. And, because abstract thinking tends to float free of any
specifications, it can easily and quickly become difficult to understand by anyone who is himself a concrete, particular, materially
embodied person living in a concrete, particular, materially
embodied world. If you have ever taken a philosophy class, you
know just how quickly discussions of such abstractions as "being"
and "essence" can become entirely incomprehensible.

Our use of language in America today is riddled with abstraction—
for several quite different reasons, two of which I would like to
discuss here. First (and I deliberately want to give priority to this
reason because I do not think we generally understand just how
important it is), our language is abstract because we simply do not
know enough, either linguistically or culturally, to express the
richness and diversity either in ourselves or in the people, places,
and events of our ordinary experience. Consider the implications
of the following statement:

It [the English language] is huge, with over 700,000 words,
and growing fast; it is also grievously under-used by its habi-

tuates. The average English-speaker's customary vocabulary is only 600 words, and monitoring experiments carried out by the Bell Telephone Laboratory show that a group of 100 common words constitute over 75% of all conversations.[6]

If I have only a few hundred words at my disposal to describe everyone and everything I know, pretty soon the people and things I know are going to start sounding like reruns of one other. Perhaps this is why so many shows on television already give this impression long before the reruns start. Perhaps this is why football viewers such as myself find ourselves assaulted weekly by monotonous comments to the effect that "this is a great game", "that was a great pass", "the quarterback is a great young man", "that was a great reception", "their coach does a great job", etc.

Language such as this is abstract not in the scientific or philosophical sense but in the repetitive and lackluster sense. Different qualities are not abstracted from concrete particulars, as the philosopher might abstract. Instead, the same qualities are applied to all concrete particulars, because the speaker simply does not know any other qualities, any other words, to apply. Hence, people, places, and events lose their specificity, their uniqueness, because we, the users of our language, simply do not know the words that would allow us to express the differences that are there.

Our use of language is also limited, as E. D. Hersch, Jr., has recently pointed out to us, by our lack of cultural literacy. The sentence "The lilies are blooming in the fields today" is meaningless to people who do not know the word "lilies" and the word "fields". But the sentence "She is one of the lilies of the field" is equally meaningless to people who know all about lilies and fields but do not know anything about the Bible. After reading Hersch's book, I conducted a short cultural literacy test in three of my classes and discovered, to my dismay, that not a single student in any one of them knew what "lilies of the field" means. Thousands upon thousands of the words we use

---

[6] Paul Johnson, *Enemies of Society* (London: Weidenfeld and Nicolson, 1977), p. 103.

not only have direct, specific meanings (denotations); they also carry with them whole ranges of associated meanings (connotations). If we do not know the connotations, something of the vividness of the word and of the thing the word signifies is irreparably lost.

To give just one small example from my own recent experience, I, like most people, learned as a small child the word "ladybug", and I have on many occasions in life observed specific creatures that are denoted by that expression. What I did not know until a couple of weeks ago is that the "lady" in ladybug is the Blessed Virgin Mary and that these bugs were so named because they eat insects that would otherwise destroy a farmer's crops. I shall never again be able to think of a ladybug without thinking of our Lady and of her benevolence toward us. Indeed, I shall probably find it impossible in the future to see a ladybug without thinking of it as a creature entrusted with a mission that links the heavens and the earth.

Unless we consciously labor both to increase the number of words we know and to recover the associated meanings attaching to them, we can expect ordinary English usage to become even more tedious and lifeless than it already is. And it is already intolerably wearisome. As Edwin Newman observed a few years ago,

> Much written and spoken expression these days is equivalent to the background music that incessantly encroaches on us, in banks, restaurants, department stores, trains, shops, airports, airplanes, dentists' offices, hospitals, elevators, waiting rooms, hotel lobbies, pools, apartment building lobbies, bars, and, to my personal knowledge, at least one museum. It thumps and tinkles away, mechanical, without color, inflection, vigor, charm, or distinction. People who work in the presence of background music often tell you, and sometimes with pride, that they don't hear it anymore. The parallel with language is alarming.[7]

The second major reason our language has become so abstract is because science exercises such an enormous influence on how we

---

[7] Edwin Newman, *Strictly Speaking* (New York: Warner Books, 1974), pp. 30–31.

think and on how we perceive reality. Theoretical physics holds the pride of place among the hard sciences, and no human being alive today is more intent on pursuing the abstract than the theoretical physicist. From Newton through Einstein to Hawking, each is seeking some grand unified theory that can be expressed in that most abstract of all languages, mathematics. For an Einstein, equations such as $E = Mc^2$ represent the highest pinnacle the human mind can ever hope to scale. Einstein himself made the point quite clearly when, in 1952, he declined the presidency of Israel on grounds that "equations are more important to me, because politics is for the present, but an equation is something for eternity".[8] Here we get a chilling glimpse into the scientific heaven, where God is replaced by the grand unified theory and beatitude is contemplation of equations.

Einstein's remark was cited in the recent bestseller, *A Brief History of Time,* by Stephen Hawking, Einstein's legitimate successor both in genius and in fame. And Stephen Hawking, in that same book, notes that because a unified theory is "just a set of rules and equations", we have to ask what its actual relationship to our universe might be. He then poses what to some people must have seemed a really stunning question: "Is the unified theory so compelling that it brings about its own existence?"[9] When someone begins to wonder if equations might possess the power to create a universe, all anyone else can say is that abstract thinking just does not get any more abstract than that.

Unfortunately, this kind of thinking has set the tone for every discipline on God's green earth that makes any claim, valid or not, to being scientific, including, of course and perhaps especially, theology, which still remembers those long, glorious centuries in which she held pride of place as the queen of all the sciences. As a result, every discipline seems, at one time or another, intent on demonstrating that its subject matter can be rendered just as abstract as the most abstract grand unified theory. Under these

---

[8] Cited in Stephen W. Hawking, *A Brief History of Time* (Toronto, New York, London, Sydney, and Auckland: Bantam Books, 1988), p. 178.

[9] Ibid., p. 174.

circumstances, sociologists become, as Edwin Newman quips, "people who pretend to advance the cause of knowledge by calling a family a microcluster of structured role expectations or a bounded plurality of role-playing individuals".[10] Educational theorists produce one tome after another of incomprehensible abstractions that never, under any circumstances, suggest that education has anything to do with living, breathing human beings. Richard Mitchell's several books, most especially *The Graves of Academe,* document well the absurdities spawned by this method. The following is just one example of the netherworld in which educational theory today dwells. Consider the following description of "instructional approaches":

> These instructional approaches are perhaps best conceived on a systems model, where instructional variables (input factors) are mediated by factors of students' existing cognitive structure (organizational properties of the learner's immediately relevant concepts in the particular subject field); and by personal predispositions and tolerance toward the requirements of inference, abstraction, and impulse control, all prerequisite to achievement in the discovery or the hypothetical learning mode.[11]

If you want to know why American education has declined so strikingly in recent years, you could do worse than begin your inquiry right here.

Theology, of course, has kept up with this sort of thing stride for stride. I will content myself here by citing an example included by Edwin Newman in his book *A Civil Tongue.* The following reflection on the subject of "piety and politics" can be found in Paul Lehman's *The Transfiguration of Politics: The Presence and Power of Jesus of Nazareth in and over Human Affairs.*

> Piety and politics belong intrinsically and inseparably together. Piety is the compound of reverence and thankfulness that forms and transforms the reciprocity between creaturehood and creativity, in privacy and in society, into the possibility and the

[10] Newman, *A Civil Tongue,* p. 13.
[11] Richard Mitchell, *The Graves of Academe* (New York: Simon and Schuster, A Fireside Book, 1981), p. 33.

power of fulfilling human freedom and joy. Politics is the compound of justice, ordination, and order that shapes, sustains, and
gives structure to a social matrix for the human practice of
privacy and for the practice of humanness in community. In
such a matrix, justice is the reciprocity of differences in creaturehood and creativity, experienced as enrichment rather than as a
threat; ordination is the insistent priority and pressure of purpose over power in the practice of the reciprocity between
creaturehood and creativity; and order is the possibility and the
power of so living in one time and place as not to destroy the
possibility of other times and places. So piety apart from politics
loses its integrity and converts into apostasy; whereas politics
without piety subverts both its divine ordination and its ordering
of humanness, perverts justice, and converts into idolatry. . . . The
human meaning of politics is to the biblical meaning of politics
as the Fall is to the creaturehood and destiny of humanity in a
world that has been created and redeemed.[12]

What does this mean? Newman thinks it means that "the Biable is
viable".[13] All I can add is that the Bible would not be viable if
Jesus Christ had permitted himself to talk like that.

Lest we think that such uncivil language is confined to academic discourse, we would do well to remember that what
starts there sooner or later filters out, through the graduates
of our colleges and universities, into government and business,
into art and literature, into law and medicine, into newspapers
and television, and, alas, even into our churches. A few examples,
to which I am primarily indebted to Edwin Newman, will,
I think, suffice. An investment company tells us, "We have
exceptional game plan capabilities together with strict concerns
for programming successful situations."[14] Making buses run on
schedule translates into "schedule adherence with emphasis on
hitting checkpoints within the targeted time".[15] Cemeteries are
now "human interment space", taxes have become "revenue en-

---

[12] Newman, *A Civil Tongue,* pp. 155–56.
[13] Ibid., p. 156.
[14] Ibid., p. 5.
[15] Ibid., p. 9.

hancement", and death is "negative patient care outcome". A young man is so moved by the kindness and compassion of an older man who had helped him in his life that he writes to the local newspaper about this person who "became an experiencing person in my life, lending an aura to my developing personality of absolute rapport and communicatory relevance".[16] A priest writes to Edwin Newman expressing the fear that his days as a pastor are numbered: "Unless the trend in language was reversed, he expected to be Coordinator of the Faith Community Dimension."[17] And surely we all remember how Nixon's coverup of Watergate was characterized by one of his aides as "maximizing the incumbency".

Such language is perhaps appropriate at a time when we are encouraged to walk about in a permanent state of open-mindedness, since these contentless words float easily in and out of such minds. G. K. Chesterton was not, however, much taken with modern notions of open-mindedness. In reference to the views of H. G. Wells, he was moved to remark, "I think he [H. G. Wells] thought the object of opening the mind is simply opening the mind. Whereas I am incurably convinced that the object of opening the mind, as of opening the mouth, is to shut it again on something solid."[18] In this debate, Chesterton is right. And it is impossible to have thoughts to think unless one has words upon which the mind can fix itself. If we fix our attention, for example, on the family, our minds can entertain real thoughts about husbands, wives, fathers, mothers, brothers, and sisters and the commitments, responsibilities, obligations, loyalties, and loves that bind them together. If, in contrast, we fix our attention on "a microcluster of structured role expectations", human thought grinds to a halt. All of us have had some experience with fathers and mothers, brothers and sisters, but none of us has ever met a structured role expectation, not on our longest day or in our wildest dreams.

[16] Ibid.

[17] Ibid., p. 15.

[18] G. K. Chesterton, *The Autobiography of G. K. Chesterton* (New York: Sheed and Ward, 1936), pp. 228–29.

THE CATHOLIC FAITH AND LANGUAGE

Edwin Newman characterizes the good use of language, or "a civil tongue", as he calls it, as "direct, specific, concrete, vigorous, colorful, subtle, and imaginative when it should be, and as lucid and eloquent as we are able to make it".[19] And common sense alone should be enough to tell us he is right. But if he is right, and if language is bound up with our perception of reality, then there must also be something about reality itself that allows us to perceive it more readily by way of specific, concrete words than by way of abstractions. To return to one of the questions raised at the beginning: Is there such a thing as a Catholic sentence?

If by that question we mean, are there sentences that convey, by their very use of language, a view of reality that is consistent with the Catholic Faith, the answer must be an unmistakable yes. What kinds of sentences are they? They are precisely the kind Edwin Newman describes, "direct, specific, concrete". Why? The answer is obvious and simple and can be found in a single verse at the beginning of John's Gospel: "And the Word became flesh." If I may draw once again on Chesterton, who said it far better than I could ever hope to:

> Whenever you hear much of things being unutterable and inde-finable and impalpable and unnamable and subtly indescribable, then elevate your aristocratic nose towards heaven and snuff up the smell of decay. It is perfectly true that there is something in all good things that is beyond all speech or figure of speech. But it is also true that there is in all good things a perpetual desire for expression and concrete embodiment; and though the attempt to embody it is always inadequate, the attempt is always made. If the idea does not seek to be the word, the chances are that it is an evil idea. If the word is not made flesh it is a bad word.[20]

In the beginning, and by his word, God spoke things into existence,

[19] Newman, *A Civil Tongue,* p. 6.
[20] G. K. Chesterton, *A Miscellany of Men* (New York: Dodd, Mead, 1912), p. 174.

and the things he spoke into existence were direct, specific, and concrete. They were, in short, materially embodied and materially bonded to one another. And God looked at what he had made and declared it to be very good.

Millions of years later, scientific man looked at God's handiwork and asked what makes it tick. And he discovered that he could only find out by taking it apart. Thus began what we might call the great deconstruction of that world—and, to some degree, the deconstruction of man himself. The result, as Guardini has observed, is that "man's relations with nature have been altered radically, have become indirect. The old immediateness has been lost, for now his relations are transmitted by mathematics or by instruments. Abstract and formalized, nature has lost all concreteness; having become inorganic and technical, it has lost the quality of real experience."[21]

Abstracted or removed from his old direct relationship with the natural order, man has also abstracted himself from his own human nature, which is to say, from his own flesh. And just as he has come to see the whole order of nature, all of its powers, its forces, as rationally understandable and subject to technological control, so also he has come to see his own body, his own physical existence, in much the same light—as rationally understandable and technologically controllable.

This "demystification of the human body", as one writer puts it, removes all of the traditional restraints that previous ages attached to the two most bodily events we know: sex and death. The result, as that same writer points out, is that

the unborn child is no longer a human person, attached by indelible rights and obligations to the mother who bears him, but a slowly ripening deformity, which can be aborted at will, should the mother choose to cure herself. In surrogate motherhood the relation between mother and child ceases to issue from

[21] Romano Guardini, *The End of the Modern World,* trans. Joseph Theman and Herbert Turke, ed. with introduction by Frederick D. Wilhelmsen (New York: Sheed and Ward, 1956), pp. 87–88.

the very body of the mother and is severed from the experience of incarnation. The bond between mother and child is demystified, made clear, intelligible, scientific—and also provisional, revocable and of no more than contractual force. . . . In just the same way the sexual bond has become clear and intelligible, and also provisional, revocable and of merely contractual force, governed by the morality of adult "consent". . . . It no longer seems to us that the merely *bodily* character of our acts can determine their moral value. Hence arises the extraordinary view that the homosexual act, considered in itself, is morally indistinguishable from the heterosexual act: for what is there, in its merely physical character, to justify the traditional stigma?[22]

This modern detachment of man from his body is most apparent in the abstract language that today in matters of sex and death replaces the direct, concrete expressions of earlier ages. Lust is free love, adultery is open marriage, homosexuality is a life-style, masturbation is safe sex, pregnancy is disease, abortion is termination of that disease, procreation is reproduction, birth prevention is birth control, natural mothers are surrogate mothers, unborn children are embryos, embryos are property, murder is mercy killing, mercy killing is assisted suicide, and suicide is death with dignity. The degree to which such language has taken over was borne in on me when I told my students that the judge in Maryville, Tennessee, had ruled that frozen embryos are children, not property. A substantial number of my students were jarred by that statement. Clearly, nothing in their perception of reality had prepared them for such a ruling. [The decision in this case was overturned on appeal in June 1992, giving the father the "right" to destroy the embryos.—ED.]

There was a time when I viewed this new language as euphemistic, that is, as a deliberate attempt to find pleasing ways to characterize nasty things in order to rationalize the doing of those things. Unfortunately, something much more ominous is abroad in the land. The people who use this language are not, from their

[22] Roger Scruton, *Untimely Tracts* (London: Macmillan, 1987), p. 205. See also Romano Guardini, *Power and Responsibility,* trans. Elinor C. Briefs (Chicago: Henry Regnery, 1961), esp. pp. 50–51, for a similar discussion of this phenomenon.

point of view, speaking euphemistically. They are speaking quite accurately, because they are operating with what Cardinal Ratzinger recently characterized as a "revolutionary vision of man". At the heart of this vision, as Ratzinger points out,

> the body is something that one has and that one uses. No longer does man expect to receive a message from his bodiliness as to who he is and what he should do; but definitely, on the basis of his reasonable deliberations and even with complete independence, he expects to do with it as he wishes. In consequence, there is indeed no difference whether the body be of the masculine or the feminine sex; the body no longer expresses being at all; on the contrary, it has become a piece of property.[23]

When it no longer matters whether the body be masculine or feminine, then it no longer matters that language reflect the masculine or feminine character of human beings; hence the feminist insistence that we employ so-called nonsexist or sex-neutral language. Men and women become persons, mothering and fathering become parenting, couples expecting a baby are encouraged to mouth such nonsense as "we are pregnant". The abstractive character of such language achieves heights heretofore undreamed of in the expression "significant other", which abstracts not only from sexual differentiation but also from every conceivable differentiation. My "significant other" can be literally anything from my pet rock to God himself (though, of course, we are no longer allowed to refer to God as a "him").

At the same time, if my body is my property, at my disposal, then there are virtually no limits to what I can do with it. I can rent it out for sex (hence current justifications of prostitution), rent out my womb for the bearing of someone else's child, view my own children as diseases to be surgically removed, or treat my own physical life as something to be ended when I wish. Women who talk about their rights to control their reproductive organs really do view their bodies, as the language suggests, in some fashion as machines producing goods, such that both the machine

[23] Joseph Cardinal Ratzinger, "Difficulties Confronting the Faith in Europe Today", in *L'Osservatore Romano*, July 24, 1989, p. 6.

and the goods are at the disposal of the person who owns them. These women have abstracted themselves from their own materiality, and hence, when they speak of freeing themselves from their biology, they are not talking euphemistically, they are talking abstractly, and they are doing so because abstract language does accurately express their perception of reality.

The most alarming feature of such language is that, by abstracting from the concrete, the specific, the materially embodied, we also abstract from the limits within which we must live our lives. Just as abstractions float free of any particular context, so human beings who perceive reality this way float free of any particular structure. The incessant use of the word "liberation" today expresses precisely the modern, abstracted perception of reality that supposes human beings to be no longer constrained by authority, by irrevocable commitments, by Tradition, by history, or even by God. Everything in creation, from our bodies to the farthest flung galaxies, now appears to us to be at our disposal. Everything is just so much Play-Doh, to be manipulated at will.

Chesterton once observed that "the Church and the heresies always used to fight about words, because they are the only things worth fighting about".[24] Battles about words are always battles about competing views of reality. And the battle today is about competing and mutually exclusive visions of man, a conflict that confronts Catholics with, in the words of Cardinal Ratzinger, a "truly fundamental opposition to Faith's vision of man, an opposition which admits no possibility of compromise but places squarely before us the alternatives of believing or not".[25]

BIG BROTHER IS REALLY BIG SISTER

If the Catholic vision of man is correct, then the present and the immediate future bode ill, for, as one modern idiom puts it, what goes around comes around. And, to mix our idioms here, the

---

[24] G. K. Chesterton, *The Ball and the Cross* (New York: John Lane, 1910), p. 96.
[25] Ratzinger, "Difficulties", p. 6.

chickens are already coming home to roost on this one. We know they are, not only because we have been forewarned by our own Faith but also because we have been forewarned from the pen of the secular writer George Orwell. In his brilliant satire on the future, *1984,* he tells us just how it is that modern abstractive thought takes its vengeance on us, and today in American society we can see that vengeance already upon us.

Big Brother and the Party operate on a very simple, but very effective, principle: "Who controls the past controls the future; who controls the present controls the past." Big Brother realizes that effective control of the past, present, and future requires total control of language—hence Newspeak. As English columnist Roger Scruton has observed, "If you want to control the world, first control language: such has been the unspoken maxim of revolutionary politics in our century."[26]

Big Brother's strategy to control language is basically four-fold. First, replace Oldspeak with Newspeak and impose this change on everyone. Second, see to it that Newspeak operates with a much smaller vocabulary than was available in Oldspeak. This strategy is conducted for two purposes, that the range of thought might be narrowed and that whole categories of words might be destroyed.

> It was intended that when Newspeak had been adopted once and for all and Oldspeak forgotten, a heretical thought—that is, a thought diverging from the principles of Ingsoc—should be literally unthinkable, at least so far as thought is dependent on words. Its vocabulary was so constructed as to give exact and subtle expression to every meaning that a Party member could properly wish to express, while excluding all other meanings and also the possibility of arriving at them by indirect methods. This was done partly by the invention of new words, but chiefly by eliminating undesirable words and by stripping such words as remained of unorthodox meanings, and so far as possible of all secondary meanings whatsoever.[27]

[26] Scruton, p. 5.
[27] George Orwell, *1984* (New York: Harcourt, Brace, 1949), pp. 303–4.

Third, control people's consciousness and memories by mandated hate sessions, lectures, and assorted activities all conducted in the language of Newspeak. Finally, and most ominously, see to it that all records of the past are translated into Newspeak and continually revised, such that the collective memory of the community, contained in its documents, can never contradict Big Brother's current agenda.

> The mutability of the past is the central tenet of Ingsoc. Past events, it is argued, have no objective existence, but survive only in written records and in human memories. The past is whatever the records and the memories agree upon. And since the Party is in full control of all records, and in equally full control of the minds of its members, it follows that the past is whatever the Party chooses to make it.[28]

Big Brother is already present among us, and he is Big Sister. It takes very little effort to discover that what the feminist movement is up to bears an uncanny and fearful resemblance to the machinations of Big Brother. First, feminism would change the "language of the body", as John Paul II calls it, into "sex-neutral" language, and feminism would have this new way of speaking imposed on everyone. Already dictionaries analogous to the various editions of the Newspeak dictionary have appeared in our midst. But that is not all. The language guidelines to which I made reference earlier are explicitly entitled "Guidelines for Non-Sexist Language", and the copy I have of them is one imposed on graduate students in the Yale University Divinity School. These guidelines, among other things, instruct the students to avoid the generic use of man and of male pronouns, to avoid masculine or masculine-only pronouns for God, and to avoid the use of feminine pronouns in reference to Israel and the Church. The student is told at the outset that

> language reflects, reinforces and creates reality. It is important that language in term papers represent as full an understanding as

[28] Ibid., p. 214.

possible of human reality. For this reason, linguistic sexism . . . is to be avoided.[29]

Clearly only one view of reality is going to be permitted under these circumstances, and that view is not going to be whatever one the student happens to bring with him to Yale's Divinity School.

Second, this new way of talking diminishes vocabulary in order to diminish the range of thought and in order to destroy words and/or their secondary meanings. With regard to this second strategy, let us first note that our society as a whole is paving the way to such reductionism, because we already restrict our own vocabulary and already blind ourselves to the connotations or secondary meanings of words. In our society, Big Brother would already have found half his task accomplished for him.

With the vocabulary that we continue to use, however, words are already, in nonsexist language, being destroyed. Man and woman are not necessary if person can cover both. Fathering and mothering give way to parenting. And significant other, as previously noted, could half empty our dictionaries in a single stroke. Secondary meanings also go by the board. *The Nonsexist Communicator,* one of those handbooks instructing us on how we are to conform ourselves to feminist Newspeak, provides us with an appendix entitled "Alternatives to Sexist Usage" and instructs us therein on how secondary meanings of words, when applied to women, must be eliminated (and that is the text's word, not just mine). To give you a sample, the following words beginning with the letter "B" are now, in their secondary application to women and in the parlance of *1984,* to be regarded as Oldspeak and crimethought: baby, baby doll, bag, ball and chain, bastard, bat, battle-ax, bearcat, beauty pageants, beauty queen, better half, bitch, boy, broad, brood mare, built, and bunny.[30] Although the "L" section of this minidictionary does not include ladybug, it does instruct us that the word "lady" ought to be eliminated as a noun.

[29] See n. 3.
[30] Bobbye D. Sorrels, *The Nonsexist Communicator* (Englewood Cliffs, N.J.: Prentice-Hall, 1983), pp. 125–27.

Third, the control of people's consciousness in *1984* bears an uncanny and chilling resemblance to feminist consciousness-raising sessions and Womanchurch liturgies, mandatory activities, it would seem, for those who seek to be truly feminist. Like the inner Party members in Oceania, whose indoctrination in doublethink is absolute, so too those in the inner circles of the feminist movement all share in similar forms of the same feminist consciousness, maintained and reinforced by activities conducted in the language of feminist Newspeak.

Finally, the altering of past documents, the collective memory of the community, is already upon us in the Christian churches, where the translation of the Bible and liturgical texts into the new language is even now well under way. If this process is carried to its logical conclusion, the day could come when nothing in the documents of our past will be found that contradicts what Big Sister says. If you have ever read the feminist revision of the Nicene Creed in use at the Episcopal Divinity School of Cambridge, Massachusetts, you know that God the Father cannot be found anywhere in it. As William Oddie observes, "The resulting document reminds one of nothing so much as a new edition of the Soviet Encyclopaedia, from which all mention of some luminary who has suddenly become a non-person is unaccountably discovered to be eliminated."[31] Or, as O'Brien, the Party rep, says to Winston in *1984*, "Posterity will never hear of you. You will be lifted clean out from the stream of history."[32]

"Who controls the past controls the future; who controls the present controls the past." Scientific/technological man (Big Brother) and feminist woman (Big Sister) both operate on the same principle and for the same reason: both are in thrall to abstraction, abstraction from the limits of nature, from the limits of history, from the limits of human bodiliness. When O'Brien tells Winston that he, O'Brien, is capable of floating right off the floor like a soap bubble, Winston, now deeply indoctrinated in doublethink, is able to figure out what O'Brien means: " 'If he

---

[31] William Oddie, *What Will Happen to God?* (San Francisco: Ignatius Press, 1988), p. 108.

[32] Orwell, p. 257.

thinks he floats off the floor, and if I simultaneously *think* I see him do it, then the thing happens.' . . . All happenings are in the mind. Whatever happens in all minds, truly happens."[33] Feminism operates along the same lines. If the feminists believe that sexual differentiation is insignificant, and if the rest of us can be persuaded by them that sexual differentiation is insignificant, then the thing happens. Sexual differentiation becomes insignificant—or so the feminists would like to think.

"TRULY A CATHOLIC SENTENCE"

Let us return, here at the end, to those three questions raised at the beginning. Is there such a thing as a Catholic sentence? Yes. What are the elements of such a sentence? The elements are those good words that, like God's own creative and salvific word, seek to become flesh, that is, seek to speak the truth about a world that is concrete, not abstract, and about human beings who are ensouled bodies, not souls possessing bodies.

Is Ms. Washington's sentence truly a Catholic sentence? Let us run it by again. "I'd like an alliance with a man who could be a comrade and a kindred spirit, and I've had such alliances in the past; even with the hassles they were *enriching* and *enjoyable* experiences." It is hard to understand how anyone really familiar with the Catholic Faith could think of that as a Catholic sentence. Of course, Ms. Washington appeals not to the Catholic Faith but to the phenomenon of religious linguistics, a phenomenon with which I personally am not familiar and, if this be the sort of conclusions it yields, a phenomenon with which I hope never to become familiar.

What is an "alliance", and what does that have to do with Ms. Washington's sex life (remember, this sentence is aimed at readers who will think she is weird if she does not say something on that subject)? What does she mean by "comrade" and "kindred spirit"? All we know for sure is that these alliances she has had

33 Ibid., p. 281.

with comrades and kindred spirits did involve men. What is an enriching experience? Eating a hot fudge sundae is an enriching experience when one considers that sundae from the point of view of fat, cholesterol, and calories. "Enriching experience" is to activities what "significant other" is to relationships. Almost anything can qualify.

Ms. Washington characterizes this sentence as "Catholic", but let us not forget that she also characterizes it as "cryptic and evasive", which it most certainly is. Why does she think a "cryptic and evasive" sentence is also a "Catholic" sentence? I must confess I have no idea why. There is only one sense in which I could regard this sentence as Catholic, and that is the sense in which it is quite proper to wax cryptic and evasive when perfect strangers, in this instance, the readers of *Ms.* magazine, start nosing about in one's sex life. In such situations, however, an even better Catholic response would be to tell such readers directly, concretely, specifically, vigorously, and, if necessary, colorfully that such matters are none of their business, followed by a firm resolve never again to write essays for magazines whose readers think such matters are their business.

I have said so much about what is not a Catholic sentence that I think it only fair to end this talk with an example of a sentence that truly is Catholic. And since I am not sure that any of my own sentences qualify, I am going to turn to a real expert on the subject, Walker Percy. He is a Catholic who knows what the Catholic Faith is. He is a novelist who knows what words are all about. He is a medical doctor by education and thus knows all about diseases and how to recognize them in their symptoms. And he is an astute physician of our age, having diagnosed the "modern sickness" as "the disease of abstraction".[34]

Happily, he also contributed to the "Writing Catholic" article and has supplied us therein with not just one but two truly Catholic sentences I cannot resist sharing, as we say these days, with all of you. The major point of his contribution is that the Catholic

[34] Lewis A. Lawson and Victor A. Kramer, eds., *Conversations with Walker Percy* (Jackson: University Press of Mississippi, 1985), p. 73.

Faith better serves the novelist than any other religion or philosophy, because of its recognition that man is a pilgrim journeying through a world that is both sacrament and mystery rather than an ego absorbed with itself in a world of abstractions and illusions. What, concretely, does this mean? Percy tells us what it means:

> Show me a lapsed Catholic who writes a good novel about being a young Communist at Columbia and I'll show you a novelist who owes more to Sister Gertrude at Sacred Heart in Brooklyn, who slapped him clean out of his seat for disrespect to the Eucharist, than he owes to all of Marxist dialectic.[35]

Now there is a Catholic sentence—direct, concrete, specific, vigorous, and colorful. And every one of us, even those of us who have never been to Brooklyn or indeed have never been in Catholic schools, know all about Sacred Heart and Sister Gertrude and just what she is capable of meting out when her high standards of respect for the Eucharist are violated. And we all know just as well how deeply indebted we are to her today for whatever reverence we have been able to retain for the Eucharist through the many intervening and difficult years in which we have had to endure that abstractive process known as "liturgical renewal".[36]

As for the second sentence, Walker Percy tells us that "in the end, 10 boring Hail Marys are worth more to the novelist than 10 hours of Joseph Campbell on TV".[37] For those of you who know anything about the phenomenon of Joseph Campbell, you will recognize that to be "truly a Catholic sentence".

---

[35] Walker Percy, "Writing Catholic", *Boston College Magazine* 48 (Summer 1989): 26.

[36] For a very interesting discussion of this process of liturgical abstraction (or "digitalization", as the author calls it), see Paul C. Vitz, "The Brain Hemispheres and the Liturgy", in CCICA *Annual* (1983): 9–29.

[37] Percy, "Writing Catholic", p. 26.

BECAUSE I SAID SO: FEMINIST ARGUMENT AND INCLUSIVE LANGUAGE

Lawrence C. Brennan, C.M.

"You haven't a real appreciation of Newspeak . . . ," he said almost sadly. " . . . In your heart you'd still prefer to stick to Oldspeak, with all its vagueness and its useless shades of meaning. You don't grasp the beauty of the destruction of words. Do you know that Newspeak is the only language in the world whose vocabulary gets smaller every year? . . . Don't you see that the whole aim of Newspeak is to narrow the range of thought? In the end, we shall make thoughtcrime literally impossible, because there will be no words in which to express it."

George Orwell, *1984*

For two decades now, the feminist movement has campaigned against what it considers to be discriminatory and sexist uses of language, conceiving this campaign as an essential component of the struggle for women's rightful place in society. The movement has criticized usages such as the diminutive direct address, "honey", "sugar", or "babe", and more obvious depersonalizing epithets such as "chicks", "broads", and the like. Most persons understand and have understood that these usages can be taken as demeaning or offensive. Social politeness had already avoided them for this reason, even before the feminist campaign.

The campaign, however, has also extended to other usages, woven more deeply into the structure of the language. Such usages would include the generic use of the word "man" to refer to personified humanity as a whole or to refer to a human individual regardless of age or sex—both usages as in "the sabbath was made for man". For the same reason, the campaign extends to compounds of "man" based on these meanings, as in "mankind", or "chairman", neither of which refers exclusively to males. Finally, the campaign extends to the generic use of the pronoun "he", as in "he who hesitates is lost"—where "he" is understood to refer to man, woman, or child. The first set of usages most understand to be demeaning, but many users do not accept the feminist objection to the second set; it is here that the issue is currently joined. The feminists have coined a term, "inclusive language", to refer to their campaign goal, but the term itself is an irritant to those who find no suggestion of exclusion in the usages in question.

The feminist campaign has been vigorous and has enjoyed noteworthy, if lamentable, success. New dictionaries (e.g., the Random House *Dictionary of the English Language* [1987] and *The American Heritage Electronic Dictionary* [1990]) tell us that the former standard usage of "man", especially as a compound, to describe a human being regardless of age or sex is declining, because some people object to an ambiguity that may be thought to exclude women. The argument will be considered presently; what is notable is the lexicographical confirmation of the feminist campaign.

The use of generic terms continues to be understood without difficulty. In fact, most people who encounter criticism for their use of ordinary English seem genuinely puzzled. Demand for "inclusive" language is an artificial sensibility and an affected usage on the part of an influential elite. To be sure, there is an opposing point of view, an attempt to maintain the prerogatives of standard usage, counter to the influence of the first group; but the attempt has had little effect, so far, on the discussion. The work of Michael Levin, *Feminism and Freedom* (Transaction Books, 1987), contains a spirited and principled objection to the feminist language campaign, an objection set in the larger context of a critique of feminist ideology as such.

Feminists have created, principally among those who consider themselves politically correct, a widespread artificial sensibility, analogous to the work of advertisers. For many educated persons in our culture, saying "man" is as uncool as ordering a "cola" instead of a Coke at McDonald's. (The feminists have succeeded so well that, in certain circles, the word "man" may not be used even to refer to male human beings.) But is "uncool" really equivalent to insensitive, as the feminists contend?

FEMINIST LINGUISTICS IN CHURCH

In the churches, the matter is particularly acute: the feminist position is no longer argued, but presumed a fait accompli. In the February 1985 issue of *Atlantic,* Barry Hoberman explained then-forthcoming changes in the Revised Standard Version of the Bible by asserting that in the English language the outcome of the move to replace "male-oriented" usages with inclusive ones is "no longer in question". His bland confidence is shared by many others in the realm of ecclesiastical administration and education. What began as a moderate effort to have Saint Paul include "sistren" in his many letters to the brethren has ended with the revelation of the God of Abraham and Sarah, Isaac and Rebecca, and Jacob and Rachel—a revelation that has even resolved the delicate hermeneutical question of which of Jacob's wives and concubines is to be included in the divine title.

In American Catholicism, the Catholic Biblical Association has revised the translation of the New Testament of the New American Bible, the National Conference of Catholic Bishops has formulated a set of guidelines for a new Lectionary based on the revised translation, and the liturgical establishment has moved diligently forward with a revision of the text of the Sacramentary. Missalette and hymnal publishers have changed the wording of dozens of classic hymns, making it impossible to sing the hymns from memory. Lectors and celebrants have changed the words of the liturgy itself without authorization. All of these changes have been in favor of "inclusive" language, and opposition, if any, has had little effect.

There are reasons for the present crisis. The authority that approves liturgical texts can impose a settlement of sorts in the matter of language, binding, first of all, on Church members during formal worship in church. Beyond the liturgy, the settlement can also affect the massive middle-level bureaucracies of the Church and the endless meetings, dialogues, papers, speeches, and formal documents that these organizations produce. Given the power of Church authority to enforce ecclesiastical policy and to offer a limited validation to feminism itself, political maneuvering to capture that authority for the feminist language project has been intense.

In principle, genuine development in standard usage should be reflected in the language of the approved translations and texts of the Church's worship—leaving aside for the moment the practical question of how to determine whether such a development has occurred. Conversely, an affected usage, such as "inclusive" language, should not be imposed. When affected usage is imposed as standard on a large linguistic community, such as the Church at worship, a serious moral issue is at stake—an issue far more important than wounded feminist sensibilities.

FEMINISM AND THE LINGUISTIC COMMUNITY

Language is a set of conventional symbols whose meaning is fixed by a tacit, inherited, and mostly arbitrary agreement among its users. Each person who learns a language submits to that agreement, and each pays the price of not being understood if he departs significantly from the terms of the agreement. Thus language actually involves a commitment to the linguistic community of its users, and it is precisely here that the moral issue of inclusive language is located.

If an assignment of linguistic meaning is to be understood as "sexist", and if, because of this "sexism", the assignment of meaning is to be changed, more than gratuitous assertion and accusation is required. The assertion itself must be supported by persuasive evidence and argument. Should the argument fail, its proponents are not justified in ad hominem arguments or other acts of cultural violence. This is a matter of elementary accountability and simple civility.

Among other problems with the feminist language campaign, its evidence and arguments are unconvincing; nevertheless, it insists on imposing its conclusions in a way reminiscent of Lewis Carroll's famous "sentence first, verdict afterwards". More to the point, its cultural tactics, in response to the failure of its linguistic argument, are identical to those of terrorism: a rejection of the standards by which it is criticized and taking the law into its own hands.

In a controversial interview several years ago (published as *The Ratzinger Report* [Ignatius Press, 1985]), Cardinal Joseph Ratzinger remarked to the Italian journalist Vittorio Messori that feminism is, in effect, another religion. He was referring to the bizarre paraliturgies and to the overtones of witchcraft that are found in some circles of religious feminism, but his comment is a useful starting point for looking at feminism in general.

The movement is very much a question of faith. The anthropological assumption that undergirds feminism is that there are no important differences between the sexes except for superficial genital differences. This cannot be empirically proven, as it is claimed. Even the popular press (see *Time* magazine, "Sizing up the Sexes", January 20, 1992) is beginning to call attention to the growing body of scientific research that supports the idea of innate and fundamental sexual differences. Evidence supporting the feminist claim is at best speculative. To refer back to Cardinal Ratzinger's thesis, the feminist leap from shaky evidence to sweeping conclusions involves a "leap of faith", an act of will. It thus persuades only those who have made this same act of will.

The plausibility structure of feminism, having begun with this "leap", moves on to a quasi-Marxist social analysis: hope that the Gender Millennium is at hand and that it necessarily will arrive through conflict (see, for instance, Kenneth Minogue, *Alien Powers: The Pure Theory of Ideology* [New York: St. Martin's Press, 1985]). Gender revisionism becomes the rule in the rewriting of history, and the opponents of feminism are considered to be in thrall to "gender alienation" that is historically destined to be overthrown. As with other Marxist analysis, this utopian hope is neither intel-

lectually vindicated by proponents nor generally accepted by
the populace at large. More to the point, feminist writers who
speak so confidently of their "tools" of social analysis have yet
to come to terms with the recent dramatic collapse of Marxism
itself.

Finally, to focus the "plausibility structure" specifically on
language, feminism imports a theory of linguistic determinism,
the idea that language itself determines thought and views of
reality, rather than the idea that the determining usually occurs
the other way around. This theory is associated with the late
linguist Benjamin Whorf and is not widely accepted by other
linguists. It is, however, held as virtual law by feminist language
proponents, for whom it explains the issue of "sexist" language
and informs the strategy by which they intend to effect change.
That is, while most linguists reject linguistic determinism, feminists
not only believe in it but also are aggressive in using this theory to
control the outcome of the debate.

Unisex anthropology, dialectical genderism, and linguistic
determinism—debatable as they are—provide the basic framework against which the arguments over languages have any
power. But before looking at the arguments themselves, it is
worthwhile to note how the basic assumptions alone corrode
commitment to the linguistic community. They are elitist and
"illuminist"—in effect, a form of gnosticism. Since the arguments
are not self-evident, they require initiation and "consciousness-
raising". The crypto-religious nature of the feminist language
project makes dialogue impossible: there can be no compromise
with the infidel.

American society maintains a deep ambivalence about the imposition of sectarian religious views on the body politic. This ambivalence may explain why the quasi-religious feminist language
campaign has not been received by society at large. The Church,
for her part, maintains a tradition that Church authority should
be reluctant to resolve issues that are disputed among the schools
of theology. The present volume is, in part, an effort to show that
no consensus exists in the matter of inclusive language. To many
in the Church, the imposition of inclusive language in the liturgy is

as unwarranted and unwelcome as, for instance, a replacement of
the Creed with the Democratic party platform.

THE ARGUMENTS FOR LINGUISTIC "INCLUSIVISM"

The driving motive of linguistic "inclusivism" is the feminist act
of faith; nonetheless, the movement introduces arguments that
must be considered. The first is undoubtedly the most effective, if
measured by the frequency with which it is cited: the argument that
the usages in question exclude women. However, it is an argument with little substance. It posits a parallel between an offensive
racial epithet such as "nigger" and a term such as "man", which
latter is said to be—*mutatis mutandis*—an equally offensive *sexist*
usage. Since the parallel pairs an epithet with standard usage, the
argument limps from the beginning. Epithets are never anything
but demeaning, while standard usage strives to be neutral.

More fundamentally, the argument is faulty in its premise. It is
based on an etymology that holds that the term "man" primarily
refers to the male of the human species and that it came to refer to
the species as a whole only as a result of the patriarchal dominance
of the male. A similar argument is adduced to explain what is said
to be the use of the masculine personal pronoun system ("he", etc.)
for the indefinite personal pronoun in the singular (again, as in
"he who hesitates . . . "). The problem with the argument in both
cases is that it represents at best a folk etymology; the folk etymology itself is demonstrably false; subsequently, the parallel that it
must support collapses.

Every dictionary, even the new ones that include feminist
definitions, must report as one of the primary meanings of the
word "man" some variation on the theme "a human being, regardless of age or sex". The new dictionaries may add usage notes, but
they may not pretend that the meaning of the word has changed.
The English usages in question are of long standing, and, as
already noted, they continue to be understood by all English-
speaking people, irrespective of their view of feminist issues. That
some persons experience a connotative reaction over and above

the strict denotation of the terms reflects a deliberate cultivation on their part. Others who have chosen not to cultivate the same sensibility do not by that measure intend an exclusive meaning to the usages; they consider their usage to be standard and politically neutral. To be sure, feminists may charge that this commitment to standard usage is *unconsciously* exclusive, since feminists see the standard-setting society as sexist. But arguments concerning unconscious motivation seem designed more to discredit than to persuade.

It is open to question that, as Hoberman states, English lacks "a common-gender singular pronoun in the third person". It is entirely possible, for instance, that this pronoun is in fact identical in form to the masculine pronoun, but a quite distinct usage or word. Nor would such a linguistic economy of service be unusual. In spoken German, the same word, *sie,* could mean either "she", "they", or the polite address "you"—though in written German, the latter meaning is specified by capitalization. That one word should serve in such a combined capacity is a matter of fairly arbitrary linguistic development, as is the development in English that the pronoun "he" can have as an antecedent either a male human being or simply a human being. English speakers are quite capable of distinguishing these two meanings, and normally the process of being educated in the use of one's native tongue attends to just such skills. Moreover, it is a far less taxing effort to make a simple distinction such as this than to recast the usage of a multinational language spoken by hundreds of millions.

Most of those who have adopted the cultivated sensibility on the usage of "man" and of the indefinite "he" have done so in an uncritical acceptance of the folk etymology that has just been described. However, some who hold this view recognize that the etymology is untenable and adjust the argument accordingly. In this revised argument, they claim that, since "man" or "he" could refer either to an individual of the human species or to the male alone, an ambiguity results that is unacceptable—due to the "exclusiveness" of the latter meaning. Thus the speakers of the language are called upon to abandon a serviceable and clearly understood usage and to do so in order to avoid an ambiguity that has been known and tolerated for centuries.

The problem with this second argument is that it demands a linguistic overrefinement or purism in its addressees: educated users, speaking in good faith, are held to be "sexists" because their employment of standard usage might be construed to exclude women. But a living, spoken language cannot aspire to such artificially created precision. If and when language should attain such a precision, it is no longer the living, spoken language: it is jargon. Not by accident does "inclusive" language have the feel of legalese. That same artificiality has destroyed much of the poetry of traditional hymns. The English language abounds in ambiguities such as homonyms and seems to be able to distinguish meanings adequately. Where there is confusion, no one minds a question for clarification—and by using such a practical strategy, the speakers of English continue to understand each other.

THE ARGUMENT FROM SENSITIVITY

A third argument is usually adduced, sometimes in place of linguistic considerations or sometimes after linguistic considerations have failed altogether to justify the cultivated sensibility. This argument holds that, regardless of the linguistic merits of the question, a good many people now believe that "man" means the male of the species alone. Their belief might result from sloppy usage, from ideological conviction, or simply from intimidation by angry feminists. But proponents of inclusive language, who have deliberately promoted the wide diffusion of this belief, contend that the indefinite usage of the terms in question is gradually disappearing. This is essentially the argument of the new dictionaries.

Proponents of this view sometimes support their argument with demographic evidence to the effect that people think of a human male when they hear the word "man"—a finding that is hardly a surprise. Or they may argue that language is a living reality and that it will continue to change regardless of uncooperative grammarians and sexists. The upshot of this argument is that sensitivity to those who have this belief in the "exclusive" meaning demands that the usages in question be changed. In effect, "sensitivity" means catering to mistaken impressions. Folk etymology, a gender purism, and a peremptory linguistic obscurantism, all unchallenged, must be allowed to rule the day. Why must you use "inclusive" language? In the end, because I said so.

The question is whether this really constitutes sensitivity. Allergies are sensitivities, too, but they are not proposed as norms for the experience of the less sensitive, who are actually the normal. Allergies are in fact hypersensitivities, and quite a few of them are developed hypersensitivities. This is exactly the sort of "sensitivity" that the feminist language proposal seems to represent. Usages that do not bother most speakers bother the feminists. The limit to the analogy of allergy, of course, is that, while allergies may develop, they are not usually self-induced. The feminist hypersensitivity to language, however, is very much self-induced. It is a cultivation or an affectation, a calculated choice to depart from the linguistic norm.

To what, then, is the community obliged? Should the feminist hypersensitivity become the norm? Must the community apply the allergens to itself, to develop the same hypersensitivity? What if the community is too sensible to do so or too healthy to have a reaction? It seems germane to observe that legislated sensitivity does not usually accomplish its goals. It creates resentment among those who must submit to it unwillingly, and, with resentment, division. It also creates a whole new realm of cultural taboo, a new set of guilt provocations to burden the conscientious and ready-to-hand insults to arm the polemicist. If someone is allergic to trees, then perhaps he should avoid walking in the woods, but does this necessitate that the woods be cut down?

A SHIBBOLETH BY ANY OTHER NAME...

In English, standard usage is a somewhat relative thing, and the very group that normally sets the standard is the group now most influenced by the feminist usage. Thus, in principle, the question of standard usage must represent more than a nose count of educated speakers behind a given turn of phrase. It must also reflect the process by which the linguistic community as a whole rejects jargon and academic trendiness and turns instead to a distilled usage accessible to everyone. As Edwin Newman and others have noted, bombast, circumlocution, and deadwood are currently suffocating American English. It seems reasonable to add that the strained constructions of "inclusive" language (s/he, his/her, his or her, etc.) have become part of the same problem. The English language needs no more to adopt the inclusive usages than it needs to use "impact" or "stonewall" as verbs or "parameters" instead of "perimeter".

While feminists present themselves as women representing women and working to change the lot of women, they are in fact women and men identified with a political agenda of radical social change, an agenda that has engendered considerable controversy—not least among women themselves. Many in our society and Church (including women) simply disagree with the tenets of feminism and with the premise that these tenets are self-evidently a matter of justice. Does the Church, then, exercise responsibility in adopting these tenets uncritically? Is it justice that opponents of feminist politics be made to worship in feminist language without even being previously consulted?

Michael Levin has suggested that the inclusive language debate, at bottom, represents a continuing referendum on the cultural strength of feminism. His suggestion seems persuasive. Political reporter E. J. Dionne, in the wake of the Clarence Thomas hearings, has described the current state of American culture as nothing less than a moral civil war. Sociologist James Davison Hunter calls it a culture war (*Culture Wars: The Struggle to Define America* [New York: Basic Books, 1991]). What is evident is that, as the cultural strength of radical feminism apparently wanes— witness the defeat of the Equal Rights Amendment, the progressive restriction of abortion "rights", etc.—feminists are escalating their assault on the culture via the language, employing the tactics of intolerance and intimidation in the academic community and in ecclesiastical bureaucracies.

The Church has her own role to play in this cultural conflict, and she has no business casting her vote with the feminist ideologues.

Her concern should be to establish, in society, a new form of the women's movement that is clearly dissociated from contraception and abortion on demand. Her concern should be to promote, within the Church herself, a movement that is truly inclusive and truly constructive, avoiding the hateful rhetoric, the revisionist history, and the polarizing politics so characteristic of the feminist movement.

In the meantime, the politically correct will continue to see inclusive language as a necessary step to achieve the heights of gender enlightenment. Others, not caring much—perhaps understanding less—will use such language as a shibboleth to avoid slaughter at the fords of the feminist Jordan (see Jg 12:6). Still others might take heart if only they remember: the word "man" is not a dirty word and may still be used in polite company—for that matter, even in church.

THEOLOGICAL LIBERALISM
ABORTING ITSELF

Jon D. Levenson

At a conference several years ago, I found myself seated at a dinner table with several other Jews but only one Christian—a professor, it turned out, at a prominent liberal seminary. In response to genial questioning from some of his dinner companions, the lone Christian explained that his institution had long ago shed its once vivid ecclesiastical affiliation. The break had occurred over the application of the historical-critical method to the Bible, a prospect that the denomination had found incompatible with its deepest beliefs. "Are there, then, any beliefs or practices required of the faculty or students now?" asked one of the company. "No," replied the seminary professor firmly. But then, as an afterthought and in an undertone, he added, "except the requirement to use inclusive language."

The professor's qualification summons to mind some most curious scenarios. Imagine: in an institution once explicitly and formally Christian and still culturally so, largely dedicated to the education of ministers, one can deny with utter impunity that Jesus was born of a virgin or raised from the dead. But if one says that he was the son of God the Father, one runs afoul of the institution's deepest commitments. If the ancient christological confession is to be retained at all—and this, presumably, is only a matter of personal preference—it must be recast in gender-neutral terms. Though our dinner companion did not say so, I assume that the older formulation may still be employed for purposes of critique, to show the alleged androcentrism of the early Church, but not for purposes of affirmation, at least not without an immediate qualification to the effect that the traditional language is a historically conditioned convention and an unhappy one at that.

The application of a feminist critique to the most basic affirmations of one's own religious tradition is a phenomenon that any practitioner of the historical-critical method should readily understand. For the twin hallmarks of that method have always been, first, its stout refusal to exempt any beliefs or practices from its merciless scrutiny and, second, its commitment to reconstructing the original and all-too-historical context of phenomena that traditionalists take to reveal the eternal and the transcendent.

The irreverence and subversiveness of historical criticism should not be taken to imply, however, that it is only skeptical and never affirmative. As Wittgenstein observed, one cannot doubt everything at once, for each expression of doubt presupposes some correlative affirmation. The affirmation underlying most of the practice of historical criticism has been some form of historicism, the conviction that existence is essentially and inescapably historical and developmental. An institution committed to the historical-critical method or even just accepting of it will tend to reject arguments that deny the historicist presupposition. What it will not do is encourage historical critique of some beliefs and practices and forbid it of others—if, that is, its critical commitment is intact. For selective critique—critique of the other person's affirmation but not one's own—is characteristic of a different sort of institution, one to which terms like "orthodox", "fundamentalist", and "unicultural" are more fittingly applied than the word "liberal".

What my dinner companion's qualification suggests is that his seminary's historic liberalism has finally capitulated under the force of an orthodoxy, not the old orthodoxy of Christian fundamentalism (which is thriving elsewhere), to be sure, but a feminist orthodoxy of which "inclusive language" is emblematic. Historicism and kindred liberal commitments, valiant in combat against orthodox forms of Christianity and Judaism in an age of rising modernism, have proven impotent against the post-modernist movements that now dominate American academic life. The effect has been to remove an increasing list of issues from serious discussion.

A parade example of such a proscribed topic is abortion. In some formerly liberal institutions the range of permissible opinions on this topic is now no broader than in their most rigidly orthodox counterparts. In one divinity school, for instance, a student who was a member of a pro-life group felt compelled to write to the student newsletter about the reception she had received:

> Knowing that most students [at the school] are repelled by what they see as an anti-liberal, anti-feminist, pro-life movement, I expected some confrontation. I hoped for some rational discussion. I never expected that my posters—even those in my own dorm where people know me and my views—would be ripped, turned around, and torn down within two days.

Ironically, the institution in which this took place is one that explicitly and repeatedly affirms its dedication to "diversity" and "pluralism". To assess what these increasingly hollow terms actually mean in context, one should contrast the inaction of the community on the pro-life student's complaint with the likely response if the vandalized posters had been associated with a feminist, black, or homosexual group. "Diversity" and "pluralism" have been degraded to the status of code words for an ideology in which certain accidents of birth or early upbringing—race, gender, and sexual instinct—are thought to signal the most important human differences. A community in which people differ with respect to these variables but conform in social and political thinking is deemed to exemplify diversity and pluralism to a high degree.

What makes the ironic term "political correctness" appropriate to this situation is not the character of the consensus itself but the dogmatic way in which it is affirmed and the aggressiveness and invasiveness with which it is maintained. It is here that the ideologization and rigidification of so many erstwhile liberal religious institutions become evident. One divinity school, for example, requires its master's students to submit a review form

with routine questions about how they plan to fulfill their distribution and language requirements and the like. But it also requires
them to answer this question: "How has your program helped
you to understand and deal with questions of race and gender?"
Students who have responded by challenging the presupposition of the question have, on occasion, been rebuffed, and in
at least one case a student was officially advised to seek out
courses in women's studies, though these were not required for his
program.

What is curious here is that an academic institution whose heritage
is that of liberal Protestantism should be sensitive to the hint of
bias only on issues of race and gender. What ever happened to the
religious and intellectual issues that are presumably still central to
the work that goes on there? The *Christian* component of that
school's identity, for example, might have led to a question about
anti-Semitism. After all, Christianity is a tradition that identifies
with God himself a man who is reported to have told a group of
Jews that their real father is not Abraham but the devil, whose
bidding they willingly do (Jn 8:44). Can we really assume that the
legacy of Christian anti-Semitism no longer informs the thinking
of today's students, even on Middle Eastern affairs?

Similarly, the *Protestant* character of the institution might have
provoked a question in which the students would be asked in
what ways their thinking on issues of self, society, and authority
are derived from assumptions that the Roman Catholic tradition
has historically deemed doubtful. Is the unqualified negative valence
of terms like "hierarchy", "patriarchy", and even, on occasion,
"father", for example, owing in part to the Protestant milieu? The
new radicalism has to a shocking degree reintroduced an old
anti-Catholicism. In one liberal Protestant institution a few years
ago, radical feminist students hooted down a centrist Roman
Catholic professor in his own class. More recently another visiting
professor, this time an ex-Catholic, telling his class of his background,
allowed that "it's nice to be in a church where you don't have to
check your brain at the door". Providing cover for the virulent
old/new anti-Catholicism are academic Catholics who are more

comfortable with the faith and morals of liberal Protestantism than with those of the Vatican. Orthodox Catholics, needless to say, are not on the list of politically correct groups deserving special protection.

Finally, I can imagine a question that would challenge the *liberalism* of the liberal Protestant institution that employs that review form—not from the left, from which there is challenge aplenty already, but from the right: "How has your program helped you understand the conservative critique of left-liberal religious, social, and political thought?" Ideally, students would include in their answer instances of liberal presuppositions that inform their own thought. The priority of rights over duties, the nonexistence of norms independent of human will, and the equation of freedom with self-determination are three examples of ideas of high import on campus today that derive ultimately from streams of thought that can justly, if broadly, be termed "liberal".

A question of this sort would perform the invaluable educative service of inviting students to reflect on why their own position is not a *bias* that they need to eliminate by taking the conservative equivalent of a women's studies course. It would help drive home the reality that much contemporary hermeneutical theory is trying so hard to deny: truth is more than a function of power; expression of aggrievement and guilt-manipulation cannot substitute for reasoned argument; and we cannot validate our beliefs merely by reference to the constituency to which we belong—whether racial, sexual, economic, or religious. Prompted to distinguish the nature of their own thinking from bias, the better students would be brought to a liberating awareness of man's need for an affirmation that goes beyond that which lies at the base of historicism—an affirmation of an enduring and transcendent truth only dimly glimpsed within history.

Conservatives often assail political correctness on the grounds of academic freedom and First Amendment rights, and here they surely have a point. Much more germane to the question of education, however, is the disastrous intellectual effect of excluding alternative positions from consideration, or even expression, as is increasingly the case on campus. The consequence of such exclusion on one's own thinking is akin to the effect on a prizefighter of refusing to spar because he deems no opponent worthy of him: he soon gets out of shape but, secure in the protected environment of his handlers, remains unaware of his own vulnerability—until he is knocked out in the next bout. Political correctness is born of the absolute certainty of left-liberal intellectuals that no contrasting position is worthy of consideration or (here is where the academic freedom and First Amendment issues creep in) deserving of free expression in a civilized community. Only someone who is bigoted or unconscionably naïve could possibly dissent.

Dialogue and debate, the intellectual's equivalent of sparring, thus become impossible, and moral indignation and the claim to be offended suppress intellectual engagement. As a result, the rigorous self-scrutiny that characterizes liberal religious scholarship and the historical-critical method long associated with it is now in acute danger. It is rapidly giving ground to a hermeneutic of suspicion that conveniently disallows suspicion about its own leftist agenda.

The failure of the politically correct is not that they exclude some positions from consideration. No community can be equally open to all ideas, and the academic equivalent of First Amendment absolutism, advocated by some conservatives, is neither possible nor desirable. Their failure, rather, lies in having drawn the circle of possible positions so tightly that education degenerates into indoctrination and the ritualized reaffirmation of self-evident truths—self-evident, that is, to those whose "consciousness" has been "raised". Though religious people touched by political correctness often like to think of themselves as prophetic, an apocalyptic or gnostic analogy actually seems more appropriate. For those of the raised consciousness are often eerily reminiscent of the elect of an apocalyptic conventicle or the pneumatics of gnosticism in their hypersectarian inability to relate to the lives of ordinary people, especially ordinary people whose lives center upon the bearing and rearing of children and the faithful transmission of a family tradition. In the theological institutions of the most liberal religious groups, those very activities are more than occasionally depicted in the harshest negatives.

I have the impression that the anti-family and particularly the anti-father ethos evident in many of these seminaries and divinity schools is owing to the disproportionate number of students—and perhaps now faculty as well—who are afflicted with various psychological and social dysfunctionalities. At one southern seminary, a surprising percentage of students exhibited such elevated scores on the Minnesota Multiphasic Personality Index as to warrant immediate therapy. Once the proportion of such wounded and needy individuals reaches a certain threshold, the pressure for classes to become therapy sessions or opportunities to act out can be overwhelming. "The most destructive aspect of the low academic standards that characterize many of the class [at one divinity school]", wrote a disgruntled recent alumnus in a student newspaper, "is that it enables the least serious students to attain the most influence on policymaking."

> Concentrating one's attention on verbalizing one's own neuroses and past traumas frees the students from the diligent work that normally characterizes graduate schools. Consequently, it is the radical element that is able to afford the time to devote to activism. . . . Serious scholars who are devoted to intellectual inquiry are seldom heard from.

The cultural changes that prepared these startling transformations in theological education among liberal elites are many. One of the most important was the radicalism of the 1960s, from which some institutions have still not recovered. A prime casualty of the radical movement, in seminaries as in universities, was required courses and demanding programs. The requirement to master one or both biblical languages was often scuttled, as were competency examinations and other devices that might have saved theological training from the "dumbing down" that has devastated the whole spectrum of American education, clearing the ground for today's rampant politicization. The 1960s also witnessed a widespread capitulation to the demand for "relevance", and social activism gave religious institutions an opportunity to demonstrate to their cultured despisers that they were not obsolete after all or—Heaven forfend!—conservative. To faculties increasingly nourished on the academic ethos, the opportunity was especially welcome. For, as several empirical studies have shown, this is an ethos both more secular and more to the left than average. The easiest way for religious academics to relieve the cognitive strain of their anomalous, bicultural status is to interpret the religious tradition as the time-conditioned vocabulary of a leftist social movement with transparent applications today—seeing, for example, the emergence of ancient Israel as a peasant revolt, or the earliest church as an egalitarian, feminist enclave that somehow emerged in the world of first-century Judaism. When the religious and the revolutionary norms are on a collision course, guess which one yields the right of way.

The most far-reaching change in the liberal institutions has been their new pluralism of religious affiliations and the lack thereof. Even in many church-sponsored seminaries, both the student body and the faculty include substantial numbers of people with religious identities other than that of the sponsoring body. Ministerial candidates hostile to religious conviction are not unheard of. The resultant loss of a common conceptual framework gravely threatens the dialogue and debate essential to education. Into that vacuum has marched political correctness, with its offer of a new conceptual framework based on leftist ideology. The political absolutism is a correlative of the religious relativism: a secular orthodoxy able to employ religious language—though only selectively and without deference to religious authority—has taken the place of the evanescent religious orthodoxy. Political correctness, however, has impeded rather than furthered the cause of real education in diverse and pluralistic settings. The problem it purports to solve is still with us.

"SEXIST LANGUAGE":
THE PROBLEM BEHIND THE PROBLEM

John R. Sheets, S.J.

(What appears below was originally an exchange of letters. A sister sent me a letter describing her reaction to an article I had written. On the one hand, she thought the article had value. On the other, she explained how the "sexist language" got in the way of the thought. Her remarks led me to think out some of the aspects of this question. Instead, then, of a short reply the response began to assume the shape of an article. I thought that the exchange might be of some service to a wider audience. It was necessary to present sister's letter which provided the stimulus and backdrop for my own. I have dropped some things and made minor changes to protect the identity of the author. I hope and pray that the publication of this exchange of letters might contribute to the discussion of a question which is troubling many in the Church in the United States today, that it might be carried on in a spirit of mutual understanding, "in the Lord".)

SISTER'S LETTER

Dear Father Sheets,

I am writing to thank you and commend you on your recent article.... However, I would like to mention to you while I am writing to you about your article the effect which your use of language had on me, and on others like me. The early part of your article is heavy with repeated use of "man" and "mankind" language that was almost sufficient to keep me from reading the whole article. I say "almost", since I did want to see what you had to say on this topic. Since, however, the topic was important to me, I did persevere.

I share this with you, however, to let you know that the offensiveness of the language is such to some of us that any message set in that context will be missed. I think that may be worth considering if your chief purpose is to communicate.

Even beyond this discomfort with the jarring repeated encounters with man was the concern about what was going on in my head about judging your position. I was tempted to expect a position that wasn't worth bothering with (given the choices we have to make about what we spend time reading) because of its lack of sensitivity to the language question that is so increasingly important to many of us. Your comments on the anthropology we need to share left me suspect of your "patriarchal anthropology" from the very beginning.

I bother to share this with you, simply to let you know that the inclusive language question is *not* a trivial issue to many of your readers—or could-be readers. But many women (and some men) won't even be able to go on with reading such articles because of being offended by the language. I also know that this is an extremely volatile issue with many people. It may be with you— and in that case, my letter and position may simply be a "red flag" as I have experienced it before.

If, on the other hand, it is an issue that no one has ever bothered to raise with you or try to dialogue with you about, then it has been worth my while to bring up the issue. I have not tried to be offensive, myself, but one always runs that risk when raising the controversial topic. I think my motive in bringing it to your notice is more the enlarging of the possibilities of your own awareness and serving the interests of your readership. Again, I thank you for the content of your article. I hope my other comments about its language problems you may also find of interest and concern.

Sincerely. . . .

MY RESPONSE

Dear Sister:

Now that I have a little more time, I would like to respond to your letter at great length. This is perhaps less an answer to you than a way of sorting out in my own mind my thinking about "sexist language". I hope you won't be put off by the length my reply might take.

Let me recall first of all a few points from your letter. You graciously distinguish there the content of my article, which you find acceptable, from the language in which it is expressed. As you say, "The early part of your article is heavy with repeated use of 'man' and 'mankind' language that is almost sufficient to keep me from reading it." You go on to say that you were even more distracted from the content by the turmoil in your own thoughts caused by the seeming insensitivity of the language. "Even beyond this discomfort with the jarring repeated encounters with 'man' was the concern about what was going on in my head about judging your position." The language of the article, you say, left you suspect of my " 'patriarchal anthropology' ".

Your reaction to the article underlines a fact of human experience. It is difficult, if not impossible, to get to the truth of a statement if it is couched in words which block my mind. We find it difficult to get through the external trappings to the reality beneath. You may recall in *The Little Prince* the incidence of the Turkish astronomer. He came to a conference in Europe to present to the assembled scholars his exciting discovery of a new planet. Because he was dressed in Turkish clothes, however, no one listened. So he went back, put on a western suit, gave his presentation, and was hailed as a genius.

Pascal makes the same point. "Let the preacher appear and let nature have given him a hoarse voice or a comical cast of countenance . . . then however great the truths he announces, I wager our senator loses his gravity."

Questions and Answers

The fact that the language in which my thought is expressed offered a block to your power to judge the content on its merits is unfortunately the pattern of our human experience, but is it always possible to adapt our clothes, looks or voice to what is acceptable to another?

Since this reply, then, is as much to help me formulate my thoughts, as well as to answer your letter, I shall approach it by asking certain questions and then attempting to answer them.

1. *What is meant by the current terms: sexist language, inclusive and exclusive language? How did the present problem arise?*

Historically, the problem came to the fore comparatively recently, within the last decade or the last couple of decades. On the face of it, it has to do with justice and injustice as found in our language. The feminist movement has raised our sensitivity to the injustices suffered by women throughout the centuries into our own time. The scope of the movement has broadened from the initial stages to take in every aspect of human life.

The movement began with concern for justice in the political sphere, aiming at the rights which belonged to them as citizens. It moved into the economic realm, demanding equality of choice of work and salaries. It moved into the family, where it stresses the equality of partners in marriage. Then into the rights of a woman over her own body, which provided the basis for abortion. The breadth of the movement took on the dimensions of the whole of reality, the meaning and nature of language, and the meaning of God, and how we speak of Him. From a movement it has turned into an all-embracing philosophy.

At the same time, it is highly effective because of its efficient methods of organization and the programs it provides to secure its goals. The natural solidarity of women with women, crossing boundaries of nationality, gives the movement tremendous cohesion.

Shift in Perceptions

To come to the particular "injustice" in what is called "sexist language", it is clear that it did not exist a few decades ago but at present it is a crucial problem. I think that I could describe the phenomenon as a *"shift in perceptions"*.

It is simply a matter of historical fact that from the very genesis of the English language, going back more than a millennium, the word "man" has had two meanings, depending on the context. One was inclusive, including every human being. The other was exclusive, meaning male in contrast to female.

Within the last couple of decades a shift in perception took place. Some women began to stress a perception of the word "man" which narrowed its traditional meaning from its traditional twofold meaning to only one meaning.

The problem does not exist, of course, in many other languages, which have two words, one to express "man" as inclusive and another which is "exclusive". This is true in Latin, Greek, and German. But then the problem exists in translations from these languages into English since we have only one word to say what is said without ambiguity through two words. There are some, though, who are offended even through translations where the one word is used. Even texts that come to us, like Scripture, which are part of our common heritage, are subjected to various kinds of tampering to try to bring them in line with the "shift in perceptions".

The "shift in perceptions" has led, then, to a *conflict of perceptions.* I would hazard that the vast percentage of men and women do not find it an issue. Even among those who are conscious of it as an issue, not everyone agrees with the solution simply to abandon the perception of our language which has been our common heritage since the beginning.

Resolution of Conflict

On the one hand, under the term "sexist language" (which is often unexamined, and takes on the ring of a slogan) only one perception is acceptable; and others feel that they still have a right to use language as it has always been used. They feel also that the manipulation of substitute adaptations does not respect the genius of the language, distracts from the content, and violates their own sense of language.

The reasons put forth for advocating that everyone change his perception of language to fit the "sexist" view of language are based mainly on the effect such language has on some women. It is "offensive", "insensitive". Even more it suggests that beneath the use of such language there is an attitude which denigrates women.

In the resolution of any conflict, one of the factors to enter into the attempt at resolution is the effect on the feelings of those involved. It is only *one* element in the process, however. There are objective issues as well, such as the nature of language itself. There is also the fact that the hurt is not felt simply on one side. Those who feel intimidated by feminist pressures also feel hurt, anxiety, harassment. This leads me to my next question: the mutuality or reciprocity of the pain coming from the conflict of perceptions.

2. *Is the pain felt in the present conflict of perceptions one-sided?*

In your letter you call attention to the fact that many are offended by the use of "sexist language". Isn't there another side to the coin, however?

It is good to take a look at what is meant by the word "offensive". There are different ways in which people take offense. Sometimes it comes from what is objectively bad, for example, bad manners, bad language, bad music, etc. At other times it comes either from what is inoffensive itself or because the truth of a statement is resisted simply because we don't like the truth. What is inoffensive in itself, e.g., art, literature, can be offensive to those who think that nudity in art, certain books of solid literary worth, though they have passages which are graphic, are objectionable. Because some take offense at them, they launch campaigns against them.

Truth can also arouse, and justly so, the antagonistic feeling of those who resist the truth, as in the case of all the prophets, and especially in the case of Jesus Christ who offended many by His speech, an offense for which He paid with His life.

When it comes to the "offensiveness" of "sexist language", it belongs to the category of what is *objectively inoffensive* but is *perceived as offensive* because of the conditioning which has taken place over the past couple of decades.

What about those of us who suffer from being constantly on edge, because of the fear of being publicly challenged and embarrassed? It is an issue which does not admit of mere rational discussion, no more than the discussions of Arabs and Jews about the Left Bank. I have never walked out on a woman or anyone else for their use of "inclusive language", but I have had a sister walk out on me for what she felt was my "exclusive language".

Even deeper than the anxiety coming from fear of personal embarrassment is the fear of what could happen to our graduate program here in Christian Spirituality. For ten summers, men and women from different parts of the world studied, played, worked and worshipped together in an atmosphere of peace and companionship. Yet deep down in my stomach I felt the fear of what could happen if this issue would polarize the group, as it has done to other programs in the States, which had to suspend their programs for a couple of years.

Pain on Both Sides

We came to the very brink of that taking place a few years ago. One of the sisters in the program asked the people to remain after Mass one afternoon. Then she told them: "I want to thank the celebrant and planners of the liturgy today for eliminating all sexist language. I hope others in the future will follow suit." One priest who was there turned to the sister at his side and said, "She has laid a heavy burden on the rest of us." The sister replied, "That's your problem."

Many were indignant at the attempt to impose on them a position which not all of them shared, and at the preemptory manner in which it was done without any consideration for their feelings. Fortunately, as events turned out, it did not become a polarizing issue.

I think the pressures are even greater on campuses where there is a strong concentration of women studying theology. You may remember the incident described in Judges 12:4–6. In order to distinguish those who were their own men from their enemies, the men of Gilead would ask them to pronounce the word Shibboleth. If the person were from the enemy tribe of Ephraim and mispronounced the word he was slaughtered. "They said, 'Then say Shibboleth.' He would say 'Sibboleth', since he could not pronounce the word correctly. Thereupon they seized and slaughtered him by the fords of the Jordan."

Perhaps to quote this text to illustrate the pressures on certain campuses to conform to the "inclusive language" position is a little strong, but having lived through the pressures of the '60s and early '70s at another university, I know that it takes something akin to heroism to keep one's integrity. One lay professor who refused to capitulate told me in tears that he was going to resign because the students boycotted his classes. A good friend of mine, a priest who directed the liturgy at one of our major Catholic universities, fell into such a deep depression because of the constant harassment and intimidation of some of the extreme feminists that he had to resign.

But that is enough of this unpleasant topic. I brought it up only to point out that there is pain, suffering and violation of sensitivities on both sides in this conflict of perceptions.

I would like to take up another question, perhaps the most important.

3. *What is the "problem behind the problem" in the conflict over "sexist language"?*

I would like to suggest that problems with language can be symptomatic of even deeper problems.

Language itself is a mysterious reality, in its origin, development and as it carries within symbolic forces which have a frightening power both to unite and to divide. (Cf. Bernard Lonergan's *Method in Theology* to tap some of the mysterious nature of language; similarly, Walker Percy's *Message in the Bottle;*

Leonard Bernstein compares language and music, both coming from the deep structure of the person.)

Not only is language a mysterious reality. Each language has a *genius* of its own, marking it off from other languages. This genius acts something like a genetic code forming the texture of the language, providing it with a certain definite form throughout all the changes. Great writers have a feel for this texture, as great composers have a feel for music. Language, therefore, is not simply a sequence of interchangeable words. They form a pattern with a rhythm like a dance. One cannot treat language, then, arbitrarily.

Never Before in History

Language is *symbolic.* It embodies the identity of a people, with all the loves, hates, fears, and prejudices identified with the people. The tensions, for example, in Canada between those who speak English or French come to a head in their languages. In Belgium Flemish-speaking northerners refuse to speak French, the language of those in the southern part, and vice versa. When words or gestures are symbolic, they can release explosive power. President Reagan learned this the hard way at Bitburg a few weeks ago.

I submit that there are two reasons for the strong feelings about "sexist language".

The first is that such language is symbolic of what is contained in the group memory of many women. It is a whole history of discrimination. As symbolic it creates a sense of a mysterious solidarity with all persons and all events of history where women have suffered injustice. In some way the whole is felt in a tiny part.

This group memory and sense of solidarity, however, carries with it a manifold concentration of emotions. The name given to such a combination of emotions is *ressentiment.* It is a word used by Nietzsche to describe the cauldron of emotions fueled by group memory of injustice: anger, hurt, envy, resentment, vengeance.

When dealing, then, with language which is symbolic, which carries the weight of centuries of hurt, we are in the realm of symbols that are charged with heavy emotional content. For this reason the question of "sexist language" calls forth emotions which seem to be all out of proportion to the issue itself, if one looked at it merely as a rational question. Its emotional power arises out of the profound non-rational aspect of our human nature.

But there is another aspect of the "problem behind the problem". Here we are getting on ground that is a little scary. The feeling of solidarity in a shared history of injustice, with the *ressentiment* which gives the emotional charge, is usually based on the fact that many share the same race, nationality, family bonds. The feminist movement, however, has created a solidarity which crosses all these areas. It is based simply on being female rather than male. This has never happened before in the history of mankind.

All symbolic language is emotionally charged, but when the symbolism incarnates the primordial mystery of sexuality, there are profound forces at work. C. S. Lewis, with a certain sense of dread, points to the primordial nature of this kind of symbolism: " . . . We are dealing with male and female not merely as facts of nature but as the life and awful shadows of realities utterly beyond our control and largely beyond our direct knowledge. Or rather *we are not dealing with them but (as we shall soon learn if we meddle) they are dealing with us*" (italics mine) (taken from his collection *Undeceptions,* "Priestesses in the Church", p. 196).

The point I am making is that there is a "problem behind the problem" of language. It comes from the fact, first of all, that the language is symbolic, hence carrying subterranean emotions which well up into the symbols. On an ever deeper level, though, the symbols are carrying the subterranean power that flows out of the primordial mystery of sexuality. And here we may be the unwitting actors in a drama of which we are not even conscious.

One of the merits of Leanne Payne's recent book, *Crisis in Masculinity,* is to call attention to this same fact. We are not so much dealing with realities as they are dealing with us when we tap into the primordial mystery of sexuality.

Next Question

This brings us to the next question, the problem of the language we use to speak to God.

4. *Is our way of speaking of God as Father the remnant of a patriarchal religion?*

One of the aspects of the "sexist language" problem which is potentially the most divisive among Christians is the name we use to speak of God.

Everyone realizes, of course, that there is no sexuality in God. In regard to the manner of addressing God as Father in the Old Testament, and not as Mother, there are only two options: either it belongs to *revealed religion* or it is *pagan.* If it is merely a patriarchal projection onto the ultimate reality, then it is pagan. This is how the pagans visualize their gods, as a kind of other-worldly copy of a this-worldly reality.

If it belongs to revelation, however, then it points to the keystone which holds together in a unity which I could call the cluster of other names that are given to God, for it points to God as transcendent, absolute source of all things, creator. The God of Israel has maternal qualities as He has kingly qualities, qualities which resemble those bound together by family ties or qualities of a husband or of a lover. But He doesn't simply have the qualities which characterize a father. He *is* Father. For it is this name which shows forth His absolute transcendence. It still awaits, however, the fullness of meaning it will find in the New Testament.

Jamming Device

Cardinal Ratzinger comments on the way the name Father finds its full revelation in the incarnate Son. "Calling God the Father in the Christian context is not the projection of the patriarchal social structure into the heavens. Rather we experience who the Father is through His relationship to the Son. This divine dialogue between the Father and the Son is the new Christian basis for understanding fatherhood, and this relationship between the two Divine Persons supplants any analogy" (Joseph Ratzinger, "Preaching about God Today", *Theology Digest* 22 [1974]: 196–201).

This is not anything new. St. Athanasius used very much the same language 1,500 years ago: "God is above all things as Father, for he is principle and source; he is through all things, through the Word; and he is in all things in the Holy Spirit."

We come to our final question, as the problem reaches out to touch us in our Christian lives, as individuals and as members of a community. In the words of St. Paul, "Be humble always and gentle, and patient too. Be forbearing with one another and charitable. Spare no effort to make fast with bonds of peace the unity which the Spirit gives. There is one body and one Spirit, as there is also one hope held out in God's call to you; one Lord, one faith, one baptism, one God and Father of all, who is over all and through all and in all" (Eph 4:2–6). The potential of the language problem to divide the community, together with the way it affects those involved in the conflict, seems to contradict each of the gifts which belong to the Spirit mentioned by Paul: humility, gentleness, patience, forbearance, charity, peace, unity.

The consciousness of "sexist language" has become so strong that either "sexist language" or the attempts to avoid it distracts us from the Word of God itself, just as you mentioned in your letter that my own language distracted you from the content of the article. For some it has become such a preoccupation that it acts like one of those jamming devices found in the Eastern bloc countries which block radio and TV waves.

5. *Is there any solution to the problem of "sexist language"?*

A few minutes ago I was talking on the phone to Leanne Payne, whom I mentioned above. In the course of the conversation, I spoke of this letter I was writing, and the fact that there didn't seem to be any way out of the problem. I was struck by her reply. "It is a problem that can be transcended only by faith. It cannot be solved by rejecting a patriarchal ideology while being caught at the same time in its opposite, a feminist ideology."

The problem, as I mentioned above, has different levels: (1) the *shift in perception* of what has been the accepted meaning of words, which gives rise to the conflict of perceptions; (2) the *symbolic nature* of language, containing group memory and group emotion; (3) the fact that symbolic language which touches the *primordial reality of sexuality* takes us into a realm where there are powers at work that are awesome.

As far as the first aspect of the problem is concerned, the "sexist language", there is no agreement among all women either on the nature of the problem or its solution. Madeleine L'Engle writes: "I will have to struggle with the old, tattered words, trying never to forget that *man* is as much a feminine as a masculine word, and if I abandon my share in it, *that* would be to kowtow to the 'm.c.p.', who would like to hog the whole human gender for himself, and is aided and abetted by the more thoughtless members of the female sex who do not realize that they are not more free by insisting on falling down personholes but are blindly relinquishing their true identity" (*The Irrational Season,* p. 8).

One Opinion

That is just one opinion, but I would hazard that many women share it.

Our own bishops, as well as the authorities in Rome, are concerned about the pastoral dimensions of the problem. Rome will set up a commission to look into the problem. Our own bishops are facing the problem in terms of liturgical texts which have been modified to meet the problem (cf. *Origins,* Apr. 18, 1985, pp. 717ff.).

The demonstration of concern by the bishops and the seeking of a way to protect the unity of our Christian community belongs to them by their consecration, but they know as well as I that consecration does not make them experts in any field. As bishops, they are not necessarily competent in the realm of language, no more than those who sat on the Galileo trial were competent in astronomy through their consecration as bishops.

Language is the realm of those whose speciality it is, poets, authors, scholars. The great literary masterpiece we call the King James Version was done by scholars of Oxford and Cambridge, not by bishops. It is, in particular, the realm of the laity who are adept in this field. It would be presumptuous to make decisions on language without input from those who have a "feel" for the language and who do not simply manipulate it with word processors.

In short, in regard to the first aspect of the problem, the shift in perceptions and the conflict of perceptions, I feel there must be a respect for the realities; respect for the nature of language itself, which cannot be manipulated at will; respect for the sensitivities on both sides; and a concern to foster once again a hearing situation which can really hear the Word of God without the jamming devices which block out the Word and allow us to listen only to our emotions.

On the second level, where language is symbolic, and carries with it group memory and group emotion, there must be group forgiveness, group patience, group reconciliation, in one's own heart, and in larger solidarity of men and women. Until that takes place, a "fixed-up" solution on the level of language only covers up the real problem and it emerges in some other symbolic gesture.

In this connection, a further question could be asked: While many women, Christians, as well as non-Christians, share the same problem, should Christians have a different way of approaching the problem, *as Christians,* than the approach of non-Christians? Should not the spirit of the Gospel be operative in the search for a solution, if we are really Christian?

On the third level, the realm of the primordial reality of sexuality, we are in the realm of *discernment of spirits.* "But do not trust any and every spirit, my friends; test the spirits, to see whether they are from God; for among those who have gone out into the world there are many prophets falsely inspired" (1 Jn 4:1–2). "For it is not against human enemies that we have to struggle but against the Sovereignties and the Powers who originate the darkness in this world, the spiritual army of evil in the heavens" (Eph 6:10–12).

Perhaps nothing is more important in this current conflict of perceptions and the search for a resolution of the problem than to "test the spirits", to see what is really at work in the deep heart.

Wormwood must keep letter 16 sent by his mentor, Screwtape, right on top of the file. "I think I warned you before that if your patient can't be kept out of the Church, he ought, at least, to be violently attached to some party within it. I don't mean on really doctrinal issues.... The real fun is working up hatred between those who *say* 'mass' and those who *say* 'holy communion'.... And all the purely indifferent things—candles and clothes and what not—are an admirable ground for our activities" (*The Screwtape Letters,* C. S. Lewis, chap. 16).

This strategy to bring about division in the Church speaks directly to our present problems over "sexist language" and the divisions the problem fosters.

Conclusion

As you see, Sister, your letter has occasioned a long response. Personally I am grateful because it has forced me to put into shape all the things floating about in my head about this problem of "sexist language". Where all of this is going, how it will affect the Church in the future, I don't know. It is a neuralgic problem with some, a non-problem for others. In any case it is a serious pastoral problem in the Church.

Ultimately it is a test of our Christian faith. Does Christianity really work to bring about peace in issues that involve conflict? If it does not work, then we are counter-witnesses to the claims of the Gospel: "If you dwell within the word I have brought, you are indeed my disciples; you shall know the truth, and the truth will set you free" (Jn 8:31).

In Christ
John R. Sheets, S.J.

FEMSPEAK AND
THE BATTLE OF LANGUAGE

Peter Berger and Brigitte Berger

Ideas are weapons. So is language. Linguistic victories are translated into political victories, and vice versa. Let us call the language which feminists are striving to impose on the public *Femspeak*.

Hardly anyone, of course, likes to admit the sociological relativity
or the political function of the language deemed "proper" in a
particular camp to which one belongs. Femspeakers obfuscate, to
themselves as much as to others, the real character of their own
linguistic campaigns. Indeed, the very phrase "feminist language"
is likely to arouse puzzlement if not resentment on the part of
those who believe in the rightness of this language. In their mind,
of course, there is no such thing; there is only the correction of the
"sexist" language used by others; it is *the others'* language that is
political language (and the alleged politics of sexism are dissected
in endless analytic exercises by feminist authors); *their own* language,
preferably called "inclusive language", is supposedly nothing but
the cleansing of speech from the nefarious political manipulations
of the sexist oppressor. As with all bowdlerizers, they set about the
job of cleaning everyone's mouth out with soap in a spirit of grim,
unquestioning moral conviction.

What is mostly at issue is the generic use of the masculine
gender in standard English (the whole issue, of course, takes other
forms or does not exist at all in other languages). Supposedly,
saying "he" when one means a person of either sex, or using
terms such as "man" or "mankind" to denote the human species as
a whole, denigrates women and linguistically supports male
dominance. Since the list of linguistic offenses is quite short, it is

61

not difficult to observe the relevant tabus once one has grasped the principle. One just has to say or write "he or she" (perhaps randomly varied with "she or he" to avoid, heaven forbid, the suggestion that the sequence of pronouns has hierarchical significance), to use such "inclusive" terms as "the human race" or "humankind", or to employ neologisms like "chairperson" or "repairperson". One's *bona fides* as a non-sexist is thus easily established, to the point where even an occasional stumbling relapse into standard usage may be graciously forgiven. Observing an individual—an academic, say, addressing a faculty meeting— carefully making his way through a minefield of possible lapses into the offending terms is a touching spectacle. It reminds one of nothing as much as the spectacle of a reformed drunk gingerly talking nice while giving testimony to his reformation at a Salvation Army rally.

All those feminist authors, of course, claim that standard usage has always been experienced by women as demeaning or excluding them. The evidence for this is typically anecdotal: some little girl, say, who thought that she was not invited to a party because the masculine pronoun was used in the language of the invitation. Let it be stipulated that little girls—and, we hasten to add, little boys—often have difficulties understanding the abstractions of adult talk. This is due to what child psychologists have called the concreteness of the child's thought. The evidence for the alleged suffering by adult women as a result of this particular feature of English is, at best, very dubious indeed. Virtually all of it is a retrojection into the past of what present-day feminists feel or have made themselves feel when they encounter the allegedly sexist elements in the language. These feelings, to be sure, are real enough. To admit this, however, in no way implies agreement with the elaborate theories of linguistic sexism erected upon them.

Sexist language is an invention of the feminist movement. Attributing it to Shakespeare, to the King James Version of the Bible, or to the way millions of people talk in those sectors of the society where feminist agitation has failed to make inroads is as meaningful as attributing blasphemous intent to an individual who says "goddamit"—or, for that matter, to attribute homicidal intentions to someone who says "drop dead". Taken literally, this is a theory that elevates infantile misunderstandings to the level of hermeneutics. But it would be a mistake to take this literally. It matters little, in the final analysis, that here is a theory of language that rests on little or nothing beyond the emotions of the theorists. What matters a lot is that the theory legitimates a linguistic offensive that is part of a general political strategy. In this strategy, every masculine pronoun purged from a text, every insertion of "person" as a generic suffix, constitutes a symbolic victory in the larger struggle. Once again, everyone involved in these affairs intuitively understands what is going on — which is precisely why emotions run so high on matters that to an outside and uninvolved observer might appear deafeningly trivial.

An example may help to clarify the point. (The example will, no doubt, offend the delicate ears of feminists. But if delicacy had been a strong concern of ours, we would never have started writing this!) English is virtually alone among modern Western languages in not distinguishing the forms of address appropriate between more or less intimate individuals. Thus French distinguishes between people to whom one says, respectively, *tu* and *vous* (and even has the verb *tutoyer*, untranslatable into English, to denote the former case), Spanish has *tu* and *usted*, and so on. In modern Italian the intimate form of address is *tu*, while more distant individuals are addressed as *lei* (which happens to be the third person plural). Sometime in the 1930s Mussolini made a speech in which he castigated the use of *lei* as an effete, indeed effeminate, mode of language. The purpose of the Fascist revolution, he said, was to restore vigor and virility to the Italian people. The good Fascist was direct in language as in action. The good Fascist, therefore, did not say *lei;* instead he said *voi* (the second person plural). Now, from a philological or semantic point of view, this was sheer nonsense. The use of *lei* had never struck anyone as effete or effeminate; it was, quite simply, standard Italian. But, needless to say, the situation changed dramatically after Mussolini's speech. From then on, everyone became highly conscious of the matter (if you will, everyone's consciousness was raised). The use of *lei* became a sign of reactionary, perhaps even subversive, attitudes. The use of *voi,* preferably in a self-righteous and highly audible manner, was evidence that the speaker (or writer) was a Fascist in good standing. Indeed, it became the verbal equivalent of the Fascist salute. Put simply, what before Mussolini's pronouncement had been an apolitical and unreflective element of the common language now forced itself on everyone's consciousness as a highly political symbol.

Feminists, eager to wrap themselves in the mystique of the civil rights movement, like to compare so-called sexist language with the linguistic etiquette used to denigrate blacks. The comparison does not withstand close scrutiny. The language etiquette of race relations in America, especially in the South, was understood by everyone *at the time* as having the purpose of humiliating blacks. Whites understood this, as did blacks, and outside observers wrote about it as far back as the nineteenth century. Thus, to call adult blacks by their first names or to deny them the use of such honorific titles as "Mister" and "Miss" was part and parcel of a linguistic degradation ceremony (to use Harold Garfinkel's apt phrase) that was in the consciousness of all participants in the situation. Racist language, in other words, was *not* an invention of the civil rights movement, retrojected into the past prior to the advent of that movement. If one wants to stay within the context of American English, a better comparison would be one suggested by the aforementioned failure of English to distinguish between intimate and distant forms of address. Imagine a movement arising in America with the avowed purpose of creating greater intimacy between all members of society. Let us call it the Intimatist movement. One of the theorists of this movement writes a book developing the point that the use of "you" to address both one's closest friends and the most casual acquaintances is one of the most dehumanizing characteristics of American speech: A language that fails to distinguish such fundamental differences between human relationships, this theorist tells us, is not only a symptom of alienation but an active cause of it. Therefore, the good Intimatist never says "you"; instead, he (or she) always says "thou". Nonsense? Of course—from a philological or semantic point of view. From a political point of view, though, it will cease to be nonsense in the exact degree to which the Intimatist movement gains influence and power in the society. We will not pursue this little fantasy any farther—the censorship imposed on textbooks and government handbooks, the boycotts directed against allegedly alienating language in the public media, not to mention the new avenues of employment for retired Episcopalian priests giving rush courses in Elizabethan syntax and writing guidelines for editors—"lift up thy voice like a trumpet, and shew my people their transgression"—as to the outside observer, he shuddereth and keepeth his tongue in dreadful silence. . . .

And so, here too, the bowdlerizers are let loose in the land (not the Intimatists; we're back with the feminists). Like their neo-traditionalist cousins in faith (albeit a different faith), they rummage through school libraries, scrutinize television programs with inquisitorial alertness, harass nonconformists in classrooms or political meetings, and try to mobilize editors of books and periodicals in the service of "proper" language. The more ambitious among them invade the nursery with their language tabus (a whole new set of linguistic no-nos for the toddlers of the knowledge class to learn) and rewrite the classics in their deplorable idiom. And (how could it be otherwise, given the state of religion in our time?) there is a new phalanx of Malcolm Muggeridge's category of demented clerics translating the Bible and the Christian liturgy into the language of *Ms.* magazine. All of this activity, of course, takes place in a spirit of unquestioning and self-righteous certitude. Bowdlerizers are not given to skepticism, moderation, or humility.

"Non-inclusive language", then, is the pornography of the critical camp in the war over the family. Actually, we need not quarrel with *this* particular phrase. It does indeed "include" some—the activists and the fellow travellers of one camp; by the same token, both symbolically and behaviorally, it "excludes" those on the other side. The basic purpose of all ideologically charged language is to draw boundaries, and if possible to expand these boundaries. As we have pointed out before, the same boundaries, to a considerable extent, are also boundaries of class.

The expansion of Femspeak beyond its original more or less sectarian circles, therefore, must be understood as part of the cultural imperialism of the new knowledge class, seeking to impose its language, values, and political control over other classes in the society.

THE SERIOUS BUSINESS OF TRANSLATION (INCLUDING RELIGIOUS TRANSLATION)

K. D. Whitehead

I

Translation is a necessary evil. That it is necessary goes without saying: without translation we would never be able to have access to the preponderance of human communication that goes on continually all over the world, much less have access to the vast heritage of human culture and achievement that has been handed down to us from the past.

Translation is especially important where religion is concerned. If it is true that, as the Letter to the Hebrews reliably informs us, God has spoken to the human race in many and various ways ("through the prophets") culminating in a definitive revelation of Himself "through His Son whom He . . . made heir of all things" (Heb 1:2), then it is also ineluctably the case that God's message thus delivered through the prophets and through God's Divine Son has had to be mediated to the world—through translation. This has been true from the time of the first generation of Christians, since neither Christ nor any of His original apostles spoke or taught in a language known to many in the Roman Empire of the day, much less to us today.

In a lecture entitled "On Translation", quite celebrated when it was delivered at Oxford University over sixty years ago in 1931, Hilaire Belloc declared that "translation has been an essential to the maintenance of religion among men . . . [since the] original pronouncement of a religion . . . needs rendering into the speech men know in each succeeding age, lest the guide should fall dumb and his lantern be extinguished. In the second place, religion is of its nature universal and its application to various societies demands the rendering of its fundamental doctrines into the idiom of each in such fashion that all the renderings shall make for unity of thought, corresponding with the thought of the original."

Thus translation always has been, and remains, utterly necessary, especially where religion is concerned. That it is a necessary evil, however, may be less apparent. People tend to take Scripture, for example, for granted as they read or hear it; they usually do not reflect upon the fact that a translator—someone with a knowledge of both Greek (or Hebrew) and English—had to take thought and grapple with the words and meanings in the original and then decide how to render them into English in a way that is understandable and acceptable to those whose language is English. One of the religious problems of recent years, of course, is that many of the faithful have perceived some of the new renderings of Scripture to be strange and un-English enough that they have been distracted from the primary meaning of what is supposed to be God's word conveyed in these translations. Most people understand without having been told that translations are supposed to be unobtrusive, as if they had been set down originally in precisely the way that we read or hear them in our own language. Some modern translations, however, unfortunately call undue attention to themselves, and this problem is only compounded when people start introducing their own variants (such as "his or her" for "his" in the text).

Translation is actually a difficult art that does not at all lend itself to such improvisations. Anyone who has ever tried to translate anything, or perhaps has even just thought of translating something, must quickly become aware that the whole process bristles with difficulties. It is impossible to translate anything perfectly; it is difficult even to do it well. A well-known Italian proverb even puns in order to state the fundamental problem and its all too probable result: *traduttore traditore;* a translator is a *traitor.* Nevertheless we must necessarily have recourse to it if some messages are to be communicated at all.

The translator must not only understand the meaning of the original text being translated but must be able to make it understandable—and natural—in a new and different medium; nothing is more fatal to successful translations than jarring, clumsy, unidiomatic constructions, however "literal" they might be. The fact is that translation can never be a word-for-word kind of thing. It can never even be a meaning-for-meaning kind of thing, since such things as context and culture must inevitably enter in as well. However, it is not thereby an entirely free-floating thing, either, for a translation is always indissolubly bound to an original text, however it is rendered; it must, that is, be rendered *correctly,* insofar as that is humanly possible. The trouble often is that the higher the literary quality of a text, the more difficult it may be to do justice to it in translation.

For most of us speaking and understanding our native language involve "doing what comes naturally"; language is native to human beings, and our mother tongue easily and naturally corresponds to our thought. We normally have neither the occasion nor the motivation to reflect upon either the variety or the complexity of human language(s) and language patterns—or, often, even on the meaning of words; we just understand them. If we ever do begin to reflect upon what we are doing when speaking or writing or even listening, we are as likely as not to begin to speak or write or understand less well, much as we might swim or ride a bicycle less well the minute we start to think too carefully about what it is we are doing.

The translator, however, is strictly obliged to think carefully and in detail about what has been set down in the original and how it has been set down and what it means—all preliminary to knowing how to set the same thing down again in another medium, the second language into which the original is being translated. Ideally, this second language is the translator's native language.

All this is said by way of establishing that every translator has two inseparable responsibilities to carry out, both of them organically related to the fundamental virtue and sine qua non of any and every successful translation, namely, *fidelity,* faithfulness. The translator must be faithful both to the original text and to the language into which it is being translated. This fidelity both to the source and to the medium is essential to the integrity and quality of any and every translation. If a translation is to be a true and authentic translation rather than an erroneous and contrived one — or perhaps even something else besides a translation — it must respect absolutely both its source and its medium.

II

Every translator knows, and most literate persons can imagine, many of the mistakes and pitfalls, even the often ludicrous boners, that can be potentially involved in any translation. Belloc in his lecture spoke of what he called "the classic instance of the word 'handkerchief' in Shakespeare's *Othello,* which translated by the French word *'mouchoir',* interrupted the tragedy with loud laughter". The reason for this, of course, is that the French word for "handkerchief", rather than suggesting the light, silky creation that the word "kerchief" does generally suggest in English, is instead formed from the down-to-earth French verb that means "to wipe or blow one's nose" (*se moucher*). In order to be more faithful to the medium of French the translator of Shakespeare was obviously obliged to seek for a more appropriate word in the context (*foulard*) for what in *Othello* was called a "handkerchief".

Many similar examples quickly come to mind. Even elementary students of French, for example, learn that *"un brave homme"* is *not* a "brave" man but rather an *honest* one; meanwhile, *"un homme honnête"* is a *polite* man. And so on. Cognate words can be particularly tricky. "Deception" in English, for example, has reference to deceit, while in French it means primarily "disappointment". Similarly, "conscience" basically means "consciousness" in French; what we call "conscience" normally has to be specified as *"la conscience morale".* Yet, "conscientious", meanwhile, does come out pretty accurately in the French *"consciencieux".* And so on, and so on. Numerous further examples could be cited: they would soon become tedious. The point is that the successful translator must know both languages thoroughly, along with their usages and nuances.

Nothing is more important for a translator, in fact, than to know how words and phrases are actually used—in both languages. This can never be a matter of mere dictionary equivalents. A few years ago a major American publisher brought out an imaginative and provocative little book on the continuing influence of Satan in the modern world by the Swiss Christian writer Denis de Rougement. The title of this book in English was *The Devil's Share*, an oddly unidiomatic phrase in English, although at first it is hard to say exactly why. Anyone with a knowledge of French, however, knowing that the original French title of the book was *La Part du Diable*, could verify that the French word *"part"* does indeed mean primarily "share" or "portion" in English, hence the English title. However, the translator in this case needed to reflect more carefully on French usage and recall the very popular proverb in French that happens to have an exact equivalent in English: "Give the devil his due"; *"donner au diable sa part"*. The book title in English should have been *The Devil's Due*, not *The Devil's Share*, which does not sound quite right for a reason we can now understand better: the translator did not get the English right because he had failed to get the French right.

There is no need to belabor this point with further examples. Even people with only a nodding acquaintance with a foreign language can probably think of their own. In this regard, the advertising and public relations problems encountered by the Chevy Nova in Spanish-speaking countries quickly comes to mind; the very name of the car, *no va*, means, in Spanish, "it doesn't go"! A salient point that we may take away from the example of the choice of Rougemont's book title in English can be that, when a translator fails to respect both the source and medium in the translation being made, it is the result that "doesn't go", and, usually, we get something much worse than "the devil's share".

III

That a translator has some discretion, but far, far from unlimited discretion, for how he renders something from one language into another, we can perhaps best illustrate by looking at an actual translation, or, rather, at several different English translations of a single text. The variations that can be found even in a relatively uncomplex text can be quite instructive.

From the time that Dante Alighieri completed his *Divine Comedy* some time before his death in 1321, this masterpiece of world literature has been translated into English perhaps as many as thirty times. We obviously cannot look at all, or even at many, of these translations. We must confine ourselves to looking at three or four variant translations of a couple of selected passages.

In Canto XXVI of the *Inferno,* while Dante is being conducted by Virgil through the circle of hell, where "fraudulent counselors" and "deceivers" are receiving their just punishments, the poet encounters the tragic figure of Ulysses, famous in Greek mythology. In recounting some of his personal story to Dante, Ulysses delivers himself, inter alia, of the following explanation of the real motive for his celebrated wanderings around the Mediterranean world following the end of the Trojan War:

> *nè dolcezza di figlio, nè la pietà*
> *del vecchio padre, nè 'l debito amore*
> *lo qual dovea far Penelope lieta*
>
> *vincer poter dentro da me l'ardore*
> *ch' i 'ebbi a divenir del mondo esperto,*
> *e degli vizii umani e del valore;*
>
> *ma misi me per l'alto mare aperto*
> *sol con un legno e con quella compagna*
> *picciola, dalla quale non fui deserto.*

> (*Inferno* XXVI, 94–102)

This passage has been deliberately chosen for its uncomplicated clearness and simplicity. Dante's Italian is usually quite clear and straightforward, as a matter of fact, much easier for the modern reader of Italian than is, for example, Shakespeare's English for the modern reader of English—not to speak of that of earlier English poets such as Chaucer, even though they came later than Dante. I supply the following—rather literal—prose translation of this con-

fession of Dante's Ulysses; we shall see subsequently what some of
the various notable English translators have made out of it:

> Neither affection for my son, nor respect for my
> aged father, nor even the love I owed to her that
> should have been making Penelope happy
>
> could conquer in me the ardor I had to gain
> experience of the wide world and learn both
> about human vices and about human worth;
>
> So I set forth out upon the depths of the open sea
> with just one ship and with the small company which
> had not deserted me.

Henry Francis Cary, who became famous during the Napoleonic
Wars as "the English translator of Dante" and came to be buried in
the Poet's Corner of Westminster Abbey as a consequence, rendered
the same passage as follows in his well-known and often reprinted
verse translation of *The Divine Comedy:*

> Nor fondness for my son, nor reverence
> Of my old father, nor return of love,
> That should have crowned Penelope with joy,
> Could overcome in me the zeal I had
> To explore the world and search the ways of life,
> Man's evil and his virtue. Forth I sail'd
> Into the deep illimitable main,
> With but one bark, and the small faithful band
> That yet cleaved to me.

This is blank verse, of course; but it is also, quite obviously,
heavily influenced by some of the conventions of the Romantic
period in English literature, an era not calculated to share Dante's
outlook or understand him, whatever some may say. The artificer
of another "Romantic" version of this passage was the American
poet Henry Wadsworth Longfellow. The latter bears a name still
known to most Americans, even in an age so little given to
reading poetry as the present one. Longfellow's translation of *The
Divine Comedy* yields the following version of the same passage
from Dante:

> Nor fondness for my son, nor reverence
>> For my old Father, nor the due affection
>> which joyous should have made Penelope,
>
> Could overcome within me the desire
>> I had to be experienced of the world,
>> And of the vice and virtue of mankind;
>
> But I put forth on the high open sea
>> With one sole ship, and that small company
>> By which I never had deserted been.

These two "traditional" translations of Dante, although they certainly succeed in conveying the basic "meaning" of the passage, do not really succeed in conveying the "poetry" of it—though both translations apparently aimed to do precisely that. Nevertheless they seem quite forced and mannered and artificial, at least to the modern ear. Both translators strain to be "poetic" (Cary: "the deep illimitable main/with but one bark"; Longfellow: "the due affection which joyous should have made Penelope"), but only succeed in being strained—a characteristic that most emphatically does *not* reflect the natural and easy poetical diction found in Dante's original. The passage in English does not sound like English; it does not ring true. Admittedly, the translators took on a difficult task. Perhaps a simple prose translation would have been better if the aim really was to make Dante available to an English reader in a real way, rather than to appear to be poetical because this happened to be a translation of poetry. For the fact is that even when writing poetry, if it is good poetry, native speakers of English do not normally resort to the contrived diction found in both translations.

Thus, there is a very important sense in which both of these translations fail to be entirely faithful to the medium of English, English as normally usually used by native speakers of English, even if they happen to be poets. These translations also fail, at least in some measure, to be faithful to their source as well, since Cary really had to know that *"aperto"*, which means "open", does *not* mean "illimitable"; and surely Longfellow could have grasped that *"alto"*, "high", when applied to the sea, means "deep" in Italian.

Dorothy L. Sayers, a modern writer best known today for her detective fiction as well as for some astringent but on the whole quite admirable Christian apologetics and social criticism—she was really quite "tough-minded" and certainly not "romantic" in the conventional sense—similarly produced a translation of Dante that also fails to render properly this fairly simple passage, probably because she elected to use Dante's own *terza rima* (even Longfellow stuck to blank verse, although he divided it up into three-line stanzas, as in the original). But *terza rima* happens to be a verse form distinctly not natural or native to English (her "medium"). Here is how Dorothy L. Sayers rendered the verses in question, and she was certainly a writer with genuine, tested literary talent:

> No tenderness for my son, nor piety
>   To my old father, nor the wedded love
>   That should have comforted Penelope
>
> Could conquer in me the restless itch to rove
>   And rummage through the world, exploring it,
>   All human worth and wickedness to prove.
>
> So on the deep and open sea I set
>   Forth, with a single ship and that small band
>   Of comrades that had never left me yet.

It is not pleasant to criticize and nitpick over the work of serious and talented writers trying to make available to English readers one of the world's literary masterpieces. Nevertheless phrases such as "the restless itch to rove / and rummage through the world, exploring it" are simply not authentically English, quite apart from the fact that such phrases represent an unwarranted embellishment on Dante's original text.

In this regard, Hilaire Belloc, in his Oxford University lecture mentioned above, lays down a rule that he styles an "epigrammatic counsel" and that surely must constitute something of an absolute rule where translation is concerned. The rule is this: "Never embellish", Belloc flatly declares. "You may indeed embellish if you are desiring to produce a work of art of your own, careless of what happens to the vile body which you are adapting, just as you may melt down some silver spoons and fashion with the material an elaborate cup. But if your object be sincere translation, never yield to the sometimes considerable temptation of making the new thing (in your eyes) better than the old." The end result of what is produced by translators who do succumb to the temptation to embellish "is not translation", in Belloc's opinion.

Belloc has stated something very basic here: a translator does not have the right to embellish—or add to—the text being translated; the translator is strictly bound by what the source says, and cannot arbitrarily decide how it might perhaps have been said better and then put *that* down as the translation.

And we have now seen enough examples of embellishments to understand what Belloc meant. Translation is a serious business. Cary and Longfellow and Sayers were all professional writers with no other apparent motive but to make Dante available in English, yet we have seen how easily they can fail when they do not give sufficient respect both to their source and to their medium. We may leave to the imagination the extent to which embellishments could be employed by translators who actually wished to mislead or deceive the reader; if talented translators with no ulterior motive can fall so short, we can imagine what translators with their own agenda could achieve in the way of mistranslations!

Nevertheless we should not conclude from all of this that the task of correct and effective translation is simply impossible: on the contrary, it can be done. In the present case this can be seen by considering another version of the same passage from Dante that we have been considering; it comes from the recent translation of *The Divine Comedy* that appears in the current Penguin Classics edition of the sacred poem. This translation, by Professor Mark Musa of Indiana University, utilizes blank verse, a form that is very much native to English, as both Cary and Longfellow realized. Yet even blank verse has to be handled properly. There is good and bad blank verse, and Professor Musa has managed to use it in a way that is both faithful to the Italian original and natural and readable in English as well; it can be done:

> Not sweetness of a son, not reverence
>   for an aging father, not the debt of love
>   I owed Penelope to make her happy,
>
> Could quench deep in myself the burning wish
>   to know the world and have experience
>   of all man's vices, of all human worth.
>
> So I set out on the deep and open sea
>   with just one ship and with that group of men,
>   not many, who had not deserted me.

Besides being written in straightforward yet highly literate English, this version has a few special felicities of its own: "the debt of love" for *"'l debito amore"*; "not many", set apart as a separate phrase, for *"picciola"*, etc. At the same time the blank verse grouped into three-line stanzas does succeed in conveying something of the austere dignity of Dante's poetry.

This brief passage from Dante, which we have examined in four published English translations, could be replicated over and over again, in Dante or in any other important text or work. If anything, the difficulties of translation are multiplied and compounded in the degree that the text is more difficult and complex in the original; we need think only of the difficulties of rendering Shakespeare, say, in another language besides English. What should emerge clearly from our analysis is the importance in any translation of fidelity both to the source—the original text—and to the medium—the language into which it is being translated. To illustrate how the problems we have identified are inherent in the very process of translation as such, we may conclude this section by reproducing without further comment another short passage from *The Divine Comedy*, followed by a literal prose translation and then by the versions produced by each of the four translators whose work we have examined. The reader can make the comparison as to whether and how each of the translations is or is not faithful both to the Italian original and to authentic English discourse.

Our second text from Dante is taken from Canto XXX of the *Purgatorio*, in which Beatrice, who will henceforth conduct Dante on his journey, comes forward toward Dante across the Garden of Earthly Paradise to meet him. The poet recognizes Beatrice not by what he sees with his eyes, for she is veiled, but by the sudden fire that courses through his veins; feeling "the mighty power of his old love", *"d'antico amor... la gran potenza"*, Dante turns around to tell Virgil what he is experiencing (although unbeknownst to him, Virgil has suddenly disappeared), saying:

> *Men che dramma*
> *di sangue m'e rimaso che non tremi:*
> *conosco i segni de l'antico fiamma.*

Literal prose translation:

> There is no drop of blood in me that
> does not throb: I recognize the signs
> of my old passion (flame).

Cary:

> There is no dram of blood
> That doth not quiver in me. The old flame
> Throws out clear tokens of reviving fire.

Longfellow:

> Not a drachm
> Of blood remains in me, that does not tremble;
> I know the traces of the ancient flame.

Sayers:

> There is scarce a dram
> That does not hammer and throb in all my blood;
> I know the embers of the ancient flame.

And, finally, Musa:

> Not one drop of blood
> is left inside my veins that does not throb:
> I recognize the signs of the ancient flame.

In the face of all these variations in the translation of one simple passage, can we doubt that mere scholarship or expertise in the original language will not necessarily yield an adequate and faithful translation?

IV

We have now said enough about the difficult art and necessary process of translation to allow us to make some points about the general question of translation as such, quite apart from what is being translated into what.

Point one must be the same point with which we have just concluded the previous section, namely, that all of the scholarship and expertise in the world, say, in a particular language and culture, will not by themselves guarantee the success of a translation if both the source and the medium are not respected in the way we have been describing. Cary, Longfellow, and Sayers were all professional, indeed famous, writers who worked for years on their respective translations of Dante. Yet in the end they failed to produce the successful translation that Professor Musa was able to produce, mostly because they were all too prone to "embellish" Dante's text whenever they felt like it in order to make it more poetic, to fit a rhyme or meter scheme, or whatever ("making it better", in Belloc's words).

Our point two must be that Professor Musa succeeded where the others failed because he was willing to sit at Dante's feet and respect the latter's plain words and unadorned diction and render them into equally plain English words recognizably put together in a way that a native speaker of English normally uses English— and in a verse form, as it happened, native to the genius of English.

Our third point is that the *judge* of the success of a given translation cannot merely be the scholar or expert able to verify in a technical sense that the meanings of the words in the original language have been correctly rendered in equivalent words in the second language. The scholar or expert has a role to play, to be sure; there would be no translations if there were no translators knowlegeable in both the source language and in the medium into which it is being translated; a translator is obviously necessary for any translation, successful or not. But the real judges of the success or even adequacy of any translation must ultimately be the readers or users of it. In spite of the long publishing histories of the Cary, Longfellow, and Sayers translations of Dante, for example, we imagine only with difficulty any English reader persisting very long in reading the clogged and stilted and often jejeune versifying being served up as "Dante" unless that reader is obliged to struggle on with the text for a literature course assignment or something of the sort—or perhaps because such a reader believes Dante represents something that is "supposed" to be read. Otherwise these particular translations are hardly the sorts of thing most of us would have on our bedside table. Meanwhile, however, Dante is somebody who really should be available to modern readers of English exercising their normal judgments and preferences about what they want to be spending their time reading, and that is where Professor Musa's translation proves so useful. Perhaps a good modern prose translation would be useful as well, just as some of the modern prose translations of the *Iliad* and the *Odyssey* have brought these epics from the dawn of our civilization within the ambit of modern readers without a classical education. However that may be, translations, if they are to be successful, must be smoothly and naturally accessible to those who are going to read them or make use of them and who therefore must also be allowed to be the ultimate judges of their success or lack of it.

This consideration brings us to our fourth and final point, which is that the reader who knows Dante, say, only through a translation that has failed to respect either its source or its medium, or both, does not get the real Dante but rather something else besides Dante, a false Dante, an ersatz Dante. Such a reader is therefore cheated. Worse, it is a failure of integrity that a "translation" should be put forward as something that it is not; it is a form of untruth. As we have said and repeated—and as should now be clear—a translation, if it is to be faithful, or even adequate, must be faithful both to its source and to its medium; otherwise it is not even a translation but some kind of fabrication.

V

When we come to the special problems of religious translation, everything that has been said about translation qua translation up to this point applies. Indeed, it applies all the more. If any and every translation must have integrity and be faithful both to its source and to its medium, how much truer must this be of a translation of an inspired text, of a medium conveying God's own word! Here, at any rate, users of translations of sacred texts must *not* be cheated! Our salvation could depend on it, however little anybody likes to talk about such things nowadays.

One fact of special importance concerning religious translation today, of course, is that we have witnessed a complete turnover in the existing stock of translations of the Bible, and this several times over. The old Confraternity Revision of the Challoner-Rheims Catholic Bible on which many of today's Catholics were brought up, for example, is not only long gone; it is practically forgotten, as is also the famous King James Version, once considered by English-speaking Protestants virtually to *be* "Scripture". In spite of the overall beauty and the many felicities in detail of these old translations, associated as they were with the initial great age of the development of English prose and poetry — in their day they certainly represented singular examples of respect for the English-language medium — it had become generally recognized that, especially with all their archaisms, they had become inadequate for continued regular use by today's English speakers. As Belloc remarked, religious translations do have to be periodically updated. Usages change; so does vocabulary. Time marches on; so does scholarship. Thus, quite apart from our ultimate judgments concerning the success or even the adequacy of some of the newer translations, we are obliged to admit that these new versions "translated from the original languages with critical use of all the ancient sources" do point to a renewed respect for the source of the Bible, and this is surely all to the good as far as it goes.

Having said this, however, we must go on to add that the convergence of all the new scholarship with the Church's perennial need for accurate translations of Scripture in contemporary language does *not* justify "the permanent revolution" in Bible translations that we have witnessed in recent years. The fact is that the modern versions of the Bible that initially replaced the older versions themselves did not last very long; the Jerusalem Bibles and the Revised Standard Versions were themselves soon replaced with yet newer versions, such as the New American Bible, and then very quickly there were revisions of *that,* not to speak of yet other "approved" versions clamoring for attention and use, such as the Good News for Modern Man and the St. Jerome Catholic edition of the American Bible Society's modern translation. For the nonspecialist the whole thing eventually becomes bewildering. Jesus Christ committed his Gospel not to specialists, however, but to ordinary men, the apostles; the successors of the latter, the bishops, should be the ones, not the specialists themselves, to decide whether and when we need a new version of God's word in English. If new and ever-changing versions continue to be pressed upon us, Scripture itself can come to seem fluid and changing and arbitrary; indeed this may be the case already, considering all the many changes that have already been made in recent years.

How can a people go on considering something "sacred" when it keeps on being changed all the time? This is simple human psychology. From a pastoral and liturgical point of view, therefore, the need for all the new and variant translations constantly succeeding one another becomes highly questionable. If translation is a necessary evil, the evil is certainly compounded where religious translation is concerned when new translations are multiplied indefinitely.

Then there is the question of the quality of some of the new translations. Are they good translations or not? Are they even adequate ones in the sense we have been discussing here? No doubt plenty of attention has been given to the ancient sources of Scripture and the modern study of these sources as far as most of these new translations are concerned. Has equal thought been given to respect for the medium of the modern English language? We saw that defective handling of the English medium was where most of the translators of Dante went wrong. Have the translators of, say, the English Jerusalem Bible or the New American Bible similarly gone wrong, at least some of the time?

To bring to some kind of conclusion this inquiry into the serious business of translation, especially religious translation, let us compare some variant renderings of a well-known Scripture passage to determine if some of the points we established in our examination of variant translations from Dante have any application to some of the new translations of the Bible. In the familiar text of Matthew 16:16–18, Jesus, questioning his disciples, elicited a response from Simon Peter that subsequently became rather celebrated. Here is the passage according to the old Catholic Confraternity edition of the New Testament, copyrighted in 1941:

> "But who do you say that I am?"
> Simon Peter answered and said, "Thou art the
> Christ, the Son of the living God."
> Then Jesus answered and said, "Blessed art thou,
> Simon Bar-Jona, for flesh and blood has not revealed
> this to thee, but my Father in heaven. And I say to
> thee, thou art Peter, and upon this rock I will build my
> Church and the gates of hell shall not prevail against it."

This is an English version upon which generations of Catholics were brought up; it is doubtful if many of them ever experienced any difficulty understanding what it meant and internalizing it as part of their faith as the latter developed and matured. Comparing it with the original Greek, with the Latin Vulgate, and with other modern translations, we can only conclude that it is an accurate, and indeed quite adequate, translation of the original text. It has some difficulties for the totally untutored reader (if such really exists)—"the Christ" as a title rather than a proper name, the meaning of "Bar-Jona", the relationship between the name "Peter" and the word "rock", and the meaning of the phrase "the gates of hell". These difficulties, however, were always easily explainable and were always in fact explained through the Church's catechesis; few of the faithful can ever have had any real difficulty with them.

It is true, of course, that the "thees" and "thous" of this version have rendered it archaic for current Church use; Scripture should not sound quaint, any more than it should sound slangy, and hence the modernization of this text was surely called for. The Revised Standard Version, for example, accomplished precisely this in a translation virtually identical with the above except that the pronouns become "you" and "the gates of hell" become "the powers of death" in the RSV version. Concerning the latter, a note informs the reader that the phrase in Greek reads "the gates of Hades" (or *Sheol* in Hebrew). The RSV similarly includes a note explaining the relationship between the Greek *Petros,* "Peter", and *petra,* "rock". It is hard to see how anyone could go wrong with this.

Some of the newer translations, however, have not been as content to let well enough alone when rendering a passage so very familiar to all instructed Christians. The Jerusalem Bible in English, for example, has Jesus telling Peter that the latter is "happy" instead of "blessed" for having been inspired to make his famous confession of faith. This is one of those favored modern render-ings that simply seem inexplicable to the layman. The French Jerusalem Bible similarly has *"heureux",* the German *"selig".* Why? The Greek is *"makarios",* and however scholars may interpret its primary meaning, the fact is that, in these modern transla-tions, it does not ring true. "Happy" is the most general of all the adjectives in the three modern languages for the general idea of "bliss"; in English, however, "happy" does not normally have any religious connotation, as to some extent *"heureux",* or better, *"bienheureux",* does in French, and as *"selig"* does in German; in English the adjective for "bliss" with religious con-notations is "blessed". Were the Jerusalem Bible in English transla-tors simply translating the French rather than the original? How-ever that may be, the very first Beatitude, where the same flat, pointless translation of "happy" appears in the Jerusalem Bible, the text itself goes on to specify that there is a very particular kind of "bliss" or "happiness" that "the poor in spirit" will enjoy, namely, possession of "the kingdom of heaven" (cf. Mt 5:3), not just happiness pure and simple. In view of all this, the substitu-tion of "happy" for "blessed" in the Jerusalem Bible was surely wrong.

Similarly, the same Jerusalem Bible cannot simply go with "the gates of hell" but has to bring in a rather clumsy and wholly un-English phrase "the gates of the underworld", adding a note indicating that "the gates symbolize the power of the underworld to hold captive", whatever *that* means. "Underworld" by any standard is a most unfortunate rendering because today the word in English refers primarily to the world of criminals and gangsters; perhaps educated people understand the meaning of "underworld" in Greek and Roman mythology, but the average person in the pews is all too likely to be thinking primarily of mobsters instead. Even the French Jerusalem Bible retains *"les portes de l'Hades"*, although it does not really succeed in explaining it with an elaborate note to the effect that " 'gates' personified refer to the power of the Evil One who, having introduced men into the spiritual death of sin, further drags them down into a definitive death in eternity. . . . The Church's mission is to rescue the elect from this empire of death, both temporal and eternal." Translators obliged to resort to such explanations as this might prudently have stayed with "the gates of hell", about which the average person is not really going to make a very serious mistake concerning its basic meaning.

Regarding the whole passage about Peter's confession and Jesus' giving him the name by which he would henceforth be known, the more the modern translations strain to try to render its obscurities and difficulties, the more obscure and difficult it seems to become. This certainly turns out to be the case for the version that follows from the New American Bible; it is this version that we now seem to be hearing at Mass, and it seems likely that a fair number of us were quite startled by it the first time we heard it and have had no little trouble being completely comfortable with it ever since:

> "And you," he said to them, "who do you
> say that I am?"
> "You are the Messiah," Simon Peter answered,
> "the Son of the living God."
> Jesus replied: "Blest are you, Simon, son of
> John! No mere man has revealed this to you
> but my heavenly Father. I for my part declare

to you, you are 'Rock', and on this rock I
will build my Church and the jaws of death
shall not prevail against it."

We cannot object to such variants in this version as "Messiah"
for "Christ" or "son of John" for "Bar-Jona"; these would appear
to be acceptable variants for translators faced with the awesome
task of translating Scripture. Nevertheless, an overall judgment
about this version as a whole would have to be that it both calls
attention to itself in a way that distracts the reader or the listener
from its meaning and also obscures that meaning, the meaning of
what Jesus is saying to Peter in this key New Testament encounter.

For starters, anyone who prefers the poetic adjective "blest" for
the regular English past participle "blessed" has no ear for the
contemporary tongue as spoken. And why "no mere man" for
the perfectly apt, familiar, and understandable "flesh and blood",
which is apparently what the original Greek says? Besides being
halting and limping, "no mere man" will in any case arouse the ire
of the radical feminists anyway, and there will be agitation to
change it *again!* "Heavenly Father", again, departs from the Greek
"Father in heaven" for no discernible reason. Coming to "I for my
part declare", we encounter some highly artificial, even ludicrous
diction as far as contemporary English usage is concerned; it is a
much inferior rendering to the simple "and I say to you" of some
other translations and, apparently, of the original Greek text.

When we reach the rendering "you are 'Rock', and on this
rock", however, the whole artificial construct that has been erected
up to this point simply collapses into absurdity. This translation is
utterly clumsy and obtuse. The simple fact that there happens to
be a play on words in the Greek between *"Petros"* and *"petra"* —
which everybody already knows about anyway — does *not* provide
a justification for eliminating the actual name that Jesus did,
after all, give to Peter, by which the latter has been universally
known for the entire two millennia since. Pedagogically as well as
logically, it is much easier to explain that the now very common
name "Peter" originally came from the Greek word for "rock"
than it is to try to explain that the "rock" in this passage actually

refers to the head apostle, whom everybody already understands to be named Peter.

Yes, it is true—and again probably already realized by everybody—that the Greek play on words just does not come out in English, as it does, for example, in Latin (*"Tu es Petrus et super hanc petram"*) or in the Romance languages (*"Tu es Pierre et sur cette pierre"; "Tu sei Pietro,"* etc.). The play on words does not come out in German, either, any more than it does in English (*"Du bist Petrus und auf diesen Felsen"*); but a play on words such as this does not have to be rendered in order for a translation of it to be adequate, especially when its meaning is so well established in everybody's consciousness anyway. It is a pretty safe bet that nobody has ever been confused by "you are Peter and upon this rock"; it is, however, absurd to say in English, "you are 'Rock', and on this rock". A simple note, as in the Revised Standard Version, could have made the distinction. But the heavy pedantry of insisting on "rock" simply fails to respect the medium of modern English.

The same thing is true of the translation "the jaws of death". What does it mean? There is no such expression native to English. Is it required by the Greek text? Apparently not, as the Jerusalem Bible translation into French makes clear by retaining "Hades" with a note that it refers to the Hebrew *Sheol*. Why have it then? It seems to be the sort of "embellishment", in Belloc's sense, that never should be resorted to by translators. Perhaps it was coined in an attempt to come up with something that just sounded better to the modern ear than "the gates of hell", since nobody wants to talk about hell today; if that was the motive, it failed because the result is not a recognizable expression in English; the RSV's "powers of death" is somewhat better, though it is not good, considering what the original says.

A mistranslation such as this underlines the error of trying to improve upon Scripture with expressions and concepts supposedly more congenial to the modern mind than what is contained in the original. The fact is that Jesus himself had no problems with the expression "the gates of hell"; it is the expression that he *used!* The idea that a concept such as this might have been something merely cultural pertaining to the time of Jesus perhaps, but not to our more enlightened times, which now has to be rendered by an unidiomatic expression such as "the jaws of death"—this represents a fatal error for modern translators to fall into. If even the so-called cultural background of the time and place in which Jesus lived is not faithfully reflected in a translation, then it also fails as a translation. God chose a particular time and place in which to reveal Himself to us, including the fullness of His revelation in Christ Jesus, God's Son. To presume to change any of this for modern consumption not only exhibits unconscionable arrogance; it also fails strictly as translation since it fails to respect both its source and its medium; it misrepresents Jesus and those words of his destined never to pass away (cf. Mt 24:35). As we saw was the case with Dante earlier, we not only get a false translation; we also get a false Jesus, an ersatz Jesus.

Similarly, we find here again, as we also found earlier, that scholarship and expertise, by themselves, cannot produce an accurate and successful translation if they are unwilling to listen to Christ's plain words and then turn them into plain English. Finally, the ultimate judges of whether and when our Scripture scholars have really produced a successful translation have to be, as we also established earlier, the ordinary Catholic faithful in the pews currently obliged to wince and cringe at such artificial English as "you are 'Rock'" and "jaws of death". (We should probably be thankful we do not have to listen to Jesus saying, "on this rock I will build my *community*".)

VI

Is it fair to judge a translation such as the New American Bible on the basis of a single example? First of all, fairness is not really the principal question here. No doubt the NAB is far from uniformly bad; it has been the "official" translation for some time now; most of us are more or less inured to it anyway. Nor can anybody really argue that we are not really being generally given the word of God in the Church today, more or less; most certainly, we are.

But where the word of God is concerned, "generally" and "more or less" are not good enough. There simply should not be, anywhere in any translation approved for Church use, anything like the mistranslation that we have found in Matthew 16:18. The occurrence of a passage like this has to be viewed as *symptomatic:* translators capable of producing even one mistranslation such as this *cannot be trusted* to go on producing official versions of Scripture for Church use without some careful oversight! When expressions such as "you are 'Rock'" and "the jaws of death" turn up, they constitute the *evidence* that the whole text has to be gone over with a fine-toothed comb and examined according to the criteria of fidelity both to the source and to the medium of modern English. The scholarship and expertise of those capable of producing such texts *cannot* simply be taken for granted and at face value.

This does not mean, in everyday practical terms, that the entire NAB translation now has to be thrown out just because an error or ineptitude has been discovered somewhere in the text. What it means is that such errors and ineptitudes, when discovered, should be corrected by proper Church authority, rather than just left to stand because that is what the scholars and experts happen to have come up with in an otherwise acceptable text. Furthermore, correcting a text in Scripture that is jarring to practically everybody is a very different thing from arbitrarily changing time-honored renditions that have been internalized by the faithful to the point where they are practically considered basic elements of the Faith. It was a mistake to change "the gates of hell" to "the jaws of death"; it would *not* be a mistake to change it back, though, even if that happened to be the only change made in the current "approved" NAB translation.

In any case, there are other examples of mistranslations that could be cited, both in the NAB and in some of the other modern versions of the Bible competing for our attention and use. No doubt there is no translation that will ever be perfect, but at least we ought to be working at achieving the best that is possible. Anyone minded to apply the kind of test we have applied here to other passages might well begin by comparing some of the modern translations of the Our Father, the Lord's Prayer, which is found in Matthew 6:9–13. The translations that come most immediately to mind in this regard are those in which what we all learned as "hallowed"—a word from the same root as "holy" and meaning to "make holy", to "sanctify"—is suddenly, inexplicably rendered as "honored", a much more secular notion. The NAB, as it happens, does retain "hallowed", but some other approved versions with genuine episcopal *imprimaturs* (Good News for Modern Man, American Bible Society) have now moved on to "honored", no doubt as part of the general secularizing trend of our times. Yet the original Greek word is derived from the same root as *"hagios"*, "sacred", from which we get, for example, "hagiography". Since the scholars who produce such mistranslations *cannot* be ignorant of the meaning of *hagios,* it would seem to follow that they are producing their translations in accordance with some other criteria than those proper for translators. Since such novelties are almost invariably in the direction of greater secularization, the hypothesis does suggest itself that they might just have some other motives than setting forth the Faith of Jesus as contained in the Gospels. And so the question arises: How do such secularized versions come to be approved and given *imprimaturs* by the shepherds commissioned to preserve the Faith of Jesus Christ, not some modern ersatz secular gospel?

It is perhaps of some significance that the Catholic bishops of the United States have regularly voted down over the years proposals to adopt new versions of the Our Father, the prayer taught by Jesus Himself to his disciples when they asked Him to teach them to pray. Thankfully the bishops as a body have understood that such fundamental elements of the religious Faith of the Catholic people as the Our Father cannot be trifled with or casually changed. This realization has not, however, prevented the bishops from approving complete translations of the New Testament containing variant versions of the Our Father; the one in the NAB, for example, includes the inept and un-English "subject us not to the trial" (the English Jerusalem Bible's "do not put us to the test" is at least idiomatic English). Nevertheless, in the matter of declining to rush into new versions of the Our Father as such, the bishops have demonstrated their understanding of the principle that the essence of the sacred is something that, precisely, is not to be touched (as is also implied in the popular expression "nothing is sacred any more", that is, it *is* now being touched or changed).

Similarly, at their general meeting in November 1991, many of the bishops reacted strongly and spontaneously to a proposed new translation for the Lectionary for Masses with Children of passages contained in Luke 2:7, 12 that read: "They dressed him in baby clothes and laid him in a feed box"; "You will find him dressed in baby clothes and lying in a feed box."

The comical absurdity of such translations as these immediately leaps to the eye, as it did to many of the bishops at their meeting when they first encountered them. Among other things it would seem to reflect the ignorance of the translators, who have evidently never been on a farm and hence are indeed ignorant of the fact that the word "manger" is the English word currently in use on American farms to denote the trough from which animals eat. A totally idiomatic English sentence that might be articulated on an American farm today, for example, could be the following: "Get some meal from the feed box and put it in the manger for the cows to eat." "Feed box" and "manger" are different words, both legitimately used for what they designate.

But such translations betray more than mere ignorance of current English usage on American farms; they indicate tone deafness to basic symbols of the Faith. Many of the bishops picked right up on this immediately in this particular instance. In doing so they were reacting exactly the way some of the faithful have unfortunately been obliged to react to some of the other "approved" translations containing sacred and symbolic elements of the Faith. The trouble is, some of these mistranslations *have* come into approved use. Only the real howlers, such as "feed box" for "manger", seem to have attracted significant episcopal notice. Too many other mistranslations, such as the NAB's Matthew 16:16–18 examined in this paper, continue in use. Nor does it appear that the responsible bishops feel obliged to look behind the howlers such as "feed box" or "jaws of death" and inquire more carefully into the work of those who have proved themselves capable of such howlers and boners. The time should have long passed when we can just automatically rely on the scholarship of the scholars or the expertise of the experts; too many attempts are being made today to implement other agendas than just aiming at translating what is contained in the original.

Translation is a serious business *because* it is a necessary evil; we cannot do without it; therefore we have to try harder to see that we get it right. This is especially true of religious translation, where the integrity of the Faith is sometimes at stake. We must therefore wish and pray for a greater sense of responsibility on the part of those learned in the sacred languages on whom we must depend to render God's word in our own tongue. We must pray and hope that they will always have the faith and courage to translate what is actually there before them in the sacred text into plain English without embellishments or attempts to improve upon it for modern consumption. We must wish and pray and hope that the bishops will encourage and approve precisely that kind of translating—and that all of us will understand and encourage translations that respond to criteria of faith, not to any other criteria, learned or otherwise, except, of course, the fundamental criterion of any and every authentic translation, namely, fidelity both to the source (the sacred text) and to the medium (the living English language).

II

LINGUISTICS: USE OF GENERIC "MAN"

GENERIC MAN REVISITED

Ralph Wright, O.S.B.

About five years ago I wrote an article in which I suggested that both men and women would be the losers if generic man was eliminated from the vocabulary of the English language. I stated that I was firmly in favor of the movement to remove language that was sexually discriminating wherever possible. I was all in favor of saying men *and* women, brothers *and* sisters, sons *and* daughters, wherever and whenever this was appropriate. But I felt that there remained contexts in which it was important to maintain the original generic sense of the word "man" and its plural "men": a human being, male or female, member of the human race. Today, January 1989, I hold this even more strongly, and, since the move to abolish the generic sense seems, at least in Catholic circles, just as strong, I am once again taking up my pen to make a few further observations. As a poet with a tendency to drift somewhat whimsically, I need to have some goading thought provoking me to the vulnerable, tiresome, and hazardous business of articulation. The current goad is: "You cannot get rid of man without at the same time getting rid of God." Clearly this raises the stakes. You cannot throw out the generic man bathwater without at the same time discarding God. Maybe the following paper will throw a little light on this somewhat stark assertion.

Although sometimes we may pretend otherwise, when we are born and learn to speak, we "inherit" a language. We do not inherit it as the potter inherits the clay—a highly malleable substance that can be formed in a myriad ways. A language is more like a genetic code. At the moment of conception we are landed with our physical and even mental makeup, and it has taken all the human beings down to our mother and father to produce the precise code that we are. Environment is going to have significant influence on how we turn out, but if the genetic code has not provided the potential, no mere environment will be able to substitute for it. The case with language is analogous. We may hope that our language rests freely in the hands of our literary experts, our grammarians, or even our liturgists so that they are free to do with it what they will or what society bids them; in fact, this freedom is severely limited. Those hands are tied. They are tied by all the literature and all the oral tradition that comprise the genetic inheritance of a language, stretching from the distant past right up to the very moment when we ourselves learned how to speak. And, because our language is living, it is constantly evolving and adapting and growing. New ideas, new discoveries, new inventions—all needing to be named. But there is an important distinction to be made between the creation of new words like "byte" and "biochemistry" and the manipulation of words already in the language, which may already have a history of usage stretching back five hundred years or more. The way such words grow and develop is much more mysterious, and only in a very limited sense can this growth be controlled by the editor or the grammarian. When the language is English, spoken as it is by so many different peoples on the planet, this process is even more complex.

The limited question that we are asking at this moment is: Can the word "man" and its plural "men" be legitimately used today in the generic sense of "human being"? The answer given by those who are in the business of renewing the liturgy in the Catholic Church is a definitive "no". I have been informed by someone who is in the midst of the process that generic man will no more return to common usage than will the words "negro" and "colored". I am told that the National Association of Teachers of English has issued guidelines for the removal of generic man from the language adopted by all textbook publishers. I have heard that the new Lutheran, Episcopal, Christian (Dutch) Reformed, Methodist, and Presbyterian hymnals have already eliminated the word or are currently working on it. Our own Worship III has done so. The revised New Testament of the New American Bible and the New Jerusalem Bible has removed it, whether piecemeal or wholesale. ICEL, for the new Sacramentary, is planning to. Am I closing the stable door after the stallion/mare has left? Quite possibly, but I believe this remains to be seen.

A Feminist Dictionary [AFD], by Kramarae and Treichler (Pandora Press, 1985), begins the entry *"man as false generic"* with the following sentences:

> Convention in English of using the word "man" to refer "generically" to people both men and women. Though custom and convention are used to defend this and related usages, sound arguments based on research demonstrate that the claims of generic meaning are false: these words do not include everyone equally (p. 247).

A little later in the same article we learn:

> The word man has been making confusion in many respects for more than a thousand years. It was certainly used in the Anglo-Saxon language as early as 825 A.D. to mean specifically the human creature in general; but about the same time it was also used to mean an adult male person; while contemporaneously the word "woman" was in use as meaning an adult female human being. And persons who have occasion to study Anglo-Saxon laws and literature, if they care anything at all about exactness, have to be constantly on guard as to whether man means a human creature in general or an adult male (p. 247).

Still later:

> In Old English the word "man" meant "person" or "human being" and when used of an individual was equally applicable to either sex. It was parallel to the Latin "homo" "a member of the human species"—not "vir" "an adult male of the species".... The combined forms "waepman" and "wifman" meant respectively "adult male person" and "adult female person". In the course of time wifman evolved into the modern word "woman" and "wif" narrowed in meaning to become "wife" as we use that word today.... "Man" eventually ceased to be used of individ-

ual women and replaced "wer" and "waep man" as a specific term distinguishing an adult male from an adult female. But "man" continued to be used in generalizations about both sexes. As long as most generalizations about people were made by men about men, the ambiguity nestling in this dual usage was either not noticed or thought not to matter (Casey Miller and Kate Swift, 1980, pp. 9–10, quoted by AFD, p. 248).

What I find particularly enlightening about these quotations is that they reveal how far back in the history of the language the roots of generic man go — right to the very beginning. The observation is true that because the language has been landed with one word carrying two distinct meanings — the generic and the male-as-opposed-to-female meanings — this has led to considerable confusion through the centuries, particularly in legal documents. No mention is made, however, of the fact that in literature, which one might dare to call the primary normative region of a language, the context normally clarifies the particular sense intended. In any case, it might well be asked whether the long usage of both these senses of the word in a thousand years of literature does not in itself question the legitimacy of labeling such an inheritance a "false" generic. There is something a little disquieting about a dictionary that is so eloquent about the shortcomings of male grammarians claiming that a usage that has been normative in all the literature of the language from before Chaucer to beyond Nemerov is simply "false".

If the feminist dictionary alerts us to the secular scene, Mary Collins, in her book *Worship—Renewal to Practice* (Washington, D.C. 20011: Pastoral Press, 1987), gives a glimpse of what is going on in the Church and the world:

Presently trade and textbook publishers, journalists, television commentators, and feminist grammarians, are acting as pace-setters for the development of the language. At these levels, the false generic has generally been discredited; lapses into such usage are perceived and treated as lapses. Various approaches to alternatives to grammatical and lexical androcentrism are being tried. If none of them are [sic] yet wholly congenial to the ear, nevertheless, large numbers of English speakers and writers have committed themselves to exploring and expanding the limits of the English language. In this regard, English is at a new stage of its continuing development. It is in this context that episcopal conferences vested with responsibility for authorizing suitable language for public prayer must reflect on the implications of this socio-cultural development for the continuing cultural adaptation of the liturgy. As with so many other matters, not to decide is to decide. The English of the liturgy will be inclusive, or it will be exclusive, androcentric, and sexist (p. 203).

Once again it is disconcerting to note that the "pace-setters" in our language development no longer include the novelists, dramatists, poets, short-story writers, biographers—those, in fact, who have been the protagonists in the development of language from its earliest beginnings; their place seems to have been taken by "publishers, journalists, television commentators, and grammarians". What is even more alarming is the fact that the translators of Scripture are now denied the usage of generic man in the name of this new development. This at times seems to be in sharp contrast to the direction in which such translators and editors would themselves wish to go. For example, the New Jerusalem Bible includes this sentence in its current Foreword:

> Key terms in the originals, especially those theological key concepts on which there is a major theological note, have been rendered throughout (with very few exceptions) by the same English word, instead of by the variety of words used in the first edition (p. v).

Sensitivity to the new dogma that generic man is no longer acceptable means that, as we shall see in a moment, this principle cannot hold good for the translation of *"anthropos"* and *"aner"*— terms that one might be tempted to call "key", since the Scriptures exist for *"anthropos"*, not *"anthropos"* for the Scriptures. It is particularly important here to claim that, in spite of what the feminist dictionaries say, there remains a valid generic sense for the word man and its plural men—a sense that we have not created but inherited. It has been preserved in our literature from the infancy of our language, and it is irreplacable, particularly in contexts where man is being compared or contrasted or merely juxtaposed to other entities—God, angels, devils, or even personifications of the river, the mountain, the sea, the earth. (In an appendix to this essay I have listed instances of both singular and plural usages of man in its generic and nongeneric senses. With minimal research it has been possible to show these words in common currency from the ninth century to December 1988, or, if you like, from Beowulf to Updike.) In such contexts the use of philosophical paraphrases or abstract nouns cannot render the meaning or the power of the original and therefore cannot be faithful renderings. This is part of what I mean by saying that if man is discarded, God has to go, too.

To examine this matter more carefully, it is important to get specific. I will refer to the Greek New Testament. (I have no knowledge of Hebrew but am conversant with Greek.) The Greek language has two key words for man: *"anthropos"*—the generic sense: a human being; and *"aner"*—the male of the human species. The fact that the translation of this word is no marginal matter is indicated by the following list of the frequency of the two terms in the four Gospels:

Matthew:	8 *"aner"*;	109 *"anthropos"*
Mark:	4 *"aner"*;	50 *"anthropos"*
Luke:	31 *"aner"*;	92 *"anthropos"*
John:	7 *"aner"*;	57 *"anthropos"*

From this it may immediately be seen that the word with the generic sense is used by the evangelists many more times than the word that means "male" as opposed to "female". Clearly the translator is faced with enormous problems if the English equivalent to this word is considered no longer valid. The first and perhaps most crucial is how to translate the title of Jesus as *"ho huios tou anthropou"* or "Son of Man". Here NJB decides to keep the traditional translation, thereby suggesting that there does still exist at least one context where the generic term man may be used. (The Inclusive Language Lectionary translates this title as "the human one".) But having made this decision, he seems to have decided to turn a blind eye to the consistency principle quoted above and to attempt a variety of ways of coping with *"anthropos"*. See the diagram on pp. 102–3 for examples. The revised version of the New American Bible New Testament is also given to show what presumably is about to become the official version for our own American Lectionary. As can be seen from the examples, the one Greek word *"anthropos"* has been translated variously in the above contexts as "people", "man", "someone", "human agency", "human", "human resources", "human beings", "humanity", "person", and "others". This is in itself disquieting, because it reveals an added distance of interpretation that has been inserted between the translator and the reader. Add to this the fact that much of the linguistic power of the original has been lost in the various kinds of paraphrase that have been required. None of this would be necessary if it could be shown that generic man is still a valid word in our language.

In the Grail inclusive language version of the Psalms, a further kind of inaccuracy is adopted as a substitute for the "false generic". This involves the decision to pluralize (turn into the plural) various singular originals or to change the person from third person to second person—this latter approach being adopted to avoid having to use the masculine pronoun "Him" to refer to "the Lord". We are not here concerned with the whole pronominal dimension of the inclusive language scene, so we will not linger on this. Suffice to say that "happy indeed is the man who follows not the counsel of the wicked" (Ps 1:1)[1] can hardly be translated "happy indeed are those who follow . . . " without obvious infidelity to the original. As teachers of Greek or Latin will confirm, this kind of change from a singular to a plural would be pointed out to a high school student as an elementary slip in translation. At college it would be regarded as deplorable. It can scarcely be claimed that the authors of this new version were showing the concern expressed in section 22 of the Vatican Council's decree on revelation that the Church "with maternal concern see to it that suitable and correct translations are made into different languages especially from the original texts of the sacred books".

[1] Cf. Ps 15:2; 16:15; 17:7; 21:25; 24:23; 34:33; 35:36; 37:36; 48:17.

Text	Greek	Revised New American Bible [RNAB]	Jerusalem Bible	New Jerusalem Bible [NJB]
Mt 4:19	anthropos	fishers of men	fishers of men	fishers of people
Mt 5:16	anthropos	your light must shine before others	in the sight of men	in people's sight
Mt 10:32	anthropos	before others	in the presence of men	in the presence of human beings
Mt 13:25	anthropos	man	to a man who sowed good seed	to a man who sowed good seed
Mt 13:44	anthropos	a person finds	a man has found	someone has found
Mt 19:12	anthropos	by others	eunuchs made so by men	eunuchs made so by human agency
Mt 21:25	anthropos	of human origin	John's baptism: Was it of God or of men	John's baptism: What was its origin, heavenly or human?

Lk 18:27	*anthropos*	for *human beings*	not possible for *men* are possible for God	are impossible by *human resources* are possible for God
Mk 8:27	*anthropos*	not as God does but as *human beings* do	the way you think is not God's way but *man's*	you are thinking not as God thinks but as *human beings* do
Mk 10:9	*anthropos*	no *human being* must separate	what God has united *man* must not divide	what God has united *human beings* must not divide
Jn 3:19	*anthropos*	*people* preferred darkness to light	*men* have shown they prefer darkness to light	*people* have preferred darkness to the light

To take one instance from the letters of Paul:

Eph 4:8	*anthropos*	gave gifts to *men*	He went up to the heights, took captives; he gave gifts to *men*	He went up to the heights, took captives; he gave gifts to *humanity*.

Another concern is poetry. Anyone with an ear for poetry will be familiar with the way in which sound and sense blend in a poem. The whole poem is built of a union between sound, sense, connotation, and rhythm in such a way that, as Judy Stix eloquently expressed it, the form and content are inextricably united. It is in this poetic area of psalmody, hymnody, and every text for worship where the expression comes closest to poetry that the question of generic man once again becomes crucial. Terms that we have just been looking at in the New Jerusalem Bible version of the Gospels—"human beings", "human resources", "humanity", and even "person" are closer to philosophy, sociology, or even speculative theology than they are to poetry, and yet the memorable classic versions of Scripture seemed so close to poetry. In a recent article for the Jesuit periodical *America*, William O'Malley wrote:

> Since the advent of English in the liturgy much of the mystique and most of the poetry have been vacuumed out of the Mass. Thirty years ago, even atheists could find themselves unwittingly drawn into the mystery through the cadence of the Latin or even the lusty convinced belting of "Holy God, We Praise Thy Name". To them it could be as fascinating as an oriental rite still is to us. Now we have a Mass with such outlandish phrases as "our spiritual drink" and such tame literalism as "This is the Lamb of God" instead of the far stronger "Behold! The Lamb of God". I'm by no means advocating a return to Latin, but let us have a Mass written by a poet rather than one that sounds written by a canon lawyer or a speculative theologian ("Mass and Teenagers", *America* [Oct. 8, 1988]: p. 217).

I would submit that the abolition of generic man is moving us one further step in the direction that the writer of the above article deplores.

But is this in fact where the rest of the poetic world is moving? Are the current secular writers—the poets and playwrights and novelists and critics of our day—avoiding generic man in their poems and in their prose? And what about the translators? Are they avoiding generic man when they put French or Polish or Hebrew or Greek into English? I do not think so. Let me take three examples.

The first two are from *The Book of Job,* the work of a contemporary poet and translator whose poem on St. Jerome may have caught your eye in a recent *New Yorker* (December 19, 1988). He has just come out with a version of the Tao Te Ching, which Huston Smith, author of "The Religions of Man" (that wretched word again!) appreciates in the following words:

> Stephen Mitchell's rendition of the Tao Te Ching comes as close to being definitive for our time as any I can imagine. It embodies the virtues its translator credits to the Chinese original: a gemlike lucidity that is radiant with humor, grace, largeheartedness and deep wisdom.

The following passage will show that this translator is far from being insensitive to the questions of sexual discrimination in language:

> The reader will notice that in the many passages where Lao-tzu describes the Master, I have used the pronoun "she" at least as often as "he". The Chinese language doesn't make this kind of distinction; in English we have to choose (Tao Te Ching, p. ix).

At the same time he shows himself quite at ease with generic man:

> Men are born soft and supple;
> dead, they are stiff and hard.
> Plants are born tender and pliant;
> dead they are brittle and dry (no. 76).

> When man interferes with the Tao,
> the sky becomes filthy,
> the earth becomes depleted,
> the equilibrium crumbles,
> creatures become extinct (no. 39).

> The Tao is great.
> The universe is great.
> Earth is great.
> Man is great.
> These are the four great powers (no. 25).

Stephen Mitchell has produced a version that is memorable. Would this have been possible if his publishers had forbidden him the use of generic man?

This point is underlined when we glance at an earlier work of his originally published in 1979 by Doubleday and republished in a revised version by North Point Press, San Francisco, in 1987. This version, too, has received high praise. The reviewer in the *Beloit Poetry Journal* says of it: "Here at last is the text for those who wish to read and teach one of the greatest of all poems—now a great English poem. Stephen Mitchell has put us all in his debt." When it comes to the use of generic man—allowed to Mr. Mitchell, almost forbidden to the New Jerusalem Bible—there is no better way to illustrate the result than to print three passages from Job side by side: 7:17; 14:1; and 14:10.

New Jerusalem Bible	Mitchell

Job 7:17

What are *human beings* that you should take them so seriously, subjecting them to your scrutiny, that morning after morning you should examine them and at every instant test them? Will you never take your eyes off me long enough for me to swallow my spittle? Suppose I have sinned, what have I done to you, you tireless watcher of *humanity*?	What is *man,* that you notice him, turn your glare upon him, examine him every morning, test him at every instant? Won't you even give me time to swallow my spit? If I sinned, what have I done to you, Watcher of *Men.*

Job 14:1

A *human being,* born of woman, whose life is short but full of trouble. Like a flower such a one blossoms	*Man* who is born of woman— how few and harsh are his days! Like a flower he blooms and

and withers. fleeting as a
shadow, transient.

withers; like a shadow he fades
in the dark.

Job 14:10

But a *human being?* He dies,
and dead he remains, breathes
his last, and then where is he.
The waters of the sea will vanish
the rivers stop flowing and run
dry: a *human being,* once laid to
   rest will never rise again,
the heavens will wear out before he
   wakes up, or before he is roused
   from his sleep.

But *man* is cut down forever;
he dies and where is he then?
The lake is drained of its water,
The river becomes a ditch
and *man* will not rise again
while the sky is above the earth.

The question that needs seriously to be asked is this: What price will be paid in poetry for the proscription of generic man? Down through the ages some of the greatest poems, hymns, carols, and meditations depend for their power on generic man as they sing of the Incarnation. The melody, the refrain, of God becoming man cannot be played if the generic chords are removed from the instrument. The terms "human beings" and "humanity" or even the bloodless "someone" or RNAB's "others" unfortunately just will not do. Our own Catholic generations are about to be deprived of the resonances of a thousand years of reflection, poetry, and meditation even while our secular culture is claiming, as illustrated above, that the generic sense is still very much alive and kicking.

(While preparing notes for this article I picked up the November 28, 1988, issue of the *New Yorker* and found a poem by John Updike that contains a generic man [see Appendix]. I also picked up *Poetry Magazine* for December 1988 from the shelves of our county library and found three instances without much search. Are all these "lapses", to use Mary Collins's term?)

Finally, there is the work of the Polish poet Czeslaw Milosz, who received the Nobel Prize for Literature a few years ago. A recent translation of his poetry by Robert Hass, with Milosz himself cooperating, was reviewed in the *New Yorker* by Helen Vendler (October 24, 1988). She calls it an "enthralling and commanding" book. One quote will suffice to give the reader a taste of this powerful writer:

> Tomorrow at the latest I'll start working on a great book
> In which my century will appear as it really was.
>
> No it won't happen tomorrow. In five or ten years.
> I still think too much about the mothers
> And ask what is man born of woman.
> He curls himself up and protects his head
> While he is kicked by heavy boots; on fire and running,
> He burns with bright flame; a bulldozer sweeps him into a
>   clay pit.
> Her child. Embracing a teddy bear. Conceived in ecstasy.
>
> I haven't learnt to speak as I should, calmly.

About generic man, neither have I.

SOME CONCLUSIONS

From its very infancy in the eighth century to the present,[2] there have existed in the English language, side by side, two different senses for the word "man" and its plural "men", one generic meaning "human being", the other specifying sex, "male human being". Both these senses remain valid. If these facts are clearly

---

[2] It was interesting to note that in his inaugural address, which was distinguished for its conciliatory tone, George Bush used generic man on at least two occasions. The first read as follows: "For a new breeze is blowing, and a world refreshed by freedom seems reborn, for in man's heart, if not in fact, the day of the dictator is over." The speech was composed by Peggy Noonan, the writer who was responsible for his acceptance speech at the Republican convention. If this word usage was considered offensive to the great majority of women, she would have found other ways of saying what she believed needed to be said. The fact that she did not, that Bush liked it as it was, and that the country as a whole seems to have reacted positively to the speech all support the conclusions of this paper.

taught, then the word will no longer be seen as discriminatory. It will no longer be considered an instance of that unfortunate androcentric shortcoming of our language where "sons" has been used to mean "male *and* female human offspring" (the complex questions that these language limitations have provoked are not our focus here). With this clarification and a new sensitivity to the kind of contexts in which generic usage is appropriate, our Christian Churches may once again feel free to use them, with the results that:

1. The term "man" and its plural "men" will once more normally be used to translate the Greek *"anthropos"* in Scripture.

2. The key scriptural title of Jesus, *"ho huios tou anthropou",* the Son of Man, will no longer be destined to become an archaism: it will no longer be thought of as "soiled" by the "false generic".

Finally, as a poet, I cannot refrain from restating what I said at the beginning of this paper. We cannot discard the generic term "man" without at the same time discarding the term "God". In the mystery and poetry of the Incarnation—the constant meditation on the God/Man oxymoron—translations of *"anthropos"* as "human being", "humanity", "someone", "others", "person" just will not cut the ice. If you discard "man", "God" goes, too.

APPENDIX

Quotations to illustrate the fact that the word "man" and its plural "men" have been used from the earliest days of the English language in two distinct senses:

1. the generic sense = human being (Latin: *homo*)

2. the sense specifying sex = male human being (Latin: *vir*)

and to show that both these senses continue to be valid today.

Man-Homo (generic man)	Men-Homines (generic man plural)	Man-Vir (male human being)	Men-Viri (male human beings)
750 BEOWULF swa hy naefre man lyhth se the secgan wile soth aefterrihte (Klaeber, *Beowulf*, N.Y.: Heath, l. 1048) of such openhandedness no honest man could ever speak in disparagement (Alexander)	**750** BEOWULF medoaern micel *men* gewyrcean (l. 69) a house greater than *men* on earth ever had heard of feasceaftum men a former race of *men* (l. 2285)	**750** BEOWULF Gang da aefter flore fyrdwyrde *man* mid his handscale. The man excellent in warfare walked across the hall. (Tr. Alexander, Penguin Classics, l. 1316)	**750** BEOWULF Thonne healgamen/ Hrothgares scop aefter medobence *maenan* scolde, (be) Finnes eaferum. when Hrothgar's bard was bidden to sing a hall-song for men on the mead-benches. (Klaeber)
850 ALFRED'S BEDE he nales from monnum ne thurh *mon* gelaered waes, ond thurh Godes gife. . . . ALFRED'S BOETHIUS Caedmon's gift of song was not from or through men learnt but was a gift from God (Bolton, *An Old English Anthology*, Northwestern, p. 1)	**850** ALFRED'S BEDE tha Godes gife in thaem *men* (Bolton, p. 3, l. 57) ALFRED'S BOETHIUS yfelwillende *men*; (*Sweet's Anglo-Saxon Reader*, Onion's ed. Oxford, 1962, p. 9, l. 16)	**850** ALFRED'S BEDE tha stod him sum *mon* (Bolton)	**850** ALFRED'S BEDE Tha gelaeredestan *men* (ambiguous) (Bolton, p. 3, l. 4) DREAM OF THE ROOD aelmihtig God for ealle *menn* geweordode ofer eall wifa cynn (Bolton, p. 99, l. 94)

950 LINDISFARNE GOSPELS, NORTHUMBERLAND GLOSS	990 DEATH OF GUTHLAC	990 AELFRIC	1023 WULFSTAN	1150 O.E.H.	1150 A MORAL ODE	1150 OLD ENGLISH HOMILIES	1150 OLD ENGLISH HOMILIES
Apud homines is translated: mid *monnum*	nanegum *men* ne alyfad to secganne; quae non licet homini narrare; which no man is allowed to relate (Bolton, p. 65, l. 34)	Sum *man* feoll on ise. (Bolton, ibid., p. 63)	Leofan *men*, dear men (Sermo Lupi ad Anglos, l. 1; Bolton, p. 125)	and gef hem bred of hevene and *men* eten englene (bred) (Morris and Skeat, p. 33 l. 103)	Mani *man* seid hwo reche pine the sal habben ende (Oxford, Morris and Skeat, *Specimens of Early English*, l. 135)	riche *men* habbeth . . . feire wifes (Morris and Skeat, p. 18, l. 37, 39)	elhc cristene *man* maketh this dai procession fro chirche to chirche (Morris and Skeat, p. 28, l. 40) and make godes weie in to *mannes* heorte (p. 29, l. 69)

Man-Homo (generic man)	Men-Homines (generic man plural)	Man-Vir (male human being)	Men-Viri (male human beings)
	1250 GENESIS AND EXODUS: And alle *men*, the it heren wilen, God leve hem in his blisse spilen Among engeles & seli *men*, Withuten ende in reste ben (Morris and Skeat, p. 170)	**1250** GENESIS AND EXODUS: Ne was non so wis *man* in all his lond (Morris and Skeat, l. 135) — Hu sulde oni *man* poure forgeten, swilke and so manige suns bigeten? (Morris and Skeat, p. 158, l. 2179)	**1250** GENESIS AND EXODUS: Fro galaad *men* with chafare *men* with merchandise (Morris and Skeat, p. 154, l. 1951)
			1250 ROBERT OF GLOUCESTER: For hi held the old usages that *men* with *men* were/By hem selves, and women by hem selves also there — *Specimens of Early English Poets*, London: George Ellis, 1845, p. 80
1350 PLAY OF NOAH: Bot yit the fals feynd Made Hym with *man* wroth (Sisam, p. 186, l. 36)	**1350** MANDEVILLE'S TRAVELS: and thei eten *men* whan thei take hem (Sisam, p. 103, l. 242)	**1350** PIERS PLOWMAN: for an hydel *man* thow semest (Sisam, *14th-Century Verse and Prose*, Oxford, p. 27)	**1350** PIERS PLOWMAN: ther Ryghtfulnesse rewardeth ryght as *men* deserveth (Sisam, p. 90, l. 32)
1350 MANDEVILLE'S TRAVELS: half *man* and half hors (Sisam, p. 103, l. 241)			
1380 JOHN WICLIF: But what *man*, on Goddis half, shulde reverse Goddis ordenaunse and his wille? (Sisam, p. 117, *De Officio Pastorali*, chap. xv)	**1380** JOHN WICLIF: And herfore freris han tauzt in Englsnd the Paternoster in Englizsch tunge, as *men* seyen in the pley of zork, and in othere	**1380** JOHN WICLIF: Also Peter saith in Dedis of Apostolis to a pore *man* that to him neither was gold ne silver; (Sisam, p. 128, l. 285)	**1380** JOHN WICLIF: And sith *men* ben holden heretikis that done azenst the popis lawe, (Sisam, p. 120, l. 45)

1422
JOHN LYDGATE

To give his men in knighthood exercise, Everyche to put other at assay in justes, listes and also in tourney (*Specimens of Early English Poets*, London: George Ellis, 1845)

1450
CAROLS

Crist charged alle His apostlis . . . to goo and preche the Gospel to alle *men* (Sisam, p. 120, l. 15)

1450
CAROL

It was dark, it was dim For *men* that lived in great sin, Lucifer was us all within Till on the Christmas day. (*AECC*, p. 164)

1450
CAROLS

for every *man* to hell gan go (*AECC*, p. 165)

the Son of God is become (*AECC*, p 159)

1536
CHRISTMAS CAROLS

He was born of a virgin pure, Not knowing a *man*, as I you assure. (*Ancient English Christmas Carols 1400–1700*, London: Rickert, 1910, p. 185)

1536
CAROLS

Jesus Christ, both God and *man* (*AECC*, p. 189, l. 2)

1537
HEYWOOD

I mean a sallet with which *men* do fyght (*Thersytes*, p. 128, l. 45, from Pollard, *English Miracle Plays*, Oxford, 1890)

1580
ALEXANDER HUME

The callour wine in cave is sought, *Mens* brothing breists to cule (ambiguous) *New Oxford Book of Christian Verse*, p. 44

1588

And showeth favour unto *men* (*AECC*, p. 198)

Man-*Homo* (generic man)	Men-*Homines* (generic man plural)	Man-*Vir* (male human being)	Men-*Viri* (male human beings)
1600 SHAKESPEARE All the world's a stage, / And all the men and women merely players; / They have their exits and their entrances, / And one *man* in his time plays many parts (*As You Like It*, 2.7.137)			**1600** SHAKESPEARE All the world's a stage / And all the *men* and women merely players (*As You Like It*, 2.7.137)
		1622 GEORGE WITHER And no *man* minds his labour (NOBCV, p. 185)	**1622** GEORGE WITHER Now every lad is wondrous trim, / And no man minds his labour; / Our lasses have provided them / A bag-pipe and a tabor / Young *men* and maids.... (NOBVC)
1630 JOHN DONNE Let *man's* Soule be a Sphere (Grierson Metaphysical Poets, p. 89)			
	1650 JOHN DONNE And soonest our best *men* with thee doe goe (Grierson Metaphysical Poets, Oxford, p. 87)		

1700
JOHN DRYDEN

Thus *Man* by his own strength
to heaven would soar;
And would not be obliged
to God for more
(NOBCV, p. 130)

1740
ISAAC WATTS

"Return ye sons of *men*" (Grierson, p. 150)

1780

At rich *men's* jests laughed loud, their stories praised; / Their wives' new patterns gazed and gazed and gazed. (Timothy Dwight, NOBCV, p. 207)

1700
JOHN DRYDEN

A parish priest was of the pilgrim train; / An awful, reverend and religious *man* (NOBCV)

1790
ROBERT BURNS

Then gently scan your brother *Man* / Still gentler sister Woman (NOBCV, p. 210)

1790
COWPER

Man thinks he fades too soon (NOBCV, p. 204)

1800
COWPER

No—the man's morals were exact. What then? 'Twas his ambition to be seen of *men*. (NOBCV, p. 192)

1800
THOMAS JEFFERSON

"I have sworn upon the altar of God eternal hostility against every form of tyranny over the mind of *man*" (Letter to Rush, Sept. 3, 1800)

Man-*Homo* (generic man)	Men-*Homines* (generic man plural)	Man-*Vir* (male human being)	Men-*Viri* (male human beings)
1850 WORDSWORTH Religious men, who give to God and *man* their dues (NOBCV, p. 213)		**1850** WORDSWORTH The oldest *man* he seemed that ever wore grey hairs (NOBCV, p. 212, l. 7)	
1866 GERARD MANLEY HOPKINS And wears man's smudge and shares *man's* smell: the soil (*God's Grandeur*, Norton Anthology, p. 887)	**1866** HOPKINS Why do *men* then now not reck his rod? (Norton Anthology, p. 887)		
		1879 GERARD MANLEY HOPKINS Who have watched his mould of *man*, big-boned and hardy-handsome (Felix Randal)	
			1880 EMILY DICKINSON Read, sweet, how others strove The river could not drown, Brave names of *men* And celestial women Passed out of record Into renown (NOBCV, p. 244)
			1930 T. S. ELIOT Then the camel *men* cursing and grumbling (*Collected Poems*, p. 68, "Journey of the Magi")

Man-*Homo* (generic man)	Men-*Homines* (generic man plural)
1984 ROBERT PENN WARREN	
Excavation next summer exposed that glory to *man's* sight (*Poems*, p. 45)	
1988 GARY GILDNER	
when it almost reached where no *man* would ever dream to touch (Poetry, Dec. 1988, p. 128)	
ANTHONY SOBIN	
perhaps millions of ages before the history of *man* (Poetry, Dec. 1988)	

Feminism, Freedom, and Language

Michael Levin

"Words are wise men's counters, they do but reckon by them: but they are the money of fools."

— Thomas Hobbes

Of all feminist initiatives, the attempt to alter language is the most apt to provoke derision. It is difficult to suppress a smile when "manholes" become "personholes". The Labor Department's replacement of "fisherman" and "newsboy" by "fisher" and "news carriers", the National Weather Service's scrupulous alternation of male with female names for hurricanes (which begins with male and female "A" names in alternate years), engage the sense of the absurd by their strenuous pursuit of the trivial.

Absurd or not, this campaign has been markedly successful, well beyond the embrace of linguistic guidelines by publishers and professional organizations. Executive officers have become chairpersons and chairs. Businessmen have become business professionals. Ships are no longer manned, but crewed by crewmembers. Hockey defensemen are "defenders" and "defensive players". "He/she's" populate public utterances and private memos. There are computer programs to insert "or she" after inadvertent "he's" (and to delete such words as *virile, manly,* and *manhood*). Schools encourage teachers to call their charges "children" instead of "boys and girls". "Man" as the inclusive name for the human biological species has become taboo, with parallel efforts under way to change other languages.

That natural language infuriates feminists is clear enough:

> Sexist language is no less noxious than racist language. As Kett
> and Underwood say in their recent book, "Avoiding *he* is equal
> to taking down the 'whites only' sign in a restaurant."[1]

What precisely is wrong with the inclusive use of "he" and related
features of natural languages is less clear. These usages are said to
be "biased", but language, which distributes nothing and takes
nothing, cannot be directly assessed by the canons of justice.
Speaking more analytically, there are four standard objections to
current speech patterns: (1) They reflect the inferior state of women;
(2) they perpetuate this inferior status; (3) they mendaciously
represent women as inferior to or different from men; and (4) they
insult women by making them "invisible". Many of these charges
are made in *The Right Word,* a booklet prepared by the National
Committee of the American Society for Public Administration.
According to *The Right Word,* current language presents a "danger"
to working women by its "perpetuation of myths and false
generalizations . . . 'active' and 'passive' are descriptive of individual personality—not gender; sometimes men are quiet [and] women
are insensitive." The pronoun "he" is objectionable because it
results in "misleading and inaccurate communication" and "reinforces
the perception of woman as an appendant to generic 'man' ", as
well as "reinforcing inequity based on gender". Or, as Marie
Shearer puts it, "Male pronouns . . . imply that everyone who is
anyone is male."[2] Similar theses are maintained in more scholarly works.[3]

These charges cannot all be leveled consistently. If women
enjoy lower status than men and have been pushed by socializa-
tion from society's mainstream, it is not a lie to represent women

---

[1] Marie Shearer, "Solving the Great Pronoun Problem: Twelve Ways to
Avoid the Sexist Singular", *Perspectives: The Civil Rights Quarterly* 13 (Spring
1981): 18.

[2] Ibid.

[3] See, e.g., Robin Lakoff, *Language and Women's Place* (New York: Harper
and Row, 1975); Mary Vetterling-Braggin, ed., *Sexist Language* (Totowa, N.J.:
Littlefield, Adams, 1981).

in this light—assuming that it is *language* that can be properly said to represent anything, rather than *speakers* who represent things by use of the means language supplies. If some traits are for whatever reason more prevalent in one sex, it is not mythologizing to reserve the appropriate epithets for that sex. One cannot coherently complain that "he" refers basically to men, and that the masculine "he" refers to *both men and women.* In fact, before going farther, we may dismiss the idea that masculine pronouns are misleading. Words are misleading when they mislead. If nobody is misled by a turn of phrase, it is not misleading, and there is no one over the age of three who has been fooled by "he" into thinking that women are unpersons. It is not possible to produce a woman who believed (until feminists cleared things up) that "He who hesitates is lost" did not apply to her. It is universally understood that "he" is used with the intention of referring to both men and women, and that this intention has settled into a convention. Nothing more is required for a purely designative expression like "he" to *mean* men and women both.

Possibly because the only difficulty created by ordinary language is that feminists do not like it, feminist linguistic reform has become a kind of ongoing referendum about feminism itself. In the absence of any clearer purpose, substituting "person" for "man" is a concession made to feminists just because feminists demand it. As a result, whatever thought is to be conveyed in the act of communication is consciously subordinated to equity, with the collateral effect of obscuring whatever is actually being said. When clergymen refer to "Our Father and Mother who art in Heaven", or "The God of Abraham and Sarah", as many now do, or when contemporary reworkings of the New Testament change the "Son of God" to "The Human One", they shift attention from religion to the struggle against sexism. Feminist linguistic reform is an attempt to make all thought whatsoever concern feminism to the exclusion of everything else.

Feminist linguistic reform is for this reason far from inconsequential. Linguistic change legislated to conform to a worldview makes people self-conscious about their own language, an uncomfortable state of mind that may properly be called oppressive. Language is the vehicle of thought, and in an important sense speakers must be unconscious of choosing their words if they are to express their thoughts. When we become entangled in decisions about how to talk, we lose contact with the reality our talk is supposed to be about. Like playing the piano, language is largely a system of acquired habits, and fluent speech accompanied by constant conscious decisions about which words to utter is as difficult as fluent pianism accompanied by constant conscious decisions about which keys to hit. The most uncomfortable moments in life—emotional scenes, first dates, delicate negotiations with the boss—are distinguished by precisely this need to anticipate what to say. There is no need to think about words when things go smoothly—the right words come unprompted. The distraction occasioned by the felt need not to offend the notional feminist watchperson hovering nearby makes everyone just that much more self-conscious about talking. As *The Right Word* admits, "the newly sensitized administrator is frequently tongue-tied". Feminists insist that this self-consciousness passes in a few weeks. The reader must judge the plausibility of this guarantee for himself.

LANGUAGE AND THOUGHT

At the end of this chapter we will look at attempts to enforce feminist linguistic reform by law. For now it suffices to remember that enforced ideological linguistic reform has been tried before, and failed. During the Reign of Terror that succeeded the French Revolution, all persons were addressed as "citizen" and "citizeness". Russians became "comrades" after the Bolshevik Revolution. In both cases these conventions swiftly became empty, for reality is not so obliging as to follow language. The ordinary worker may be officially entitled to address the First Secretary of the Party as "comrade", but that has not made them friends or equals in any substantial way. Russians must still privately distinguish genuine comrades from pro forma ones, thus undercutting the reform. The failure of "comrade" and "citizen" to induce political equality suggests that language does not and cannot shape thought in the manner or to the extent supposed by egalitarian reformers. Attempts to alter putatively biased thinking by altering the language which expresses this thinking reverse cause and effect. At the same time, these attempts have negative short-term effects of the sort mentioned in the previous section.

The beginning of wisdom on this complex subject is to reject the idea, advanced by a number of contemporary anthropologists and philosophers, that language shapes rather than reflects reality, and the related thesis, usually called the Whorf hypothesis, that a speaker's language is a significant factor in determining his conception of the world, particularly the social world.[4] In my view, the Whorf hypothesis completely reverses the direction of the causal arrows connecting language, thought, and reality.[5]

Speakers mark a distinction linguistically when the distinction becomes important, and name a phenomenon when the phenomenon becomes salient; things do not *become* important *because* the means to describe them have been enlarged. Imagine a community of cavemen who call all furry animals by the single word *furry* (or, to avoid anachronism, a word best translated into English as "furry"). Suppose that one kind of furry animal begins to attack members of the community. The community would almost certainly coin a special name for that special animal—"leopard", say. Cave children would thereafter be warned about leopards, and the next generation of adults would see leopards as particularly dangerous. It is surely implausible to attribute these changes in outlook to the addition of "leopard" to the communal vocabulary. The cavemen fear leopards because leopards attack them, not because "leopard" has fearsome connotations; quite the reverse— the coinage "leopard" acquired fearsome connotations because leopards themselves are menacing.

Feminist monitoring of language can be simulated in this situation by a shamanistic injunction to remove "leopard" from the

[4] See Benjamin Whorf, *Language, Thought, and Reality,* ed. J. E. Carroll (Cambridge, Mass.: MIT Press, 1956).

[5] See Michael Levin, *Metaphysics and the Mind-Body Problem* (London: Oxford University Press, 1979), pp. 152–56.

cave vocabulary because using "leopard" is sinful. In that case, a viable cave community would simply *reinvent* a synonym for the old word *leopard,* or some handy descriptive device for capturing the difference between harmless and dangerous furry animals. The least likely outcome would be for speakers of the newly "leopard"-less language to cease fearing leopards. Speakers desirous of obeying the shaman would experience short-term difficulties in heeding the distinction between leopards and other things, to be sure, and aversion to the guilt attendant on verbalizing leopard-thoughts would generalize to aversion to leopard-thoughts themselves. No one would want to think about, much less talk about, leopards. Even though the use of "leopard" does not cause leopard-thoughts, thoughts are sufficiently associated with words for both to come to control a response originally keyed on just one. George Orwell was right to think that tinkering with language disrupts thought, but wrong to think that this was because language determines thought. The disruption is in fact the product of two vectors: positive reinforcement by reality for calling things as they are seen, and fear of pain conditioned by harassment for calling things as they are seen. The effect Orwell identified might be compared to the flickering of a flame caused by a blockage in the ventilation shaft.

The perception- and reality-dependence of language is illustrated by anthropological data commonly thought to illustrate the language-dependence of perception. Take the variety of Eskimo words for snow. In fact, Eskimos differ from speakers of English, not in seeing as different what speakers of English see as similar, but in having short phrases for the different kinds of snow that speakers of English can distinguish only clumsily. The availability in Eskimo of distinct words for differently textured snow is a linguistic adaptation to the importance of weather in Eskimo life. English speakers can say whatever Eskimos can say and describe any kind of snow Eskimos can describe, albeit more longwindedly. There has been no pressure on speakers of English to compress the description "dry, powdery snow that cannot be packed into snowballs" because, in the environments in which the typical speaker of English finds himself, the texture of snow is unrelated to vital interests like the location of food. Or consider the Hopi, who use different words for the spilling and pouring of powders, but the same word for the spilling and pouring of liquids.[6] It is better to explain Hopi usage in terms of the Hopi sense of similarity—the Hopi find the spillage of different substances less similar than they do the spillage and pouring of the same substance—than to explain the Hopi sense of similarity in terms of Hopi usage. The latter explanation cannot address the question of where the Hopi usage itself came from, while numerous non-question-begging explanations can be suggested for the origin of particular similarity spacings. To have interesting empirical content, the Whorf hypothesis must predict that the Hopi *disregard* the difference between spilling and pouring liquids—that, for instance, Hopi mothers punish their children for naughtily pouring water from jugs *and* for accidentally spilling it, in contrast to English-speaking mothers who punish water mischief but not water accidents. So far as I know, this has not been observed to be a trait of Hopi behavior. In fact, so many observations are at variance with the Whorf hypothesis—primitive people with no word for "jet plane" notice and become quite worked up about the first jet plane that flies low over their heads—that its defenders usually reformulate it in terms of *inclinations* created by language to heed or ignore phenomena. It is not clear that hypotheses about inner mental models of the universe that lack behavioral manifestations are empirically significant.

I believe social scientists are led to suppose that speakers of differing languages see the world differently through identifying the expressibility of a thought in a language with the presence in that language of a single word for the thought. That this *is* an error is plain enough from the undoubted expressive equivalence of French with English despite the French use of pairs of syncategorematic particles to express negation. Neither *"ne"* nor *"pas"* means quite what "not" means, yet *"Je ne danse pas"* means exactly what "I do not dance" means (to the extent that synonymy can survive the attacks

[6] See J. B. Carroll and J. B. Casagrande, "The Function of Language Classifications in Behavior", in *Communication and Culture,* ed. A. G. Smith (New York: Holt, Rinehart, and Winston, 1966), pp. 489–514.

of the philosopher Quine). Social scientists sometimes stumble over this point in their very attempt to describe incompatible linguistic frameworks. Carol Eastman writes: "American English does not have a kinship term which refers to one's daughter's husband's brother."[7] It does, of course—"one's daughter's husband's brother".

Still, might not concepts for which no single word exists be more *difficult* to utilize than those for which there is a single, familiar word? (So that it would be *harder* to be sexist in a gender-neutral language.) There is evidence that this is not so when the environment is sufficiently demanding. The Nigerian language Wolof contains no single word for "blue", a single word denoting both "red" and "orange", and a vague word most nearly equivalent to "yellow". Bruner, Greenfield, and Olver[8] found that children who speak Wolof classified toy trucks with respect to color and function just as French children do.

A language expresses a culture and its patterns of thinking—"A language is a form of life", in Ludwig Wittgenstein's Whorfian apothegm—in the sense that much may be inferred about the culture and environment of a group from its language, particularly its vocabulary. An observer can infer a great deal about the Eskimo's world from the large number of Eskimo words for "snow". In this sense, but in no stronger sense, language is continuous with culture. An observer, then, who knew nothing of the human race, could infer from its "sexist" languages that human beings perceive the sexes to be dimorphic. And, just as he would conclude that Eskimos would not have coined so many words for different kinds of snow unless there *were* different kinds of snow, he will conclude that human discourse probably reflects some truth about sex dimorphism. What really bothers feminists about language is that virtually every natural language records a fundamental recognition of sex differences. The feminist quarrel is not with language but the reality behind language and the human recognition of this reality. When the demand is made that "men

<hr />

[7] Carol Eastman, *Aspects of Language and Culture* (San Francisco: Chandler and Sharp, 1975), p. 88.

[8] *Studies in Cognitive Growth* (New York: Wiley, 1966), p. 385ff.

working" signs be replaced by "people working" signs (as the state of New York is spending ten million dollars over a ten-year period to accomplish), the aim is not fairness but the denial of sexual dimorphism. Feminists want language to be the way it would have been had the sexes been the same. Because the feminist argument reverses the causal arrow between the perception of sex differences and the origin of this perception, it is not altogether clear whether feminists expect a neutered language to change the reality behind it, or whether they simply regard the avoidance of acknowledgment of this reality as intrinsically desirable.[9] Either expectation is an attack on the messenger.

EXAMPLES

An example of the confusion of words with their referents is Robin Lakoff's observation that people look askance at men who have mastered the vocabulary of sewing. This observation, although correct, has nothing to do with language. People take mastery of any specialized vocabulary to indicate familiarity with its subject. Since in our culture most men are unfamiliar with seams, hems, and other details of sewing, a man who speaks competently about them is anomalous, and draws the suspicion normally directed at any anomaly, because he shows an anomalous familiarity with sewing itself. This is a fact about people's attitude toward men and sewing, not their attitude toward men and words about sewing. Assuming it desirable to change this attitude, this change

[9] Robin Lakoff does acknowledge that "social change creates language change, not the reverse" (*Language and Women's Place*, p. 59), a conclusion very vexing to Virginia Valian: "While we are curing the disease, no overnight affair, we can use a little relief from the symptoms ... not only is reduction of suffering a good in itself, it often gives the patient the strength to fight the disease more effectively.... The disease ... is not social inequality but lack of power over one's life; all forms of oppression—be they economic, psychological, social, or linguistic—are merely symptoms of it" ("Linguistics and Feminism", in Vetterling-Braggin, p. 76). As the example mentioned at the beginning of the next section indicates, it is not clear that Lakoff herself is always consistent on the direction of the causal arrow.

cannot be induced by encouraging people to say "John fingered the damask" with a straight face (as Lakoff herself seems at times to realize).

An extensive subgenre of feminist writing on language is directed against sexual slang.[10] Feminists correctly observe that sex described from the male point of view is always active (men "conquer" and "score", "screw" and "hump") while sex described from the female point of view is passive (women "put out" and are "satisfied"). The anger provoked by these idioms is probably beyond the reach of reason, but it is worthwhile pointing out that in sex men *do* aggress while women are receptive. A man must achieve erection and a woman must relax. The ability to sustain an erection no matter what is a point of pride for many men, whereas women do not regard the ability to relax sexually as a comparable achievement. It is hardly surprising that metaphors for sexual intercourse should reflect these facts, or that these metaphors should involve the insertion of prongs into orifices. Parental investment theory predicts that sex for men will be accompanied by feelings of mastery, and sex for women by feelings of surrender—psychological realities merely reflected in language.

The neologism *Ms.* also puts the linguistic cart before the horse of reality. "Ms." was explicitly introduced by feminists as a device to mask the marital status of women just as "Mr." does for men, it being felt that the "Miss/Mrs." distinction disadvantageously "defines" women in terms of their relations with men. More recently, there have been efforts to replace "Ms." by the even more sex-neutral convention of designating women by their last names alone in contexts in which men are so designated. Whether these notational changes can contribute to making marital status no more important for women than it is for men depends on the function of "Miss" and "Mrs." As the most adaptive strategy for K-selected males is the aggressive pursuit of many females, while

[10] See, e.g., Barbara Lawrence, "Four-Letter Words *Can* Hurt You", in *Philosophy and Sex,* ed. Robert Baker and Frederick Elliston (Buffalo, N.Y.: Prometheus, 1975); Stephanie Ross, "How Words Hurt: Attitudes, Metaphors, and Oppression", in *Sexist Language,* pp. 194–216; Robert Baker, " 'Pricks' and 'Chicks': A Plea for Persons", in *Sexist Language,* pp. 161–82.

the most adaptive strategy for females is monogamous surrender to the male who vanquishes his competitors, it must be the K-selected male who initiates courtships. So as not to waste calories pursuing already mated females, a male must be able to gauge the availability of females he encounters. The female, who does not initiate courtship, needs no such gauge; a male's initiation of mating rituals—showing off his tailfeathers, requesting a date—is itself a signal of his interest. Every human society will evolve a device to signal the male about the availability of females. (Male philanderers send false signals by approaching females as if unattached; on the whole, married women are less inclined to stray because one mate is all a woman needs for maximum reproductive success. In any event, social signals evolve to fit the average.) The wish to collapse "Miss" and "Mrs." into Ms.'s who resemble Mr.'s is the wish that women be thought of as selecting sexual partners in the way and with the purposes characteristic of men. It is a wish for the terms of address and marital status that would have evolved had there been no differences in the sexual nature of men and women. (I suspect that the conventional prefixing of some title to female names reflects an unconscious desire to soften the harsh functionality of bare name reference, which *is* thought appropriate for men.)

The more deeply language is probed, the more traces it reveals of the beings that produce it. The gender of nouns in languages with masculine and feminine words are usually appropriate; "house" is usually feminine and "key" masculine. The neuter in classical Greek coincides with the masculine more often than with the feminine, and never with the feminine alone—perhaps reflecting some dim perception that men have a greater affinity with neutral things. The *absence* of gender from a language has no correspondence with a cultural history in which women experience unusual political equality with men or are accorded unusually extensive participation in male spheres. Turkish lacks gender, but Turkish women lack many rights enjoyed by women in countries with more "sexist" native tongues.

DOES LANGUAGE INSULT WOMEN?

That natural languages reflect sex differences makes natural languages anti-woman only on the assumption that typically male traits are better than typically female ones and that any reflection of sex differences is a reminder of female inferiority. In fact, language cannot be misogynistic (or be biased against anything else) for the simple reason that anything at all about men and women, indeed anything at all about anything, can be said in any natural language. Take the word *shrew,* whose presence in English is sometimes cited as an instance of linguistic bias against aggressive women. Now, English cannot force anybody to believe that there are strident women, for if it did it would be impossible to say in English that there are no shrewish women, which is easily done by uttering the sentence "There are no shrewish women." Nor does the admitted negative weight of "shrew" compel dislike of certain forms of female behavior, for English and other natural languages contain devices for neutralizing evaluative connotations. Anyone who does not mind the behavior normally called shrewish need only say "I don't mind the behavior normally called 'shrewish' ".

There remains the charge that "he", "mankind", and their cognates slight women by referring to them by words that are also used to refer to men alone, thereby implying that women are not important enough to deserve a name of their own. This charge is silly for the same reason it is silly to say that "he" does not refer to women. Just as reference is secured by a mutually recognized intention to refer—so that "he" refers to women as well as men because everyone realizes that it does—so an insult is a word or gesture used with the *intention* of causing affront through the recognition of that intention.[11] In the all-important point of their history, words like *he* and *man* are neutral names for the human race as a whole; whatever the reason that the collective name for

[11] A large philosophical literature has developed a theory of linguistic meaning in terms of nested intentions; its primary contributors are H. P. Grice, P. F. Strawson, John Searle, Jonathan Bennett, David Lewis, J. L. Austin, and Stephen Schiffer.

males is also the collective name for males and females, nobody ever adopted this usage *with the intention* of causing feelings of shame and inadequacy, or with the intention of expressing contempt. The word *nigger,* by contrast, *is* intended to affront by expressing contempt. It has acquired this conventional force because its original usage was known to be accompanied by contempt, so that its continued use by a speaker, who would be presumed to know that feelings of contempt would be imputed to him, amounted to the intention of expressing contempt. The generic "he" has no similar history.

No matter what distress it may cause, a word or gesture is not insulting unless accompanied by or known to be conventionally associated with malice. If my passing remark about your tie causes chagrin because of some event in your childhood unknown to me, I have not insulted you. Were ordinary pronouns insulting to women, every utterance ever voiced in English before 1970 was an insult. It would follow that Shakespeare unintentionally insulted women when he had Hamlet say "I'll make a ghost of him who lets me" without threatening Ophelia. The idea of an unintended insult makes no more sense than that of unintended discrimination.

The use of "he" has doubtless *become* provocative, but only because the feminist movement has made it so. By announcing that they will respond belligerently to "he", feminists have turned it into a fighting word. They have so raised linguistic consciousness that some decisions on pronouns have become unavoidable; if one is not profeminist in one's usage, one declares oneself defiantly antifeminist. It is of course the feminists' privilege to transform a previously inoffensive pronoun into a fighting word, as it is the privilege of the saloon brawler to announce that touching an intrinsically inoffensive chip on his shoulder will henceforth be construed as a challenge to fight. It is, however, quite absurd for feminists to decide to take offense at the English language and then complain that offensive remarks are constantly falling on their ears.

WHAT FEMINIST REFORM ACCOMPLISHES

Embedded sex differentiations do not desensitize language to social change. World War II produced "Rosie the Riveter", just as the popularity of Charles Dana Gibson's drawings produced the "Gibson girl" in a previous era. But such changes cannot be predicted, let alone dictated, for they arise from the same unconscious depths as speech itself and in response to the unpredictable contingencies in the extralinguistic world.

Because language reflects reality and not vice versa, universal adoption of feminist usages will do nothing to "upgrade" women. Indeed, there is an inconsistency between the claim that such coinages will beneficially raise consciousness and the demand that these coinages become the unconscious standard, for if "he or she" comes to be used as "he" now is (or was until very recently), namely, as an indexical device, it will prompt no thoughts of sexual equality. The change will simply sprinkle a great many "she's" where none would otherwise have been found, a protocol as empty as calling everyone "comrade". If sprinkling "she's" is to have a point, the point must be kept in mind; if "he or she" becomes the *un*conscious norm, it will leave everything as it is. The same perceptions which once created "he" will continue to operate. Suppressing one or many of their linguistic manifestations will simply leave these perceptions in temporary tension with a language forbidden to express them—temporary, because they will find other expressions.

These points are unintentionally illuminated by an experiment taken by its designers to show that "he" suppresses thoughts of women.[12] It was found that people are more likely to think of a man first when "he" is used in sentences than when "he or she" is used. An alternative interpretation of this experiment comes to mind when its unsurprising result is redescribed as the greater readiness of people to think of a woman first when "he or she" is used than when "he" is used. It is surely more plausible to suppose

[12] Janice Moulton, George M. Robinson, and Cherin Elias, "Sex Bias in Language Use", *American Psychologist* (Nov. 1978): 1032–36.

that "he or she" prompts previously unentertained thoughts of women than that "he" quashes previously excogitated thoughts of women ready to enter consciousness. Consider the same experiment with "she" replaced by "a kangaroo". No doubt people are more likely to think of a human being first if "he" is used than if "he or a kangaroo" is, but does this mean that "he" inhibits thoughts of kangaroos, or that "he or a kangaroo" produces thoughts of kangaroos that would not otherwise have existed? The experiment as conducted relies on the current novelty value of "he or she". There is no reason to think the effect would continue should "he or she" simply *replace* "he" as the standard, unconscious conventional mode of reference used by English speakers from birth. People would continue to think first of whomever experience showed to lead the way in most activities, which would still be men.

It is extremely unlikely that "he or she", "he/she", "s/he" or similar neologisms will acquire purely indexical status, since they are syntactically complex. The mind seeing an "or", overt or disguised by a slash, wants to construct the meaning of the complex or-phrase from its components. The only practical replacement for "he" would have to be a completely new word bearing no syntactical relation to "he". The prospects for injecting such a word into a natural language by fiat are nil.

While its oppressiveness and clumsiness may sink feminist newspeak of its own weight, this tampering with language can, as noted, carry important negative consequences. Punishing words creates an aversion to the thoughts these words normally express, and while nothing can make people permanently disregard what they see, people can be made to *worry* about acknowledging what they see. This happened during the Victorian era, when an unwillingness to acknowledge sex openly drove people to clothe the "limbs" of tables and devise elaborate euphemisms for anything vaguely corporeal. Considerable damage was done in the way of hysteria and repression (although sex itself seems to have survived). Feminists seek to make taboo the acknowledgement of anything having to do with sex differences, and particularly with masculinity. For all their good words for forms of sexual behavior the Victorians would have abhorred, feminists are rather akin to Victorians.

LANGUAGE AND GOVERNMENT

Insofar as the feminist invasion of the mind is a private effort, there is nothing further to be said about it than to point out the errors on which it rests. It is up to each individual whether or not to lower his mental portcullis. The extent to which the government has taken the feminist side in this invasion is so far relatively minor. Still, neutering language is presented as a matter of rights, and the censoring of "discriminatory language" is increasingly equated with antidiscriminatory legislation.[13] Some feminists hold "sexist language" to violate Title VII and Title IX; during a television discussion in which I participated, it was asserted that control of the language of textbooks was a matter of "civil rights".[14]

The state has, somewhat tentatively, accepted the invitation to enter. In 1980, the secretary of health and human services prohibited the use of "sex biased" terms in departmental communications and sent copies of *The Right Word* to all regional officers. A "right to be free of sexist language" is cited in Iowa's ban on language that "excludes women" in its public schools. This right is also cited in section 1604.11, the federal ban on "sexual harassment", which gives legal effect to the theory that language may serve as an oppressive force against women. "Sexual harassment" conjures up images of sexual blackmail, and there might be a case for treating sexual blackmail as a problem of some sort, if not perhaps a federal tort, if a precisely and narrowly defined case could be made for its prevalence. This condition is not met in section 1604.11, whose central provision run as follows (emphasis added):

---

[13] See Susan Salliday, Letter to the Editor, *Proceedings of the American Philosophical Association* 52 (Aug. 1979): 869.

[14] *Straight Talk,* WOR–TV, New York, June 21, 1982.

Section (a)(3): *verbal* or physical conduct of a sexual nature constitute[s] sexual harassment when such conduct has the purpose *or effect* of unreasonably interfering with an individual's work performance or creating an intimidating, hostile or *offensive* work environment.

Section (c): an employer is responsible for its acts and those of its agents and supervisory employees with respect to sexual harassment regardless of whether the specific acts complained of were authorized or even forbidden by the employer and *regardless of whether the employer knew or should have known* of their occurrence.

Section (c): An employer may also be responsible for the acts of nonemployees.

Section (f): An employer should take all steps necessary to prevent sexual harassment from occurring, such as affirmatively raising the subject, expressing strong disapproval, developing appropriate sanctions, informing employees of their right to raise and how to raise the issue of harassment under Title VII, and developing methods to sensitize all concerned.[15]

This language is aimed less at sexual blackmail than at any communication involving sex which, intentionally or unintentionally, bothers someone. It is consistent with (a)(3) that use of the epithet "bitch" is a tort; whether it actually is such will depend on the discretion of the federal judiciary. It is consistent with (a)(3) that an epithet need be directed at no particular individual to be harassing; if a woman is offended by an argument in the workplace using off-color language, she has standing and a prima facie case, as does a woman being pestered for a date. If a woman in a workplace dislikes a male coworker's sexual boasts, or the pinups in his locker, she may have a legally sound complaint; its "reasonableness" is a matter for judicial determination. Heated insistence on sex differences in an office argument will also be tortious if the federal courts see it as sufficient grounds for offense. (When section 1604 was issued for preliminary public comment before publication in the Federal Register, feminists argued strenuously for the deletion of the (a)(3) reasonableness test.)

---

[15] *Federal Register,* 45, 219, sec. 1604.11 (Nov. 10, 1980), p. 74667. Sec. 1604.11 was issued by the EEOC as an implementing regulation of Title VII.

The strict liability created by (c) for an employer for any sexual harassment by an employee or, per clause (e), any passerby, codifies *Miller,* in which the Bank of America was found responsible for a supervisor's firing a subordinate for denying him sexual favors. The application of a strict standard of liability is notable beyond its transformation of a tort that one would have thought inherently intentional. Strict liability, the threat to inflict punishment for events beyond the tort-feasor's control, is rare in the law. Some jurists regard it as a holdover from a time before the concept of individual responsibility had been developed. Jurists who do see a place for strict liability in Western law regard it as a means for promoting vigilance against serious mishaps. A restaurant owner is held strictly liable for his patrons' food poisoning even if he has taken reasonable precautions against it, on the theory that food poisoning constitutes such grave harm that restaurant owners must be made to take extraordinary precautions against it. In effect, section 1604 holds that remarks capable of giving sexual offense are as harmful as food poisoning.

Clause (f) outlines the measures an employer must take to maintain this heightened vigilance. In tandem with strict liability, the affirmative obligations of clause (f) strongly encourage employers to raise a commotion when there is no prior evidence of a need to. One thinks of the shock the required steps might bring to the average male and female office workers. They are probably not bothered by "sex harassment", and perhaps have never heard of it. They may enjoy the mild flirting that goes on, and, if unmarried, may hope to find a marriageable partner at work. Suddenly, on government orders transmitted by the local AA/EEO office, comes a flood of memoranda, posters, videotapes, lectures, warnings, instructions for bringing lawsuits and incitements to file anonymous grievances. An employer who takes section 1604 seriously may make periodic sweeps of the janitor's locker room, and to be on the safe side dismiss any employee who asks a co-worker for a date. Chase Manhattan Bank, fearful of 1604 litigation, now forbids all physical contact between employees and discourages "verbal pats on the back". The employer must still anticipate inadvertently offensive remarks by nonemployees who happen onto the premises.

The owner of a diner might feel safest by putting signs around his parking lot warning "Don't whistle at our waitpersons".

This neo-Victorian obsession with sexual misbehavior is designed to mix everyone's awareness of sex with the thought of legal reprisal, to suppress speech with any sort of sexual content, and, ultimately, to chill normal relations between men and women. It is difficult to understand a "civil rights" policy which insists via quotas on "sexually integrating" the workplace, and then threatens reprisal when men and women placed in proximity, often in situations of stress, refuse to pretend they are neuters.

To place 1604 in perspective, the reader might recall the Supreme Court doctrine that no speech, however disrespectful, contemptuous, or advocatory of violent change, can be prohibited unless it is inciteful of and imminently likely to produce lawless action.[16] Under this doctrine the Supreme Court has protected topless dancing, American flags worn on the seat of the pants in public schools, and neo-Nazi marches through Jewish neighborhoods. Yet making a pass at work is no longer protected against state action.

[16] See *Brandenburg v. Ohio*, 395 US 444 (1969).

INCLUSIVE LANGUAGE RE-EXAMINED

Joseph C. Beaver

Evidence continues to mount in the secular world that the use of so-called inclusive language has peaked, and is, in fact, on the wane. On January 1, 1981, a letter was read on National Public Radio's "All Things Considered" from a listener who objected to NPR's reference to the flight around the world by the "Voyageur" as an example of what "man" can achieve (one of the two pilots, of course, was a woman). In the February 23, 1987, issue of the *New Republic,* the "Washington Diarist" reported that one reader could not countenance the *NR's* "stubborn" use of "gender-specific" pronouns. And in a letter to the editor of the Barnard College Alumnae magazine for Spring 1987, one Ruth Halseth states at length that she has no objection to "chairman" or "mankind", since both are generic nouns. These are just a few of many instances that could be cited showing the gradual demise of inclusive language in the secular world, and demonstrating that many have grown tired of the pretense that generics are words that somehow "exclude" women.

But the same tendency is asserting itself, perhaps somewhat timidly, in religious circles as well, where the push for inclusive language has not yet abated, where revised hymnals, prayer books, lectionaries, and the like have appeared in many denominations, and others are considering putting out "language-sensitized" versions. It is as if many who have been quietly enduring changes in which they didn't really believe are beginning, at long last, to speak up (and, frankly, to take a position against inclusive language is taboo in many seminaries and churches).

In an exchange with Alvin Kimel, an Episcopal priest who had deplored in an earlier issue the fallacy of regarding "man" as a "gender-specific" word, the Reverend Jimmye Kimmey, a female priest serving in a New York Diocesan position, admits in a letter to the editor of *The Living Church,* July 20, 1986, that the credal phrase "and was made man" does include all of us — correctly so, since man is anarthrous (without an article). And Barbara Brown Zikmund, dean of the Pacific School of Religion, in a *Christian Century* article on the Trinity and feminism (May 1987), admits that she, too, has never felt personally excluded by generics. (This testimony, which one hears from so many women, leads one to wonder who, indeed, ever did feel excluded, until they were artificially instructed that generics are a "sexist" product of the language.)

So, we witness today two opposing trends, the gradual disappearance of insistence on inclusive language in secular society, and — in seminaries and churches — a continued push for it, though voices are now heard once again in opposition. National church councils and committees which have not yet officially recommended expensive new "inclusive lectionaries" and the like would be well advised to consider these trends and the linguistic facts that are dealt with in this article. These data should be weighed carefully before final decisions are made. The same would apply to local churches which have some autonomy with regard to the adoption of such "language-sensitized" versions.

How did the whole phenomenon begin? What were the origins of inclusive language? We shall see that inclusive language sprang from a fallacious analogy, and that it is based on a false linguistic premise. We shall maintain that inclusive language is doomed, therefore, to ultimate failure, though it may well survive somewhat longer in religious circles than in secular society. If this is correct, it is indeed a sad situation, because new prayer books and lectionaries are expensive, and their continued promulgation may regrettably turn more away than had been anticipated from the liturgies of the mainline churches.

The '60s was the decade which witnessed the height of the civil rights movement, in the sense of maximal media coverage. It will be recalled that a succession of terms to refer to members of the black race occurred in the '40s, '50s, and '60s. First, there was "negro" (as well as its vulgate counterpart), taken directly from Portuguese and Spanish, a form meaning "black"; then, "colored" (this was the approved form as late as the era of Martin Luther King, who used it himself); then several short-lived forms, such as "Afro-Americans". For some dozen or fifteen years now, "black" has been the acceptable form. This progression of terms to refer to the same people was accounted for by the fact that black leaders found each term in succession to be pejorative. They were probably right.

The current feminist movement began later than the equal-rights-for-blacks movement, and, in fact, it began exactly when the terms to be used for blacks were undergoing debate and fairly rapid change. It was logical and natural, viewed from a certain standpoint, for some in the feminist movement to conclude that what was needed was a change of terminology with respect to women.

However, in searching for such a change, feminists faced a linguistic problem they did not recognize and which blacks had not faced. For blacks, it was a question only of settling on new *nouns* (what linguistics call pure lexical items—words having clear, specific referential content). Nouns may be invented rather freely by the speakers of a language, and speakers move with relative ease from one term to another for the same referential object—witness the succession of terms that have been employed this century, in English, for "automobile". But the feminists could not propose language changes of this type. They did not propose, for example, a new term to substitute for "women". The nouns referring to members of the female sex in general were, in fact, not pejorative (except marginally—in the view of some extremists at that time who taught that the term "lady" was pejorative and wanted to ban it).

So, the feminist activists focused attention on the so-called "generics" of the language, nouns of a somewhat different kind, not always clearly and specifically referential in their content, and, indeed, sharing some linguistic elements (lack of stress, for example, in certain instances) in common with pronouns. Thus began the war against "mankind", and also the generic "man" and "men".

Jimmye Kimmey correctly observed that such nouns are typically "anarthrous", that is, they are generic when used without an article. "Mankind", of course, never accepts an article. "Man" and "men" may accept articles ("the" or "a"), and when they do they are clearly not generic, but "gender-specific". Even such an expression as "A man's got to have a little drink now and then" conveys a clear notion of gender-specificity because of the article in front of "man", even though the person who uses such an expression might mean it generically. To be sure, it is also true that "man" and "men" may occasionally be anarthrous and yet gender-specific. But, in general, speakers of the language recognize quite clearly when these words are generic and when they are not. There is no real problem here—only the fiction that these words have only one meaning, as if we were to teach that "bank" always and everywhere refers to the side of a river, never to a commercial financial establishment.

But the feminists, working from a false analogy with the black experience, which was admittedly in many other respects parallel (status, pay, etc.), created a problem. They began to teach the fiction that generics were gender-specific. Thus came the call for "language" which did not "exclude women": "men and women" and "humanity" were asked for instead of "men" or "mankind", despite the fact that many such proposed phrases clearly exclude teenagers and children, hermaphrodites and others, as has been noted by a number of earlier writers on this subject, such as Brigitte and Peter Berger.

Generic pronouns also came under scrutiny. In English, as in many Indo-European languages, when a singular pronoun is used to refer to a noun of unspecified gender (say, "writer", or "author"), "he" is regularly used, but it is not a gender-specific "he". A number of awkward and unworkable solutions to this imaginary problem have been tried—the wordy "he or she", the computer-like "he/she" (now rarely encountered), and even "she", with the militant and linguistically naïve implication that "she" could serve as a generic pronoun. But the forces of *grammar* are not as malleable as are items such as nouns used to describe things of clear and specific referential content. Linguistically viewed, pronouns fall in the domain of grammar rather than the domain of the "lexicon" (the list of words referring to things of specific referential content— broadly speaking, nouns, verbs, and adjectives). It is a simple matter to devise a new referential lexical noun—it happens all the time. It is not easy, perhaps it is impossible, to invent a new preposition or pronoun, and the attempt to use "she" generically has also failed.

It is sometimes argued by more extreme advocates that people *do* mean male sex only when they say or write "man" or "men", and always have, if only subconsciously. Because of the nature of generics, actual evidence bearing on this claim is a little difficult to come by. Nevertheless, there is some evidence at hand indicating that speakers and writers do have generics internalized as referring to both sexes. In Shakespeare's play, at one point, Hamlet says, "Man delights not me—no, nor woman neither, though by your smiling you seem to say so" (II.ii.). Like all of Shakespeare's plays, *Hamlet* abounds in puns, word-play, and jokes. Hamlet has uttered his feelings; Rosencrantz, to cheer him up, to divert him from his gloom, as it were, assumes a friendly leer, making a joke (probably referring to Hamlet and Ophelia) out of the two-way possibility in Hamlet's "man". In smirking, Rosencrantz implies the gender-specific "man"; by adding the conjunctive phrase "nor woman neither", Hamlet asserts he meant the generic. If "man" had not been generic, there would have been no joke.

A vivid, straightforward bit of evidence is to be found in Anglican Bishop Lancelot Andrewes' 1614 sermon on Isaiah 7:14, where he discusses the virgin birth:

> To make Him *man,* it is well known there wanted not other ways: from the mould, as Adam; from a rib of flesh, as Eve. . . . Adam was not son to the mould, nor Eve daughter to Adam . . . howsoever of the body of *man* there may engender that which is not of the same kind, yet by way of conception there cometh of *man* nothing but *man;* nothing but of the same nature and substance that *he* was conceived of (*Works,* I., pp. 139, 140—italics mine).

A clearer illustration of the genericism of "man" and "he" could scarcely be desired: Eve is overtly stated to be included by "man", and, since Jesus was born of Mary, Mary is quite clearly also included. We have also, in Genesis 1:27, "So God created man in his own image, in the image of God he created him; male and female he created them"—thus in the RSV, and similarly in the NEB and other translations.

It would appear that the burden of proof lies with those who assert that the use of generics indicates conscious or unconscious exclusion. Such real evidence as I have been able to uncover indicates the contrary.

So the early movement to change the language to be "inclusive" was based on faulty linguistic conceptions and analogies. What the feminists attempted to do, in fact, *was,* however, almost exactly analogous to what Brigitte and Peter Berger noted in *The War Over the Family* (1983) and described in the chapter entitled "Goshtalk, Fem-speak, and the Battle of Language". In the 1930s, the Italian Fascist dictator Benito Mussolini made a speech in which he castigated the pronoun *lei* as effete. The word *lei* is a third person plural pronoun in Italian but has been used for centuries by Italian speakers as the formal morpheme for the second person singular. Many Indo-European languages (English among them) have, or had, two second person singular pronouns— one for familiar address, one for formal, as in modern French, *tu* and *vous.* The familiar second person singular in Italian is *tu,* but, as has English, the language has lost one of the two forms (English has lost the familiar "thou" and its variants). Good fascists, Mussolini declared, will say *voi* (actually the second person plural). Accordingly, public use of *lei* became viewed as reactionary, even subversive (as a preacher who dares say "mankind" now in certain churches might be viewed). Everyone's "language consciousness" was raised, we might say. But Mussolini's dictum never took complete hold, and after the war the Italians quickly resumed the use of *lei.*

So, the feminist notion that their desired reforms were comparable to what was going on in the civil rights movement was mistaken (as the Bergers also note, on p. 64). The Mussolini/*lei* phenomenon, however, is almost exactly parallel, involving as it does decrees on the part of a minority having to do with grammatical aspects of language, as opposed to lexical aspects. Also, the proposed list of items to be changed is small: in the Mussolini instance, only one; in the current feminist movement, no more than three or four are at stake. Finally, the terms involved are essentially grammatical rather than lexical. As one of my correspondents on this subject said to me (personal correspondence), "All I want is to be permitted to use my language naturally."

But in addition to being based on a faulty analogy to one aspect of the civil rights movement, the argument of inclusive language advocates was also based on a linguistic premise which has been shown to be invalid. It was thought that by eliminating generics one could change the *attitudes* of people toward women, just as it was thought by blacks that changing the lexical designation of their race would result in a change of attitude. That, in the latter case, such a change did occur would be denied by many, perhaps by most, blacks. But, in any event, the language problem involved was different. As we have seen, though you can coin and substitute real lexical items, you cannot blithely alter the glacial-like grammatical functionaries.

But the very notion that either grammatical forms *or* lexical items reflect the outlook or attitudes of the speakers of a language is unsound. The notion that language "shapes thought" is a very old one. Benjamin Whorf, an American linguist who early in the century did considerable work with American Indian languages, was impressed by the great contrast he found between those languages and the Indo-European. He noted, for example, that the Hopi, if they wish to refer to a hole in the ground, are compelled by their language to add a grammatical suffix to the word for "hole" to indicate whether the hole is in general circular or four-sided. (Cf. English, where, if we want to use a principal verb in a clause, we are forced to put it into past or present form, English being grammatically a two-tense language.) From this and similar observations, Whorf concluded that the language of speakers *did* shape their world outlook—that a Hopi actually did tend to see holes more as circles or squares than a non-Hopi, that speakers of a language that has no tense at all may *not* consider time as important as do speakers of a language that has tense, etc.

This theory became known as the theory of "linguistic relativity". Its pertinence to our subject is immediately apparent.

Following Whorf, a number of different studies were conducted by linguists to determine if the theory was valid. For example, one series of studies was devoted to certain African languages where the lexicon has only two, three, or four words for the different colors of the spectrum, as compared with the seven or eight found in most Indo-European languages, including English. Did it follow that these African language speakers would be less sensitive to color gradations than were speakers of languages which had more names for colors? None of the studies confirmed Whorf's theory. Since inclusive language advocates assume the validity of such a theory (though, of course, most of them have never heard of it), it would seem clear that all our present efforts to "language-sensitize" our liturgies and prayer books and lectionaries will prove to be like the house built on sand.

In conclusion, I suggest that inclusive language, while well-intentioned, has turned out and will turn out for most people to be a fad. In the secular world it has passed its peak. In secular prose, in TV advertisements, generics are almost as common as they ever were. Ultimately, for the linguistic reasons I have briefly sketched, I believe the same thing will happen in the churches, synagogues, and seminaries. The publications of such institutions remain as a kind of temporary bastion. There is also the considerable financial investment in "language-sensitized" hymnals, prayer books, and so forth. But, just as inclusive language came to the religious scene later than to the secular world, so it will depart later, though that departure be delayed because of this investment.

Deva is a clothing mail order house located in Burkittsville, Maryland. It has as a kind of credo the following: "Deva is a community of the heart. We know that miles are not distance to the spirit and that all who have the greater good in their hearts belong to the community of man." In the "Most Asked Questions" department of one of their catalogues a reader recently queried, "Why do you use the word 'man' instead of 'person'?" The answer was, "We thought about it long and hard. The word 'man' comes from the Sanskrit *manas,* which means to think, to be human. No matter how sadly that meaning has been twisted in contemporary society we feel that the original concept is valid. We would hope for a change in *understanding* rather than a mere shift in grammar. What we *mean* when we relate to each other is what is truly important."

III

HERMENEUTICS/SCRIPTURE

OLD TESTAMENT ICONOLOGY AND
THE NATURE OF GOD

Paul V. Mankowski, S.J.

We believe in one Lord, Jesus Christ, ... who was crucified
under Pontius Pilate, suffered, died, and was buried. On the
third day he rose again in accordance with the Scriptures. He
ascended into heaven, and is seated at the right hand of the
Father.

Let us linger for a moment over these words from the Creed. We
profess that we believe that Jesus Christ is seated at the right hand
of the Father, *kathezomenos en dexia tou patros,* according to the
symbol of Constantinople.[1] But there is a problem here. God is
spirit and therefore possesses in himself no property characteristic
of bodies. Yet "right" and "left" are notions that are in the strict
sense *only* attributable to bodies and must therefore be denied of
God. Are we at liberty, then, to say that Jesus is seated at the left
hand of the Father, since the physical associations of left and right
are equally inapplicable to God?

A partial answer is to say that the term "right" is used anal-
ogously in this instance and that its use entails no theological
embarrassment. But what are the terms of the analogy? For while
it is true that right- and left-handedness have a basis in nature, it is
less obvious to what extent right-handedness is *naturally* superior
to left and hence naturally appropriate in a description of Christ's
seat in glory. Again, it must be acknowledged that there is an

[1] DS 150 (381 A.D.).

overwhelming cultural preference accorded to the right hand over the left (in virtue of which this passage in the Creed becomes intelligible); yet at the same time much of the social and linguistic priority accorded to right and right-handedness is purely conventional, even arbitrary. Do we have the license, then, to reverse the terms of our Faith statement?

The situation is further complicated by the fact that the dominance of right-handedness in most civilizations has led to foolish, and sometimes cruel, impositions on those people who are naturally left-handed. Since God has no part in folly or cruelty, are we obliged to make amends in this respect by purging our theological language of a bias that has sometimes been pernicious?

I raise these questions only to leave them hanging and to move on to something more pertinent to my brief. Consider three recent statements concerning the attribution of sexual imagery to God:

> In itself, [God's] "generating" has neither "masculine" nor "feminine" qualities. It is by nature totally divine. It is spiritual in the most perfect way, since "God is spirit" and possesses no property typical of the body, neither "feminine" nor "masculine". Thus even "fatherhood" in God is completely divine and free of the masculine bodily characteristics proper to human fatherhood.

> The anthropomorphic language of the Scriptures and of the doctrinal formulations of Trinitarian life should not be taken literally, as if God were male rather than female. God is neither; God is pure spirit.

> While it may still be true "that to be human is to be male is to be the Son of God", we are proposing a reversal of that equation which will enable women to experience that: to be human is, for them, to be female is to be the Daughter of Goddess. For a woman to accept the divine Person as male can bring no other consequences than the destruction of her own personhood.

The first of these statements is by Pope John Paul II in his meditation *Mulieris dignitatem;*[2] in simple terms: God does not have the

---

[2] *Mulieris dignitatem,* 8. Translated in *Origins* 18, no. 17 (Oct. 6, 1988).

physical properties of masculinity or fatherhood. The second is from the second draft of the U.S. bishops' pastoral on women;[3] here: God is neuter. The third is from a recent essay on fundamental theology by Eleanor Rae and Bernice Marie-Daly:[4] God also is a goddess and must be experienced as female by some humans.

The "gender" of God is obviously a pretty hot topic today, while the positioning of Christ in glory is not, but theologically the problems are comparable. Gender, like handedness, is most obviously known in its corporeal realizations, and since God is not a body, no bodily extension of gender can be predicated of God. This leads the Pope to deduce that God does not share the "hardware" of human paternity, while it leads the authors of the women's pastoral to make a further step and deduce that God is neuter. Again, like handedness, gender contrasts have acquired an enormous load of cultural content, including much that is conventional and some that is pernicious, and this fact has led Rae and Marie-Daly to maintain that all gender predication is purely arbitrary and can be changed according to the sexual status and appetites of the believer. Are we, in fact, at liberty to profess that Jesus Christ is seated or standing on the right or left hand of our Mother/Father?

The position I wish to defend is that a Christian is obliged to acknowledge God as masculine, as a "he", in the fullness of the Godhead and in the Persons of the Trinity severally; corollary to this is the conviction that it is heterodox to picture God as neuter (as do the authors of the bishops' pastoral), or as hermaphrodite, or as feminine. Without straying from the Creed, we can find a number of contrasts whose correlative pairs are given or implied, each of which is crucial to our understanding of God, thus: he vs. she; father vs. mother; father vs. son; right vs. left; light vs. darkness; ascent vs. descent; above vs. below. It is absurd, as I have suggested, to reason that, because none of these notions can be

[3] "One in Christ Jesus", *Origins* 19, no. 44 (Apr. 5, 1990): para. 135. In the same place we read of "God, who is without gender".

[4] *Created in Her Image: Models of the Feminine Divine* (New York: Crossroad/Continuum, 1990).

predicated of God in a "physical" sense, we are equally correct in predicating either correlative of Him. If a contrast is invoked in the first place, there is at least *prima facie* ground to think that there is a point in using one member of the contrast-pair in our doctrinal formulations to the exclusion of the other. Yet, even if we agree that it makes theological sense to attribute masculinity to God, we still need to ask whether, and to what extent, that which has been revealed to us gives us grounds for so doing.

For some contemporary theologians, the Sacred Scriptures have of themselves no extraordinary authority in matters of belief or — what comes to the same thing — the Bible is revelatory not of God but of the attitudes of those who have managed the religion business throughout the history of Israel and the early Church. Although I think there are sound objections to this conspectus, I am not going to give them but will simply nail my colors to the mast. I will take as a given that the Bible is a sacred text and a preeminent source of our knowledge of God.

Among those of like conviction, there was little doubt until recently that the Bible did reveal God to be masculine in some sense. The challenges are recent, and I will marshal those that seem to be the most formidable or at least the most often repeated.

First: the androcentric culture of the biblical authors made it impossible to conceive of God as other than male.

Second: the theological naïveté of the sacred authors resulted in anthropomorphic images of God that are in themselves of no consequence.

Third: the Bible gives evidence of God as "she" as well as "he".

Fourth: the notion of God as "Father" was a late innovation, largely the work of single Nazarene rabbi, and represents a regression from the purer Faith of the Old Testament.

[It should be noticed, by the by, that these theses are often mutually incompatible. It is hard to argue, for example, that the bias of Israelite culture excluded the possibility of a feminine God, while also maintaining that, if you look hard enough in the right places, you find evidence for the goddess anyway. The fact that such assertions *are* often found in the same authors is evidence that this discussion is carried on in terms more often political than theological.]

For the remainder of this essay I would like to look at something rarely adduced by current disputants of the question, namely, the evidence. I will limit myself to that pertinent to the Old Testament—partly out of personal interest, but largely because it is here that the disputed territory really lies, that Nazarene rabbi having hampered discussion among the New Testament scholars by insisting, with remarkably bad taste, that God was to be called Abba, Father. Hardly a starting place for open and fruitful dialogue. If I can make my case for the Old Testament, then, it should apply a fortiori to the New.

EVIDENCE FROM THE GREATER SEMITIC PANTHEON

Why is evidence for the culture, or worldview, of the biblical authors important? Because, if an idea can be shown to be so universal in a given society that no alternative was thinkable, the fact that this idea is simply repeated in such-and-such a place has little significance for the historian; conversely, any departure from otherwise universal belief is very significant indeed. Many contend a feminine God was unthinkable among the Jews. What are the facts?

As a Semitic people, the Hebrews were part of a larger civilization, comprising a number of related languages and sharing a number of practices and beliefs about law, warfare, religion, and so on. It is disputed as to when precisely the Israelites became monotheistic in the strict sense, but it is generally thought that they *were* monotheistic by the start of the first millennium before Christ and that they were absolutely unique among Semitic nations in this respect. The other Semites might be called "promiscuously polytheistic", by which I mean that they not only enjoyed a domestic pantheon of several deities but also had little theological scruple in incorporating the gods of foreign peoples when it was politically expedient to do so. Now, every Semitic pantheon of the OT era, with the sole exception of Israel, included clear goddesses as well as male deities. We can determine the gender of these deities with great accuracy and from several sources. First, we can tell by grammatical inference, that is, seeing whether the various parts of speech that refer to gods in the texts are masculine or feminine. Second, in many cuneiform sources a special sign is placed before personal names indicating that the bearer is female, and many goddesses are identifiable in this fashion. Third, there is often a mythological context in which sexual relationships are specified and the gender of the deities is obvious. And finally, among the non-Israelites there is a mass of engraved and sculpted material in which gods and goddesses are clearly represented.

Again, with the glaring exception of the Hebrews, there seems to have been no scruple among the Semites in attributing a wide range of sexual antics to the pantheon. The gods took husbands and wives (as well as indulging in more irregular recreations); their genital endowments and mating rituals were described in exuberantly specific terms; the goddesses gave birth to offspring, and both gods and goddesses were assigned the natural attributes of father- and motherhood. A passage from a poem in the Ugaritic Baal cycle will the make the point:

> Baal the Conquerer obeyed.
> He fell in love with a heifer in the desert pasture,
>   A young cow in the fields on Death's shore:
> He lay with her seventy-seven times,
>   He mounted her eighty-eight times
> And she became pregnant,
>   And she bore him the Master.[5]

Not, in short, the Hebrew instinct. In fact the difference could hardly be greater. The great OT scholar Gerhard von Rad has summarized the data with succinctness:

> For the historian of religion, what is most astonishing is Jahwism's self preservation *vis-à-vis* the mythicising of sex. In the Canaanite cult [that is, in the religion of Israel's immediate neighbors], copulation and procreation were mythically regarded as a divine event; consequently, the religious atmosphere was as good as

[5] Michael Coogan, *Stories from Ancient Canaan* (Philadelphia: Westminster, 1978), p. 108 (adapted).

saturated with mythic sexual conceptions. But Israel did not share in the "divinisation of sex". YHWH stood absolutely beyond the polarity of sex [though *not* of gender!], and this meant that Israel could not regard sex as a sacral mystery.[6]

There is yet another source of information about the iconology of Semitic gods—that derived from personal names. A very large percentage of Semitic personal names, in particular among Israel and her neighbors, were in the form of short sentences. A well-known Hebrew example is Michael, that is "Mi ka 'El" = "Who is like God?" Another common sentence name form, and one with particular relevance to our topic, is that which is composed of a god's name and the word for father, mother, brother, sister, etc.; thus we get the Old Babylonian names Ummi-Ištar, "My mother is Ištar", and Šamas-abi, "Šamaš is my father." The composite of personal names proper to a given people or region is called its onomasticon. Now it is interesting that several Semitic peoples[7] had personal names in which the same god, usually male, figured both as father and mother: so Šamas-abi, "My father is Šamaš", vs. Ummi-Šamaš, "My mother is Šamaš." Presumably calling a god as one's mother or father one invoked a special kind of tutelary relationship, the kind of protection and partiality proper to a parent. Now the Hebrew onomasticon is rich in names in which the "father" element figures, but in no instance do we find a name with a word for mother or sister—not even among the names of women. The departure is striking. The upshot is that Semites were perfectly capable of viewing their gods as female, and in fact attributed motherhood both to female as well as (in a less obvious sense) to male deities; yet Israel, while sharing so much in the way of Semitic religious practice, had *no* part in this kind of attribution.

A word about the ambiguity of the concept of culture. If we are not careful, we can fall prey to a confusion that many champions of the theory of cultural determination have used to their own advantage. Most communities should be viewed as having

---

[6] Gerhard von Rad, *Old Testament Theology* (New York: Harper and Bros., 1962), p. 27.
[7] Including the Akkadians and Amorites.

not one but several cultures, imagined perhaps in terms of concentric circles of increasing diameter, each of which is part of the matrix in which social choices are made. Thus, when we make general statements about the culture of such-and-such a community, we have to be as clear as we can regarding *which* of its cultures we are talking about. Now, some argue that the "culture" of the Hebrews excluded a female deity. But what do they mean? If they mean the larger culture of the northwest Semites, they are simply wrong; goddesses were as common as houseflies. If, in contrast, they refer solely to the religious culture upheld as normative by the Bible and ignore the larger culture, they are not much better off, for it is perfectly plain that Israel *was* cognizant of this larger culture and took pains to separate itself from it. To sum up: we can only say a given belief is "determined" by a culture if no alternative is conceivable. However, the narrow culture of Israel clearly regards a polymorphously playful pantheon as the ordinary state of affairs among nations and Israel itself as the blessed exception; the ridicule and abhorrence it expresses toward these notions is evidence *against* cultural determination and *for* a system of conscious and deliberate theological decisions. This consideration should guide our thought also on other aspects of the uniqueness of the religion of Israel.

THE MASCULINITY OF ISRAEL'S GOD

My next task would have been regarded as pointless by most readers of the Bible throughout history: to give the evidence that the God of Israel was imagined as masculine; but times change. The divine name YHWH[8] revealed to Moses at Exodus 3 and used as the name of God some 6,800 times in the OT,

---

[8] I have argued elsewhere that Catholic scholars should abandon the practice of writing and pronouncing the name YHWH (such as was fostered by the Jerusalem Bible) in favor of a return to the traditional substitution. See "The Crisis of the Sacred and the Old Testament", in *Recovering the Sacred*, Proceedings of the Twelfth Convention of the Fellowship of Catholic Scholars, pp. 114f.

is almost certainly a Semitic verb in the imperfect tense—that is, equivalent to the English present or future tenses. Its meaning is not sure, although most scholars have given wary assent to William Albright's suggestion that it is a causative form of the verb *hayah,* meaning "he causes to be" or "he calls into being".[9] Others[10] have suggested derivation from a root meaning "to be passionate or strong". In either case it must be a third person *masculine* form of the verb. (Unlike the case in European languages, Semitic verbs were inflected for the gender of the subject as well as person and number.) Therefore, the form of the verb that is God's name must point to a grammatically masculine referent. Further corroboration is to be had from the fact that *'elohim,* the word for "God" as opposed to the proper name, is also masculine in form, as is the word *'adonai,* which is the *gere'* or substitute pronounced for the letters YHWH.[11] Similarly, every adjective, every pronoun, every participle that refers to YHWH is unmistakably masculine. The grammar of the Bible is unanimous in this regard.

The imagery of the OT—metaphoric language in the broadest sense—provides a more complex picture, but one that is still unambiguous as to import. In rough terms, every image that is *predicated* of YHWH, that is, every instance in which we find a statement of the kind "YHWH is X", the predicate is either masculine or entirely compatible with maleness. The much-discussed feminine attributes, however, are never predicated of YHWH but only suggested in the form of similes, where the precise limits of the analogy are put forth. So Isaiah 66:13, "As one whom his mother comforts, so I will comfort you [says YHWH]." That is, in respect of consolation, God is *like* a mother. The case is quite different regarding the masculine.

The notion of a warrior goddess, for example, was common in the ancient Near East. The Canaanite goddess Anat or Astarte is one instance, as is her Mesopotamian counterpart Inanna, whom Ham-

---

[9] W. F. Albright, *Yahweh and the Gods of Canaan* (New York: Doubleday, 1968), pp. 168–72.

[10] R. Mayer, "Der Gottesname Jahwe im Lichte der neuesten Forschung", *B2* n.s. 2 (1958): 25–53.

[11] So too the LXX *kyrios.*

murapi calls "the mistress of battle and strife, she who bears my weapons". The OT picture of YHWH as leading armies in battle is not therefore inherently masculine. Yet in Exodus 15, by all accounts one of the most ancient passages of the Bible, we read *YHWH 'is milhamah,* "YHWH is a man of battle"—a male, a *vir proelii.* In Psalm 24 we find that YHWH is designated not as a fighter simply but as a *gibbor,* a word laden with specifically masculine overtones, such that it would be a solecism to use it of a female warrior.[12] "Who is this King of Glory? YHWH the strong one, the warrior, YHWH is a warrior of battle." Notice: we do not read, "Like a warrior leading the charge, so YHWH shall lead us"; rather we have a simple predication: YHWH *is* a warrior, with no qualification or limitation.

The onomasticon is likewise unambiguous. Putting aside for a moment the names with a "father" element (which is a large part of the evidence), we still find unanimity on the question of gender. The name *'ahiyya,* "My brother is YHWH", is used of five individuals in the OT, one of whom is female; four individuals share the name *yo'ah,* which means the same. By contrast, there is no occurrence of the counterparts meaning "my sister is YHWH" or "sister of YHWH". The name *malkiyyah,* "My king is YHWH", is used of twelve persons, again with no "queen" counterpart. Of the fifty-five recorded Hebrew sentence names that are composed of the name YHWH and a verb, each shows the masculine form of that verb. The evidence is exceptionless.

EVIDENCE FOR A FEMININE YHWH

Next I want to examine the evidence for the feminine nature of YHWH. This may involve some rather tedious demolition work, and I apologize beforehand if the technicalities are sometimes hard to follow. But there is so much bogus pedantry floating around in the literature and discussion of this question that I feel obliged to

---

[12] In Aramaic, the GBR root comes to mean male simply. Cf. the semantic history of Greek *aner:* in Homer, it means a hero or warrior; later, it means a male as opposed to female, *vir* against *mulier.*

try to set the record straight, even if being inoculated with the antidote is a bit painful.

An article that assembles much of the goddess evidence, evidence that has become the standard lore on the question, was published by Phyllis Trible in the supplementary volume to the *Interpreter's Dictionary of the Bible* in 1976. Careful scrutiny of her evidence severely undercuts the strength of the claim that the OT permits a feminine portrait of YHWH.

A significant part of Trible's case centers around the OT use of the root RHM in its various forms. She writes:

> Designating a place of protection and care, the womb (*reḥem*) is a basic metaphor of divine compassion. The metaphor begins with a physical organ unique to the female and extends to psychic levels in the noun *reḥamim* (mercies), in the adjective form *raḥum* (merciful), and in the uses of the verb *raḥam* (to show mercy). It moves from the literal to the figurative, from the concrete to the abstract.[13]

A number of serious linguistic questions are here given very summary treatment. In the first place, we have no evidence whatsoever that any such metaphoric usage "begins" with "a physical organ unique to the female". In the absence of a well-documented process of semantic change, it is almost never possible to judge which uses of a word are "primitive" and which are "extended". The problem is, simply put, that even if we are able to establish a cognate relationship between two words, we have no way of knowing whether they are related as siblings—that is, both secondary derivations from a common parent—or as mother and daughter—that is, where one usage is more primitive and the second is an extension of the first. A fortiori, we cannot say *which* is mother and *which* daughter. Now, the etymology of the word under discussion is far from clear. With no argument or evidence to support her, Trible posits that *reḥem* as womb is the mother usage and *raḥum* as compassion is the daughter, the derived usage. But *reḥem* has also been compared with the Arabic word *raḥuma*,

[13] P. Trible, "God, Nature of in the OT", *Interpreter's Dictionary of the Bible* (Supp., 1976), pp. 368f.

meaning "it is soft". Given this semantic triad—womb/compassion/ soft—it is easy to see how any of the three could be the mother of the other two, and it is logically impossible, without historical textual evidence, to decide in favor of one possibility over another. Indeed, the tendency of analogous semantic shifts where we do have a well-attested history lengthens the odds that Trible has guessed right. The Semitic word for "liver" *can* be demonstrated to have been derived from the word meaning "heavy". (The liver is the heavy organ, just as in older English the lungs are called lights.) The analogy would put the meaning "soft" or "gentle" as primary and the organ word, womb, as derivative.

But the problems do not end here. Trible goes on to say:

> Distinctive in the Mosaic faith is the assertion that YHWH is merciful (*raḥum*) and gracious. Used only of the deity, *raḥum* is not language for a father who creates by begetting but for a mother who creates by nourishing in the womb.

Let us assume—what we have no logical grounds for doing— that Trible is right is taking *reḥem*-womb as primary and *reḥem*-compassion as derived. She makes two inferences from this premise: first, that the notion of "womb" was somehow before the minds of the authors who used the word for compassion; second, that the kind of compassion such authors imagined was specifically motherly. Is either inference justified?

The first inference is a classic instance of what is called the etymological fallacy—that is, that the earliest semantic value of a word is that word's *real* meaning, and this more real meaning somehow "shines through" all subsequent changes. This is patent nonsense. We can hoist Trible on her own petard by consideration of the relation between Greek *hystera,* "womb", and the English word "hysterical". This has none of the problems associated with the Hebrew words for womb and compassion, because we know the lexical history of hysterical. Yet we can be certain that, except for its use by pedants, the word "hysterical" when used by English speakers carries none of the more primitive semantic value of "womb", and a foreign scholar who thought otherwise would be writing nonsense. A word to the wise.

The second inference fares no better. Even if it were granted that the compassion of Hebrew *raḥum* were heard as womb compassion, must it be for that reason a motherly, womanly trait? By no means. Already by 1885 the scholar Theodor Nöldeke had proposed that the connection was one of brotherly, rather than motherly, love.[14] He compared to *raḥum* the Greek word *adelphos*, which is composed of alpha-copulative plus the word *delphus*, womb, and which means "he of the same womb" (Latin *frater uterinus*), a distinction that would have been important in a society in which concubinage was common. If the analogy holds, *raḥum* means not "mother love" but "philadelphia", which I think we all agree is a sobering thought.

Trible claims that the use of this word to attribute compassion to the deity is "distinctive" of the Mosaic religion. This is simply false. One scholar has collected fifty-two distinct Semitic personal names of sentence form, from a single people and period, that are composed of a divine name plus a form of the verb under discussion,[15] for example, Irimanni-Marduk, "Marduk is compassionate toward me." That alone is fatal to Trible's assertion, but it is still more interesting that, of these fifty-two names, only five designate a deity who is female. The fact that *rḥm* compassion was commonly entreated from or predicated of male deities in the Near East centuries before the biblical period shows that we should be cautious in our theological employment of speculative Semitic gynecology.

Trible, however, is not so easily dismayed. "Uteral speech", she says, "functions as a major symbol throughout the history of Israel. In this symbol, divine mercy is analogous to the womb of a mother." Our confidence does not increase when we see her at work as an exegete. She argues:

Jeremiah intensifies this [uteral] language in a poem replete with

[14] T. Nöldeke, review of W. Robertson Smith, *Kinship and Marriage in Early Arabia*, in zDMG 40 (1986): 151. For the etymology of *adelphos*, see P. Chantraine, *Dictionnaire etymologique de la langue grecque* (Paris: Klincksieck, 1968), pp. 194f.

[15] A. T. Clay, *Personal Names from Cuneiform Inscriptions of the Cassite Period* (New Haven, Conn.: Yale, 1912), pp. 194f.

female imagery (31:15–22). Over against Rachel's lament is the word of YHWH: "Is Ephraim my dear son? Is he my darling child? For as often as I speak of him, I remember him still. Therefore my inner parts yearn for him; I will surely have motherly compassion on him (*raḥem 'araḥmennu*) says the Lord" (31:20, author's trans.). As Rachel mourns the loss of the fruit of her womb [says Trible], so God yearns from her own inner parts.

The Hebrew-less reader with only Trible's article to hand would be led seriously astray here. Trible presents an artful antithesis wherein YHWH's compassion plays off against Rachel's mourning for "the fruit of her womb". But Rachel simply mourns "her sons" (*banim*), and Trible's rendering is, at best, tendentious in the extreme. Similarly, the word *mea*c, which Trible translates "inner parts" and connects with the womb, is used of both men and women as the belly, the seat of deep emotion. Jonah was carried in the *mea*c of the whale. Trible, significantly, neglects to mention this.

I pause here to explain why I think it important to tackle these issues in such detail. The scholarship I am trying to expose belongs not to the fringe but has provided the stock "database" for recent discussion about the biblical image of God. These are the arguments behind nonsexist translations of the Bible, which appear to be becoming a nonsexist version of our Catholic lectionary. These are the arguments behind changes in the liturgy to which the bishops responsible have proven all too receptive. These are the arguments behind a revolution in Christian theology and spirituality wherein "God our Mother" is to be invoked without a qualm. A Jesuit professor of theology in Cambridge, hardly a radical, opined recently that it is heresy to maintain that God could *not* be addressed as mother—a heresy that he claims will be declared explicitly in the next pontificate. Again, the arguments I am taking on are in the background of such an attitude. I beg you to believe that I am *not* belaboring the obvious but am working against what has become the conventional wisdom of mainstream academic theology.

With this apologia, let us move from womb-imagery to a more elevated subject: the breasts. Trible has this to say about the Biblical epithet of God as *'El Shaddai:*

Gen 49:25 parallels the God of the Fathers with the God Shaddai. These epithets balance masculine and feminine symbols. [The OT scholar Frank Moore] Cross holds that Shaddai had the original meaning of breasts, a meaning that is preserved here through paronomasia [that is, a play on words]. The God of the breasts gives the blessing of the breasts (*shadayim;* cf. Hos 9:14).

What Cross in fact says is "the epithet *šadday* proves to mean 'the mountain one' ".[16] He does *not* translate *'El Shadday* as "God of the breasts". While he takes "breast" as a primary and "mountain" as an extended meaning of *shadday,* he stops well short of saying that this meaning is "preserved" by the play on words. Indeed, the frequency with which other Semitic deities were styled as "the Lord of the mountain" or simply as "the Mountain" makes the proposed semantic connection even more remote. YHWH is God of the mountains much as He is the Lord of hosts: what is represented is not an iconic attribute but an area of dominion.

A feminine God, then, had no place in the religion of the Hebrews. But it is easy to make the evidence say too little or too much. The stupidity of idolaters in trying to make images of their own gods is almost incomprehensible to Israel; a fortiori it would be perverse to attribute characteristics of physical humanity to YHWH. We are not surprised that the Bible absolutely excludes sexuality from its conception of God. But this is not the whole story. Notwithstanding the insistence of the OT on the incomparability of God to man and its abhorrence of suggesting physical features of gender apply to Him, it is not therefore equivocal about His iconology. God is not sometimes "He" and sometimes "She". God is not a brother in some personal names and a sister in others. The name YHWH does not govern masculine verbs in J documents and feminine forms in P. The testimony of Israel is as clear on the masculinity of God as it is that this masculinity is utterly remote from biology, from sexuality however conceived. With this caveat before us, we can proceed to examine that fatherhood that Israel attributed to God.

---

[16] F. M. Cross, *Canaanite Myth and Hebrew Epic* (Cambridge, Mass.: Harvard Press, 1973), p. 55.

THE FATHERHOOD OF YHWH: BIBLICAL EVIDENCE

The question of the fatherhood of God is, of course, an entirely distinct question from that of His masculinity, since one can admit the former and not the latter, and I have tried not to blur the distinction. The treatment of the fatherhood of YHWH by the OT should be seen against the background of the polytheistic mythologies that surrounded it, wherein potency and fertility were ritually divinized and the gods were portrayed as frankly sexual beings who lust, mate, give birth, and enjoy the prerogatives of parenthood—all of which Israel is loath to attribute to its God. For all that, we do find in the religion of Israel—from the earliest stages on—a clear, limited, and very precise confession of the fatherhood of YHWH. It is, in fact, a *primary* datum of OT belief.

I do not have the time to give full-dress arguments for what follows, though I believe such arguments are important and the evidence in their favor is ample. What I offer are conclusions, not the scaffolding for what purports to be a demonstration.

The OT is careful to remove YHWH from any notion of father as physical progenitor. The fatherhood of YHWH is, rather, *supervenient;* that is, YHWH comes upon an already existent Israel and gratuitously, deliberately, lovingly, *makes* Israel into His firstborn son. Israel comes into being as a people in the event of the exodus, when God says to Moses, "You shall say to Pharaoh, 'Thus says YHWH, Israel is my firstborn son, and I say to you, let my son go that he may serve me'" (Ex 4:22–23). God's fatherhood is supervenient because it *intrudes* into the history of an already living body; it is inceptive of a profoundly new relationship.

The imagination of Israel is irrevocably marked by the power of this encounter: unsought, undeserved, unlikely—were there not larger and stronger and wealthier nations? Yet YHWH *chose* Israel for His own. Even in prophetic remonstrance over the apostasy of Israel, this astonishment at the tenderness of YHWH's soliticitude is patent. So Hosea 11:

> When Israel was a child, I loved him,
> And out of Egypt I called my son. . . .

> It was I who taught Ephraim to walk,
> I took them up in my arms;
> But they did not know that I healed them.

Here again it is the election of Israel, an election beyond hope or expectation, that provides the basis for the prophet's rebuke. The picture here, I believe, is not of a father teaching his own infant son to take his first steps but of one who is helping an injured youth, most probably a slave lamed by mistreatment, to regain the power to walk. God comes upon Israel enslaved in Egypt the way a man walking in the countryside might come upon a young beaten slave, whom he nurses and takes to his bosom as a son. Fatherhood is a finding, a purely gratuitous extension of partiality: "Out of Egypt I called my son."

The evidence from the onomasticon ought to prove an embarrassment to anyone unwilling to acknowledge that YHWH was seen as a father, in some sense, in ancient Israel. The scholar Jeffrey Tigay has well expressed why this evidence is important:

> The use of personal names as evidence of religious belief presupposes that their meaning was understood and intended at least to some extent. This is sometimes doubted by scholars, probably because in the modern Western world names are frequently not understood because they did not originate in the language or dialect of those who use them. But in preexilic Israel most personal names were in Biblical Hebrew and could be understood by any Israelite. Even if factors extraneous to meaning—such as fashion, tradition, or aesthetics—may have influenced some parents' choice of names, what is important for present purposes is that the divine name within Hebrew theophorous names [that is, a personal name which itself contains the name of a god] could not have gone unrecognized. Sensitivity to the theophoric element was so great in Israel that in later times scribes felt compelled to change names that seemed pagan in manuscripts of Samuel, and perhaps of Chronicles as well.[17]

[17] J. Tigay, "Israelite Religion: The Onomastic and Epigraphic Evidence", in P. D. Miller, P. Hanson, and S. McBride, eds., *Ancient Israelite Religion: Essays in Honor of Frank Moore Cross* (Philadelphia: Fortress Press, 1987), p. 159.

We have already noted that names compounded with the word for "mother" are entirely missing from the Hebrew onomasticon. What we do find is that the name *'abiyya,* "YHWH is my father", is used of eight individuals in the OT, including two women. In addition, three persons bear the name Joab, *Yo'ab,* "YHWH is father." And since there is no instance in the OT where a clear awareness of 'El as a Canaanite deity distinct from YHWH is manifest, we are on firm ground in enlisting the 'El- names as additional support for the attribution of divine fatherhood. Thus we can add *'eli'ab,* which is used of five persons, and *'abi'el,* used of one. As for the meaning of fatherhood in these names, I suggest that the notions of patronage and partiality evidenced by such names as "My father is help" and "My father is deliverance" supply the semantic content of divine fatherhood.

CONCLUSIONS

The loudest silence of the OT is in the absence of a consort for YHWH. He is utterly alone. Surely YHWH's solitude is the most immediately remarkable and distinctive thing about Him, given the rampant polytheism of the Near East. Surely His masculinity is iconologically beyond question, and, since YHWH is also a creator, surely a female partner in creation—the one to be acted upon—is called for in the Semitic worldview; it is almost a conceptual necessity. It is a remarkable fact about the religious genius of Israel that it convinces us so totally about YHWH's maleness at the same time that it convinces us that He is "beyond sexuality". It is the unique circumstances of YHWH's fatherhood in which this is accomplished. He becomes a father not by approaching a woman but by electing a son, an election that in virtue of itself *creates* the son.

The fatherhood of YHWH is thus also a kind of creation, but it is a creation that shatters and completely replaces the sexual creation metaphor. "Thus says YHWH, Israel is my firstborn son." It is not surprising that, when Israel did begin to speculate about cosmogony, the beginning of the world was pictured not as the sowing of seed or the bursting of a ripe womb but as election, the deliberate and benevolent creation of order out of chaos. The fatherhood of God is effected not by chance but by choice, not by lust but by unhoped-for love.

This paper has principally been an exercise in demolition; I have attempted to knock apart for your benefit four grandiose but harmful constructions: that the masculinity of God was a cultural imperative, that the sacred authors were theologically naïve, that the OT shows us a hermaphroditic God, and that the idea of God as Father is a feature of late Galilean piety. When engineers drop really large buildings, they do not bring out the bulldozers but place small explosive charges at the critical junctures, the places where things are tied together. So too I have tried to use philology—the science of how language ties things together—to explode individually the impostures that have held these mental constructs together. The work can be painstaking, even tedious, but when all goes well, the building comes down like a house of cards. The end is not demolition for its own sake but that theology might have a level ground on which to build, so that a faith seeking understanding might encounter in the Sacred Scriptures, not the resentments spawned by our own age, but the unalloyed love of Him whom we seek with minds and hearts. And besides, if we are going to talk about the Bible, why not get it right?

APPENDIX A

THEOPHOROUS BIBLICAL NAMES
COMPOUNDED WITH *'ab*

Name	Identification	Reference
'abi	M of Hezekiah (FN)	2 Chron 29:1
'abi'el	GF of Saul	1 Sam 9:1
'abiyya	1. S of Samuel	1 Sam 8:2
	2. S of Jeroboam	1 Kings 14:1
	3. M of Hezekiah (FN)	2 Kings 18:2
	4. Priest	Neh 12:4
	5. W of Hezron (FN)	1 Chron 2:24
	6. Benjaminite	1 Chron 7:8
	7. S of Rehoboam	1 Chron 24:10
	8. Priest	2 Chron 11:20
'eli'ab	1. Zabulonite	Nb 1:9
	2. F of Dathan	Nb 16:1
	3. B of David	1 Sam 16:6
	4. Warrior	1 Chron 12:9
	5. Levite	1 Chron 15:8
yo'ab	1. Warrior	1 Sam 26:6
	2. Judahite	1 Chron 4:14
	3. S of Pahath-moab	Ezra 2:6

APPENDIX B

SELECTED LIST OF BIBLICAL NAMES
COMPOUNDED WITH 'ab

Name	Lexicology	Reference
'abi'asaph	My father has gathered	Ex 6:24
'abida'	My father knows	Gen 25:4
'abidan	My father is judge	Nb 1:11
'abi'ezer	My father is succor	Nb 26:30
'abigayil (FN)	My father exults (?)	1 Sam 25:14
'abihayil (FN)	My father is might	Nb 3:35
'abihud	My father is majesty	1 Chron 8:3
'abimelek	My father is king	Gen 20:2
'abinadab	My father is noble	1 Sam 7:1
'abino'am	My father is delight	Jg 4:6
'abiram	My father is exalted	Nb 16:1
'abishalom	My father is peace	2 Sam 3:3
'abishua'	My father is deliverance	1 Chron 8:4
'abishur	My father is a rampart	1 Chron 2:28
'abital (FN)	My father is dew	2 Sam 3:4
'abitob	My father is goodness	1 Chron 8:11
'abram	Exalted father (?)	Gen 11:26
'abyatar	The Great One is father (?)	1 Sam 22:20

BIBLIOGRAPHY

Ahlstrom, G. *Psalm 89.* Lund: Haakan Ohlssons, 1959.

Albright, W. F. "Northwest Semitic Names in a List of Egyptian Slaves from the Eighteenth Century B.C." *JAOS* 74 (1954): 222–33.

———. *Yahweh and the Gods of Canaan.* New York: Doubleday, 1968.

Avalos, H. "Biblical Feminine Names in the Light of Northwest Semitic Onomastics." Unpublished seminar paper, Harvard NELC, 1987.

Benz, F. L. *Personal Names in the Phoenician and Punic Inscriptions.* Studia Pohl 8. Rome: Biblical Institute Press, 1972.

Bird, P. "The Place of Women in the Israelite Cultus". In P. D. Miller, P. Hanson, and S. McBride, eds., *Ancient Israelite Religion: Essays in Honor of Frank Moore Cross.* Philadelphia: Fortress Press, 1987, pp. 397–419.

Chantraine, P. *Dictionnaire etymologique de la langue grecque.* Paris: Klincksieck, 1968.

Clay, A. T. *Personal Names from Cuneiform Inscriptions of the Cassite Period.* YOS 1, New Haven, Conn.: Yale, 1912.

Clines, D. J. A. "X, X ben Y, ben Y: Personal Names in Hebrew Narrative Style". *VT* 22 (1972): 266–85.

Coogan, M. "The Use of Second Person Singular Verbal Forms in Northwest Semitic Personal Names". *Orientalia* 44 (1975): 194–97.

———. *West Semitic Personal Names in the Murašu Documents.* HSM 7. Missoula, Mt.: Scholars Press, 1976.

———. *Stories from Ancient Canaan.* Philadelphia: Westminster, 1978.

Cross, F. M. *Canaanite Myth and Hebrew Epic.* Cambridge, Mass.: Harvard Press, 1973.

Eissfeldt, O. *"Adhon".* In *Theological Dictionary of the Old Testament.* Vol. 1. Grand Rapids, Mich.: William Eerdmans, 1974, pp. 59–72.

Engnell, I. *Studies in Divine Kingship.* Uppsala: Almqvist and Wiksells, 1943.

Fitzmyer, J. "Abba and Jesus' Relation to God". In *A Cause de l'Evangile: Etudes sur les Synoptiques et les Actes. Lectio Divina* 123, Paris: Cerf, 1985, pp. 15–38.

Fowler, J. D. *Theophoric Personal Names in Ancient Hebrew.* JSOT Supp. 49, Sheffield: *JSOT,* 1987.

Freedman, D., and F. Andersen. *Hosea.* Garden City, N.Y.: Anchor Bible, 1980.

Gesenius, W. *Hebrew Grammar.* Ed. E. Kautzsch, rev. and trans. A. E. Cowley. Oxford: Clarendon, 1910.

Grapow, H. *Die bildlichen Ausdrücke des Ägyptischen.* Darmstadt: Wissenschaftliche Buchgesellschaft, 1983.

Gray, G. B. *Studies in Hebrew Proper Names.* London: Black, 1896.

Grondahl, F. *Die Personennamen der Texte aus Ugarit.* Studia Pohl 1. Rome: Pontifical Biblical Institute, 1967.

Herdner, A. *Corpus des tablettes cunéiformes alphabétiques découvertes à Ras Shamra-Ugarit* I/II (*CTA*). Imprimerie Nationale. Paris: P. Guethner, 1963.

Hess, R. S. "Personal Names from Amarna: Alternative Readings and Interpretation". *UF* 17 (1985): 157–87.

Huffmon, H. *Amorite Personal Names in the Mari Texts: A Structural and Lexical Study.* Baltimore: Johns Hopkins Press, 1965.

Jacobsen, T. *The Treasures of Darkness.* New Haven, Conn.: Yale Press, 1976.

Jouon, P. *Grammaire de l'hébreu biblique.* Rome: Institut Biblique Pontifical, 1923.

Kerber, G. *Die religionsgeschichtliche Bedeutung der hebräische Eigennamen im AT.* Freiburg: Mohr, 1897.

Key, A. F. "The Giving of Proper Names in the Old Testament". *JBL* 83 (1964): 55–59.

Lagrange, M. J. "La Paternité de Dieu dans l'AT". *RB* 5 (1908): 481–99.

Lawton, R. B. "Israelite Personal Names on Pre-exilic Hebrew Inscriptions". *Biblica* 65 (1984): 330–46.

Lipinski, E. *Studies in Aramaic Inscriptions and Onomastics I.* Orientalia Lovanensia Analecta, 1. Leuven University Press, 1975.

Lohr, Max. *Die Stellung des Weibes zu Jahwe-Religion und -Kult* Leipzig: J. C. Hinrichs, 1908.

Mayer, R. "Der Gottesname Jahwe im Lichte der neuesten Forschung". *BZ* n.s. 2 (1958).

Miller, P. D., P. Hanson, and S. McBride, eds. *Ancient Israelite Religion: Essays in Honor of Frank Moore Cross.* Philadelphia: Fortress Press, 1987.

Nestle, E. *Die Israelitischen Eigennamen.* Haarlem: Bohn, 1876.

Nöldeke, T. Review of W. Robertson Smith, *Kinship and Marriage in Early Arabia,* in *ZDMG* 40 (1886): 148–87.

Noth, M. *Die Israelitische Personennamen im Rahmen der gemeinsemitischen Namengebung*. Stuttgart: Kohlhammer, 1928.

———. "Mari und Israel: Eine Personennamenstudie". In *Beiträge zur historischen Theologie* 16. Tubingen: Mohr, 1953.

Ohana, M., and M. Heltzer. *The Extra-Biblical Tradition of Hebrew Personal Names*. Haifa: University of Haifa, 1978.

Peritz, I. "Women in the Ancient Hebrew Cult". *JBL* 17 (1898).

Pritchard, J. *Ancient Near Eastern Texts Relating to the Old Testament. ANET.* Princeton, N.J.: Princeton University Press, 1955.

von Rad, G. *Old Testament Theology*. Trans. D. M. G. Stalker. New York: Harper and Bros., 1962.

Ringgren, H. "'abh". In *Theological Dictionary of the Old Testament*. Grand Rapids, Mich.: Eerdmans, 1974, pp. 1–19.

———. "'elohim". In *Theological Dictionary of the Old Testament*. Grand Rapids, Mich.: Eerdmans, 1974, pp. 267–84.

Schult, H. *Vergleichende Studien zur alttestamentlichen Namenkünde*. Bobb: Rheinische Friedrich-Wilhelms Universität, 1967.

Silverman, M. H. "Aramaic Name-Types in the Elephantine Documents". *JAOS* 89 (1969): 691–709.

———. "Hebrew Name-Types in the Elephantine Documents". *Orientalia* 39 (1970): 465–91.

———. "Servant ('ebed) Names in Aramaic and Other Semitic Languages". *JAOS* 100 (1980): 361–66.

———. "Biblical Name-Lists and the Elephantine Onomasticon: A Comparison". *Orientalia* 50 (1981): 265–331.

———. *Religious Values in the Jewish Proper Names at Elephantine*. AOAT 217, Neukirchen-Vluyn: Neukirchener Verlag, 1985.

von Soden, W. *Akkadisches Handwörterbuch*. Wiesbaden: Otto Harrassowitz, 1972.

Stamm, J. J. *Die akkadische Namengebung. MVAG* 44, Leipzig: Hinrichs, 1939.

———. *Beiträge zur hebräischen und altorientalischen Namenkünde*. Göttingen: Vandenhoeck and Ruprecht, 1980.

Tigay, J. *You Shall Have No Other Gods: Israelite Religion in the Light of Hebrew Inscriptions*. HSS 31, Atlanta: Schwartz, 1986.

———. "Israelite Religion: The Onomastic and Epigraphic Evidence". In P. D. Miller, P. Hanson, and S. McBride, eds., *Ancient Israelite Religion: Essays in Honor of Frank Moore Cross*. Philadelphia: Fortress Press, 1987.

Trible, P. "God, Nature of in the OT". *Interpreter's Dictionary of the Bible.* Supp., 1976, pp. 368–69.

Winter, Urs. *Frau und Göttin: Exegetische und ikonographische Studien zum weiblichen Gottesbild im Alten Israel und in dessen Umwelt.* Göttingen: Vandenhoeck and Ruprecht, 1983.

A FEMINIST PSALTER?

Chrysostom Castel, O.C.S.O.

In recent years an escalating feminist ideology concerned with equal rights and dignity for women has affected nearly all areas of secular and Church society. Instances of discrimination in both these milieus can be found which justify this feminist concern and require rectification. In secular society, e.g., one could cite unequal job opportunities and unfair pay scales. While in the society of the Church, women are sometimes prevented from equally sharing their talents in the ministry of the Gospel or in the administration of parish life.

There are other areas, however, such as the whole complex question of language, where feminists allege discrimination but where often none in fact exists or was ever intended. And until recently, in this as in other areas, feminists seemed to offer a unified front in presenting themselves as representative of the consensus of all women, or at least the majority, in their grievances against the Church. Surprisingly, however, there have now emerged several organized women's groups, national and international, within the Church who are vigorously disclaiming association with or any representation by the feminist movement and its agenda for the Church. The fact that this emergence is inspired not by "male chauvinism" but arises spontaneously from the concerns of women themselves has seriously questioned and undermined the validity of many feminist grievances.

One of the areas already mentioned which these non-feminist women's groups contest and claim as misrepresented by the feminists is that of language—the area with which this article will be particularly concerned. Specifically, it is the question of the generic-inclusive use of terms such as "man/men/mankind" and their pronominal substitutes. Although the majority of today's literati (e.g., poets, journalists, playwrights, etc.) continue to regard and employ these terms as inclusive of women in their traditional generic sense,[1] feminists still insist that such usage excludes women and must be expurgated from the language. Non-feminist women's groups, on the contrary, vigorously contest this allegation and claim they do not feel excluded by these terms but rather affirm their continuing validity as generically inclusive. The antiquity of this inclusive meaning has been well documented in fact in an important article by Suzanne Scorsone who

[1] David Littlejohn, Professor of Journalism; Chairman, Committee on Senate Policy, University of California, Berkeley (Letter to Roderic B. Park, Vice Chancellor, April 30, 1985), p. 1. The following excerpts are taken from this letter responding to Roderic B. Park's concerned letter to Professor Littlejohn regarding an admonition from the U.S. Department of Education's Civil Rights Division to the University of California, Berkeley. This admonition advised the omission of terms like "man, men, mankind" in the University's catalog of courses. Excerpts of Professor Littlejohn's reply follows:

I have circulated the March 4, 1985, letter . . . from the U.S. Department of Education . . . , for comments to a number of leading journalists, editors, and others for whom the correct and sensitive use in the English language is a daily professional responsibility. I then compared current standards of usage given in the style books of the *New York Times,* the *Washington Post,* the *Los Angeles Times,* and United Press International.

The Consensus Response

Every professional authority, and many of the individuals consulted, . . . without exception, regarded the use of "man" or "mankind" for humanity in general (and such time-honored terms as "the common man", "man in the street", and "manmade") as sanctioned by historical usage, universally understood to encompass males and females, and resisted by certain militant feminists on what can only be considered as political grounds. "The traditional forms often carry desirable nuances of meaning" (*Los Angeles Times Stylebook*). "Traditional forms are in many cases more appropriate" (*Washington Post Deskbook on Style*). The argument against the long-accepted universal use of "man" and "mankind" is political, not linguistic or logical. It may be compared to the mandated universal use of "comrade" (or the abandoning of titles) in "classless" societies. [*Signed:* David Littlejohn.]

equally contests this feminist allegation.[2] And indeed, these non-feminist women have actively urged great caution on the Holy See and the U.S. Bishops to beware of a precipitous approval of any liturgical changes of language influenced solely by the feminist ideology. They contend that not only do they not feel excluded by the generic use of these terms, as we said, but that further: as members of the Church, they have a right to an unadulterated and faithful transmission of the Liturgy and the Scriptures.

This countermovement of non-feminist women, however, seems to have had little bearing on the revision of the popular Grail Psalter we will be considering here. Apparently influenced wholly and solely by the feminist optic of "sexist" language, the Grail translators have revised their original 1963 edition[3] in an "Inclusive Language" version conforming to feminist lingo.[4] This revised Grail version has even appeared now in a handsomely bound calligraphy edition produced by the Cistercian nuns of the monastery of Glencairn in Ireland.[5]

It is important to note, however, that this 1983/1986 "Inclusive Language" Psalter has not been approved for liturgical use either by the U.S. bishops or by the Holy See. Although submitted to them for approval as an alternate liturgical Psalter, the U.S. bishops did not accept the new Grail revision because of the

> lack of clarity concerning which psalms were messianic in character, either in themselves or in the exegesis given such psalms in traditional liturgical usage, and whether such psalms should or could be revised for inclusive language.[6]

---

[2] "In the Image of God: Male, Female, and the Language of Liturgy", by Suzanne Scorsone, *Communio* 16, no. 1 (Spring 1989): 139–51.

[3] *The Psalms,* The Grail (England), A Fontana Book, 1963.

[4] *The Grail Psalms: An Inclusive Language Version,* The Grail (England) (G.I.A. Publications Inc., 7404 S. Mason Avenue, Chicago, IL 60638, 1983, 1986).

[5] *Psalms and Canticles* [*The Grail Psalms: An Inclusive Language Version*] (Conference Book Service, 55 Waltham Tce. Blackrock, Co. Dublin, Ireland, 1988).

[6] "The Revised Grail Psalter", Statement of Archbishop Pilarczyk, *Bishops' Committee on the Liturgy Newsletter,* 21 (Apr. 1985): 13.

Consequently, Grail's "Inclusive Language" Psalter has also not been approved by the Holy See for liturgical use in the United States, nor indeed anywhere else.

[When this essay first appeared it was believed the feminist language *Grail Psalter* was a dead issue as it had been rejected by the Vatican. Apparently it has been resuscitated. In the report from the U.S. Bishops' Committee on the Liturgy, which appeared in the documentation for the November 1991 meeting of the NCCB, we read the following: "The Liturgy Committee agreed to reexamine the revised *Grail Psalter (Inclusive Language Version)* and will establish a mechanism to recommend to the publisher changes required by the *Criteria for the Evaluation of Inclusive Language Translations* which the NCCB approved last November. *Once all problems have been satisfactorily resolved, the Committee will recommend that the NCCB authorize this version of the psalter for liturgical use*", (emphasis added).

[Later on the same page we find: "Finally, the Liturgy Committee took note of P.S. (Position Statement) 1990 E on the use of a variety of images when speaking of God." Evidently, the translators and publishers have far too much invested in these projects to be willing to abandon them simply because the Vatican disapproves or rejects the Commitee's efforts. So far, there is no sign that this process, which has been so highly effective in coercing the bishops and the Holy See to capitulate to the demands of contemporary reformers will be unsuccessful.— Ed.]

In what follows, we would like to determine whether the reservations of the U.S. bishops concerning this feminist version of the Grail Psalter are substantiated. The next part of this article will be concerned therefore with sampling a group of psalms from the first part of the Psalter, in which typically altered verses from the revised Grail will be compared with the earlier Grail version. The pertinent verses from the 1963 Original Grail [OG] will first be given, with the altered words underscored. This will be followed, in italics, by the revised 1983/1986 Feminist Grail version [FG] of the same verses, with the correspondingly altered words underscored. Next will follow any relevant New Testament and/or Patristic citations, or liturgical uses, indicating the traditional Christian and liturgical exegesis of these verses. New Testament texts will be taken from the Catholic Revised Standard Version, while Patristic citations will be taken largely from Dom Claude Jean-Nesmy's collection of Patristic texts on the Psalms: *La Tradition médite le Psautier chrétien* [=TPC].[7] Other sources, when cited, will be identified in their place.

PSALM 1

[OG]: 1a—
   "Happy indeed is the man
   who follows not the counsel of the wicked . . . "
[FG]: 1a-
   "Happy indeed are those
   who follow not the counsel of the wicked . . . "
ORIGEN: "What better beginning for the Psalter than this prophecy and this praise of the Perfect Man in the Savior!" [TPC, 2a:15].
EUSEBIUS: "Every man desires bliss; that is why this first psalm describes 'He who' is truly happy. The first blissful One is the Savior. This psalm concerns Him who is the 'Bridegroom' of His Church."
AUGUSTINE: "Jesus Christ 'had not gone off following the way of the Wicked One', He refused an earthly kingdom, while the Rebel had wanted to raise his throne in the North" [TPC, 2a:17].
[OG]: 3—
   "He is like a tree that is planted
   beside the flowing waters,
   That yields its fruit in due season
   and whose leaves shall never fade;
   And all that he does shall prosper . . . "

---

[7] *La Tradition médite le Psautier chrétien,* by Dom Claude Jean-Nesmy (Paris: Editions Tequi, 1973), vol. 2a.

[*FG*]: 3—

> *"They are like a tree that is planted*
> *beside the flowing waters,*
> *That yields its fruit in due season and*
> *whose leaves shall never fade;*
> *And all that they do shall prosper. . . . "*

EUSEBIUS: "The tree is at once the Son of God (near the rivers, that is, the Divine Scriptures which announce Him) and the just man who, always attached to the Divine Law, is irrigated by all the spiritual rivers" [TPC, 2a:19].

HILARION: "The tree of life is Christ . . . " [TPC, 2a:19].

GREGORY THE GREAT: "In Holy Scripture the tree symbolizes sometimes the Cross, sometimes man (just or unjust), and sometimes incarnate Wisdom" [TPC, 2a:19].

RUPERT OF DEUTZ: "Job says (14:7–9) in announcing Christ: 'The tree has a hope: If it is cut down it grows green again and its branches are multiplied.' What is this tree if not that very one which at the moment it was being cut down said: 'If they do this to the green tree, what will be done to the dry?' If it is 'cut down it grows green again'—we understand here the third day: the Resurrection" [TPC, 2a:20].

HIPPOLYTUS: "In place of the wood (the forbidden tree of Paradise), this wood (the Cross) takes root. In place of the sinful woman's hand once put forth with impiety, it stretches forth with piety its immaculate hand, showing thus of itself that truly life is hung on the tree. . . . We eat of it and we do not die" [TPC, 2a:21].

PSALM 3

[OG]: 3b–4, 6—

> "There is no help for him in God. But you, Lord, are a shield about me, my glory, who lift up my head. . . . I lie down to rest and I sleep. I wake, for the Lord upholds me."

[*FG*]: 3b–4, 6—

> *"No help will come from God.*

But you, Lord, are a shield about me,
my glory, who lift up my head. . . .
I lie down to rest and I sleep.
I wake, for the Lord upholds me."

IRENAEUS: "The Spirit of Christ says now through David: 'I lie down to rest and I sleep. I wake . . . ' He calls death a sleep because He will be resuscitated" [TPC, 2a:31].

GREGORY OF NYSSA: "Through a sudden illumination of the Spirit, the prophet receives a revelation of the Mystery of the Passion, puts on the very person of the Lord and exclaims: 'I lie down to rest and I sleep. I wake . . . ' " [TPC, 2a:32].

ORIGEN: "It is Christ who speaks, knowing that the Father 'will uphold' Him and exalt Him as Philippians 2:9 says" [TPC, 2a:33].

AUGUSTINE: " . . . this Psalm is to be understood in the Person of Christ. . . . It is clear that if they had any idea that He would rise again, assuredly they would not have slain Him. . . . Therefore, neither would Judas have betrayed Him, if he had not been of the number of those who despised Christ, saying, "There is no salvation for Him in His God' " [*Enarrationes in Psalmos,* PL 36:67ff.].

PSALM 7

[OG]: 2b —
"From my <u>pursuer</u> save me and rescue me
lest <u>he</u> tear me to pieces like a lion . . . "
6a —
"then let my <u>foe</u> pursue me and seize me,
let <u>him</u> trample my life to the ground."
[*FG*]: 2b —
"From my <u>pursuers</u> save me and rescue me
lest <u>they</u> tear me to pieces like a lion"
6a —
"Then let my <u>foes</u> pursue me and seize me,
let <u>them</u> trample my life to the ground."

GREGORY OF NYSSA: "The psalm announces the Resurrection of

the Lord and the mystery of His Passion. . . . The Enemy is one
by nature, but he multiplies himself by his lieutenants and his
delegates" [TPC, 2a:53].

AUGUSTINE: "It is Christ who speaks. . . . 'Let him trample my
life': the foe is the serpent. . . . The patience of David announces
the Passion of Christ" [TPC, 2a:53, 54].

RUPERT OF DEUTZ: "Christ prays in His Passion" [TPC, 2a:54].

[OG]: 15–17—
"Here <u>is one who is</u> pregnant with malice,
<u>conceives</u> evil and brings forth lies,
He <u>digs</u> a pitfall, digs it deep;
and in the trap <u>he has</u> made <u>he</u> will fall.
<u>His</u> malice will recoil on <u>himself</u>;
on <u>his</u> own head <u>his</u> violence will fall."

[FG]: 15–17—
"Here <u>are enemies</u> pregnant with malice, <u>who conceive</u> evil and
brings forth lies,
<u>They dig</u> a pitfall, <u>dig</u> it deep;
and in the trap they have made <u>they will fall</u>
<u>Their</u> malice will recoil on <u>themselves</u>;
on <u>their</u> own head <u>their</u> violence will fall."

ORIGEN: "It is a question of the devil" [TPC, 2a:54].

EUSEBIUS: "It is a matter of the traitor" [TPC, 2a:54].

ATHANASIUS: "It is the enemy of our life" [TPC, 2a:54].

AUGUSTINE: "The trap is prepared by the devil for Christ" [TPC,
2a:54].

JEROME: "The Serpent is crushed to the earth" [TPC, 2a:54].

AUGUSTINE: "He [the devil] becomes a slave again" [TPC, 2a:54].

PSALM 8

[OG]: 5–7—
"What is <u>man</u> that you should keep <u>him</u> in mind,
mortal <u>man</u> [Lit.: "son of man"] that you care for <u>him</u>?
Yet you have made <u>him</u> little less than <u>a god</u>;
with glory and honor you crowned <u>him</u>.

Gave <u>him</u> power over the works of your hand,
put all things under <u>his</u> feet.
[*FG*]: 5–7–
"What are <u>we</u> that you should keep <u>us</u> in mind?
<u>*men and women,*</u> *that you care for <u>us</u>*
Yet you have made <u>us</u> little less than gods;
and crowned <u>us</u> with glory and honor.
Gave <u>us</u> power over the work of your hand,
put all things under <u>our</u> feet."

NEW TEST.: " 'What is man that thou art mindful of him, or the
son of man, that thou carest for him? Thou didst make him for a
little while lower than the angels, thou hast crowned him with
glory and honor, putting everything in subjection under his
feet.' Now in putting everything in subjection to him, he left
nothing outside his control. As it is, we do not yet see everything in subjection to him. But we see Jesus, who for a little
while was made lower than the angels, crowned with glory and
honor because of the suffering of death..."
[Heb 2:6–9 RSV].

"For [Christ] must reign until [God] has put all his enemies
under his feet. The last enemy to be destroyed is death. 'For
God has put all things in subjection under his feet' " [1 Cor
15:25–27 RSV] "...and [God] has put all things under his feet
and has made him the head over all things for the Church..."
[Eph 1:22 RSV].

"...we await a Savior, the Lord Jesus Christ, who will change
our lowly body to be like his glorious body, by the power
which enables him even to subject all things to himself" [Phil
3:21 RSV].

IRENAEUS: "After the Passion of Christ and His Ascension, God
put all his adversaries under His feet, and he was elevated above
all" [TPC, 2a:55].

ORIGEN: "Glory and honor applies first of all to Christ..."
[TPC, 2a:56].

CYRIL OF ALEXANDRIA: "It is a question of Christ, crowned
with glory in so far as He is man; therefore we also are crowned
with Him" [TPC, 2a:56].

PSALM 13

[OG]: 6—

"You may mock the poor man's hope, but his refuge is the Lord."

[FG]: 6—

"You may mock the hope of the poor,
but their refuge is the Lord."

JEROME: "The Counsel [= Grail's 'hope'] of the Poor Man is the plan of Christ who, rich as He was, became poor to enrich us" [TPC, 2a:68].

AUGUSTINE: "This Counsel [= Grail's 'hope'] is the coming of the Son of God for the redemption of the world. Through His humble coming, He wanted to make those called put their hope in God alone, not in earthly things" [TPC, 2a:68].

BEDE: "The Counsel [= Grail's 'hope'] of the ancient disposition, of the new regeneration, of eternal happiness. You had wanted to confound the coming of Christ, because the Lord was His hope: He did not present Himself with the pomp of the power-ful of this world" [TPC, 2a:68].

PSALM 14

[OG]: 2–5—

"He who walks without fault
he who acts with justice
And speaks the truth from his heart;
he who does not slander with his tongue;
He who does no wrong to his brother,
who casts no slur on his neighbor,
Who holds the godless in disdain,
but honors those who fear the Lord;
He who keeps his pledge come what may;
who takes no interest on a loan
And accepts no bribes against the innocent,
such a man will stand firm forever."

[FG]: 2–5 —

> "*Those* who walk without fault,
> *those* who *act* with justice
> And *speak* the truth from *their hearts*,
> *those* who *do* not slander with *their* tongue,
> *Those* who *do* no wrong to *their kindred*,
> who *cast* no slur on *their neighbors*,
> Who *hold* the godless in disdain,
> but *honor* those who fear the Lord;
> *Those* who keep *their word*, come what may,
> who *take* no interest on a loan
> And *accept* no bribes against the innocent,
> such *people* will stand firm for ever."

BERNARD: "One alone among the sons of men has entered without spot into this life: the Emmanuel. And for our sakes He was clothed with curses" [TPC, 2a:70].

ROMAN LITURGY: "*Christ* is the perfect and the just Man par excellence (v. 2). God welcomes Him for ever (v. 5c) under His tent (v. 1a) and upon His holy mountain (v. 1b), because He has passed through the mountain of Calvary (v. 1): Cf. *Matins of Holy Saturday;* Ant. v. 2b, 1.[8]

PSALM 15

(This Messianic psalm, traditionally interpreted as a prayer of Christ to His Father—as witnessed by New Testament citations, the Fathers of the Church and the Liturgy—has been rewritten by [FG] in verses 3, 7 and 8 in the second person. Clearly this is to avoid third person masculine references to God as it stands in [OG] and the Hebrew and is therefore an obvious departure

[8] *Le Psautier de la Bible de Jerusalem,* by Didier Rimaud, S.J., and Joseph Gelineau, S.J. (Les Editions du Cerf, 29, Boulevard de Latour–Maubourg, Paris, 1955), p. 48. [Although this work refers to the pre–Vatican II structure of the Roman Breviary, it is an excellent source book for the traditional liturgical exegesis of the Messianic Christology in the psalms and could have been cited for all of the psalms treated in this article.]

from and rejection of Christ's own manner of addressing God in masculine terms, which Scripture and Tradition have always followed.)

[OG]: 3—

"He has put into my heart a marvelous love
for the faithful ones who dwell in his land.
Those who choose other gods increase their sorrows."

[FG]: 23—

"You have put into my heart a marvelous love
for the faithful ones who dwell in your land.
Those who choose other gods increase their sorrows."

[OG]: 7–8—

"I will bless the Lord who gives me counsel,
who even at night directs my heart.
I keep the Lord ever in my sight:
since he is at my right hand, I shall stand firm."

[FG]: 7–8—

"I will bless you, Lord, you give me counsel,
and even at night direct my heart,
I keep you, Lord, ever in my sight;
since you are at my right hand, I shall stand firm."

NEW TEST.: "For David says concerning [Christ], 'I saw the Lord always before me, for he is at my right hand that I may not be shaken. . . .'" [Acts 2:25–28 RSV]

ORIGEN: "Christ speaks through the prophet . . ." [TPC, 2a:71]

ATHANASIUS: "Christ speaks in the name of the whole human race, of His Church which is His flesh." [TPC, 2a:71]

AUGUSTINE: "Christ came into the transitory, but He never detached His gaze from the Eternal: after having fulfilled all His program, He returns there with haste." [TPC, 2a:72]

PSALMS 17 AND 18

(As with the preceding Psalm 15, these two psalms have been rewritten by [FG] in the second person of direct address wherever God is addressed in the third person in [OG] and the original

Hebrew. This is obviously again in order to avoid any masculine references to God, contrary to Christ's own usage in the New Testament and, hence, throughout Tradition and the Liturgy.)

This sampling of psalms from the first part of the new Grail "Inclusive Language" Psalter is typical of the extensive editing and rewriting policies used by Grail under the influence of feminist ideology in the Church. Given, however, the clear witnesses cited above from both New Testament and Patristic exegesis, as well as liturgical usage regarding the Messianic Christology contained in just these few initial psalms of the Psalter, it would seem that the U.S. bishops' witholding their approval of this revised Grail Psalter for liturgical use is indeed amply justified. It will be recalled that their concern was "whether such [Messianic] psalms should or could be revised for inclusive language", implying that perhaps their christological content might thus be violated or completely eliminated. And this, in fact, seems here to be the case. The Grail's feminist rewriting of such psalms manifests a seemingly total ignorance of, or cavalier disregard for, their Messianic Christology as witnessed by Tradition. As a result, they have been virtually *dechristianized.*

In the Gospel of Luke we are told that, as the two disciples of Emmaus were telling the eleven and those gathered together with them about how Jesus appeared to them on the road and explained to them the Scriptures, suddenly Jesus himself again appears in the midst of all of them. After eating something to prove he was not a spirit, he then tells them that " 'everything written about me in the Law of Moses and the Prophets *and the Psalms* must be fulfilled'. Then *He opened their minds to understand the scriptures*" (24:44–45 RSV). It has been the belief of the Church down the ages that the exegetical principles which Jesus then gave to the Apostles and disciples of Emmaus by "opening their minds to understand the scriptures" concerning him have been faithfully handed down in Tradition through the exegesis of the Apostolic and post-Apostolic Fathers, as also in the Liturgy which follows their guidance in finding Christ in the Scriptures, and especially in the psalms.

Crucial to this Christology of the psalms—as of the rest of the Scriptures—is precisely the *singular* form of "man" and its pronominal substitutes used in the original Grail and Hebrew texts. In its generic-singular form so frequent in the psalms and throughout Scripture, "man is not only inclusive of *both* sexes—as is its plural counterpart "men" or "mankind"—but in the terminology of depth psychology, it functions at a yet deeper level as an archetypal symbol of the Universal Man: the image of "corporate personality" so important in the Bible, wherein the single individual mystically embodies the whole people, nation, or entire human race. In this function "man" often carries and conveys the whole theology of the "first and Second Adam" which St. Paul elaborates in his first Letter to the Corinthians (15:21–49). And it resonates as well with all the Christology of the "Son of Man" logia scattered throughout the Gospels.

These Adamic/Christic resonances, nuances, of the generic-inclusive singular form of "man" have been well perceived by some of our contemporary literati. The poet J. E. Cirlot, e.g., says this of "man" in its generic form:

> Between man as a concrete individual and the universe there is a medial term—a mesocosmos. And this mesocosmos is the "Universal Man". . . . He symbolizes the whole pattern of the world of manifestation, that is, the complete range of possibilities open to mankind. . . . This concept of the "Universal Man" implies *hermaphroditism,* though never specifically. For the concrete, existential human being, in so far as he is either a man or a woman, represents the dissected "human" whole, not only in the physical sense but also spiritually.[9]

The modern English poetess Kathleen Raine makes this even more explicit. Extolling Edwin Muir's poetry in one of her books, she writes:

> In writing his Fable of Man, Muir turned naturally to those great symbolic figures who are not men, but *Man*—Adam, and Prometheus; the Israelites, with their strange god-bearing

[9] J. E. Cirlot, "Man", *Dictionary of Symbols,* (New York: Philosophical Library, 1962). English translation by Routledge and Kegan Paul Ltd., 1962.

destiny; and, inevitably, the figure of *Christ*... [10] [emphasis added].

As both woman and poet, Kathleen Raine's unabashed and uninhibited use of "man" in its traditional generic-inclusive sense is an eloquent judgment on the feminists' problem with it. In her poem "Dust", e.g., which is obviously referring to the whole race "corporately contained" at once both in Adam and in Christ, the Second Adam, she writes:

> Man's passion is predestined in the tree.
> The cross-beams of the heavens, vegetation,
> The thorns, the iron, and the organic thirst
> From the beginning raise his calvary. [11]

So too, Thomas Merton, who had corresponded with Raine, intimates the same idea:

> Our growth in Christ is measured not only by intensity of love but also by the deepening of our vision, for we begin to see Christ now not only in our own deep souls, *not only in the Psalms,* not only in the Mass, but everywhere, shining to the Father in the features of men's faces. The more we are united to Him in love the more we are united in love to one another....
>
> In this union we discover ... that there is so to speak *"One mystical Person"*, after all, chanting the Psalms. ... *It is the Eternal Christ....* The *One Man* who suffers in the Psalms, who cries out to God in them and by God is heard, this *One Man* is the *Whole Christ....* Our vision goes out to embrace the whole Mystical Body, in all the scattered members in every part of the world. And wherever they be, those men and women are also here, and we are there with them, because we are all *"one Man".* [12]

But all of this Messianic Christology contained in the Psalter's generic singular form of "man", however, is effectively obliterated

[10] Kathleen Raine, *Defending Ancient Springs* (Oxford: Oxford University Press, 1967), p. 11.

[11] *The Collected Poems of Kathleen Raine* (London: Hamish Hamilton Ltd., 1972); p. 80.

[12] Thomas Merton, *Bread in the Wilderness,* A New Directions Book, James Laughlin, (New York: 1953), pp. 92, 94.

by rewriting such verses in the plural, as Grail has done throughout the psalter. Hence, by this feminist ploy of recasting all singular forms of "man" into the plural, the Christ whom Tradition has always held to be hidden under the "species" of the word is thereby made virtually inaccessible to one who reads or prays this emasculated, de*Christ*ianized Psalter.

Standing in stark contrast, however, to this feminist agenda for rewriting Scripture—long touted as a necessary corrective to "sexism" and the chauvinism of patriarchal discrimination—is a joint statement by a coalition of *non*-feminist *women's* groups in the Church. This feminine alliance of non-feminists, already mentioned earlier in this paper, comprises the international: *Women for Faith and Family,* a group of lay women; *Consortium Perfectae Caritatis,* an organization of women Religious; and *The Forum of Major* (women) *Superiors of the Institute of Religious Life.* Their ten-point statement released April 18, 1989, aims at combatting the false allegations of the feminist factions which until now have vociferously, and often belligerently, claimed to represent the universal attitudes and beliefs of women in the Church today. [13] While on the contrary, according to an article in *30 Days,* it is rather this non-feminist coalition of women which probably represents the actual opinions of the vast majority of women in the Church on the issues addressed in their public statement. [14] The joint statement registers their mutual concern about the pervasive influence and destructive effects of radical feminism, and strongly objects to its "ideologically motivated" liturgical and linguistic innovations of precisely the kind we have seen above in the psalms.

And yet, from the male segment of the Church, particularly bishops, priests, and male religious, we witness an astounding support for the revolutionary agenda of the feminists, especially in the area of language—*the Word*—so crucial to the Tradition of the Faith. We see a gallant, headlong rush to defend and comply with

[13] "Statement on Feminism, Language, and Liturgy" appears below in Appendix A, pp. 323ff., nos. 2, 6, 8.

[14] Joseph Fessio, S.J., "The Last Word: A Rumor and Response", *30 Days,* English edition, Ignatius Press (May, 1989), p. 82.

their revisionist demands that seems truly chivalrous. But how will these knights-errant now respond to help this countergroup of ladies in distress? Will their bold chivalry prove equal, and as swift, to *their* defense? Or will their anguished cries but be that "sign of contradiction" proving just what spirit spurs these cavaliers?

AUTHORITY AND THE
LANGUAGE OF THE BIBLE

Donald G. Bloesch

AUTHORITY IN FEMINISM

Feminists are surprisingly united, not only in the area of goals, but also in their understanding of authority. For nearly all feminists, the final court of appeal is human experience, particularly feminine experience.

Rosemary Ruether is typical in this regard: "Human experience is the starting point and the ending point of the hermeneutical circle. Codified tradition both reaches back to roots in experience and is constantly renewed or discarded through the test of experience."[1] Although making a place for revelation, she sees this, not as a supernatural communication of information about God through historical events or even directly to the human soul, but instead as a breakthrough into a higher level of consciousness or as a new awareness of self and the world. Revelatory experiences are "breakthrough experiences beyond ordinary fragmented consciousness that provide interpretive symbols illuminating . . . the *whole* of life".[2] The ultimate never intrudes as a foreign element into experience but is in fact a dimension of all experience.

Ruether sees an underlying affinity between feminist and liberation theologies: both have their genesis in the experience of oppres-

---

[1] Rosemary Ruether, *Sexism and God-Talk: Toward a Feminist Theology* (Boston: Beacon Press, 1983), p. 12. Ruether contends that what makes feminist theology unique is its appeal to women's experience.

[2] Ibid., p. 13.

sion, and both seek a world free from exploitation. "In rejecting androcentrism (males as norms of humanity)," she says, "women must also criticize all other forms of chauvinism: making white Westerners the norm of humanity, making Christians the norm of humanity, making privileged classes the norm of humanity."[3]

The more radical feminists are inclined to have a mystical criterion for faith, reflecting a monistic rather than a dualistic world view. (The mainstream feminists are also closer to monism than to dualism, but they draw back from pantheism.) What is decisive is not human experience as such but making contact with the deepest within human experience — the creative powers within nature. Meinrad Craighead calls for a religion "connected to the metamorphoses of nature: the pure potential of water, the transformative power of blood, the seasonal rhythms of the earth, the cycles of lunar dark and light".[4] Charlene Spretnak states that "the worldview inherent in feminist spirituality is, like the female mind, holistic and integrative. We see *connectedness* where the patriarchal mentality insists on seeing only separations."[5] In the words of Starhawk, "Justice is not based on an external Absolute who imposes a set of laws upon chaotic nature, but on recognition of the ordering principles inherent in nature. The law is the natural law."[6] In fact, for her: "Individual conscience — itself a manifestation of the Goddess — is the final court of appeals, above codified laws or hierarchical proclamations."[7]

Obviously, men who embrace the cause of feminism do not appeal to feminine experience, nor are they as inclined to celebrate the cycles of nature. Instead, their authority is the new conscious-

[3] Ibid., p. 20.

[4] Meinrad Craighead, "Immanent Mother", in Mary E. Giles, ed., *The Feminist Mystic and Other Essays on Women and Spirituality* (New York: Crossroad, 1982), p. 79. Similarly, Dorothee Sölle declares: " 'Source of all that is good', 'life-giving wind', 'water of life', 'light' are all symbols of God which do not imply power of authority and do not smack of any chauvinism" (*Beyond Mere Obedience,* trans. Lawrence W. Denef [New York: Pilgrim Press, 1982], p. xix).

[5] Spretnak, *The Politics of Women's Spirituality* (New York: Doubleday, 1982), p. xxiii.

[6] Ibid., p. 416.

[7] Ibid., p. 417.

ness of living in a male-female world, a world in which hierarchy and duality are replaced by mutuality and unity.

Both men and women in the feminist orbit align themselves with the cultural vision of a holistic humanity characterized, not by separation between the sexes, but by an androgynal unity. The norms for feminism are therefore cultural rather than ecclesiastical, experiential rather than biblical.

THE BIBLE IN FEMINISM

This is not to deny that the Bible has a role (sometimes important) among Christian feminists, though it is not the ruling norm but an aid in bringing to people a new horizon of meaning. It is treated, not as an inspired witness to a unique and definitive revelation of God in the history of the people of Israel culminating in Jesus Christ, but as an illuminating record of the struggles of the people of Israel for liberation from political and economic enslavement.

Elisabeth Schüssler-Fiorenza contends that only those parts of the Bible that lend support to the struggle for liberation should be accepted as authoritative. She calls for a "depatriarchalizing" of the Bible in which we interpret the Bible in the light of a canon within the canon. Those passages promoting equality between the sexes and races become the norm by which we weigh the validity of other parts of the Bible. For, she argues, "only the nonsexist and non-androcentric traditions of the Bible and the nonoppressive traditions of biblical interpretation have the theological authority of revelation if the Bible is not to continue as a tool for the oppression of women".[8] Thus the paradigm of "emancipatory praxis" is the criterion or norm for biblical interpretation.[9] The Bible is to be understood not as an archetype but as a prototype —

[8] Elisabeth Schüssler-Fiorenza, "Toward a Feminist Biblical Hermeneutics", in *Readings in Moral Theology No. 4*, ed. Charles E. Curran and Richard A. McCormick (New York: Paulist Press, 1984), p. 376. Also see Elisabeth Schüssler-Fiorenza, *In Memory of Her* (New York: Crossroad, 1983), pp. 4–67.

[9] Fiorenza, "Toward a Feminist Biblical Hermeneutics", p. 378.

"one critically open to the possibility, even the necessity of its own transformation".[10]

Reflecting the influence of David Tracy, Sallie McFague asserts that "the authority of Scripture is the authority of a classic poetic text".[11] Therefore "its interpretation is flexible", meaning that "the world it presents is open to different understandings".[12] The Bible is to be seen as "great literature" rather than a document of divine revelation. "The Bible as model", she says, "can never *be* the word of God, can never capture the ways of God. As model, the Bible can never be an idol. As poetic classic, the Bible continues, as does any great poetic work, to speak universally."[13] It should be interpreted "as other poetic texts are interpreted — existentially, flexibly, openly".[14] She emphasizes "the relative, groping character of this very human work" rather than its inspiration and canonicity.[15]

Most radical feminists do not hesitate to disavow the Bible either as a means to discover the reality of God or as an aid in the struggle for women's liberation. Carol Christ says bluntly that the "symbol systems cannot simply be rejected, they must be replaced. Where there is not any replacement, the mind will revert to familiar structures."[16] For Naomi Goldenberg, witchcraft is "the only Western religion that recognizes woman as a divinity in her own right".[17] Rita Gross suggests that we enrich our imagery of female divinity by meditating on the Hindu goddesses.[18]

Feminists on the left of the ideological spectrum who make a place for the Bible generally emphasize its insufficiency as a norm for faith and conduct because of its roots in a patriarchal culture.

[10] Ibid., pp. 376, 377. She is here citing Rachel Blau DuPlessis.

[11] McFague, *Metaphorical Theology: Models of Gods in Religious Languages* (Minneapolis: Augsburg Fortress, 1982), p. 59.

[12] Ibid.

[13] Ibid., p. 62.

[14] Ibid.

[15] Ibid.

[16] Spretnak, *The Politics of Women's Spirituality,* p. 73.

[17] Ibid., p. 217.

[18] Carl Olson, ed., *The Book of the Goddess Past and Present* (New York: Crossroad, 1983), pp. 217–30.

Sister Ann Patrick Ware, former associate director of the Commission on Faith and Order of the National Council of Churches, contends that the Word of God "is in need of correction", since it has been "corrupted by the mores of the culture in which it was received".[19]

In summary, the so-called mainstream or reformist feminists are willing to use the Bible—but with drastic selectivity. Those passages supportive of a patriarchal world view (teaching subordination, distinct roles for men and women, etc.) are to be relegated to the marginal areas of the canon, whereas those upholding equality in Christ are to be seen as determinative and binding. Yet even here the final authority is not the biblical witness but the current cultural understanding of equality and wholeness which is informed by the social sciences, particularly psychology and sociology.[20] The Bible is read in the light of this cultural understanding, which is not simply intellectual but also experiential. The fact that the cultural vision of a new humanity is an object not only of our hopes but also of our experience means that in the final analysis the authority for faith is experiential and subjective.

THE LANGUAGE OF THE BIBLE

The relevance of this discussion to the debate on the language of faith, and especially the language of the Bible, is very clear. Biblical authority is inextricably tied to how we conceive of the imagery or symbolism of the Bible.

Those who accent the total otherness and inaccessibility of God are inclined to view the Bible as more or less opaque in relation to the Word of God. Opaque in this context means virtually impene-

[19] See Nadine Brozan, "In the Religious Life, a Conflict of Faith and Feminism", *New York Times* (Mar. 8, 1980), p. 18.

[20] This is made abundantly clear by Burton H. Throckmorton, Jr., in his "Why the Inclusive Language Lectionary?" *The Christian Century* 101 (1984): 742–44. Throckmorton appeals to "humanity's understanding of itself" as the norm by which to determine whether the Bible can be heard as the Word of God.

trable to understanding.[21] God is known not by thought but by the blind groping of love.[22] What is given in the Bible are "glimmerings of transcendence" (Carl Rasche) rather than real knowledge of God. It is commonly held that we can say of God only what he is not (*via negativa*). This category embraces not only the main strand of feminist theology but also a great many of those in all theological traditions who have been unduly influenced by either Gnosticism or Neoplatonic mysticism.[23]

Those who affirm God as utterly transcendent but not wholly dissimilar to humanity are inclined to view the Bible as translucent to the Word of God. These are the people who stress the middle way of analogy as opposed to univocity on the one hand and equivocity on the other. We can have an imperfect but nevertheless real knowledge of God. We can know the ways of God by faith in Jesus Christ, but we cannot comprehend his essence. Here we find the centrist tradition of Christian faith—Augustine, Thomas Aquinas, Martin Luther, John Calvin, Karl Barth, and Thomas Torrance, among many others.

[21] For the meaning of "opaque" in relation to "cloudy", "murky", and "turbid", see S. I. Hayakawa, ed., *Modern Guide to Synonyms and Related Words* (New York: Funk and Wagnalls, 1968), p. 227.

[22] The fourteenth-century anonymous author of the mystical work *The Cloud of Unknowing,* trans. Clifton Wolters (Baltimore: Penguin Books, 1967), contends that we do not have real knowledge in the state of contemplation but only "a blind groping for the naked being of God" (p. 64). He acknowledges that God may on occasion "send out a shaft of spiritual light, which pierces this cloud of unknowing between you, and shows you some of his secrets, of which it is not permissible or possible to speak" (p. 87). *The Cloud of Unknowing* stands in the mystical tradition of pseudo-Dionysius, who described God as "the Transcendent Darkness" that is "beyond being and knowing". In this kind of orientation, conceptual knowledge is replaced by a mystical silence.

[23] Mysticism the world over denies that man can have adequate conceptual knowledge of God. The names of God in mysticism are equivocal, since God is beyond essence, being, and intelligibility. See James F. Anderson, *The Bond of Being: An Essay on Analogy and Existence* (St. Louis: B. Herder, 1949), pp. 65, 66. Lao-tse says: "The name that can be named is not the enduring and unchanging name." *The Texts of Taoism,* trans. James Legge (New York: Julian Press, 1959), p. 95.

This general orientation is reflected in Elizabeth A. Johnson, "The Incomprehensibility of God and the Image of God Male and Female", *Theological Studies* 45, no. 3 (Sept. 1984): 441–65.

Those who stress the congruity and homogeneity between God and humanity are prone to regard the Bible as transparent to the Word of God. While acknowledging that the Bible contains symbolism and metaphor as well as historical firsthand report, they nevertheless contend that the basic affirmations of the Bible concerning God and his self-revelation to humanity can be comprehended by human reason (though not exhaustively) and can therefore be stated univocally. These are the people who prefer to think of the Bible as a verbal revelation from God or as a document of revealed propositions. This general position is forcefully argued today by conservative evangelicals like Carl Henry, Gordon Clark, Ronald Nash, and Roy Clouser.[24] It was anticipated by the medieval scholastic theologian Duns Scotus, who believed that it is possible to have a univocal knowledge of God, since every analogy must have a univocal core.

Rationalistic philosophy (as distinguished from the theological rationalism noted above) aims for a univocal rather than merely symbolic knowledge of God, but it usually relegates the biblical language as well as the language of piety and devotion to the category of myth and poetry. Philosophers as different as Whitehead and Hegel argue that we must not abandon the poetic or mythical language of the Bible, but we must clarify it by translating poetic insight into conceptual truth.

Most feminists, as has been indicated, fall into the first position, namely, seeing the Bible as giving us only intimations of transcendence. Gail Ramshaw-Schmidt describes the scriptural

[24] Clouser, who identifies "God's revelation" with Sacred Scripture, contends that religious language purports "to give univocal truth about God. It should not be seen as giving us something *like* what is true of God, while it is all really beyond our comprehension, as the analogy theorists maintain. Nor should it be understood as merely our resolve to talk about God *as if* he had such characteristics, as Kantians and pragmatists have maintained. Rather it should be seen as quite ordinary language purporting to ascribe to God properties which he really has and relations in which he really stands." Roy Clouser, "Religious Language: A New Look at an Old Problem", in Hendrik Hart, Johan Van Der Hoeven, and Nicholas Wolterstorff, eds., *Rationality in the Calvinian Tradition* (Lanham, Md.: University Press of America, 1983), pp. 394, 395.

language about God as metaphorical rather than univocal or analogical. "A metaphor", she claims, "says something radically other than what we want it to say."[25] Thus the biblical language is characterized by catachresis—using a word or phrase that does not fit.[26] Because God is radically other than humanity, we can only dimly perceive him; he always escapes and transcends our definitions. This is why "human language cannot properly or adequately describe God". I would argue that human language cannot exhaustively describe God, but it can certainly give an adequate description if it is inspired by the Spirit of God—adequate not for a comprehensive knowledge of metaphysical reality but for life and salvation.[27] Ramshaw-Schmidt draws upon Meister Eckhart, the thirteenth- and fourteenth-century Rhineland mystic, who stressed the utter incongruity of human language about God.[28]

In radical feminism, the emphasis is on knowing God by intuition and feeling rather than conceptually or propositionally. The language about God is mythical and poetic, and this is all we need in order to realize our potential as bearers of divinity.

Those feminists who link up with process philosophy and theology are willing to use Scripture because it offers provocative lures that lead us into the promise of the future. From Scripture we gain not conceptual knowledge of God but instead a new awareness of self and the world, which enables us to embark or continue on the glorious adventure of life.

In opposition to the agnosticism that mysticism spawns, evangelical theology contends that we can speak about God truly, but not exhaustively, because God first speaks to us and awakens within us a possibility to engage in dialogue with the transcendent.

---

[25] Gail Ramshaw-Schmidt, lecture at the Twin Cities Presbytery meeting, Hope Presbyterian Church, Richfield, Minn., May 8, 1984.

[26] See Paul Ricoeur, *The Rule of Metaphor* (Toronto: University of Toronto Press, 1977), p. 291.

[27] In my debate with Gail Ramshaw-Schmidt, she seemed open to this last suggestion.

[28] Eckhart could say that God "is nonloving, being above love and affection". *Meister Eckhart,* ed. Raymond Blakney (New York: Harper, 1941), p. 248.

Our words in and of themselves cannot reach God, but our words can be adopted by God as means by which we can bear witness to his saving deeds. Our words can also be received by God when they are offered in the form of prayer. Karl Barth has stated it well:

> By the grace of God we shall truly know God with our views and concepts, and truly speak of God with our words. But we shall not be able to boast about it, as if it is our own success, and we have performed and done it. It is we who have known and spoken, but it will always be God and God alone who will have credit for the veracity of our thinking and speaking.[29]

Evangelical theology in the classical tradition upholds revelational translucency over both mystical ineffability and rational transparency. We can know God—partially and yet truly—when we are known by God in the event of the awakening to faith. Faith signifies not the rational grasping of the truth of revelation but the state of being grasped by this truth. The role of reason is neither to prepare the way for revelation nor to measure its validity but instead to serve revelation as we pursue our vocation to be signs and witnesses of the One who is revealed.

THE RETURN TO THEONOMY

Whereas many traditional religionists are inclined to heteronomy—locating authority in an external standard or institution (such as creed, church, or magisterium)—feminists locate authority in the self—in conscience, experience, or mystical insight (autonomy). Feminist theology is therefore anchored in the Renaissance and Enlightenment, which celebrated the infinite possibilities of man, rather than in Catholic tradition or the Reformation, which emphasized submission to the authority of either the Church or the Bible.

[29] Karl Barth, *Church Dogmatics,* eds. G. W. Bromiley and T. F. Torrance, trans. T. H. L. Parker, W. B. Johnston, Harold Knight, and J. L. M. Haire (Edinburgh: T. and T. Clark, repr. 1964), vol. 2, pt. 1, p. 213.

It is my position that we need again to retrieve theonomy in order to overcome the present polarity between liberal and conservative religion. The Church at its best, both Catholic and Protestant, has maintained a theonomous understanding of authority—in which the final court of appeal is the living Christ himself—the center and ground of human personhood as well as the head of the Church and the primary focus and ultimate author of the Bible. In theonomy the self is not negated as in heteronomy, nor is it given free rein to go its own way, as in autonomy; instead, the self is fulfilled in God by losing itself in the service of God.

Against Tillich, however, who freely makes use of this typology, I insist that locating authority in God, the transcendent ground and goal of the self, also entails submitting to his self-revelation in Jesus Christ, the content of the Bible and the basic message of the Church. God is known only as he reveals himself in his Word—revealed, written, and proclaimed. We have the infallible norm for faith and practice, not by plumbing the depths of our consciousness, but by seeking the Word of God in Scripture primarily and in Church tradition secondarily.

This is not, however, to make of either the Bible or the Church heteronomous authorities (as has been the case in much theologizing in the past and present). The Bible is not in and of itself infallible or absolutely normative; yet by virtue of the Spirit of God acting upon its words and also moving within our hearts, the Bible directs us to the One who alone is unconditionally infallible—Jesus Christ, the incarnate Word of God, the Son of the Father, the source and ground of all truth. Similarly, the Church is not in and of herself infallible, but she becomes infallible when her words become translucent to the living Word of God who stands over the Church as her transcendent head but at the same time works within the Church as her immanent guide and teacher.

In the light of the feminist protest against sexism and patriarchalism, I believe that we as orthodox Christians must acknowledge that too often in the past we have confused the patriarchal garb in which divine revelation comes to us with the truth of revelation itself. We have been inclined to absolutize cultural expressions and modes of behavior that belong to a cultural past and not to the dogmatic content of the faith itself. We have been guilty of absolutizing certain directives in the Bible that were intended not as universal divine commands but as specific injunctions pertaining to a particular situation in the Church (such as Paul's admonition that women keep silent in the churches).

At the same time, we must resist the prevailing practice in modern theology to separate the divine content from the cultural form and to place it in a new symbolic garb. The divine content of the Bible only comes to us in and through the language of Canaan, and though we can supplement this language, we cannot abandon it. Moreover, this language is not an obstacle to the understanding of God but the catalyst and conduit through which we come to the right understanding.

The biblical witness is normative not simply because it points to revelation but because it participates in this revelation through the action of the Spirit; it thereby becomes a part of the revelation itself. We cannot say that Paul was mistaken in his view of subordination, since this is to denigrate the authority and normativeness of his affirmations. Neither dare we say, as does process theologian Lewis Ford, that the Bible has lost its credibility as a norm for faith because of our "greatly expanded world history, a scientific understanding of nature and man, and a drastically altered social and ethical situation".[30] The norms of theology, in his opinion, must now be "purely philosophical criteria".[31]

In the evangelical view, the Bible derives its authority not from its concurrence with one's self-evident preconceptual experience or with the latest findings in the social and natural sciences. Rather its authority is derived from the self-disclosure of the living God in the history that it records and celebrates. The fact that God really did reveal himself in the person of Jesus Christ, the fact that the Word became flesh and dwelt among us, the fact that Jesus Christ really rose from the dead — this is the ineradicable basis upon which Christian faith stands or falls. The authority for faith, however, has not only a historical but also a pneumatic

[30] Lewis S. Ford, *The Lure of God* (Philadelphia: Fortress, 1978), p. 16.
[31] Ibid., p. 135.

dimension: it rests partly on the outpouring of the Holy Spirit, who brings the Church into a renewed appreciation of the facts of sacred or biblical history, who opens the minds of believers to the significance of these facts, not only for biblical times, but also for the times in which we live. We look to the Bible, not because it is an outstanding piece of religious literature, a religious or poetic classic, but because it contains the revelation of God's will and purpose for all mankind. It yields not simply glimmerings of transcendence but the knowledge that is able to instruct us for salvation (2 Tim 3:15). This is a knowledge available only to faith, however, not to natural reason, which can attain a historical knowledge of the biblical revelation but not the redeeming knowledge that gives us the existential significance of this revelation. Feminists are right that we need a new horizon of meaning, but this comes to us when we are brought into a saving relationship with Jesus Christ through the preaching and hearing of the gospel (Rom 10:8–17), not through a comparative analysis of cultures or a phenomenological treatment of religious experience.

Our hope lies neither in making contact with the depths of human consciousness nor in blindly submitting to the dictates of Church authorities. Instead it lies in joyfully embracing the gospel of reconciliation and redemption, in gladly responding to the great invitation of our Lord to become his sons and daughters on the basis of the promises recorded in the Bible and reaffirmed by our fathers and mothers in the faith through the ages.

IV

LITURGICAL AND
SPIRITUAL DIMENSIONS

ON PRAYING "OUR FATHER":
THE CHALLENGE OF
RADICAL FEMINIST LANGUAGE FOR GOD

Roland Mushat Frye

First showing the simplistic falsity of the feminist slogan, "Since God is male, the male is god", this paper discusses the "Our Father" as the quintessential Christian prayer, exemplifying the meanings of the divine patronymic in the Bible and Early Church. Efforts to replace this ancient usage have been disastrous both theologically and liturgically. Finally the paper recommends the ancient principle that the Church should "gauge God's assertions concerning Himself by the scale of His own glorious self-revelation".

I. INTRODUCTION: PURPOSE AND STRUCTURE

My purpose in this essay is to make a straightforward defense of biblical language for God: for almost two thousand years, without interruption, this has been the Church's language of public worship and private prayer, doctrinal theology and the discourses of faith. But today, ancient and universal Christian God-language, especially "God the Father", "God the Son", and their attendant masculine gender pronouns, have been subjected to sustained disparagement and outright rejection by relatively small but highly activist radical feminist groups, with support from other trendy theological camps.[1] In effect, church people are being told that

---

[1] Objections are also raised to such other "sexist words" as King and Lord.

the founding and sustaining words of the Christian Faith have been weighed in strange new balances, found wanting, and are now marked down for destruction. This is not done in the name of truth, but in the name of various political, social, and sexual liberation agendas.

This is indeed a remarkable phenomenon of our time.[2] I propose to consider it critically in historical and doctrinal perspectives. We shall thus begin with the first model of Christian prayer, move out into past and future from that point, then into other important aspects of the language-for-God issue, and finally return to considering the Lord's Prayer for deeper understandings of the Christian meaning of God as Father.

Observing Jesus at prayer, one of the disciples asked him to teach them to pray. Jesus replied in these familiar words:

> Pray then like this: Our Father who art in heaven, hallowed be thy name. . . . [3]

From early on, that prayer has been a central part of the public and private worship of Christians and Christian churches of all kinds and places around the globe. Jesus' references, throughout his ministry, to the Fatherhood of God and his namings of God as Father amounted to several times more than the total of all previous biblical references to God as Father, important though these were. "Father"—whether as "the Father", "my Father", "your Father", or "our Father"—was the most distinctive expression for God in the teaching and example of Jesus.[4] The fact that Jesus

[2] See also my earlier analysis, "Language for God and Feminist Language: Problems and Principles" (Princeton, N.J.: Center of Theological Inquiry, 1988), which has also appeared in whole or part in *The Scottish Journal of Theology, Interpretation,* and elsewhere.

[3] See Mt 6:9 and following in the Revised Standard Version, which I cite here because of its wider liturgical use. For the most part I shall hereafter cite the New Revised Standard Version because it faithfully maintains biblical language for God while judiciously introducing inclusive language for references to humanity.

[4] To my knowledge, no published liturgy, lectionary, or "translation" of the Bible has yet jettisoned "our Father" from the Lord's Prayer, but this omission is patently only tactical and temporary.

Christ was by far the most persistent and effective biblical advocate for such language has not prevented radical advocacy groups from judging all references to God as Father to be "simply unacceptable".

II. SUBSTITUTIONS, ALTERNATIVES, AND "EQUIVALENTS"

Substitutions and alternatives for such references to God as Father appear in a number of current publications. I shall illustrate with some representative examples from two of these, beginning with *An Inclusive Language Lectionary* (hereafter ILL) prepared in conjunction with the Division of Education of the National Council of Churches. The ILL editors tell us that "In this lectionary, 'God the Father and Mother' is used as a formal equivalent of 'the Father' or 'God the Father'." This is surely one of the more extravagant claims to be made even in our rhetorically extravagant century. What it appears to wish to say, without quite saying, is that "Father and Mother" means the same as "Father": that is, on the face of the thing, simply not so. At all events, ILL renders Jesus' prophesy to the Samaritan woman at the well in John 4:23 as "the true worshipers will worship [*God*] the [*Mother and*] Father in spirit and truth, for such are those whom God seeks as worshipers", while Philippians 2:10–11 in ILL tells us that at the name of Jesus every knee should bow and every tongue confess "that Jesus Christ is Sovereign [*or Lord*] to the Glory of God the Father [*and Mother*]."[5]

Such revisions and additions in the biblical texts are reminiscent of a 1929 Hollywood movie based (more or less) on Shakespeare's *The Taming of the Shrew* and issued with the following credit line:

By William Shakespeare.
With Additional Dialogue by Sam Taylor.

[5] *An Inclusive Language Lectionary: Readings for Year A,* rev. ed. (Atlanta, New York, and Philadelphia, 1986), pp. 269, 43, 92, carefully following the editor's punctuation and typography.

In ILL, none of the "additional dialogue" is a "formal equivalent" of anything in either the Greek New Testament or the Hebrew Old Testament. Joined with the obvious damage inflicted upon Christian substance and English style from these carpet-bombing assaults on readings from Scripture, at least two dangerous confusions are introduced into the doctrine of God. Both can be recognized by common sense and illustrated by history.

Those who advocate such phrases as "God the Father and Mother" may not be fully aware of the implications of such language, but the Early Church was neither ignorant nor naïve on the subject. "Mother and Father" language for God can suggest outright polytheism (to which we will turn shortly), or a grotesque kind of monotheism, represented in the "mother-father (matropater)" or "bisexual Power" of the Gnostics.[6] In the second century, St. Irenaeus warned against the belief of Valentinus and other Gnostics in a "masculo-feminine" deity with "the nature of a hermaphrodite", while two centuries later Gregory of Nazianzus still found the need to ridicule the "hermaphrodite God" of Gnostic religions.[7] Many radical feminists seem unaware that this historical, religious meaning inheres in the God-language they advocate for liturgy and worship, but Rita M. Gross candidly approves "imagery of bisexual androgynous deity".[8] That religious conception also fits rather neatly with New Age fashions today. And there is a second problem, at least equally disturbing.

Common sense will also recognize the polytheistic implications of calling God both the Father and the Mother, and history will

[6] Elaine H. Pagels, "What Became of God the Mother? Conflicting Images of God in Early Christianity", *Signs, Journal of Women in Culture and Society* 2 (Winter 1976): 293–303, with direct citations from 294 and 296–98.

[7] Irenaeus, *Against Heresies* 1.11.1 and 5, in *Ante-Nicene Fathers of the Christian Church,* vol. 1, p. 336; and Gregory of Nazianzus, "Fifth Theological Oration: On the Spirit", cap. 7, in *Christology of the Later Fathers,* ed. E. R. Hardy and C. C. Richardson (Philadelphia, 1954), p. 198.

[8] Rita M. Gross, "Female God Language in a Jewish Context", in *Womanspirit Rising,* ed. Carol P. Christ and Judith Plaskow (New York, 1979), p. 173.

again illustrate the point. In the pagan and Gnostic cults of the Roman Empire in the early Christian period, pairs of male and female gods technically known as syzygies were sexually linked (whether literally or allegorically). Irenaeus relates that some Gnostic groups baptized their converts in the name of the unknown father of the universe, and of Truth the mother of all things, and of the spirit who descended on Jesus.[9] This imitation (or parody?) of the Christian sacrament of baptism clearly involves a threesome, with father and mother counting as two and "spirit" as the third. If God the Father and Mother are not taken as hermaphrodite, but as a pair of separate deities, then their believers are committed to a polytheistic pantheon, utterly incompatible with the subtle balances of the Christian Trinity in unity. There are grave dangers here, dangers and confusions into which the *Inclusive Language Lectionary* editors walk and would lead the churches when they assure us that God the Father and Mother is "a formal equivalent" of God the Father.

We have seen two major hazards produced by substitute language for God, but there is also another: where God the Father is changed to "the Mother" or "the Goddess" the result is likely to be pantheism. Joseph Campbell has observed from his wide acquaintance with myths that "when you have a Goddess as the creator, it's her own body that is the universe. She is identical with the universe."[10] Not only is this not catholic Christianity, but it goes far beyond even heretical Christianity.

The Standing Liturgical Commission of the Episcopal Church in its *Supplemental Liturgical Texts: Prayer Book Studies 30* was careful not to introduce the word mother "as a substitute for Father", and so has avoided several dangers into which ILL has fallen. But I regret to say that it was not careful enough.[11] In the Second Supplemental Eucharistic Prayer we read that the Spirit at the creation "brought to birth the heavens: sun, moon, and stars; earth, winds, and waters; growing things, both plants and animals;

[9] Irenaeus, op. cit., I.II.2I, p. 346.

[10] Joseph Campbell, *The Power of Myth*, (New York, 1988), p. 67.

[11] *Commentary on Prayer Book Studies, Containing Supplemental Liturgical Texts* (New York: The Church Hymnal Corporation, 1989), p. C-10.

and finally humankind." The sound is impressive but the sense is troubling: "God giving birth to ... the whole creation", as the gloss in the "Introduction" puts it, while the introductory note to The Holy Eucharist calls this "the central metaphor of God bringing to birth".[12] My ellipses signal an omitted phrase, "and nurturing", which, being orthodox, may distract attention from the otherwise pantheistic implications that must not be ignored. Christian and Jewish doctrines hold that God summoned the whole created order into being out of nothingness, by the power of his Word, and not by any kind of gestation and parturition. In contrast, this "birthing" language unfortunately introduces both ancient and current New Age style pantheisms into the eucharistic service, for if the physical universe was "birthed" by God it invites the pagan interpretation "it is divine", and not the biblical "it is good". Whether or not the implied pantheism was intentional (and I am confident that it was not) it is, at the very least, unchristian. And yet the Standing Liturgical Commission was so enamored of this "birthing" conception that they repeated it in the last collect of the liturgical texts: "O God who brought all things to birth in creation. . . . " I am aware of a few biblical words that presumably lie behind these birthing passages, but they run counter to the major biblical accounts of creation. We should not seize such "stray" passages as we may like and magnify them beyond the major and persistent emphases of Scripture, and we should surely not call them "the central metaphor".[13] Unfortunately, *Supplemental Liturgical Texts* falls into such errors and potential heresies all too frequently in its search for feminine language for God.

The Holy Trinity is of course a necessary subject of any Chris-

[12] Ibid., "Texts", p. 70, "Introduction", C-30, and "Concerning the Eucharistic Rite", p. 58.

[13] Ibid., p. 81. I am generally persuaded by the arguments of Professor Mayer I. Gruber of Ben Gurion University, who finds in the Hebrew Scriptures only four unequivocal female images for God, all in Second Isaiah (42:14; 45:10; 49:15, and 66:13). He regards arguments from gynomorphic etymologies as of dubious value. See Gruber, "The Motherhood of God in Second Isaiah", *Revue biblique* (1983): 351–59; and Frye, "Language for God", p. 11, cited above in n. 2.

tian liturgy. The Episcopal Standing Liturgical Commission affirms that "trinitarian language is a very perplexing issue". I presume that their use of "perplexing", rather than the more Catholic "mysterious", is due to the nature of the challenge they faced. Of this they say:

> We are challenged with being faithful to the creedal tradition of the Church, while, at the same time, naming God who is "One in Three and Three in One" in non–gender specific terms.[14]

That stipulation does indeed restrict their capacity to name God in theologically faithful ways; it may very well even preclude it.

The Gloria Patri has traditionally been used in the Book of Common Prayer, but the Liturgical Commission feels that it must, under its charge, find an "alternative" to it. The following lines are presented as "theological equivalent" (which they are not) to the Gloria Patri:

> Honor and glory to the holy and undivided Trinity,
>   God who creates, redeems, and inspires:
> One in Three and Three in One,
> for ever and ever. Amen.[15]

I am told that in at least one of the leading Anglican seminaries the students call this the "Gloria non Patri".

To the extent that these lines sound plausible, that effect was achieved by concentrating on the "undivided Trinity" and avoiding any concrete naming of the triune Persons. A very impressive verbal legerdemain operates here. In place of the identification of the Persons, we have two references to "Three", linked to three active verbs. Some may assume that the "God who creates, redeems, and inspires" refers, in order, to Father, Son, and Holy Spirit, but that cannot be, because there is an overlapping of these operations between the Three Persons (peri-choresis or circumincession). Those active verbs apply to the operations of the "undivided Trinity", not of its members, as

[14] Ibid., C-20.
[15] Ibid., C-20, p. 56.

the Liturgical Commission was presumably aware. The Catholic or Orthodox conception is that the *ad extra* or external operations of the Godhead (such as creating, redeeming, and inspiring) are undivided and cannot be assigned to the Persons "individually", so to speak. So these lines are not only "non–gender specific" but also non-Person-specific.[16] It is well to remember Rosemary Ruether's judgment that "feminist theology cannot be done from the existing base of the Christian Bible".[17] One of the implications that repeatedly arose from my study of *Supplemental Liturgical Texts* is that the authors apparently operate with a sub-Christian, and surely sub-Catholic, understanding of the authority of Scripture. We will return to that subject in the last section of this paper.

Clearly, members of the Liturgical Commission were unable to accomplish *both* tasks set before them: to be faithful to the creedal tradition of the Church, and at the same time to name God in non–gender specific language. They did avoid masculine language for God, but in so doing they produced an inadequate, even truncated, naming of the Christian God. This is to say (and it must be said) that they failed in their task, but I do not sense that this was because they lacked energy, intelligence, and stylistic resourcefulness. They were, to speak analogically, told to square the circle, and of course they could not do it. I have a good deal of sympathy for the Liturgical Commission, although not much admiration for the Texts they produced. I worked for six years as a member of the committee assigned to compose "A Brief Statement of Faith" for the Presbyterian Church (USA), in the course of which I read many, and perhaps most, of the major efforts to find ungendered equivalents of Father and Son language. But there really are none. We Christians are simply faced with an either/or choice. As the impressive and promising young Anglican theologian Alvin F. Kimel, Jr., put it a

[16] As one example of how the Supplemental Texts formula fails to identify any Person, recall how Scripture associates "creating" with all three Persons.

[17] Rosemary Ruether, *Womanguides: Readings Toward a Feminist Theology* (Boston, 1985), p. ix.

few years ago, we must decide between Ashtoreth and the Holy Trinity.[18]

This brings me to one final observation on such efforts as the Episcopal and ILL texts: It is indeed ironic that all the ingenuity expended upon providing feminine gender words for God to match masculine gender words has replaced essentially non-sexist emphases with explicitly sexist ones.[19] Surely, neither the Bible nor the Christian tradition has ever taught the sexual maleness of God. Indeed, both Bible and tradition have repeatedly denied that God has any biological identity of any kind. Which brings us to our next subject.

III. "SINCE GOD IS MALE..."

In 1974, Mary Daly published her now famous slogan that "Since God is male, the male is god."[20] Like most slogans, this one minimized evidence while increasing conviction, and it has served as a powerful rallying cry for radical feminism. In that landmark year of 1974, the assault upon biblical and Christian language for God began in earnest. It is also relevant that at about the same time Daly summarized "the significance of the women's revolution as anti-Christ and its import as anti-church".[21] Through her writings, she probably contributed as much as anyone to establishing the radical feminist attitude toward traditional Christian language for God. Thus when *Newsweek* published an important article entitled "Feminism and the Churches",

[18] See Kimel's two fine articles: "The Holy Trinity Meets Ashtoreth: A Critique of the Episcopal 'Inclusive' Liturgies", *ATR* 71 (1989): 25–47; and "A New Language for God? A Critique of *Supplemental Liturgical Texts — Prayer Book Studies* 30", Reports from Episcopalians United, no. 2, Shaker Heights, Ohio, 1990.

[19] See Paul Minear, "Changes in Metaphor Produce Changes in Thought", *Presbyterian Outlook,* Dec. 19–26, 1983.

[20] Mary Daly, "The Qualitative Leap Beyond Patriarchal Religion", *Quest* 1 (1974): 21.

[21] Daly, *Beyond God the Father* (Boston, 1973), p. 140. Daly also renounced the Christianity in which she had been reared.

it found the heart of the issue to be the "identification of God as a male".[22]

So Daly's slogan has been immensely effective, even though it runs directly contrary to the evidence. Neither the Bible nor the Christian and Jewish traditions have ever taught that God is male, and, in terms both explicit and implicit have repeatedly denied that he is. In this, both the Christian and Jewish traditions stand in stark opposition to pagan and gnostic religions which recognized a host of "genital gods", or *dii genitales,*[23] as Cicero's Roman contemporaries called them. One would have thought this to be obvious, but because radical feminism so dogmatically argues from the claim of God's "maleness", and lest some people may be confused, it should be helpful to clarify matters by consulting the primary evidences, even at the risk of boring those who are already familiar with much of this.

References to God as Father can be traced well back into the Old Testament. In Deuteronomy 32:6, Moses uses a rhetorical question to teach that God is Father to the Children of Israel: "Is not he your Father who created you, who made you and established you?" And in Isaiah 63:16, the prophet directly addresses and professes God in just those terms: "For you are our Father. . . . You, O Lord, are our Father." Within the biblical framework, such passages cannot be taken to mean that God is to be considered male, or biologically masculine, or biologically identifiable in any sense. For example, Numbers 23:19 declares that "God is not man" and again in 1 Samuel 15:29 we read that "the Glory of Israel . . . is not a man". And God speaks directly to the prophet in Hosea 11:9 to say that: "I am God, and not man."[24]

One of the most dramatic repudiations of any "identification of God as a male" (or female either, for that matter) comes in Moses's "last address" to the Children of Israel. Reminding them of the scene at the foot of Mount Horeb when the Ten Commandments were given, Moses reiterates the prohibition of every form of

[22] *Newsweek,* Feb. 13, 1989, p. 58.
[23] Cicero, *De Oratore,* III.xxxviii.154, in Loeb Classical Library edition, vol. 2, pp. 120–21.
[24] The last three citations are from RSV.

idolatry, including perverse religious conceptions of God as either male or female: "Since you saw no form when the Lord spoke to you at Horeb out of the fire, take care and watch yourselves closely, so that you do not act corruptly by making an idol for yourselves, in the form of any figure—the likeness of male or female. . . . "[25] In biblical terms, God is never confused or conflated with the blatant sexuality of the male and female pagan gods, the *dii genitales* to whom Cicero referred. God's fatherhood of the Children of Israel does not consist in sexual generation, but in his calling of them to be his chosen people, and his adoption of them by his grace. It is comparable to God's creation of the universe out of nothing by his powerful word, as will also be true of the angelic messages to and about the young Mary.

As for the followers of Christ in the New Testament, they like Israel are related to God by adoption. As Paul puts it in Ephesians 1:3–6, "the God and Father of our Lord Jesus Christ . . . destined us for adoption as his children through Jesus Christ, . . . " John 1:12–13 similarly speaks of our becoming children of the Father, through the Logos: "to all who received him, who believed in his name, he gave the power to become children of God, who were born not of blood or of the will of the flesh or of the will of man, but of God." And 1 Peter 1:3 likewise affirms, "blessed be the God and Father of our Lord Jesus Christ! By his great mercy he has given us a new birth into a living hope through the resurrection of Jesus Christ from the dead." Climactic, perhaps, are the words of Galatians 4:5–7:

> But when the fullness of time had come, God sent his Son, born of a woman, born under the law, in order to redeem those who were under the law, so that we might receive adoption as children. And because you are children, God has sent the Spirit of his Son into our hearts, crying "Abba! Father!" So you are no longer a slave but a child, and if a child then also an heir, through God.

For believers, this intimate and familial association into which they have been invited directly by Jesus has always been one of

[25] Dt 4:15–16.

the most basic and most appealing elements of Christian faith and life. Mark 14:36 tells us that, during the Agony in the Garden, Jesus prayed to God as "Abba, Father", where the Aramaic word *abba* indicates the closest and most intimate of father-child relationships. "Abba, Father" established itself quite early in Christian invocations of God, as we see in Romans 8:14–16 and Galatians 4:6.

But, again, it does not signify that God the Father is male, in the sense that he has any biological identity or function, as was made abundantly clear by the Fathers of the Early Church. Thus Hilary of Poitiers declared that the "Divine and eternal must be one without distinction of sex", and Gregory of Nyssa spoke to the same effect: "The distinction of male and female does not exist in the Divine and blessed nature."[26]

Repeated instances of such teachings indicate the care with which the Early Church guarded against any confused identification of God with the male. To clarify the issue in grammatical as well as theological terms, Arnobius wrote "that no thoughtless persons may raise a false accusation against us, as though we believed God whom we worship to be male—for this reason, that is, that when we speak of him we use a masculine word—let him understand that it is not sex which is expressed, but his name and its meaning according to custom, and the way in which we are in the habit of using words. For Deity is not male, but his name is of the masculine gender."[27]

Conversely, if God is not male in any ordinary sense, neither is human maleness to be confused with the fatherhood of God, as Jesus emphatically indicated when he told his disciples to "call no one your father on earth, for you have one Father, the one in heaven".[28] That saying powerfully clarifies the issue, as we might expect. To it we may append as a kind of gloss this laconic advice

---

[26] Hilary of Poitiers, *On the Trinity* 1.4, in *Nicene and Post-Nicene Fathers of the Christian Church,* second series, vol. 9, p. 41; and Gregory of Nyssa, *On the Making of Man* 22.4, in *Nicene and Post-Nicene Fathers of the Christian Church,* second series, vol. 5, p. 412.

[27] Arnobius, *Against the Heathen,* III.8, *Ante-Nicene Fathers,* vol. 6, p. 466.

[28] Mt 23:9 NRSV.

from Hilary: "Remember that the revelation is not of the father manifested as God, but of God manifested as Father."[29]

So understood, there is only one true Father, God, "our Father who is in heaven". In Ephesians 3:14–15, he is called "the Father from whom every family in heaven and on earth takes its name". The correct human understanding of proper human fatherhood should be derived from the divine fatherhood, rather than assuming that the divine fatherhood is derived from ordinary human relationships. Athanasius wrote that "we men . . . are called fathers of our own children" because "God is properly, and alone truly, Father of his Son".[30]

New Testament accounts of the virginal conception of Jesus remind us of the Genesis accounts of the creation of the universe: by God's will and Word alone, life is called out of nothingness into being. The Virgin Mary out of virginity conceives by hearing and obeying the call of God. As Matthew 1:18 and 20 put it, Mary was "found to be with child from the Holy Spirit" and as an angel from God told Joseph in a dream, "the child conceived in her is from the Holy Spirit". The account in Luke 1:26–38 is more dramatic. Gabriel announced to Mary simply that "The Holy Spirit will come upon you, and the power of the Most High will overshadow you; therefore the child to be born will be holy; he will be called Son of God." None of this places "the Most High" in a class with the gentile *dii genitales,* who had unmistakably sexual, genital contact with "the daughters of men" as well as with goddesses. For centuries, Christian painters chastely, but rather literally, represented Mary as conceiving by the entrance of God's creating Word into her ear, borne by the dove of the Spirit on a beam of divine light from the mouth of the Father in Heaven. Mary, hearing the word of God, received it, conceived, and brought forth the Son of God.

The living example of Jesus shaped the New Testament understanding and language for God. His teaching and practice not

[29] Hilary of Poitiers, op. cit., 3.22, p. 68.

[30] Athanasius, *Against the Arians* 1.23, in *Nicene and Post-Nicene Fathers of the Christian Church,* second series, vol. 4, p. 320.

only referred to God as Father much more frequently than had the Old Testament but also decisively moved such references in the direction of the language of familial intimacy and affection. In a 1985 publication called *Harper's Bible Dictionary* (but prepared and copyrighted under the aegis of the Society of Biblical Literature), we read that "for Jesus, 'Father' was the principal and most frequent designation of God" and that "the concept of God as Father expressed the personal relationship to God affirmed by Jesus and the church (e.g., Mt 11:25–27)... "[31] Men and women of faith are thus accepted by adoption through Christ as children and heirs of God the Father.

The array of evidence we have reviewed in this section should make it unmistakably clear that, in the biblical and churchly understandings, God is not male. That being so, it will be appropriate to replace Professor Daly's slogan. I suggest the following as a substitute: "Since God is not male, the male is not god." That conception should help us all.

IV. THE LORD'S PRAYER

"Our Father who art in heaven, hallowed be thy name" is perhaps the most revealing invocation in Scripture and liturgy. But it is also the most habitual. We have almost tamed it out of meaning. We are so accustomed to it, almost inured to it, that we need to get beyond its customary facade, to see it fresh, to recognize it as gospel, as good news.

Those opening words are explosive on impact. How can we poor, ignorant, sullied mortals dare to address the Lord God Almighty, maker of heaven and earth, as "our Father"? For Jesus Christ to do so is one thing, but for us it seems presumptuous, even impertinent. That must have been one of the first wonderments of the listening disciples, as it has been ever since. Faced with those

---

[31] Paul J. Achtemeier, general editor, et al. *Harper's Bible Dictionary* (New York, 1985), p. 684, col. B, s.v. "Names of God in the New Testament".

words, Augustine suspended his incredulity and embraced the wonder: "See how our Creator has condescended to be our Father!"[32] Hilary of Poitiers observed here how the remoteness and impersonality we may instinctively feel distancing us from God the Creator, master of the galaxies, has been converted into the familial warmth of the Son's relationship with God the Father into which Jesus invited and introduced his followers. As Hilary wrote: "But the work which the Lord [Christ] came to do was not to enable you to recognize the omnipotence of God as Creator of all things, but to enable you to know him as the Father of that Son who addresses you."[33]

That last phrase is the key: the Lord Christ came "to enable you to know God as the Father of that Son who addresses you". It is only through the words and actions of the Son that we can fully know his Father as our Father. Cyprian quite properly put it in the context of grace: "But how great is the Lord's indulgence! how great his condescension and plenteousness of good toward us, seeing that he has wished us to pray in the sight of God in such a way as to call God Father . . . , a name that none of us would dare to venture on in prayer, unless he himself had allowed us thus to pray."[34] And Cyprian beautifully caught the essence of the prayer: "It is a loving and friendly prayer, to beseech God with his own word, to come up to his ears in the prayer of Christ."[35]

John Chrysostom emphasized the everyday implications of the Lord's Prayer and of its initial postulate that God is our Father in fact and in word. When our Lord teaches us to pray "Our Father who art in heaven," Chrysostom said that

> he takes away hatred, and quells pride and casts out envy, and brings in the mother of all good things, even charity, and exterminates the inequality of human things, and shows how far the equality reaches between the king and the poor man, if at

[32] Augustine, "On the Lord's Prayer", Sermon 7.2 (Benedictine ed. Sermon 57), *Nicene and Post-Nicene Fathers of the Christian Church*, ser. I, vol. 6, p. 281.

[33] Hilary of Poitiers, *On the Trinity* 3.22, op. cit., p. 68.

[34] Cyprian, "On Prayer", par. 11, in *Ante-Nicene Fathers . . . before 325*, vol. 5, p. 450.

[35] Ibid., par. 3, p. 448.

least in those things which are greatest and most indispensable, we are all of us fellows. . . . For to all has he given one nobility, having vouchsafed to be called the Father of all alike.

The implications for human conduct and dignity of this condescension by God the Father in "ennobling" us as his children were then spelled out:

For he who has called God Father, and a common Father, would be justly bound to show both such a conversation [i.e., behavior] as not to appear unworthy of this nobility and to exhibit a diligence proportionate to the gift.

And in the petition "hallowed be thy name", Chrysostom observed that God

commands him who prays to seek that he [i.e., God] may be glorified also by our life.[36]

The remarks of Augustine, Hilary, Cyprian, and Chrysostom on the opening verse of the Lord's Prayer reintroduce themes to which we were introduced earlier in this essay, biblical and churchly understandings of God the Father and God the Son. But surely many or most of those whose energies have been deeply vested over the last fifteen or twenty years in rejecting the use of any masculine gender language for the Father and the Son, or any grammatical expression of such language, whether through nouns or masculine gender pronouns or in other ways—many or most of these may very well continue to insist on replacing such language in Scripture, theology, worship, and Christian discourse with non-Christian verbal concepts like Father-Mother God, or God the Father and Mother, or even Goddess, or God/ess, and so forth. If their commitment to the authority of the Bible and of catholic Christian doctrine is not enough to persuade them otherwise— and I deeply hope that it yet may be—then it is difficult to see what might persuade them.

Even so, important things can be done. In the first place, it can

[36] Chrysostom, Homily 19 (Matt. 6:1), in *Nicene and Post-Nicene Fathers of the Christian Church,* ser. I, vol. 10, p. 134.

be made clear by faithful Christian people, and to faithful Christian people as well, that Mother-Father, *matro-pater* kinds of language are not harmless variants on biblical and churchly language for God. To say that they are either "formal equivalents" or "theological equivalents" is naïve, whatever else it may be. At all events, such verbal strategies sound more than a little like the clever lawyer in the Gilbert and Sullivan operetta

> who can demonstrate with ease
> That two and two are three, or five, or anything
>   you please;
> . . . who can make it clear to you
> That black is white — when looked at from the
>   proper point of view;
> A marvellous philologist who'll undertake to show
> That "yes" is but another and a neater form of "no".[37]

The first important thing to do, then, is to recognize that two and two are not "anything you please", that black is not white, and that "yes" is not another and a neater form of "no" — and similarly that "God the Mother", and "God the Mother and Father" and the rest are not acceptable Christian alternatives or equivalents for Father and Son.

The second important action is to keep steadily before the Church the difference between catholic, orthodox Christianity and heretical or schismatic sects.[38] The most widely accepted test of catholicity is the often cited Vincentian Canon: *quod ubique, quod semper, quod ab omnibus creditum est,* or "what has been believed everywhere, always, and by all".[39] This threefold test of universality or ecumenicity, and antiquity, and consent can help us to distinguish between faithful and unfaithful doctrine in the Christian Church.

---

[37] W. S. Gilbert, *Utopia Limited,* act one, in *The Savoy Operas,* 2 vols. (London and New York, 1963), vol. 2, p. 317.

[38] It will be recognized by the theologically knowledgeable (whether laity or clergy) that "catholicity" is not used here in a sense excluding all churchly bodies not in communion with the Church of Rome, but that point should nonetheless be made clear out of consideration for others who may read this essay.

[39] Vincent of Lérins, *A Commonitory* 2.4 and 6, in *Nicene and Post-Nicene Fathers of the Christian Church,* ser. II, vol. 11, p. 132.

These tests were given their present form by the fifth-century St. Vincent, a member of the once famous monastery at Lérins, and they were recorded in his *Commonitory* or *Remembrancer.* They acknowledge the primary authority of Scripture as governing in the Church (to which we will return), but where there is a major dispute about the interpretation of Scripture, the threefold rule is applied to decide the merits of the issue. Vincent showed how these tests had been used by the Church in disposing of major controversies and schisms.

It will be helpful to consider the relevance of these criteria to our current controversy.[40] First, for ecumenicity, "the faith of the whole Church" around the globe, the rejection of simple biblical Father and Son language for God is certainly not "universal" in the Church but even in the West is advocated by only a small minority of middle class, largely professional and upscale people, largely in the United States. The same is true for the reverse side of this advocacy, the substitution of Mother and perhaps occasionally Goddess language. As for antiquity, "that which has been held from the earliest times", advocates of such substitutes can make no claim to that, their movement extending back less than twenty years. Finally, consent, or what "has been the acknowledged belief of all or of almost all" surely cannot describe the opponents of Father and Son language for God. Sociologically, the radical opponents of traditional biblical and theological language for God appear to represent a small but highly vocal group of political activists. Thus far, this group has demonstrated either minimal or no concern for fidelity to Scripture and the central doctrines and traditions of the Christian faith. What they do show is a deep concern for imposing their own program upon the Church, and that program is far removed from the universal, ancient, and consensual commitments of the Christian Church.

[40] The phrases I quote in this paragraph are cited from the Introduction by the editor of Vincent's *Commonitory,* the Canon of Christ Church Cathedral and Lady Margaret's Professor of Divinity at Oxford, C. A. Heurtley, in the edition cited just above.

V. ON NOT GAUGING GOD'S NATURE
BY THE LIMITS OF OUR OWN

The biblical and catholic expressions for God that I have sought
to uphold are among the profound mysteries of Christian faith.
Of such mysteries, Hilary of Poitiers wrote that: "What man
cannot understand, God can be." In a longer passage, worth
reading in its entirety, Hilary cautioned that we men and women

> must not measure the Divine nature by the limitations of [our]
> own, but gauge God's assertions concerning Himself by the scale
> of His own glorious self-revelation. For the best student is he
> who does not read his thoughts into the book, but lets it reveal
> its own; who draws from it its sense, and does not import his
> own into it, nor force upon its words a meaning which he had
> determined was the right one before he opened its pages. Since
> then we are to discourse of the things of God, let us assume that
> God has full knowledge of Himself, and bow with humble
> reverence to His Words. For He Whom we can only know
> through His own utterances is the fitting witness concerning
> Himself.[41]

Perhaps the best brief example of Christian understandings
of language for God is found in Origen's reply to the attack
upon Christianity by the second-century pagan Celsus. Celsus
had argued that God "is not to be reached by word", and
that "he cannot be expressed by name". Origen, in his response, established a crucial distinction: God cannot be revealed
by words or names that we originate, but he is revealed by
his Word to us. In other words, God can be expressed by the
name he names himself in disclosing himself to us "in order to
lead the hearer by the hand, as it were, and so enable him to
comprehend something of God, so far as attainable by human
nature".[42]

[41] Hilary of Poitiers, *On the Trinity* 3.1 and 1.18, pp. 62 and 45 in *Nicene and Post-Nicene Fathers of the Christian Church,* second series, vol. 9, pp. 62 and 45. The divine pronouns were capitalized by Hilary's editor, Professor W. Sanday of Oxford, in 1898.

[42] Origen, *Against Celsus* 6.65, in *The Ante-Nicene Fathers,* vol. 4, p. 603.

The deep mystery remains, but along with it there is the clarity of the Scripture and of the Christian tradition. God is *not* male but we may, on the gracious invitation of Christ and in the unbroken tradition of the Faith, address him as "our Father who art in heaven, hallowed be thy name", and in similar words. Not to do so comes very close to being the sin against the Holy Spirit. The Apostle Paul put it this way:

> When we cry, "Abba, Father, it is the Spirit himself bearing witness with our spirit that we are children of God."[43]

---

[43] Rom 8:14–16. See also Gal 4:6.

IN THE IMAGE OF GOD:
MALE, FEMALE, AND THE
LANGUAGE OF THE LITURGY

Suzanne R. Scorsone

There are those who feel that the only way to ensure that women are treated at long last as men's equals is to banish any male-evocative words from the liturgy—and from the rest of religious and secular culture. The argument of this small contribution to a large debate is that the conflict is unnecessary to the equality of women, that it is probably counterproductive, and that the best way to assure the equality we all want is to recognize the gender-inclusive and the feminine, rather than to censor out the masculine. We can then turn our attention back to the two great commandments, to the one thing necessary, free of at least this distraction.

It may be useful to examine some of the points of departure from which I, as one Catholic woman among a like-minded many, have come to this perspective.

1. The English language has always, from the earliest days of which we have any written record, used the word "man" in two senses. Always there have been the generic (equivalent to the Latin *homo*) and the male gender-specific (equivalent to *vir*).

So much by way of pseudoetymology and claims from history based on little or no research has been scattered across the liturgical language debate that I must ask your patience while I do some documentation of at least an illustrative sort. Those who find the English language breathlessly intriguing, as I do, may even enjoy it.

For Old English, Anglo-Saxon, that craggy and evocative, stirring language, a few examples should suffice. I use a number of such examples because it is here that the language begins at its most primitive. If "man" had sexist roots, they should appear here, but they do not. Aelfric's *Grammar,* an ancient dictionary, puts it precisely: "aegPer is man ge wer ge wíf" (either is man ye male person or ye female person).[1] L. K. Shook, in fact, would translate Aelfric's definition as meaning "Both *wer* (= Latin *vir*) and *wíf* are covered by *man.*"[2] *Wíf,* incidentally, did not mean some sort of subordinate identity derivative from the man to whom she was married (the ideological underpinning of the neologism "Ms"). A *wíf* was the genderspecific term for a woman of any age, married or unmarried.[3] A girl was a *wífchild*[4] and a widow remained a *wíf.*[5] A female friend to man or woman was a *wíf-freond.*[6] Being a man's *wíf* was more like the converse of what we would mean by saying a male was "her man".

The very words "woman" and "women" in contemporary English are derived from *wíf-man* and *wíf-men.* Over time the word was simplified by dropping the "f"; to this day the spoken, pronounced form of the plural (wimen), as distinct from its spelling, retains this original Anglo-Saxon form. The word means "female man", i.e., "female person", translated by Bosworth as "foemina homo".[7] Thus our very term designating women, including the women's movement itself, has its genesis in the generic meaning of the word "man".

The Anglo-Saxons, however, took this even-handed understanding of *man* or *mann* beyond Aelfric's technical definitions to applied usage. *The Anglo-Saxon Chronicle* for 640 A.D. speaks of

[1] Joseph Bosworth and T. Northcote Toller, *An Anglo-Saxon Dictionary* (London: Oxford University Press, 1898), p. 668.

[2] Personal communication.

[3] Bosworth and Toller, *An Anglo-Saxon Dictionary,* p. 1217.

[4] Rev. Joseph Bosworth, *A Compendious Anglo-Saxon and English Dictionary* (London: Gibbons & Co., Ltd., 1901), p. 252.

[5] Bosworth and Toller, *An Anglo-Saxon Dictionary,* p. 1218.

[6] T. Northcote Toller, *Supplement to An Anglo-Saxon Dictionary by J. Bosworth* (London: Oxford University Press, 1921), p. 745.

[7] Bosworth, *A Compendious Anglo-Saxon Dictionary.*

"Aorcengota, hálifémne and wundorlíc man" (Aorchengota, a holy virgin and a wonderful man [person]).[8] Aelfric's (another Aelfric) *Lives of Saints* places in the mouth of the soon-martyred St. Agatha the words *"Eala du min drihten, Pe me to menn gesceope..."* (Oh, thou, my Lord, you who shaped me a man).[9] One does doubt she is claiming that she is not guilty of the capital charge of consecrated virginity on grounds that she is really a male in disguise.

The earliest use of "man" as an inclusive term having been established, let us trace that same usage forward in time.

The court of King James I of England and IV of Scotland considered it altogether unexceptionable that the new English translation of the Bible should declare that "God created man in his own image, in the image of God created he him; male and female created he them."[10] This was normal usage in the court of a king who was the heir of two highly educated sovereign queens, one his mother, Mary Queen of Scots. The other was the relative who provided for his upbringing and from whom he inherited his English throne, Elizabeth I, one of the most powerful monarchs in the world of that day.

So too with more modern English. In 1863, when Abraham Lincoln spoke at Gettysburg of "a new nation, conceived in liberty, and dedicated to the proposition that all men are created equal",[11] it never occurred to any of his hearers that his policy implied the abolition of the slavery only of males. And in 1936, G. K. Chesterton said of Alice Meynell that "since she was so emphatically a craftsman, she was emphatically an artist and not an aesthete...."[12] Chesterton is clearly speaking of a woman, using "craft*man*" in the unselfconsciously inclusive sense. His

---

[8] Dorothy Whitelock et al., trans., *The Anglo-Saxon Chronicle* (Brunswick, N.J.: Rutgers University Press, 1961), p. 19, and Bosworth and Toller, *An Anglo-Saxon Dictionary.*

[9] Walter W. Skeat, trans. and ed., *Aelfric's Lives of Saints* (London: Oxford University Press, 1881), pp. 206–7, and L. K. Shook, personal communication.

[10] Gen 1:27.

[11] Abraham Lincoln, "Gettysburg Address", 1863, in John Bartlett, *Bartlett's Familiar Quotations,* 13th ed. (Boston: Little, Brown, 1955), p. 540.

[12] G. K. Chesterton, *Autobiography* (London: Hamish Hamilton, 1986), pp. 286–87.

distance from sexism in this usage is understood from the company in which his reminiscences place her—Hilaire Belloc, William Butler Yeats, and George Bernard Shaw, among others. Chesterton was not cramped by the ideology of pronouns; he was simply using his vivid and precise command of the language to say something wonderful about someone he thought of as "a message from the sun".

For that matter, when Canadian children sing "Oh Canada", designated as the national anthem as recently as 1980, the girls are not bracketing themselves out as born subversives every time the words "true patriot love in all thy sons command" pass through their earnest, straight-standing selves.

Inclusive usage is not confined to the high-falutin' literati. Two entirely non-ideologized girls from the South Bronx or Brooklyn and the surrounding area may express anything from greeting, through surprise or admiration, to warning or anger by different inflections of "Hey, man!"[13]

None of this is to deny that women have suffered from discrimination and disability. It would take an entirely different, and far longer, piece of work to document the extent, and the limits, of those disabilities. The rights and activity of women have varied by era, by class, by region and even by individual personality.

Nor is it to deny that, once a woman has absorbed the notion that "man" is solely exclusive, hearing it used in Scripture and liturgy can become hurtful and alienating. I recall, indeed, the day my (female) eighth grade English teacher told the class that "he" was the pronoun to use when one did not know the gender of the individual. When the explanation given was that it was considered better to be male, and the choice of "he" gave the unknown individual the benefit of the doubt, I was the first, as it happens, among several in my all-girl class to say that it was unfair. We knew we were as good as boys—better, in our opinion. She meant to indicate usage, but her explanation took the form of a mistaken moral and philosophical position. Unwittingly mixing levels here, as it so often does, led us down the garden path. If many teachers

[13] Personal observation.

of that era taught the indefinite pronoun that way, perhaps taking it out of some cloned teaching manual scattered across the continent, it is no wonder many of those girls, now women, are angry. The fact is, however, that the teacher, who in other respects had many virtues, did not understand this aspect of the language clearly. She is not alone; feminist neologizers construe "he" as she did. And a great deal of sloganeering, real pain, and literary contortion has turned on that truncated and incorrect understanding of the language.

One might note, too, that this is more a North American problem than a pan-English problem. In British English, one can use "one" when one wants to keep one's own or anyone else's gender indefinite. Having dropped "one" as too formal or too arch, North Americans are left to choose their indefinite pronoun from among "you" (too colloquial and aggressively personal for literary use, even for North Americans) and "he"—now expanded to "he and she", "he/she", or leapfrogging the two by paragraph. The irony of dropping the formal but non-sexist English usage, then, is that it has resulted in the creation of a vacuum filled only by the usage which, while essentially non-sexist, can be interpreted in sexist ways, or by a self-conscious, stilted neo-formalism.

This essay, however, confines itself to saying that, during a social history both of women's disability and of women's strength, the speakers of English have always recognized both inclusive and gender-specific uses of the word "man". Such disabilities as there have been arise from other causes. Were the word "man" to be decisive for the perception of women, then Latin, which makes a clear distinction between *homo,* the inclusive, and *vir* and *mulier,* the specific, should have been the language of a fully egalitarian society. Yet women in Roman society had fewer rights and were far more under the authority of father and husband than was ever the case for English-speakers at any point in their history. No English-speaker has ever had the unlimited authority over property and person, even to the point of capital punishment, possessed by the early Roman husband who held his wife in *manus* and his male and female children under *patria potestas.*

Both languages had a generic form (*homo, man*) as well as a gender-specific form, yet the society in which the generic overlapped

234   LITURGICAL AND SPIRITUAL DIMENSIONS

the gender specific was arguably the less sexist. Important as language is for perception, therefore, it cannot be a simple one-for-one determinant of behavior. Sexism exists, but truncating the language, particularly when it actually bears non-sexist, inclusive meaning, seems a futile exercise in shooting the messenger.

This double use of "man" is not a source of confusion: it rather carries important nuances of meaning which cannot be conveyed by any alternative phrasings. English is a highly contextually construed language, the sense of many words being identified by reference to surrounding structures and content. Obvious examples are the discrimination of present or past tense in the word "read", or even, in spoken colloquial English, of whether one is referring to a riverine plant, part of a woodwind, or a literary experience when speaking of "a good read/reed". It is therefore a simple and entirely familiar mental operation for the speaker of English, from the most literary to the most colloquial, to sort the generic from the gender-specific uses of "man". The generic sense of "man", moreover, carries its own connotations of emphasis on the individual person representing the whole (a form of synecdoche). It is only very imperfectly replaced by such alternatives as "person" (Greek-derived, with its legal and role implications) or "human" (Latin-derived, with the implied taxonomic distinction from animal, alien or even angelic species).

The identification of the word "man" as solely a male designator and hence as discriminatory is an artifact of the past two or, at most, three decades. This identification is a political/ideological construct, a straw man (gender-specific) set up largely so it can be knocked down. It has no real basis in the millennium and a half of development of the English language. A far more effective, because accurate, feminist understanding of the language would emphasize the always-existing inclusion of woman in the word "man", rather than promoting a bowdlerization of the language to find other, less suitable (or euphonious) words or constructs to include the woman who had never been excluded in the first place.

Many women, feminist women, and I among them, refuse to allow other feminists to exclude us from the word "man", to which we have as much right as do men. We will not be excluded from all the English literature of the past fifteen hundred years, nor do we want a misdirected political agenda, however well-meaning, to create in us a false sense of consciousness-raised (or razed) "rage" every time we read the word "man" used in the generic sense. We love the English language and its literature too much, we understand it too well, and we have enough else to deal with in life without this unnecessary aggravation. Much that comes to me from other Catholic women indicates that this is not a minority view.

What is being called "inclusive language" is not truly inclusive; it is rather a highly exclusive construct which cuts away meaning-bearing words and the vitality of both masculine and feminine images. It excludes anything which is not neutral, or perhaps neutered. It thereby impoverishes the language. It also impoverishes our culture, as the vast majority of our works of literature are falsely dismissed as "male chauvinist"—and our Scripture and liturgical texts with them. The multivalent word "man" is being destroyed as a unifier as males and females are increasingly being viewed as different—and mutually antagonistic—species. This is the final irony of an ideology of word use which was in theory intended to unify male and female by language, but sought in praxis to do it by a methodology of conflict and rejection.

2. Scripture is the Word of God. However, much we may learn about the interpretation of this or that aspect of it, we cannot tamper with its wording beyond arranging translations (always inexact) in ways which make it maximally comprehensible. The "wisdom" of one age, or of one class, or of one culture—all operative in the secular and Church manifestations of the women's movement—has something valid to contribute, but it may not see or know something that appears quite obvious to another age, class or culture. To package interpretation as translation (which is what changing scriptural wording would be) is to limit the Word of God to only one possible manifestation of its richness. Some interpretation is inevitable in the business of translation, but systematic shifts of wording which is clear in the original (from "Father" to "Creator", from "he" to "he and she", from "Father" to "Mother" or even "Father/Mother") are going beyond the inevi-

table to the inadmissible. This is true not only of the Liturgy of
the Word itself, but of all those sections in the many liturgies
of the Church which are quotes, paraphrases or allusions to
Scripture.

3. Those changes which can be made should be such as would
be unnoticeable. They should simply be a constructive part of the
liturgy in what it is doing. One example of such a change would
be the shift from "for all men" to "for all"—unnecessary but
unobtrusive.

Many of the "inclusive" changes suggested in recent years are so
obvious, and stick out like such verbal sore thumbs, that the
ideological point being made takes precedence in the hearers'
minds over the actual content of the liturgical or scriptural phrase
itself. We can pass over the merely silly, like one bishops' conference committee document on labor that placed "fisher-people"
among a list of occupations.[14] Rather, I think here of hymns
addressed to "faithful Parent", or transmogrifications like baptism
"in the Name of the Creator, the Sanctifier and the Vivifier".
Something like that last, ironically, could undo the ecumenical
work of decades by throwing the mutual recognition of baptism
by the various Christian churches into doubt, an illustration of the
principle that any single idea, even a good one, pursued to its
extreme, will become counterproductive by its interference with
other good things.

In liturgy, the ideology of language should not distort or
replace the interpenetrating acts and ideas, the interaction between
God and Man, are what the liturgy is and without which it has no
point. I would not have us ending our prayers with "we ask you
this, O Parent, in solidarity with Jesus our Sibling, in the androgynous power of the Holy Spirit".

4. Related to this is the principle that all liturgical language
should be aesthetically suitable to, and expressive of, the reality
being transmitted. Most of the time that means that the words

[14] Episcopal Commission for Social Affairs, Canadian Conference of Catholic
Bishops, "Free Trade: At What Cost? A Message on the Occasion of the Feast
of St. Joseph the Worker", May 1987, p. 2.

should be so crafted as to be beautiful, evocative, and a means of leading the hearer beyond himself (generic) to God and to the service of his children. Much political/ideological jargon (and it matters not in what field) is far from euphonious or transcendent; it sounds more like a machinery instruction manual or like political sloganeering. It speaks to its own initiates but not to the general mass of people. (That liturgical pun—based on two highly diverse, contextually distinguished meanings of homonyms—is entirely deliberate. Just so is English rich with puns.)

The Catholic liturgy is for everyone and should speak to everyone well. The English translation of the liturgy has been so bereft of image and vivid language (which still exist untranslated in the Latin) as it is that it seems a pity to threaten it with yet another form of banality.

5. Changes made to the liturgy should not alter the theology of the liturgy. To use just one example, the word "Father" is, indeed, gender-specific. Yet to replace it with "Creator" would be to remove the "Father-child" relationship and replace it with something more impersonal. "Creator" is certainly true, but "Father" is also true and our vision is obscured without it. "Parent" is a role designation but not a personal name, so it will not do either. In English we have only an impersonal use of the neuter, so God cannot be "It". "He" is short of the whole truth, but so is "She", and taking turns between them would be glaringly artificial.

God is not only beyond gender himself; he invented it for creatures at a certain level of structural complexity who needed to reproduce. Once he had, by evolution and/or other means, created human beings (here the term is appropriate), he made gender into a union of difference which could mirror, if distantly, his own trinitarian unity in love and creativity. He is not just beyond gender; he is prior to it.

There are those who argue that there is reason for identifying the first person of the Trinity with fatherhood, which is masculine. Insofar as this is so, then that reason has to do with certain things that we see as the highest in fatherhood, rather than with maleness as such. What is being evoked has to do with strength, with authoritativeness, with unwavering protectiveness, with faithful cleaving to both mother and children, with justice gentled by mercy, with wisdom and understanding. These attributes are associated (although of course *not* exclusively) with human fathers at their best; human fathers are in fact male.

This is, however, a large world within a large universe, and we have to see clearly that none of these things is predicated upon biological maleness in itself. God did not create males and then add females as an afterthought to help out. (Nor did he create Adam, look at what he had made, and say "Hmm—not bad for a rough draft, but I can do better.") Let us prescind for a moment from the fact that our high concept of fatherhood is better fulfilled by some human fathers than by others. Gender is, as we have mentioned, something we share with a mind-boggling number of other complex organisms. Among mammals, all mothers nurture by taxonomic and functional definition, but "fatherliness" is far less universal. Wolf fathers and gibbon fathers do bond to their mates for life and do nurture their offspring. Male chimpanzees couple promiscuously in a troop and will play with, teach and protect any infant in the group (allowing for individual personality variation). Male African lions will support females in nurturing their own offspring but will kill the cubs of defeated males while taking over a pride of females. Female polar bears give birth alone, nurture and protect alone, and drive off any nearby males, genetic father or not, knowing that males are inclined to kill any cubs they find. Among nonmammals, the picture is still more diverse. Some male birds nurture their own young; others do not. Among many (not all) reptiles, such as turtles, or among amphibians such as frogs and most fish, neither mother nor father nurtures the young; they are left to hatch and fend for themselves. All possible permutations seem to exist, including a nurturant male seahorse, in whose body the female deposits her eggs.

Our image of the fatherhood of God—indeed our images of both fatherhood and motherhood—are therefore not inherently derived from biological maleness or femaleness as such (let male chauvinists and militant feminists both take note). Fatherhood and motherhood as concepts are an understanding of roles carried by males and females among *Homo sapiens.* God created this species to be like other species in most things but unique in that it bears his image. Yet we have to bear that image in the terms of the incarnational reality that we are. Thus we use our own most powerful terms of relationship, those of family, of fatherhood, of motherhood, of the union of Father and Son, of the love of God the Father toward us his children, and of our love in return.

That does not make God male. Nor does it make woman any the less God's image; all the faithful love, wisdom, protectiveness and strength we associate with motherhood also originate in God. The attributes we associate with the masculine and with the feminine must both be equally derived from God, since "God created man in his own image . . . male and female he created them."[15] We are evoking attributes and relationships which are in fact beyond and independent of biological gender.

In another sentient species the image might be expressed differently. Yet we have to perceive God's image in terms of what we actually are as he has created us. He has taken that physical and spiritual reality and made it into an image of himself. So we call God Father and human fathers happen to be male. That is not an exaltation of maleness; it is simply a statement about the fatherhood of God.

Perhaps truth is found, not in the neutering of language, but in the full, vital recognition of both the feminine and the masculine, which subsist in all of us in varying proportion. Perhaps the truth is most nearly touched by a rejoicing in the feminine and the masculine rather than a rejection of them.

All icons are less than the reality, and words are no better than pictures. Our age and culture may have too literal and linear a faith in words, without seeing them as image and icon—no more, though no less. Both word and picture are attempts at portraying a revelation which is perceived by grace but which precedes and is not simply reducible either to word or to icon.[16] Liturgical words are not the tedious but analytical and narrowly defined terms of a

[15] Gen 1:27.
[16] Cf. Cardinal Joseph Ratzinger, "Cardinal Frings' Speeches During the Second Vatican Council", in *Communio* 15, no. 1 (Spring 1988): 137.

monograph in particle physics. The realities they convey are not so manipulable. Liturgical words are the poetic terms of a metaphysics which struggles to be as precise as it can about a vast, revealed reality which it can do no more than evoke—that it may evoke.

6. Relatively few women feel excluded by the word "man". I myself did not learn that I was supposed to feel excluded from the words of Scripture, liturgy and hymns until I was well into my twenties. From childhood I quite naturally applied all the generic senses of the word "man" to myself and to all men (generic) with no difficulty at any age in distinguishing them from the gender-specific uses of the word. That "God saved man" meant me, as did the fact that "God made man in his own image". I have heard from many other women, from all points on the political spectrum on other issues, who say that the word "man" and so-called inclusive language are a non-issue for them. As one woman, a volunteer for an international development organization in the Canadian Church and no right-winger, put it to me: " 'Man' is an image. Language has to use images. We call the Holy Spirit a dove, but nobody thinks he's a bird. We just use images because we have to, but we know that's what they are."

There are, in fact, large numbers of women who are exasperated with the bickering about inclusive language. Let those who doubt this go (to listen, not to lecture) among any grassroots gathering of women, Catholic or Protestant. When I am asked to a parish to speak, I make a point of raising issues other than my topic with those who sit near me over lunch and then of sitting back and listening. Let those who want to hear the grassroots go, not to feminist conferences, but to the neighborhood fabric store, as I did while writing this article. One woman, having seen me scrawling away at a coffee shop a few minutes before, asked what I had been doing. Upon hearing, the eyes of all half-dozen women about the counter—educated, community active mothers of children, single women and one grandmother—lit up with recognition. A very heated conversation ensued. "It's so silly", said the older woman. "I have always seen 'man' as meaning all of us, men and women." "Next they are going to be wanting to change the Lord's Prayer", said a mother of three young children, member of her local United Christian Church Education Committee. She was, of course, quite right. These women are strongly in favor of equal rights, equal education, equal opportunity, and all those things that feminism originally represented; none of them sees this more radical feminist extreme as representing them as women or as in any way essential to those central issues of equality. They are not alone.

If we are to be a Church which consults broadly and accurately with the people as a whole, rather than with small sub-segments of an elite with special interests, we should ensure that liturgical writers staffing episcopal conferences or publishing houses, with their small numbers and disproportionately huge distributional impact, are not pressured into taking positions which do not represent the feelings of the majority of women. If the bishops were to do a valid, large, random-sample poll of Catholic women, they would find that the neutering of language was desired by relatively few.

Our own poll findings in this archdiocese show that Catholics, and especially women, want two things more than anything else from the Church: contact with God in the sacraments, and Christian education and formation for their children. Inclusive language was seldom even raised by respondents.[17] Even in these years of reduced church attendance, Catholics attend more often than Protestants and women attend Mass more frequently than do men (83 percent compared to 68 percent, regularly or occasionally). In other respects, too, women are far more active in the Church, on average. Even the drop in Mass attendance over recent years is less pronounced among women than among men.[18] One should also note that it takes the form of reduced frequency rather than of outright lapse or leaving the Church. So, any notion that women are leaving in droves over the use of pronouns simply does not reflect observable reality.

Some indication of what a poll of Catholics on the specific issue of language might find is given by a Decima Research poll done

[17] Archdiocese of Toronto, Sharelife, unpublished report, "Awareness and Donation Support Study", Gallup Poll, released June 1985.

[18] D. Grelet and Decima Research, "Lay Catholics and the Church", unpublished report, Archdiocese of Toronto, released 10 May 1988.

for the *United Church Observer* in March of 1988.[19] The United
Church is the quintessential embodiment of liberal Protestantism
in Canada. Women have been ordained to its ministry since 1936,
and its national staff has a very active interest in women's issues.
One would expect, therefore, that "inclusive language" would
draw the greatest support among any church population from
United Church Observer readers, who tend to be the more active
and committed members of their Church.

To lend added weight to this expectation, the question, as
asked, was somewhat loaded toward the interpretation of the
traditional language as exclusive rather than inherently inclusive.
Readers were asked whether they would prefer that the language
of Scripture, church services and business meetings "continue to
be male-oriented" or contain "both male and female images". Yet,
the responding population favored the continuation of "male-
oriented" language 63.4 percent to 36.4 percent! There was no statis-
tically significant difference between male and female respondents;
the small spread there was showed women more in favor of the
traditional language (65.0 percent) than were men (59.4 percent).
Even education showed no significant difference. Those under 40
did show a significant difference, but even they responded 56.3
percent to 42.5 percent in favor of "male-oriented language".

One would suspect that, had the question been phrased in such
a way as to include the possibility of the egalitarian definition of
language, the response would have been even more overwhelmingly
in favor of the traditional usage. I would interpret these figures,
not as revealing a woeful, intractable sexism in the pews and
among the women of the United Church, but as demonstrating a
clear comprehension of the egalitarian, inclusive meanings of the
words at issue. If this is the status of the question among members
of the United Church of Canada, it is only reasonable to expect
that a similar survey of Catholics would show an even stronger
preference for the use of traditional language.

I wonder whether the grassroots women of the churches do not

---

[19] David Allan, *United Church Observer,* personal communication, referring to
United Church Observer Decima Survey and derived article, July 1988.

have a stronger sense of their own dignity and equality as women than do the few in rarified, elite factional networks who have taken prominence upon themselves as our unelected, unrepresentative spokesmen.

7. Catholic doctrine, as such, is silent on the precise social relationship of male and female. A socioeconomically role-equivalent approach is possible. So is a more gender-separated, complementary interpretation of roles. How it is viewed may vary from culture to culture, class to class, age to age.

It would be most unfortunate if the bishops, or those writing translations of liturgies, were to take up one allowable position on male-female roles and, by enshrining it in the central Catholic interaction of the liturgy, impose it on all those Catholics who hold a different but entirely legitimate view. The roles of male and female, and with them the relationship of masculine and feminine, are largely a lay matter, and the laity have by no means reached a consensus on it. Nor, perhaps, need they. Perhaps this is one of those areas in which a plurality of views engenders freedom and vigor within the Church. If people can be Catholic and hold various views, they should be allowed to do so. *"In essentiis, unitas; in dubiis, libertas, in omnibus, caritas."*

The liturgy should not become an ideological Procrustean bed used by one faction to silence all other views. It is the Church's worship of God—not a political tool. If people of one view can convince others in the Church of the merit of their position, more power to them. Liturgy used as a weapon, however, would not only be grossly unfair in implying that God himself gave one side the big battalions; it would also be a deflection of the liturgy from its real purpose, which is direct contact with God. Sexual politics, rather than prayer, would become the reality of the action. People should be allowed by the liturgy to pray in their own way, and with their own approach, letting the ideological positions stand or fall on their own merits—separately.

This is what we will do if we truly believe in legitimate and authentic freedom and plurality within the unity of the Church.

CONCLUSION

In this era we need peace among Christians if we are to work together for peace in the world at large. Perhaps every era has the same need, but this is especially our own. The point that the full equality of women with men must be recognized in word and action has been made and has been generally accepted, although bringing it consistently down to the ground of everyday relationships has some way yet to go. We will not, however, succeed in bringing peace between men and women if we proceed on a class conflict model, trying to strike down the masculine at every turn, obliterating all that is not feminine or neuter. We will succeed far better and far more quickly if we love one another, which is probably what the Lord would prefer in any case.

One might see and apply, therefore, certain general principles to bring peace, equality and mutual acceptance to men and women in our liturgical language. Underlying these principles is Occam's Razor, the philosophical principle that whatever is the most simple and direct, and the least unnecessarily multiplied and complex, is that which is most likely to be closest to the truth.

A. We can recognize and make abundantly explicit in our teaching at all levels that the word "man" and the pronouns "he", "him", and "his", along with occasional and related others like "son", do, in certain contexts, mean both males and females. It is, if you will, authentically feminist to affirm that the word "man" belongs to women as much as to men—and let us rely on the proven linguistic intelligence of people to tell the humans from the males as they have always done.

B. Our liturgists can be put to work, not in expunging masculine imagery from Scripture and liturgical language, but in identifying and making better use of feminine imagery. Scripture compares God to a mother—to one who, though a mother should forget her child, will never forsake us, and to the woman who seeks for the lost coin until she finds it. The *Ruah,* the Spirit-breath of God, is largely a feminine image. So is Holy Wisdom, which Pope John Paul II, following tradition, applies both to

Mary and to Christ.[20] Christ himself wished to gather all Jerusalem, and with it all the world, as a hen gathers her brood under her wings—but we would not.[21]

If Christ would gather us rather than have us bicker and negate among ourselves, then let us allow ourselves to be gathered, opening ourselves—and our language—to one another. Our difference is created, not for conflict, but for synergy. Male and female are not meant to be joined in a struggle for power, acting out some ideological model of class conflict rooted in biology. Our biology is meant, rather, to be rejoiced in, to be a unifier and to be transcended both in this world and the next. Class conflict between the sexes, therefore, is fundamentally foreign to the Christian vision. Interwoven as our relationships and our biological gender identity are, it is the relationships that will live in eternity. "In the resurrection they neither marry nor are given in marriage, but are like the angels in heaven."[22] Or again, as real and as much an element of ourselves as our gender identity is, it is not meant to cause division between us. "There is neither Jew nor Greek, there is neither slave nor free, there is neither male nor female; for you are all one in Christ Jesus."[23]

Through the centuries people have found it difficult to maintain the fullness of balance in perceiving Christ as true God and true man. Perhaps we have a parallel difficulty in perceiving both the full, earthly, biological reality and the transcendent reality of our own human selves. So, in one era we tend to absolutize the spiritual; in another, such as our own, we seem to absolutize the biological. Yet, the balance is the fullness of both. We are male and female, but we are meant to be united in the concrete reality of that difference, a difference which we are ultimately intended to transcend. Our vision is one of complementarity and unity, not of conflict.

[20] Pope John Paul II, Homily on the Feast of Our Lady of Sorrows, Downsview, Ontario, Sept. 15, 1984.
[21] Lk 13:34.
[22] Mt 22:30.
[23] Gal 3:28.

Medieval Christians were nearer the mark when they used the poetic model, not of conflict, but of all creation in harmony, moving in solemn and joyful dance to the music of the spheres. Nor is this merely an obsolete, archaic image; the sciences themselves have shifted from perceiving chaos to perceiving an overarching order and unity at all levels, from the vast to the infinitesimal. The name of God is again being spoken by some among the astrophysicists.[24] Our biological and spiritual beings are part of and transcend the larger cosmic unity of his universe.

T. S. Eliot, the consummate image-painter in modern English, touched the poetry of it:

> ... The association of man
>   and woman
> in daunsinge, signifying
>   matrimonie—
> A dignified and commodious
>   sacrament.
> Two and two, necessarye
>   coniunction,
> Holding eche other by the hand or
>   the arm
> Whiche betokeneth concorde.
>   Round and round the fire ...
> Rustically solemn or in rustic
>   laughter ...
> Earth feet, loam feet, lifted in
>   country mirth
> Mirth of those long since under
>   earth
> Nourishing the corn.[25]

Liturgy is act and word, immanence and transcendence, the physical and the spiritual, rational thought and evocative poetry,

[24] E.g., Stephen W. Hawking, *A Brief History of Time: From the Big Bang to Black Holes* (Toronto: Bantam Books, 1988), pp. 173–75.

[25] T. S. Eliot, "East Coker" of "Four Quartets" in T. S. Eliot, *The Complete Plays and Poems of T. S. Eliot* (London: Faber and Faber, 1969), pp. 177–78.

movement and music. It is the at once immanent and transcendent invitation of God who is the great Unifier. So we, biological and spiritual beings, male and female, are invited to tread handfast the measures of the Great Dance, in the image of the ineffable God.

THE SPIRITUAL PATERNITY
OF "INCLUSIVE LANGUAGE"

Paul M. Quay, S.J.

When the American Bishops' Committee on the Liturgy (BCL) first raised the question of "noninclusive language" in the fall of 1979, its concern was for a "full and active participation of the entire assembly in the liturgical action", something obstructed by the "fact that some members of our eucharistic assemblies feel excluded or alienated from the prayer of the Church by the words" used. The same concern is expressed in the bishops' guidelines for liturgical and biblical language that issued from their conference in November of 1990.[1]

The problem pointed to has been a real one. But nothing that has thus far been made public indicates that the BCL ever addressed the obvious question: Do these feelings of alienation point to something truly wrong with the incriminated wordings, or, instead, do they evidence misunderstanding or even spiritual weakness in those who feel them?

To one who has read the statements of those who claim to represent these alienated members of our eucharistic assemblies, the second alternative seems not wholly unlikely. Admittedly, many feel it impolite, ungentlemanly, even to raise this possibility for discussion. Yet, in a non-sexist Church, surely what is sauce for the gander may be considered sauce for the goose. Hence, a "hermeneutic of suspicion", if in order for feminist analysis of biblical and liturgical language, might also be used concerning the complainants' sense of isolation and anguish at

[1] *Origins* 20, no. 25, (Nov. 29, 1990): 406–8.

"noninclusive language". More importantly, however, no one who truly desires people's spiritual welfare can be of help to them if he is unwilling to call them to face squarely the large part that sin has in the lives of all of us.

For this matter is, for the Church, a spiritual one. The question of "inclusive language" was first raised in this country by the New Left and quickly became one of the chief "causes" espoused by Liberal orthodoxy. But whatever the pros and cons of such linguistic usage in the secular domain, any judgments by the Church concerning the language to be used within the liturgy can only be made on the basis of her own principles: the truths of the Faith and the effects of such usage, as judged by faith, on the spiritual lives of Catholics.

To judge whether some line of action, proposed by those who claim that it is desired by the Lord, is in accord with God's will, one must see:

I. that there be nothing contrary to reason or to sound faith in what is proposed;

II. that the actions in question be such as to bring about the spiritual upbuilding of those who will be affected;

III. that an accurate assessment of the spiritual character of the persons urging the line of action shows some intrinsic probability that God might be working through them.[2]

I. REASON?

The first question is, of course: Is the language that is labeled "noninclusive" truly such, i.e., does it fail to include women on an

---

[2] Cf. the long letter of St. Ignatius Loyola to St. Francis Borgia on this subject in *Letters of Saint Ignatius of Loyola,* trans. William J. Young, S.J. (Chicago: Loyola University Press, 1959), pp. 195–211. (Original in *MHSI, Monumenta Ignatiana,* 12:632–54.)

equality with men in those passages in which all members of the human race or of the Church are intended?

In fact, there are in English no such things as "inclusive" or "noninclusive" language, "sexist" or "nonsexist" words. Employment of such phrases begs the question and surreptitiously settles the issue in advance. There can be only sexist, inclusive, or other *usage* of an already determinate language.[3] Hence, the proper way to pose the issue would be in terms of "ordinary English usage" and "feminist English usage".

Now, "man", "mankind", and the like have had for centuries a wholly inclusive meaning, referring to any member of the human race, as can be seen from any good dictionary.[4] This was their original meaning and the one from which "woman" (= female man) was derived. So also, "he" and "him", when referring to an indefinite antecedent such as "person", "someone", or the like, merely keeps alive the older generic use of this pronoun without regard to sex, even though in other circumstances it has been replaced by "she" or "it".

It is urged, however, that our language is changing, that outside the Church, in the surrounding culture, there is a strong drive to eliminate "sexist language" everywhere. Hence, while ordinary English usage might be good in itself, it is certain increasingly to be misunderstood by contemporary congregations.

Yet if the secularists within our culture have, in fact, brought about such a change,[5] ought not the bishops to oppose this introduction of implicit falsehoods into Catholic life rather than to accept them into the liturgy? For if people take a certain usage to mean something that it has never meant in the minds of those

[3] Cf. Vernard Eller, *The Language of Canaan and the Grammar of Feminism* (Grand Rapids, Mich.: Eerdmans, 1982), pp. 18–20, 23–27, and esp. 29–30. One need not agree with all that Eller says to see that neither the International Commission on English in the Liturgy (ICEL) nor the American BCL has begun to deal with the issues he and others have raised.

[4] For a brief introduction to this topic, cf. Donald De Marco, "Neutered Prayers: Is Exclusive Language Really Bad?" *Fidelity* 10, no. 1 (Jan. 1991): 24–32.

[5] Justification of this attribution of source is given below in "Spiritual Character of Originating Movement?"

who use it, if they choose to read meanings into words that have not been there hitherto, especially if they do so at the promptings of the more-than-pagan culture that surrounds them, they are, knowingly or not, assenting to falsehood. The bishops could initiate resistance to this pervasive secularism, say, by a pastoral letter pointing out the errors, express and implied, in the use of "inclusive language", in daily life as well in the liturgy.

Let us not forget that God's people have always had their own manner of speech, considered barbarous by those around them yet indispensable for the utter novelties Christian revelation brought to the world. Think only of what the New Testament does with *tapeinosis* (lit. lowness, connotes humility in NT) *aletheia* (lit. truth, connotes fidelity), or what the Fathers did with *persona,* or the early Councils with *pisteuomen eis* (salvific belief *in* Christ). We have a long tradition of liturgical usage that forms the pagan cultures around it far more than it lets itself be formed by them, even though it is their tongue that it speaks.

But it is far from clear that, apart from those unduly influenced by the academicism of the universities, any such change in usage has taken place. Thus, "man" and its compounds are accented differently in speech when used in the generic sense than when they indicate a sex. "For you and for *all* men" is instantly taken to be different in meaning from "for you and for all *men*", which latter accentuation *would* exclude women. In the few cases where accent does not distinguish, grammar almost invariably does. Of the examples contained in the present Sacramentary or Lectionary, are there any in which one cannot, if reading them aloud, tell at once whether the use is generic or indicative of the male sex?

Further, as Walter Ong, S.J., has shown at some length,[6] it is a highly distinctive feminine trait that women adopt for themselves many of the locutions, manners, and practices of men. Women easily make these masculine identifiers their own without anxiety

---

[6] *Fighting for Life: Contest, Sexuality, and Consciousness* (Ithaca, N.Y.: Cornell, 1981), pp. 71–76.

or threat to their sexual identity. So, girls today call each other "guy" and seem unconcerned if the boys call them such (though, as far as I have heard around our campuses, the young men tend to shy away from this). Men, on the other hand, avoid as the plague any indications of femininity. No normal man would dream of calling another man "gal" or let himself be so addressed. Women have no psychic problem in wearing slacks or jeans (however much, in time, they modify them into something obviously feminine). But no man will wear a dress. Thus the feminists' outraged sensitivity to "sexist language" really conceals a movement toward a profound defeminization of woman—hardly an appropriate function for the liturgical worship of Christ's Bride.

Once upon a time I argued that the BCL would never have allowed as even a temporary option any liturgical usage of ordinary English if this could reasonably be taken as exclusive of women. Once called to the bishops' attention, the matter would clearly have been too important to leave its correction for some indefinite, future reworking of the liturgical books.

Unfortunately, however, that argument soon collapsed. Quite some years ago now, the ICEL composed, entirely on its own and without Latin model, the current Preface for Thanksgiving Day: "It happened to our fathers, who came to this land, as if out of the desert, into a place of promise and hope. . . . " This truly is language that excludes, expressly ignoring the millions of Catholic descendants of African slaves as well as of the earliest inhabitants of this land. Yet the BCL has never moved to change this racist phrasing, even though it appears not in some peripheral prayer but as part of the central eucharistic action. The wonder is that there are still more blacks and American Indians in our churches than bitter and alienated women.

Despite the BCL's unconcern for genuinely exclusive usage, however, it remains true that the use of ordinary English in the liturgy is neither exclusive nor demeaning of women. Rather, as I shall argue in Section III, the push for feminist usage in the Mass represents, however unconsciously, an exact parallel to the current radical feminist effort to remake both the vernacular and the culture. It is a coercive attempt not to adapt the liturgy to our culture but to force the alien linguistic and cultural patterns of a small group upon the majority, and this through the Sacred Mysteries.

II. FAITH?

The relations between Catholic Faith and the call to replace ordinary English by feminist usage are discussed in Section III, where they can be set out more concisely and with less overlapping of categories.

BUILDING UP THE CHURCH?

Recasting liturgical and scriptural usage into a feminist mold would represent a sharp break with all past English usage.[7] All previous Christian speech and writing, including biblical translations, would quickly become subject to irrevocable misunderstanding. Since feminist English is an ideological artifact and not the product of the slow modifications that occur naturally and spontaneously, its acceptance would make past English, profane no less than sacred, inaccessible in its true meaning, cutting still more of Americans' cultural roots and further widening the breach already opened by ICEL between present liturgical language and the English of our scriptural and cultural heritage.

Since we think almost entirely in terms of language, the proposed changes would gradually make it impossible to think about man in biblical language. But since we have only one language in which to speak to God or about Him, i.e., the "horizontal" language we use with other men, if this is distorted, so also are our ways of speaking of God. Worse yet, not only would we lose biblical language for speaking of God, we would

[7] Cf. Eller, p. 3.

also lose the only kind of language He has used in speaking to us.[8]

Seemingly as a matter of principle, the ICEL and BCL have paid serious attention only to the urgings of a mysteriously influential but relatively small segment of the Church, mostly from among the college-trained, especially sisters and priests. But what of the anguish and pain of nonfeminists? At present, feminist usage merely provokes ridicule among most Americans, whatever their religion. But if brought into the liturgy or the Bible, it seems certain to arouse fierce opposition.[9] If, then, one judges that action should be taken to ease hurts inflicted by liturgical language, then something should be said about those ordinary Catholics, men and women alike, who are already confused at best, bitter or alienated at worst, by the poverty-stricken English already in use.

Many of these suffer quietly, without clamor and loud protest, but no less really. Will the adoption of feminist usage in any but the simplest situations do more than augment their pain? Or will it not alienate many more than it could possibly please? To taint what is most sacred by the introduction of ideological jargon will only dishearten the faithful still more and threaten even further the unity of the Church.[10]

Any major change would be widely publicized as showing that the Vatican had finally admitted that women have, in fact, been

[8] Cf. Eller, pp. 22–36, 49–55.

[9] Consider the fracas among Episcopalians over the revised Book of Common Prayer.

[10] There is every indication that the drive for the Tridentine Mass has little to do with Latin or with ceremonies and is mostly a misdirected response to the lack of a suitable English translation of the Novus Ordo that people could follow with devotion. Note should also be taken of those conservative Catholics who have already stopped going to Mass or have joined the movement begun by Archbishop Lefebvre because of what they regard as a threat to their faith from present translations (and, of course, the graver abuses in which the prescribed forms of the Mass are changed or omitted at the whim of the celebrant), though they often have little or no desire for a return to Latin. A glance at the literature of the Lefebvrist movement shows clearly that its strength and emotional force come from the evils it thinks to find in the current liturgy—not that officially approved by the Vatican (though that is what the Archbishop was concerned about) but that of their vernacular.

excluded from the Church's liturgical prayer and worship; that, until this "reform" was forced on her, the Church, through her official and public worship, taught a grave and fundamental error. It takes small imagination to picture the consequent growth of confusion and dissension among Catholics already divided in their "ecclesiologies".

Further, the proposed changes would be taken as a "Vatican mandate" to use feminist English and would be so trumpeted on all sides by the media. It would soon be impossible for any priest to preach or teach or write in ordinary English. Unwillingness to employ feminist usage seems likely to make still worse the shortage of priests of sound pastoral and doctrinal attitudes. Some would be moved, in effect, to early retirement. Others, young men pondering a possible vocation but virile enough not to capitulate to feminism, would decide against the priesthood, already perceived as "soft".

A fortiori, these changes will make ecumenism more difficult, especially with the Orthodox Churches, which in this country are well aware of the heterodox sources from which the current proposals have grown.[11] Conservative Protestants, who are still the great majority of Protestants though often profoundly at odds with their "liberal" leadership, are not likely to approve. Indeed, it is the Orthodox who are receiving more and more converts from the Evangelical branches of the mainline Protestant denominations, precisely because these converts see Catholicism as, in practice, unfaithful to its Tradition. Yet it is with those groups that we have most in common and the greater hope of being reunited in the fullness of faith, not with those denominations that are strongly influenced by feminism, that are now declining rapidly in numbers and still more in doctrine.

III. SPIRITUAL CHARACTER OF INDIVIDUALS?

It is an ancient and basic spiritual principle that one is unlikely to accomplish the will of the Lord by carrying out proposals for

[11] Cf. "Spiritual Character of Originating Movement?" below.

action that are attended by bitterness, resentment, falsehood, or weakness of faith, still less if motivated thereby. Such things are not signs of God's action upon the soul. It is not He but the demons that provoke us to resentment, alienation, or false doctrine. If He asks us for difficult things, it is with the grace to do them with charity and a certain peace, even when we have a storm of prideful reactions to hold in check as a result.

Yet those Catholic women who have been calling for "inclusive language" have usually declared themselves "anguished", "enraged", "bitter", "alienated", etc., at its absence. How often does one find a feminist religious who speaks of the putative oppression these women suffer in terms of the joy of having something to suffer for the love of Christ? When do they speak with obvious consolation of our Lady and their desire to be like her? Few are the signs given of charity or of patience for those who oppose them.

All this is not a matter of succumbing to momentary irritations and passing flarings of anger. Rather, everything indicates a settled mood of the most profound sort of self-pity—another name for wounded pride, something most assuredly not from God. But the Church's spiritual Tradition is firm that whatever movement of thought or spirit brings about such desolation is automatically to be set aside as a guide for action, at the very least until there is no trace left of desolation when the matter is considered or discussed.

More serious is the fact that the Faith itself is often put in question. Many Catholic feminists demand sacerdotal ordination for women. Many are unashamed openly to engage in worship of Mother Earth, the goddess, or deities "borrowed" from paganism. Jesus and His Father are, at best, tolerated alongside these, more often, simply ignored or "made female" or rejected entirely.[12] Strangely, not only do secularist feminists demand approval of contraception, legal toleration of any and all abortions, and social acceptance of lesbian and "gay" relationships on a full equality with marriage, but also many sisters, priests,

[12] Cf. Prof. William Oddie, *What Will Happen to God?* (London: SPCK, 1984), and Donna Steichen, *Ungodly Rage: The Hidden Face of Catholic Feminism* (San Francisco: Ignatius Press, 1991).

and other Catholics leading the drive for feminist English publicly agree with them.[13]

In many places, episcopal toleration of liturgical abuses long since reprobated by the Church Universal is no secret. Yet the priests engaging in such abuses and the bishops who tolerate or encourage them are usually in the forefront of those who are urging feminist English. Their doctrinal discussions in defense of their liturgical practice are at least as destructive.[14] So, also, moral theologians who urge the adoption of feminist English are, to my knowledge, "proportionalists", "consequentialists", or "revisionists", and it would be hard to find any of these latter who do not do so.

But not merely do the majority of the women who actively seek the elimination of ordinary English think that the Church is in error on these doctrinal matters. She is publicly reviled by them and her authority rejected. Their anger at the Church as she exists concretely seems boundless. Only read the material from their "Woman Church Speaks" convention in Chicago a few years ago or the similar convention in Cincinnati a bit later, and other examples abound. Many—sisters especially—declare their hatred for the "patriarchal Church" and their intent to abandon her if she does not change as they wish.

Some people speak of the danger of losing feminists of high quality from the Church. This would seem to miss the point that most of those so endangered have already been, at least temporarily, lost to the Church. For any who threaten to leave Christ's Church if what they desire is decisively refused them—if serious in their threat—have already left in heart and mind, even if not externally.

Nor should the bishops (or others) be overawed by the sometimes impressive scholarly efforts of these people. Pertinent as

[13] Cf. the copious literature cited by De Marco, Steichen, and Oddie. Also, cf. Rosemary Radford Ruether's *Women-Church: Theology and Practice of Feminist Liturgical Communities* (San Francisco: Harper and Row, 1985), for the liturgies she has collected or composed for lesbian unions, abortions, and other feminist aberrations—a particularly interesting example since, I am told by those who know her well, these are things in which she has no personal involvement.

[14] An example can be found in *National Jesuit News* 18, no. 8 (Apr. 1989): 4, to which general Jesuit reaction was strong and negative.

James' admonition is to academics generally, it seems particularly relevant to feminist scholars.

> If you have bitter jealousy and selfish ambition in your hearts, do not boast and be false to the truth. This wisdom is not such as comes down from above, but is earthly, unspiritual, devilish. . . . But the wisdom from above is first pure, then peaceable, gentle, open to reason (James 3:14–17).

One can only wonder what spirit it is that stirs feminist animus. Why do so many strain out the gnats of ordinary English usage and swallow so easily grave errors of both doctrine and basic Christian morality. Surely, worse injustices are inflicted on women, to give but one example, by the male irresponsibility that has brought about legalized abortion and that refuses to support a child "since it was her decision to have it—she could have aborted it". And yet few indeed are the leaders of the drive for feminist English in the liturgy who have shown much interest in ridding the country of legal abortion. Though vigorously involved in many other social issues related to basic human rights, they have been remarkably cool not only toward the prolife movement but also to any effective working against legal toleration and funding of abortion.

SPIRITUAL CHARACTER
OF ORIGINATING MOVEMENT?

Similar questions can be asked concerning the character and experience not only of individuals but also of the movement in which they are caught up.

Neither Catholic feminism nor the drive for feminist English is native to the Church but has entered her from without. Contemporary American feminism is largely the outgrowth of the New Left of the early 1960s, a product of the West Coast universities, under such mentors as Marcuse. Unsurprisingly, then, this feminism retains at least one deep root in Marxism, manifest not only in its language and concepts but also in its modes of understanding society and the world.[15]

Largely in reaction to the maltreatment of women in the movement by its men through the looseness of "free" or "communal" sexual encounters, some of the most prominent leaders became militant lesbians. Contraception is taken as self-evidently good for whoever wishes it, and their determined insistence on abortion on demand is notorious and undisguised. Needless to say, the movement has been intensely anti-Christian from its inception.

Among many of the more prominent activist Catholic feminists there have been similar patterns of attitude, though these patterns seem to have originated elsewhere than in the New Left. Thus, much of the push for feminist English in liturgy arose from religious and clergy heavily tainted by homosexuality, both male and female. In particular, the liturgical movement of the post–Vatican II era in the United States was much contaminated therewith, a fact known to most bishops and priests and in many cases long public. Though Catholic acceptance of contraception prepared many for an acceptance of secularist feminism and was strengthened greatly thereby, its source was other than in the latter. So, too, consequentialist moral theology, however related to the surrounding culture, was developed as a response to *Humanae Vitae*[16] and was not directly concerned with feminism.

Thus, a structure of attitudes toward Catholic doctrine closely paralleling that of Marxist feminism had already been formed, apparently independently, within the Church in this country. The singular effectiveness of the latter feminism within the Church is, then, not entirely due to its own power.

[15] If anyone needs convincing on this point, let him glance, e.g., at any of the major biographies of Alexandra Kollontai, an old Trotskyite bolshevik feminist who left child and husband in order to become a disciple of Lenin in Switzerland; or, at a less scholarly level, at *The Decade of Women: A MS. History of the Seventies in Words and Pictures,* ed. Suzanne Levine and Harriet Lyons (New York: C. P. Putnam, 1980).

[16] Cf. John Finnis, *Moral Absolutes: Tradition, Revision, and Truth* (Washington, D.C.: Catholic University of America Press, 1991), chap. 4.

Given, however, this confluence of Marxist feminism with Catholic doctrinal dissent that has characterized the movement for feminist English in the liturgy, the bishops should have serious doubts about the wisdom of making even small concessions. It is hard to see how it is the will of the Father that is truly being sought by Catholic feminists, or how growth in firm but humble charity is the driving force behind their movement.

The American media—by their own account, the most strongly secularist and antireligious segment of our society—have promoted in season and out the feminist agenda. Their ubiquitous employment of feminist usage gives the appearance of linguistic change and development that has misled the bishops and, indeed, many feminist women. Many women who have been attracted to feminism may be largely unaware of its basic ideology. Feminist leaders are the ones, however, who set the tone and, more importantly, the agenda for the movement.

CONCLUSION

In sum, then, Catholic spiritual principles would indicate that "the father of lies" has deceived the proponents of feminist usage. What they propose is not itself well grounded in reason. Implementation of their proposal would aggravate current divisions within the Church and would tend to damage rather than build up the moral and spiritual lives of Catholics and other Christians. The doctrinal and moral physiognomy of the proponents, considered individually or as a movement, does not give confidence that they have any special light from the Lord on this matter. Rather, the indications are that they have been, not only in this matter but also in many more basic ones, tricked or blinded.

APPENDIX

DOCTRINAL PROBLEMS WITH
CURRENT [1973] ICEL SACRAMENTARY

ICEL's record gives small confidence that ICEL has either the scholarly competence in language, liturgics, and theology or the spiritual sensitivity needed for its tasks. Yet it seems rather carefully to have shut out from serious participation in its activity those who do possess such competence and to have insulated itself from those, in many countries, who have labored much to assist it in its work of translation. As soon as a viewpoint different from whatever currently fashionable one ICEL has already espoused is made evident, true discussion ceases, and such scholars are not admitted even as observers to ICEL's discussions.

The impression of one-sided secrecy is augmented when one sees how ICEL's output is laid before the bishops. There is not adequate time for them to read over this material in advance or to obtain professionally competent advice. The translations are voted on in haste, with one position adopted by the BCL and no fair presentation of alternative or opposing viewpoints.

ICEL's and BCL's spiritual insensitivity to racial considerations in composing the Thanksgiving Preface was noted above. But even from the perspective of feminist usage one may wonder whether ICEL would prove helpful. Surely the First Preface for Independence Day and Civic Observances must be the worst in the Missal from the point of view of "sexist" language. Yet it is ICEL's own, composed without benefit of a Latin original. The Preface for Thanksgiving could not be regarded as much better.

Let pass the fact that ICEL has shown small concern, over many years now, for the large number who have been hurt and troubled by the jejune and wretched language it has often employed. What is serious is its spoliation of the spiritual wealth furnished in so many of the great prayers of the Mass, still present in the Novus Ordo. One need go no farther than the setting aside of what has often been the occasion for people's first introduction to contemplative adoration: "We give you thanks for your great glory" in favor of the banality of "We praise you for your glory!" Any glory calls forth praise, but God alone can we thank for His glory, even at those times when our sinfulness makes it seem that we may never behold it.

But questions of spiritual sensitivity aside, the present Sacramentary is crawling with doctrinal errors, both express and implied, though many are undoubtedly unintentional. Requiring correction of these should surely have had a higher priority with the BCL than remedying putatively "sexist" language. Yet Vatican intervention was required to rid us of the "Arian" preface in the Fourth Eucharistic Prayer and the seeming reference in the same, after the Consecration, to mere bread and wine.

Before taking up the difficulties, I should indicate that I am not opposed on principle to all alterations of sense in translations, even in the Roman Canon. Thus, "a sacrifice in spirit and in truth" seems to me a genuine acquisition, with its strong scriptural resonance and striking appropriateness at this point in the Mass.

The difficulties to be mentioned fall into two classes.

I

The first group contains statements or implications that, according to the accepted use of words in American English, are false but that, so far as I know, represent no effort at false teaching. These are due presumably to simple incompetence. That they have not been remedied long since is due, apparently, to the tendency of well-instructed Catholics to read such prayers in a doctrinally acceptable sense, unconsciously forcing the language actually used to mean what they know, in faith, it ought to say. The danger remains, however, for the generation of poorly instructed Catholics now in early adulthood.

1. In the Creed, one reads: "We believe in one holy catholic and apostolic Church."

There is no ground for using this language in connection with the Church, as if in exact parallel with the Persons of the Godhead. If it seems pastorally prudent to reiterate the "we believe" here, it should be followed by "that there is one, holy, . . . " or, even, "that the Church is one, holy, . . . " Catholic Tradition has never countenanced saying that one "believes *in*" anyone other than God.[17]

"One in being with the Father". This is, at best, ambiguous. It would seem better simply to drop "in". But the matter is important enough and difficult enough to get a complete rethinking and revision.

2. Preface of Eucharistic Prayer IV: "In the name of every creature under heaven, we too praise your glory" (supposedly a translation of the Latin, *"nos et, per nostram vocem, omnis quae sub caelo est creatura nomen tuum in exsultatione confitemur"*). But travesty aside, this is antiscriptural and false in its doctrine.

If one looks, e.g., at Ephesians 5:20, he sees that "we give thanks always for everything in the name of our Lord Jesus Christ". It is *in the name of Jesus* that we ought to do everything, above all in the Eucharist (the Thanksgiving). Further, since to do something in someone's *name* is to do it as his delegate, not merely as his substitute, this text makes man inferior to the rest of the creatures under heaven, instead of showing him to be the agent through whom even the nonspiritual, even nonanimate world is enabled to praise God.

3. The First Preface for Christmas: "In him we see our God made visible and so are caught up in love of the God we cannot see."

Taken *ad litteram,* this speaks of two Gods. One God is "made visible", and "we see" Him; the other is "the God we cannot see". The sense intended is presumably, "In Christ we see the Word, who is our God, made visible, and so are caught up in love of the Divine Being that we cannot see, even in Christ." But, then, the referent of "God" in the actual text is different in each case. In the first instance, "God" refers to the Person of the Word; in the second, to the Godhead — hardly a help to clarity in the mind of the hearer. Worse, the use of the definite article with the second

[17] On all this, cf. H. de Lubac, *The Christian Faith* (San Francisco: Ignatius Press, 1986), 173ff.

"God" serves to pick out one category of "God", the one specified by the restrictive "we cannot see". The two defects coalesce to assert two Gods.

It should be noted that almost any English Missal before Vatican II has a reasonable, if not excellent, translation of this preface, which used to be the only one for Christmas.

4. The worst of trinitarian falsification is reserved, with some irony, for the Opening Prayer for the Feast of the Most Holy Trinity:

> *Father, you* sent *your* Word to bring us truth and *your* Spirit to make us holy. Through them we come to know the mystery of *your* life. Help us to worship *you,* one God in three Persons, by proclaiming and living our Faith in *you.* Grant this through our Lord Jesus Christ, *your* Son, who lives and reigns with *you* and the Holy Spirit, one God. . . .

What, supposedly, this translates is:

> Deus Pater, qui, Verbum veritatis et Spiritum santificationis mittens in mundum, admirabile mysterium tuum hominibus declarasti, da nobis, in confessione verae fidei, aeternae gloriam Trinitatis agnoscere, et Unitatem adorare in potentia majestatis. Per Dominum. . . .

Quite apart from any question of translation, it should be clear to any Catholic that the Father is not "one God in three Persons". Yet all through, "you" and "your" are made to refer to the Father only and personally. Nor is it trivially easy to straighten out the mess without getting into as bad or worse. Better go the route of true translation:

> God our Father, who in sending the Word of truth and the Spirit of holiness into the world, make known your wondrous mystery to men, grant us, by professing the true Faith, to acknowledge the glory of the eternal Trinity and to adore the Divine Oneness in the power of Its majesty.

5. In Eucharistic Prayer IV again: "You formed man . . . and set him . . . to rule over all creatures."

Do we rule over the angels? Are we really given that kind of dominion over even inanimate or subhuman creation? The Tradition has always held that we hold the world in stewardship, and stewards are not monarchs. Today especially, this is likely to provoke and irritate any "ecology buff" who hears it. The Latin wisely says: *"eique commisisti mundi curam universi ut, tibi soli Creatori serviens, creaturis omnibus imperaret"*. Here "imperaret" is indeed strong (though it says power to command rather than simple autonomy), but it is situated in a context that subjects man's commanding and ordering to God's service, i.e., makes him the Lord's steward, in charge of things indeed, yet subject always to a will that is not his own. Note, too, since *mundus* refers ordinarily only to the visible world, that *creaturis omnibus* is correspondingly limited.

6. Preface of Eucharistic Prayer II: "He put an end to death".

This seems a strange statement when so many are dying every day in all parts of the world. The Latin has *"ut mortem solveret"*, indicating His *purpose,* not a fact. He "revealed the resurrection" is not so patently false; but *"manifestaret"* does not signify that He *has* revealed it but that He did all this so that He *might* reveal it, in His own Resurrection first and then in ours. It is a phrase based on 2 Timothy 1:10 but modified in the early Church as witnessed by Justin, Irenaeus, and others. It is neither trite nor wrong and should not be made such by the translation.

II

The second set of difficulties arises from modes of expression that, whether or not directly false, are tendentious; i.e., in the current climate of theological thought in the English-speaking world, these expressions or omissions are more or less deliberate options for false teaching.

1. In all the Prefaces in which, in the Latin, the listing of the various groups or choirs of angels is maintained or even extended,[18]

---

[18] For this very considerable verbal but also doctrinal extension in the Novus Ordo, cf. my article "Angels and Demons in the New *Missale Romanum*", *Ephemerides Liturgicae* 94 (1980): 401–10.

the naming of the choirs has been dropped in the English version. The only exceptions are the phrases "all the choirs of angels" and, four or five times, "angels and archangels". In a climate of opinion such as ours today, this is at least unhealthy, since the doctrine of the existence of angels and of demons is an essential article of our Faith.[19]

2. In the Creed, one reads, "maker . . . of all that is seen and unseen".

The bad grammar requires a choice of possible sense. Since there is no verb "to unsee", we may suppose that we are not dealing with two passives and, instead, supply the needed comma to make "is" existential, "seen" a participle, and "unseen" a simple adjective: "all that is, seen and unseen".

The terms "seen" and "unseen", however, are not doctrinally adequate to "visible" and "invisible". The former pair is technically correct, since its contradictories exhaust all possibilities. But this pair fails to honor the intent of the Council whose formulation is used (I Constantinople), where as evidenced by local conciliar decrees of that period, the Council uses "invisible" to refer to the angels and demons. But there is nothing in "unseen" that suggests what is intrinsically incapable of being seen by men. Once again, then, language that is intended to speak of angelic beings is omitted.

3. The *"gloria virginitatis"* should be restored to the First Preface of Mary. Surely today, virginity cannot be taken for granted as something all Catholics spontaneously see as glorious.

4. The two Offertory Prayers have been greatly weakened, so that they do not in fact indicate that we offer either the bread or the wine, still less ourselves with or through them. The Latin texts: *"accepimus panem quem (vinum quod) Tibi offerimus"* both are explicit as to our making the offering at the moment and by the very fact that we say them. These are turned in English into "we have this bread (wine) to offer". We have it to offer; we are not said to offer it, now or later.

[19] Cf. Paul M. Quay, S.J., "Angels and Demons: The Teaching of IV Lateran", *Theological Studies* 42 (1981): 20.

Were it not for some of the sacramental theology that identifies offering and sacrifice and that, therefore, rejects any offering that is not uniquely that of Christ Himself, this might pass doctrinally; but hardly today.

In passing, one might note some further weaknesses of ICEL's rendition of this prayer. "Through your goodness, we have ... " both flattens the style and distorts the doctrine of *"de tua largitate, accepimus. . . . "* "Goodness" is less specific and therefore less appropriate and convincing than a literal "bounty" or "liberality" (i.e., "From your bounty [liberality], we have ... "). "We have" suggests simple possession; but, as St. Paul asks, "What have you that you did not receive? If then you received it, why do you boast as if it were not a gift?" (1 Cor 4:7)—a reproach he could not level at the Latin text, which says that we have received. Moreover, "through" implies a source in some way antecedent to the goodness of God, which latter has mediated the bread or wine to us; whereas "from" would indicate God's liberality itself as the source of our gifts.

5. Consider the Opening Prayer for the Annunciation and contrast ICEL's version with the Latin.

> Deus, qui Verbum tuum in utero Virginis Mariae veritatem carnis humanae suscipere voluisti, concede, quaesumus, ut, qui Redemptorem nostrum Deum et hominem confitemur, ipsius etiam divinae naturae mereamur esse conformes.

> God our Father, your Word became man and was born of the Virgin Mary. May we become more like Jesus Christ, whom we acknowledge as our Redeemer, God and man.

ICEL explicitates the reference to the Father—fine. But, though addressing Him, it gives Him no further role at all save to be a listener. In the Latin, in contrast, He willed that the dramatic event commemorated should take place. Further, He is asked to grant what we could not dream of having of ourselves—not merely standing by, as in ICEL's version, to hear us express a wish or a desire. (This changing of a petition or request to a mere expression of a wish seems to be a matter of policy in ICEL prayers, being well nigh universal. It is hard to see how this policy will not result in a quasi-Pelagian attitude that will be spiritually damaging to people.)[20]

Moreover, being "born of the Virgin Mary" is largely irrelevant to the mystery being celebrated. Christ's conception is what the feast commemorates, not His birth. It is God's taking to Himself the reality of human flesh in this woman's womb that is all-important. And to merit (by His grace, of course) to be conformed to His divine nature says vastly more than that "we become more like Jesus Christ", both of which names emphasize His human nature.

Comparison with others of its texts should disarm the suspicions some have voiced that at this point ICEL is deliberately avoiding reference to our Lord's life in Mary's womb before birth. Yet, in these days of easy abortion, the matter is not negligible, even if unintentional. (Recall, too, that prolifers have long complained about the ICEL version of the Creed for use in the United States, which, whether or not intended to do so, teaches that His becoming man [and, therefore, ours] takes place only at birth. To render *"et incarnatus est de Spiritu Sancto ex Maria Virgine et homo factus est"* by "by the power of the Holy Spirit He was born of the Virgin Mary and became man" is, on any construal, a mistranslation of this article of our Faith. Further, assigning the primary activity of the Holy Spirit to Jesus' birth rather than to His Incarnation and conception gives a much stronger emphasis to Mary's *virginitas in partu* than either the Greek or Latin texts. Whether, when weighed against the doctrinal distortion involved, this is a gain is doubtful.)

In passing, one may note that no connection between the two sentences in the prayer for the Annunciation is suggested in ICEL's version, nor is there any obvious connection between the three parts of the latter sentence. If "God and man" were inserted after "Christ", it would be at least a little better. But why not redo the version altogether? E.g.,

God our Father, you willed that your Word should take to Himself, within the womb of the Virgin Mary, the reality of our

[20] On this, cf. the excellent article by Richard Toporoski in *Communio* 4 (1977): 226–60.

human flesh. Grant, we beg, that we who proclaim our Redeemer to be both God and man may merit to be conformed even to His divine nature.

This list could be made much longer. But enough evidence has been provided, I think, to show that the Vatican is being given advice by groups of people (ICEL, BCL) who are—one must speak frankly—demonstrably incompetent both in doctrine and in the use of English, and this quite apart from any question of feminist usage.

V

ICONOLOGY: REVISING GOD

"INCLUSIVE" LANGUAGE IN AN EXCLUSIVE WORLD

Donald De Marco

Does so-called "exclusive language" discriminate against women? If so, should its use be banned in the interest of removing one more barrier that separates women from full equality with men?

This essay examines the arguments and the counterarguments on this highly volatile issue. It also investigates some of the consequences the "inclusivist" position has produced on various levels of thought, as well as the practical influence it has had in the specific areas of administration, education, and religion.

Discrimination against women surely exists, both in action and in speech. One should be zealous and steadfast in opposing these practices. But in this essay I will attempt to show that truncating the language, particularly of words that have non-sexist, inclusive meanings, is a futile, if not counterproductive, enterprise.

The inclusive/exclusive dichotomy is essentially an ideological invention. Like all ideologies, this one suffers from its inability to harmonize and cooperate with other ideas. It is a truism that any single idea, even a good one, when pushed to the extreme, will become counterproductive by creating conflict with other good ideas.

The moral goals that animate "inclusivists" are, by and large, praiseworthy. But censoring grammatically legitimate and morally unassailable uses of generic terms is not a means that will bring about these ends. In fact, it appears to be an effective means of deepening the division both between and within the sexes.

THE DISCUSSION

The Argument for Inclusive Language

"Exclusive" language allegedly excludes women. But it is said to do more than that. The word "boy" does not include "girl", just as the word "old" does not include the notion of "young". But these examples do not illustrate "exclusive" language. Language is said to be "exclusive" when a word is used that is supposed to include both men and women but verbally appears to include only men and thus treats women as if they did not exist or are not important enough to bother mentioning. Such language is therefore said to be "sexist" as well as "exclusive".

In recent years some people have claimed that the generic use of the word "man" is "false". As a consequence, the use of this "false" generic is morally illicit since it is presumed to discriminate against women and imply that they belong to an inferior gender. The issue of "exclusive" language, therefore, transcends mere linguistic considerations, such as the need for clarification and consistency. Indeed, since it involves the equitable treatment of women, it is an issue that assumes social justice proportions. Critics argue that "exclusive" language must be expunged from the language since it perpetuates sexist attitudes.[1] Furthermore, many go as far as to compare this form of "sexism" with racism and other "isms" that oppress specific classes of human beings and prevent them from achieving their full potential. Accordingly, one feminist states:

> Sexist language is no less noxious than racist language. As Kett and Underwood say in their recent book, "Avoiding *he* is equal to taking down the 'whites only' sign in a restaurant."[2]

[1] Mary Vetterling-Braggin et al., eds., *Feminism and Philosophy* (Totowa, N.J.: Littlefield, Adams, 1978): Janice Moulton, "The Myth of the Neutral 'Man' "; Carolyn Korsmeyer, "The Hidden Joke: Generic Uses of Masculine Terminology".

[2] Marie Shearer, "Solving the Great Pronoun Problem: Twelve Ways to Avoid the Sexist Singular", *Perspectives: The Civil Rights Quarterly* 13 (Spring 1981): 18.

In a discussion on the pronoun "she", researchers Julia Stanley and Susan Robbins find that the generic function of the pronoun "he" implies that women are "nonhuman":

> Since the female pronoun always designates females—while the male pronoun designates all humans as well as all males, patriarchal language, as manifested in the pronomial system of English, extended the scope of maleness to *include* humanity, while restricting femaleness to "the Other", who is by implication nonhuman. Any speaker internalizing such a language unconsciously internalizes the values underlying such a system, thus perpetuating the cultural and social assumptions necessary to maintain the patriarchal power structure.[3]

In expressing her approval of this passage, Mary Daly remarks that the pronoun "he", which "allegedly" includes women, actually "silences" them by "splitting" them from a term that explicitly acknowledges their humanity. Thus, the word "he" as well as the "pseudogeneric" *man* are "false" generic terms. Dr. Daly goes on to say that not even terms such as "people" and "person" are true generics. Her sole defense of this assertion, however, is a reference to the expression "people and their wives", which she does not document.[4]

The Counterargument

The generic use of terms such as "he" and "man" is grammatically and linguistically legitimate. The English language has, from the earliest days of which we have any written record, used these terms without implying in any sense that women are inferior to men. Virtually everyone, from time immemorial, understood the generic use of "man" to include both men and women. Consequently, they did not regard such statements as "All men are

[3] Julia P. Stanley and Susan W. Robbins, "Going through the Changes: The Pronoun *She* in Middle English", *Papers in Linguistics* 9, nos. 3–4 (Fall 1977).

[4] Mary Daly, *Gyn/Ecology* (Boston: Beacon Press, 1978), p. 18.

created equal" and "He who hesitates is lost" as offensive, exclusive, sexist, or discriminatory.

By surveying the literature on the subject, we gain a better appreciation of the degree of moral significance some people attach to the issue of "exclusive" language as well as its prevalence in contemporary society. Let us begin by examining the gender-specific and generic uses of "he" which appear to be so central to the exclusivist's argument.

Pseudo-Etymology

Stanley and Robbins commit a fundamental mistake when they fail to recognize that the pronoun "he" is not the same as the male pronoun. The former has a generic meaning which includes both sexes, while the latter's meaning is confined to the male. It is not correct to say that "patriarchal language extended the scope of maleness to *include* humanity". This implies a confusion between *word* and *reality,* suggesting that the word has the power to change reality. The truth is that the generic use of "he" included all humanity to begin with. The word "he", in its generic use, refers equally to women and men just as the word "animal" refers equally to dogs and cats. In no sense does it exclude women or imply that they are "nonhumans".

Abundant examples of how "man" was, in fact, used as a generic term in the Middle Ages can be gleaned from the *Middle English Dictionary:* (1) in a poem called the *Ormulum* (c. 1200), "Mary was the wisest of all men [*manne*], Filled with steadfast love"; (2) a Middle Ages homily (with an Old English original) reads: "[The serpent came] to two men [*mannum*], first to the wife"; 3) in the late-twelfth-century *Rule for Anchoresses* is found: "God Almighty bowed down to man [*mon*], to Mary and to Joseph." Moreover, the word "woman" illustrates the generic use of "man", since it derives from the Old English "wif-man", meaning "the man who is a wife".

Stanley and Robbins also misrepresent the history of the female pronoun, first person singular. According to the *Oxford English Dictionary,* one of the forerunners of "she" was the word *hi.* This word actually served double duty as the generic third person plural, referring to women *and* men.[5] Thus one could say that *hí*, referring to the female as well as females and males together, discriminated against men and implied that they were inhuman. Such a conclusion, however, would be entirely unwarranted. Language is not univocal or rigidly consistent; it is multivalent, multi-faceted, and polygenetic.

The plain fact is that the word "he" is a true generic term and does refer equally (or "inclusively") to men and women. Every dictionary affirms this point. *Webster's Third International Dictionary* states: "he: 2. that one whose sex is unknown or immaterial (He that has ears to hear, let him hear—Mt 11:15)." According to *The American Heritage Dictionary of the English Language:* "he: 2. Used to represent any person whose sex is not specified: (Everyone knows he is mortal)." *Webster's New World Dictionary of the American Language:* "he: 2. the person; the one; anyone; as (he who laughs last laughs best)." *World Book Encyclopedia Dictionary:* "he. 2. anyone; person; one; (He who hesitates is lost)."

The generic "man", like the generic "he", belongs to men and women equally. The "inclusive/exclusive" dichotomy is an ideological invention. To say that these *inclusive* terms exclude women is actually to deny women what is really theirs. As one Christian feminist protests:

> It is, if you will, authentically feminist to affirm that the word "man" belongs to women as much as to men.[6]

Ironically, it is the "inclusivists" who are excluding women and not so-called "patriarchal exclusive language".

---

[5] As an example, the sentence "*Hí* (*hí* or *héo*) is the Queen and *hí* (*híe* or *héo*) are her subjects", could be deemed "sexist" since the male subjects to which the second *hí* refers tend to be identified as female by virtue of the fact that the first pronoun, *Hí*, exclusively refers to the female.

[6] Suzanne Scorsone, "In the Image of God: Male, Female, and the Language of the Liturgy", *Communio* (Summer 1989): p. 144.

The Behaviorist Fallacy

The attempt to eliminate sexist attitudes by eliminating terminology that is believed to be its cause betrays a fundamental misunderstanding of language. Language itself does not have the capacity to convince one of anything. Take the word *shrew,* whose presence in the English language is said to be an instance of bias against aggressive women. But the existence of this word cannot compel people to believe that there are shrewish women or that a particular woman is shrewish. It is a simple matter to construct linguistic phrases that dissociate women from shrewishness. One can say, for example, "There are no shrewish women", or "only men are shrewish". It is the perception of shrewishness in the *person* that convinces the observer that one is shrewish, not its existence in the *language.* Language reflects reality and not vice versa.

In the healthy outlook, the mind is incomparably more flexible and unpredictable than the word. A given word, which can appear in a variety of linguistic settings, does not compel anyone to interpret it in a fixed and predictable manner, let alone to allow it to determine attitudes and shape behavior. Indeed, if the feminists' behavioristic theory of language were true and, as they claim, "sexist" language has made women invisible and caused them to feel inferior, then, given this negative conditioning, it would be impossible for them to assert their equality with men in the powerful and effective way they have demonstrated. Thus, their own impressive display of insuppressibility and transcendence refutes their thesis.

The point may be illustrated in a variety of ways. For example, the expression "being doctored" has a clear negative connotation. Things that are said to be "doctored" (or tampered with) are in a worse condition than if they were left alone. On the other hand, "being nursed" always has a positive connotation and implies an improved condition. Nonetheless, these usages do not prevent or discourage people from seeking the help of doctors rather than nurses when they have a serious illness. Moreover, these expressions do not condition society to assign the nurse a greater social status. Indeed, it is the doctor, rather than the nurse, who earns more money, commands more respect and enjoys more prestige.

Another example may be found in the way we inquire about a person's age. We usually phrase the question using the word "old" rather than "young". Thus we ask, "How old is the child?" We probably do this because the direction of time is such that everyone is always getting older and no one is getting younger. Nonetheless, the word "old" covers the entire spectrum of age, including the elderly as well as the newly conceived. One might say this is a biased use of the word "old" that conditions people to prefer "old" to "young". However, in contemporary society, "old" is viewed in a strongly negative manner, while youth is much admired and highly prized. Once again we see that the preferential use of a particular word does not produce a personal preference for the reality that word signifies.

The Versatility of Words

Because of the spiritual nature of the mind, it is always far ahead of the word. The healthy mind is not intimidated by mere words, does not regard them as commands or factors that condition and control behavior. People do not hesitate to put cups and saucers into their "dishwashers", to order tea when dining in a "Coffee Shop", or to acknowledge they possess ten "fingers" even though they are well aware that two of these fingers are thumbs.

Latin and Greek, unlike English, have different words for the generic man (including men and women) and gender-specific man (men alone). In Latin, the word for all humans is *homo* and the word for male is *vir;* in Greek, they are, respectively, *anthropos* and *aner.* These are instances of what we might call "linguistic equality", ostensively more congenial to male-female equality. Yet this differentiation between the generic and the male gender does not translate into cultural equality between the sexes. Ancient Rome's "Paterfamilias" gave the father a disproportionate control over everyone in his family. In Greece, as one commentator has pointed

out, " 'male chauvinism' flourishes more than in many places".[7]
In other words, language by itself cannot bring about cultural
changes.

Another example comes from China. Chinese pronouns have
no gender. Yet the practice of female infanticide is well-known
and well-documented.[8]

The Turkish language is completely devoid of gender. The
same third person word (o) means "he", "she", and "it". There are
no male, female, or neuter nouns, and inflected endings are invari-
able regardless of gender. Nonetheless, Turkish women lack many
rights enjoyed by women in countries whose citizens use presumably more "sexist" native tongues.[9] The sullying of a family's
honor (namus), for example, is more easily associated with female
rather than male misbehavior. In rural areas of Turkey, female
children are sometimes held out of school; and even in cities, a
single woman is severely limited by social etiquette in where she
can go and what she can do.

"Inclusive" language is no guarantee against an "exclusive"
world. The verbal inclusion of the sexes has little to do with their
social inclusion. In fact, preoccupation with "inclusive" language
tends to exacerbate division, not only between the sexes but also
between the "inclusivists" themselves and those whom they exclude
for not agreeing with them. In some schools in North America
teachers have warned students that they must use "inclusive"
language or fail exams and outside assignments.

When a word is placed in a literary context, it gains a life, a
resonance, and a richness that it does not have as a mere word.
The practice of isolating words from a living context and inter-
preting them not according to their meaning but in terms of a
feminist ideology is, as Mary Midgley and Judith Hughes have
explained, "misleading and senseless".[10]

[7] John Wilson, Love, Sex, and Feminism: A Philosophical Essay (New York:
Praeger, 1980), p. 64.

[8] Mary Midgley and Judith Hughes, Women's Choices: Philosophical Problems
Facing Feminism (New York: St. Martin's Press, 1983), p. 145.

[9] Michael Levin, Feminism and Freedom (New Brunswick, N.J.: Transaction
Books, 1987), p. 257.

[10] Midgley and Hughes, p. 144.

Words are not like magnetic poles, with a single charge. They are far too versatile for that. There is hardly any word so complimentary that it cannot sometimes serve as a stinging insult, or so rude that we shall not sometimes greet it with delight. In any case, conversation contains an amazing amount of irony, ambivalence, understatement, euphemism, innuendo, double meaning, friendly abuse, barbed compliment, ritual and celebratory swearing, magical precaution and general emotional conjuring. Words are the complex tools suited to this game, so if one cares to pick single meanings for them it is not hard to prove all sorts of strange theses.[11]

The expressed desire to delete words from the language such as "virility", "manly", and "manhood"[12] seems to be based more on ideology than insight. This also appears to be the case with the effort to banish phrases such as "a gentleman's agreement", "a grandfather's clause", and "a bachelor's degree", or the attempts to remove commercial expressions such as "mix-master", "Master-Charge", and "Mr. Muffler". Expressions such as "Mother Nature", "Father Time", "Old Man River", "Mother-of-Pearl", "Grandfather Clock", and "Daughter Cells" provide language with a diversity and richness of imagery that enliven and humanize our efforts at interpersonal communication.

Language is an invention of sexual beings. Hence it bears the mark of its creators through and through. To object to a language that is sexually imprinted is to object to human language itself. Perhaps the zenith of this mistrust of sexualized language is Mary Daly's insistence that lesbians learn from the language of "dumb" animals "whose nonverbal communication seems to be superior to androcratic speech".[13] Daly lists several communications she supposedly had with animals and translates a few of them.[14] Commenting on these conversations, Jean Bethke

11 Ibid., p. 145.
12 Levin, p. 250.
13 Daly, p. 414.
14 Ibid., p. 466. A few examples: "It's fun to spin": a Belgian Shepherd, Wellesley, Mass., June 1976; "We spin together": two cats (sisters), Watertown, Mass., October 1976; other examples cited include a monkey in Venice; a hermit crab in Onset, Mass.; a blackbird in Bergen, Norway; a group of sheep near Heraklion, Crete, etc.

Elshtain, who as a political scientist is more interested in communications between citizens, makes the trenchant observation that "all the animals shared her perspective and none contested her position".[15]

THE CONSEQUENCES

Grammar

Because of arbitrarily regarding generic terms such as "he", "his", "him", "mankind", etc., as "sexist", people are willing to violate grammar, employ distracting verbal concoctions, and enlist awkward phraseology in order to avoid them. Thus, we find "s/he" for both she and he; "wo/man" for woman and man.[16] The sentence "Everyone thinks *he* has the right answer" changes to the grammatically incorrect, but "nonsexist", counterpart, "Everyone thinks *they* have the correct answer." "One should choose *his* friends carefully" is converted to the less graceful expression, "One should choose *one's* friends carefully."

Some consciously alternate the phrase "men and women" or "his and hers" with "women and men" or "hers and his" in order to free themselves from the charge of expressing any residual sexism by according second place to the female sex. The state of New York is spending ten million dollars over a ten-year period to replace "men working" signs by those that read "people working."[17] After changing "man-hole cover" to "maintenance-hole cover", Toronto's city councilors took pride in altering "grandfather clause" to "grandparent clause". "We're moving forward, progressively", states Mayor June Rowlands. "Instead of grandfathering clauses, we'll talk about grandparenting situations." Finally, some feminists in the United States have reclassified seminars as "ovulars".

---

[15] Jean Bethke Elshtain, *Public Man, Private Woman* (Princeton, N.J.: Princeton University Press, 1981), p. 214.

[16] See *A Comprehensive Grammar of the English Language* (1988), p. 316.

[17] Levin, *Feminism and Freedom*, p. 255.

Obscurity

The moral dimension of the "inclusive" language issue can occasion a degree of self-righteousness that obscures what a particular author is expressing or what a specific text actually states. In his commentary on the Vatican Instruction *Donum vitae,* Peter Hebblethwaite finds the traditional Church teaching that no person has a right to another person and therefore that no one has a right to a child to be a "hard saying". He cites the offending passage in the document where he alleges Pope John Paul "tries" to justify this claim: "the child is not an object to which one has a right . . . nor can he be considered as an object of ownership." Hebblethwaite then makes the following comment: "You will have to forgive, if you can, the sexist language here."[18] Apart from the fact that Hebblethwaite seems unaware that the Pope did not write the document, it is particularly significant that in his zeal for spotting "exclusive" language, he completely overlooks the Instruction's inclusive message. The Instruction makes an appeal for the lives of all human beings, including those newly conceived, to be respected. In addition, it argues against a radical subordination of any human being to any other human being by pointing out that no one person has the right to own any other person.

The "sexist" language to which Hebblethwaite refers is the generic use of the word "he", although he does not provide the reader with the original text which was written in Latin. In its initial form, the passage contains the word *filius.*[19] The Latin word for children, *liberi,* does not have a singular form. Hence, the word *filius* is employed as the generic word for child and does not refer to male or female specifically. Hebblethwaite's complaint is unfounded. He is more concerned about language than meaning, although he does not take the pains to examine the language thoroughly. He tolerates exclusive morality and asks only that it

[18] Peter Hebblethwaite, "Vatican Instruction Seen as Warning to Doctors and Scientists", *National Catholic Reporter,* Mar. 20, 1987, p. 23.

[19] *Acta Apostolicae Sedis* 80, no. 1 (Jan. 12, 1988): 97: *"Filius nullo modo aliquid est quod debetur, neque considerari potest ut obiectum proprietatis."*

be expressed in "inclusive" language. Rather than offer his readership an analysis of an important moral document that attempts to
include all human beings under a canopy of life-protecting rights,
he distracts his readers by informing them of his allegiance to an
ideology of inclusive language.

The Pope, on the other hand, whom Hebblethwaite recklessly
accuses of employing questionably forgivable "sexist" language,
takes a much broader, more insightful view of words. In *Love and
Responsibility,* he looks into the word "matrimony" which, although
referring to the union of both man and woman, is etymologically
rooted in the Latin word for mother (*mater*). Far from seeing it as
a "sexist" word, the Pope understands how it directs the husband
toward the future when his wife will become a mother, a time
when he must *husband* his wife and lovingly protect his family.
"The man expects a child from the woman", he writes, "and for
this reason takes her into his care (*matris munus*) by marrying
her."[20] Here, the Holy Father allows words to speak their specific
meaning and highlight a particular aspect of the reality they
illuminate. He does not stifle them in a mood of ideological
intolerance.

Exclusivity

Many people find "inclusive" language offensive precisely because
it self-righteously parades an allegiance to a presumed morally
superior position. Peter Berger, for example, professor of sociology at Boston University, has remarked that "inclusive" language
is offensive and literally exclusive. "It is not what people pretend it to be—namely, a rectification of a past discrimination of
exclusion. . . . " It is "an ideological jargon whose purpose is to
compel ideological allegiance in a symbolic fashion. That is why I
find it offensive."[21]

"Inclusive" language is really exclusive in that it excludes people

[20] Karol Wojtyla, *Love and Responsibility* (New York: Farrar, Straus and
Giroux, 1981), p. 295.
[21] Peter Berger, *Religion and Society Report,* June 1988.

who do not endorse it because they do not believe it is necessary (as well as offending them by implying that they are "sexist"), whereas generic terms said to be "exclusive" are really inclusive since they include all that their names signify ("mankind" includes all human beings). Terms such as administrator, aviator, actor, and author are all generic, although they can serve double duty in specifically referring to the male. Their female counterparts are: administratrix, aviatrix, actress, and authoress.

Politics

Mussolini tried to "reform" the Italian language in the 1930s. He regarded the accepted word for formal address, *lei* (You), as a degenerate, effeminate usage. Since the purpose of the fascist revolution was to restore Roman virility, he insisted that people use the word *voi* in the place of *lei*.[22] As a result, everyone who used either *voi* or *lei*, depending on his political allegiance, was conscious of making a political gesture. Because these words were so politically charged, their use inevitably offended someone. This is precisely the problem with the politics of "sexist" language.

Science

Today, certain feminist epistemologists find masculine bias present in science and want to infuse that enterprise with a more feminine quality. They see male dominance at work in the "master molecule" theory of DNA functioning, in the concept of forces "acting on" objects, in the description of evolution as the result of the "struggle" to survive, and in the economic notion of "competition".[23] Feminist author Alison Jagger objects to the fact that "Copernican theory replaced the female(earth)-centered universe with a male(sun)-

[22] Ibid.
[23] Eric Retzlaff, "Scholar Warns of Feminist Attack on Scientific Method", *The Wanderer*, Jan. 21, 1988, p. 1.

centered universe".[24] At the same time, however, other feminists object to scientists using feminine images, such as employing female terms to designate nature.[25]

Ideology

On the other hand, it is possible to use terms that are entirely innocuous in themselves, such as the pronouns "we" and "they" in an exclusive manner that is both sexist and ideological. Some feminists use "we" not only to exclude men and emphasize the embrace of "sisterhood" but to exclude even those women with whom they do not have sufficient ideological identification.[26] The we/they dichotomy is easy enough to employ, but the fact that it can be used to promote an ideology that is both exclusive as well as sexist is not justification for removing "we" and "they" from the lexicon. Blind adherence to an ideology of "inclusive" language does not automatically bring about a more inclusive world. One can faithfully employ "inclusive" language, while unconsciously promoting an exclusive world. It is the use of language that is critical, not the words themselves.

INCLUSIVE LANGUAGE: THE INFLUENCE

Administration

Despite the weakness and fallacies inherent in the "inclusivist" position, the demand for inclusive language has already deeply affected administrative, educational, as well as religious thought and practice. The National Committee of the American Society for Public Administration has produced a booklet which discourages the use of the generic term "he". According to *The Right*

[24] Ibid., p. 8.
[25] Daly, p. 467.
[26] Ibid., p. 25.

Word, the pronoun "he" is objectionable because it allegedly results in "misleading and inaccurate communication" and "reinforces the perception of woman as an appendant to generic 'man' ".[27]

A Feminist Dictionary begins the entry MAN AS FALSE GENERIC with the following explanation:

> Convention in English of using the word "man" to refer "generically" to people both men and women. Though custom and convention are used to defend this and related usages, sound arguments based on research demonstrate that the claims of generic meaning are false.[28]

Education

The National Association of Teachers of English have issued guidelines for the removal of generic man from the language adopted by all textbook publishers.[29] Following its American counterpart, the Toronto Metropolitan Separate (Catholic) School Board has published a guideline called *Equality in Language* which discourages the use of generic "man" because it "perpetuates the invisibility of women and contributes to the concept of women as a subspecies and inferior persons (sic)".[30] Since, as we have seen, the generic "man" does include women, it is difficult to find any real basis for these fears. What evidence is there that expressions such as "No man lives by bread alone" cause any woman to think she is part of a "subspecies" of the male? Nowhere in the animal kingdom (though some may find the word "*king*dom" to be sexist) is there such a thing as a male species to which a group of females is related as a "subspecies". The term "subspecies" is taxonomical (like "suborder" and "subclass"), referring to how

[27] Levin, p. 251.

[28] Kramarae and Treichler, *A Feminist Dictionary* (New York: Pandors, 1985), p. 237.

[29] Ralph Wright, O.S.B., "Generic Man Revisited", *Fellowship of Catholic Scholars Newsletter,* June 1989, p. 3.

[30] *Equality in Language: Guideline,* Metropolitan Separate School Board, Toronto, 1987, p. 6.

animals are classified. It conveys no connotation whatsoever of inferiority. Such charges are indeed reckless and intemperate. It is a curious thing that educators never suspected that the pronoun "he" or the generic "man" could cause women to feel inferior until the decade of the seventies.

The Toronto guideline confidently states that "exclusionary" words can be replaced by "inclusionary" words "without undue distortions of language". It lists several replacements: adulthood for manhood, reporter for newsman, and ancestors for forefathers. A closer examination shows that the suggested replacements are not synonyms at all. "Adulthood" refers to age in a way that "manhood" does not; "manhood" conveys a moral implication that "adulthood" does not. We speak of "adult books" and never of "man books".

A "reporter" may report any number of things other than the news, which is the business of the "newsman". Moreover, a "newsman" may not "report" the news but merely gather or process it. The word "ancestors" lacks the immediacy and identifiability suggested by the word "forefathers". "Forefathers' Day", which celebrates the landing of the Pilgrims at Plymouth, Massachusetts, is not likely to be changed to "Ancestors' Day". Although *Equality in Language* explicitly objects to "imprecision in communication", it goes to absurd lengths to encourage it.

Ontario's Wilfred Laurier University has published a guideline called "Equity in Communication", which advises students, faculty, and staff to use "people in general" rather than "the man in the street", "formidable job" as opposed to "man-sized job", "crafted" instead of "man-made", "security guard" in lieu of "watchman", "birth name" as a substitute for "maiden name", and so on. "All men are mortal" should be written "All men [*sic*] are mortal"; "He lets his wife hold an outside job" becomes "He says he 'lets' his wife hold an outside job." The author of the guideline, a university professor, blithely notes that "exclusion in language can occur when certain nouns or pronouns are used in a generic or generalizing way that excludes some persons". George Orwell may have underestimated the affinity for "doublethink" that exists in academe.

As one social observer has remarked, "there is no one over the age of three who has been fooled by 'he' into thinking that women are unpersons".[31] One wonders what all the fuss is about. In fact, through the imposition of artificial restraints, a course of action is taken that logically *increases* the alienation and distrust between the sexes.

Some critics are making a plea for tolerance. "If someone finds it natural to say, 'A creator or creatrix of a work of art should look to his or her audience'," writes a Harvard philologist, "I uphold his right to say it, and my own to wince. In return I ask for the same freedom to doubt, to question, to poke fun when appropriate, and (most of all) to speak in my own mother tongue without *ipso facto* incurring the charge of injustice. Pluck thy pronouns, if they offend thee; but include me out."[32]

But tolerance is *not* called for when truth is being sacrificed on the altar of ideology.

Liturgy

One may laugh at feminist neologisms such as "herstory" and "himicanes".[33] Another might find purely gratuitous the claim that sisterhoods of religious congregations of women are really "minibrotherhoods".[34] Someone else may consider it an exercise in trivia to find objectionable such words as "virtue", "virtuoso", "defensemen", and "fatherland". But when the war against "sexist" language enters the arena of liturgy—the official prayer of the faithful—the picture changes dramatically.

The appropriately reverential expression of sacred liturgy precludes laughter and derision. Liturgy is intended to communicate

[31] Levin, p. 251.

[32] Paul Mankowski, "Inclusive Language Reconsidered", *Homiletic and Pastoral Review* (Feb. 1989): 50.

[33] Virginia Valian, "Linguistics and Feminism", in Vetterling et al., op. cit., p. 164.

[34] Mary Daly, "The Qualitative Leap Beyond Patriarchal Religion", in Marilyn Pearsall, ed., *Women and Values: Readings in Feminist Philosophy* (Belmont, Calif.: Wadsworth, 1986), p. 199.

the eternal Word of God. Therefore, wholesale adaptations to passing fads are out of place. Since a church is a place of community worship, ideological tensions are incompatible with its proper atmosphere of peace and unity. These factors of reverence, eternality, and prayer community enshrine language and give it a context of truth. The more radical proponents of "inclusive" language want to influence liturgy precisely because they want to distract the worshipper from the liturgy itself. Suzanne Scorsone makes an important and valid point in stating that any of the "inclusive" changes suggested in recent years are so obvious, and stick out like such "verbal sore thumbs", that "the ideological point being made takes precedence in the hearer's minds over the actual content of the liturgical or scriptural phrase itself".[35]

The attempt to rewrite Scripture and change liturgy in the interest of adapting to a narrow ideology is not new. During the 1960s, many people wanted to delete the agricultural imagery of the Bible since very few ghetto children had ever seen a lamb or were familiar with other examples of agrarian culture. Donald Bloesch, in his book, *The Battle for the Trinity: The Debate over Inclusive God-Language,* documents attempts in the 20s and 30s to accommodate Christianity to National Socialism. He cites Third Reich Bishop Mueller's revision of the Sermon on the Mount. The King James version of Matthew 5:5 reads: "Blessed are they that mourn for they shall be comforted." Bishop Mueller's version is: "Happy is he who bears his suffering like a man; he will find strength never to despair without courage." Joachim Niedlich, founder of the league for a German Church, urged that hymn books and liturgy be purged of Jewish expressions.[36]

[35] Scorsone, p. 144.
[36] Donald Bloesch, *The Battle for the Trinity: The Debate over Inclusive God-Language* (Ann Arbor, Mich.: Servant Publications, 1985).

The Bible

The extremism that characterizes some of the more enthusiastic and influential proponents of "inclusive" liturgy clearly delineates the threat of using feminist ideology to supplant the Word of God. Canadian theologian Mary Malone asserts that "in the language of the Church, women do not exist", that "liturgy is mostly for men", that "women are not challenged by the Word of God", and that "at the most important moment in the life of the local Church, women are excluded, they are nonpersons".[37] Boston theologian Mary Daly sums up the feminist point of view even more forcefully: "The ethos of Judaeo-Christian culture is dominated by The Most Unholy Trinity: Rage, Genocide, and War."[38] Not too surprisingly, Mary Daly has left the Church. Another radical feminist who, while denying a number of basic Christian doctrines, remains in the Catholic Church in order to change it is Rosemary Ruether. She states that "History has been the holocaust of women". She deplores "patriarchal theology" because it "uses the parent image for God to prolong spiritual infantilism as virtue and to make autonomy and assertion of free will a sin".[39] This is the same author whom Mary Hayter, in her book about the use and abuse of the Bible in the debate about women and the Church, claims is "one of the less extreme and more reputable feminist theologians".[40]

Elisabeth Schüssler Fiorenza has stated, in her book *Bread Not Stone,* that "all biblical texts are formulated in androcentric language and reflect patriarchal social structures. There is a need for feminist critical interpretation." The Liturgy Commission in the Catholic Archdiocese of Edmonton, Alberta, has been zealous in its attempt to rid Scripture of such patriar-

---

[37] Mary Malone, *Women: Christian* (Dubuque, Iowa: Brown, 1985), p. 143.

[38] Daly, 1986, p. 199.

[39] Rosemary Ruether, *Sexism and God-Language* (Boston: Beacon Press, 1983), p. 69.

[40] Mary Hayter, *The New Eve in Christ: The Use and Abuse of the Bible in the Debate about Women in the Church* (Grand Rapids, Mich.: Eerdmans, 1987), p. 7.

chal vestiges. A few examples of its transmogrifications are as follows:

Revised Standard Version	Archdiocese of Edmonton Version
1 Peter 3:5	1 Peter 3:5
So once the holy women who hoped in God used to adorn themselves and were submissive to their husbands. . . .	The holy women of the past, like Sarah, hoped in God.
1 Peter 3:7	1 Peter 3:7
Likewise you husbands, live considerately with your wives, bestowing honor on the woman as the weaker sex. . . .	Husbands must also treat their wives with consideration in their life together.
St. Paul to the Ephesians 5:21–23 (excerpt)	St. Paul to the Ephesians 5:21–23
Be subject to one another out of reverence for Christ. Wives, be subject to your husbands, as to the Lord. . . . Husbands, love your wives, as Christ loved the Church and gave himself up for her. . . .	*Expunged from the lectionary or presented in the preaching as "unacceptable today".*

The Commission's subcommittee on inclusive language does not accept the generic use of "man". Nor does it recognize the dictionary as an "objective arbiter" in determining whether "man" does have a generic use. In an interview for the *Western Catholic Reporter* (Sept. 10, 1991), one of the subcommittee members, Kathleen Quinn, rejected the dictionary since "the dictionary was put together by someone with a subjective view of reality".

Symbolism Threatened

Wherever a particular moral or ideological focus is the inspiration for revising Scripture or changing the liturgy, the danger exists of destroying the kind of understanding of God's Word that operates on a deeper, more symbolic level. One must always be aware that fervor is not an acceptable substitute for competence. Nonetheless, enthusiasts of "inclusive" language have made many inroads into the liturgy.

For "Father, Son, and Holy Spirit", some feminists substitute "Creator, Redeemer, and Sanctifier"; others use "Creator, Redeemer, and Comforter".[41] The United Church of Canada's 31st General Council (1986) overwhelmingly adopted a recommendation calling for a reversal of "male domination in religion". The Church will no longer use the word "man" and will replace it with "people". Similarly, Father, King, He, and Master will no longer be used. Instead, the Church will say God, Creator or Father-Mother.[42] The Ontario Peel-Dufferin Separate (Catholic) School Board has endorsed a report by its board that recommends using the terms God, Creator, Friend, and Everlasting One, instead of referring to God as Father.[43]

The United States National Council of Churches has produced *An Inclusive Lectionary* in which "brethren" is changed to "friends", "watchman" to "watcher", and "Lord God" to "God the Sovereign One".[44] Not only does ideology triumph over theology, but it often triumphs over style, as the following passage from the Gospel of St. John indicates: "For God so loved the world that God gave God's only Child, that whoever believes in that Child should not perish but have eternal life." The Lectionary also strips Jesus of His sexuality (He is the "Human One" or "The Child"); it invests God with bisexuality (God is the "motherly father of the

[41] Pamela Abramson et al., "Feminism and the Churches", *Newsweek,* Feb. 13, 1989, p. 60.

[42] "Church Moves from Male God", *Vancouver Sun,* Aug. 18, 1986.

[43] Allan Thompson, "Catholic Students Urged to Pray to Non-sexist 'God and Friend'", *Toronto Star,* July 28, 1988.

[44] Lois Sweet, "Revised Church Tract Eliminates Sexuality", *Toronto Star,* Feb. 9, 1984, p. D1.

Child who comes forth"). This prompted even a former Moderator of the United Church of Canada, Rev. Lois Wilson, to exclaim: "Surely Christian women aren't so insecure and self-conscious as to require a de-sexing of Jesus in order to relate to His message."[45]

The *Revised New Testament of the New American Bible,* which replaces the previous version issued in 1970, avoids the use of "man" in reference to both men and women. Typical of the change is the verse from Matthew 4:4, "Not on bread alone is man to live" has been revised to read, "One does not live by bread alone."[46] Some critics have complained that the revision did not go far enough. For example, the Greek word *adelphoi* (literally, "brothers") is still translated as "brothers". This was found "indefensible". Yet the substitute phrase, "my dear people" (which has appeared in other revised versions), singularly fails to convey the meaning that since members of the community are adopted children of God, they are all members of the same family.[47] In this instance, "my dear people" is actually *exclusive* since it excludes the intended reference to Christ's children as members of the same family.

As one female Bible scholar sensibly points out: "When the biblical images of God as father, bridegroom, and other 'masculine' metaphors are rightly interpreted, it is clear that there is nothing 'sexist' about them."[48] The Bible does not need to be changed; it needs to be understood. And the more people read and understand the Bible, the more they realize their own need to be changed.

Many who are especially zealous about purging Scripture of its "sexism" seem unaware of their own penchant for female bias. Some feminists instruct their children to pray the Lord's Prayer by

[45] Ibid.

[46] Ari Goldman, "Bible Text Is Purged of Sexism", *Toronto Globe and Mail,* Apr. 6, 1987.

[47] Myles Bourke, "Justifying the Need for a Revised New Testament", *The Catholic Answer,* Mar. 1989, p. 35. In the context of the article, the question may be raised as to whether the "City of Brotherly Love" (Philadelphia) is "sexist" and should be changed to the more inclusive generic—Philanthropia. Similarly, Adelphi College in New York might change its name to Anthropi College.

[48] Hayter, p. 33.

saying "Our Mother".[49] Others adorn their "women-church" liturgies with replicas of "Christa", a crucifix with a nude female body.[50] One feminist theologian urges a trinity of "Mother, Lover, and Friend".[51] Rosemary Ruether proclaims that the divine reality is best understood as an empowering "Primal Matrix", the great womb "in whom we live, move and have our being".[52] Male critics are routinely discounted and the male authors of the Gospel are often regarded with suspicion precisely because they are male.

The Hebrew Bible proclaims a Creator who is qualitatively different from His creation and thereby rejects the mother images of God that resurrect Near Eastern fertility goddesses and the human sacrifices associated with the likes of Baal and Astarte. The effort to remove "sexist" language from the Bible is merely the first phase of a program aimed at radically altering its meaning. Rev. Ralph Garbe, past chairman of Canada's United Church Renewal Fellowship, has remarked that "The evidence is beginning to mount that what is happening in our church is not simply a change in language, but a change in faith. . . . The Bible is being distorted by the ideology of feminism."[53]

Feminist Naomi Goldenberg is willing to state the matter far more graphically. She writes: "The feminist movement in Western culture is engaged in the slow execution of Christ and Yahweh.[54] . . . It is likely that as we watch Christ and Yahweh tumble to the ground, we will completely outgrow the need for an external God."[55]

The meaning of male and female, of marriage and sexuality, is at once so human and profound that we cannot alter their scrip-

[49] Catherine Bolger, "The Grave Dangers of the Feminist 'Theology' ", *Sacred Heart Messenger,* June 1987, p. 16.

[50] Abramson, p. 61.

[51] Ibid., p. 60.

[52] Ibid.

[53] Bolger, p. 17.

[54] Naomi Goldenberg, *Changing of the Gods* (Boston: Beacon Press, 1979), p. 4.

[55] Ibid. p. 25.

tural descriptions without at the same time diminishing Scripture's human significance. A culture that is as time-bound as the present one is—given its obsession with fads, novelties, and expediency; its materialism, secularism, and individualism; its rejection of the past, its dissatisfaction with the present, and its apprehension of the future—is hardly in a position to correct the timeless and universal Word of God. "All that is not eternal is eternally out of date",[56] wrote C. S. Lewis, the same man who noted, quite correctly, how odd it is that "the less the Bible is read the more it is translated".[57]

---

[56] C. S. Lewis, *The Four Loves* (San Diego: Harcourt Brace Jovanovitch, 1971), chap. 6.

[57] C. S. Lewis, *Letters* (May 25, 1962).

FATHER, SON, AND SPIRIT—
SO WHAT'S IN A NAME?

Deborah Belonick

The last few years have seen vast changes in many churches in liturgical rites and educational instruction in regard to proper language for God. The United Church of Christ, to give just one example, has published "Inclusive Language Guidelines" urging members to "avoid the use of masculine role names for God, such as 'Lord, King, Father, Master, and Son'", and instead to "use nonexclusive role names, such as 'God, Creator, Sustainer, Mother/ Father'. Or use non-sex-specific words relating to the qualities of God, such as 'Spirit, Holy One, Eternal One, Rock'". Feminist theologians chide those using the traditional terms as being sexist, ignorant of feminine images for God in Scripture, or unaware of the "oppressive patriarchal structure" which "invented" these terms for God.

A study of history proves that questioning language for God is not a new pursuit. We must not think that we in the twentieth century are the only ones who ever wrestled with the traditional doxology for God: "Father, Son, and Holy Spirit". The ways that the issue has been raised, and the ways Christians in the past have responded to it, have much to teach us today as we seek to respond to accusations by feminist theologians that patriarchalism and human imagination are responsible for the traditional trinitarian terms for God.

Specifically, Christians of the fourth century have much to teach us. The fourth century was the period of the all-consuming questions: Who and what is Jesus Christ? His humanity, divinity, person, and nature were the topics of great debates, which examined his relationship to humanity, as well as to the other members of the Trinity. During these fourth-century debates, the traditional doxology for God—"Father, Son, and Holy Spirit"—was also challenged and debated.

A study of the Christian controversies of the fourth century leads to two important conclusions. First, the terms "Father, Son, and Holy Spirit" have a precise theological meaning which is not communicated by any other terms for God. Second, the traditional doxology did not emerge as a reflection of patriarchal culture.

IS "CREATOR" ENOUGH?

On the first point, two fourth-century theologians who were embroiled in controversies over the proper terms for God, Athanasius and Gregory of Nyssa, are especially worthwhile for our study.

Athanasius was defending the traditional trinitarian names against the Arians, a group which preferred to call the First Person of the Trinity "Creator" rather than "Father". Arians claimed that Jesus Christ was not the Son of God but merely a superior creature; therefore, "Father" was a fleshly, foolish, improper term for God. In reply to the Arians, Athanasius tried to explain the importance of the biblical divine names, "Father, Son, and Holy Spirit".

Using a term such as "Creator", said Athanasius, makes God dependent on creatures for his existence. If creation did not exist, he asked, would this Creator-God cease to be? If creation had never existed, what would be the proper term for God?

In addition, Athanasius argued, the word "Creator" could be used to describe *any* of the members of the Trinity. It would be wrong to refer to the Father alone as Creator because the Bible states:

"In the beginning God created the heavens and earth. The earth was without form and void, and darkness was upon the face of the deep; and the *Spirit of God* was moving over the face of the waters" (Gen 1:1–2).

"In the beginning was the Word, and the Word was with God, and the Word was God. He was in the beginning with God; *all things were made through him,* and without him was not anything made that was made" (Jn 1:1-3).

According to Scripture, the Trinity acts in concert. They all create; they all save (Jn 5:21; Acts 2:24; Rom 1:4); they all sanctify (Eph 5:26; 1 Th 5:23).

Athanasius argued that the names of God had to describe more than God's action toward creation. There are, as it were, two different sets of names which may be used for God, explained Athanasius. One set (Creator, Savior, Sanctifier) refers to God's deeds or acts, that is, to his will and counsel. The other set (Father, Son, Holy Spirit) refers to God's own essence and being. Athanasius insisted that these two sets should be formally and consistently distinguished.

In Athanasius' view, we should use the terms "Father, Son, and Holy Spirit" when speaking about the existence of God as three persons in a community of love, when speaking about the relationships among members of the Trinity without regard to their acts toward creation. God's "being", Athanasius reasoned, has priority over God's action and will: "God is much more than just 'Creator'. When we call God 'Father', we mean something higher than his relation to creatures" (*Against the Arians*).

THREE DISTINCT PERSONS

Gregory of Nyssa faced similar problems when dealing with a sect known as the Eunomians, who believed that Christ was unlike God the Father by nature and instead was a "created energy". For this reason, Eunomians refused to call God "Father". In response, Gregory sought to explain the character of the Holy Trinity, and the Church's insistence on the traditional terms, "Father, Son, and Holy Spirit".

First, said Gregory, there was no more adequate theologian than the Lord himself, who without compulsion or mistake designated the Godhead "Father, Son, and Holy Spirit" (see Mt 28:19).

Further, Gregory said, these names are not indications that God is a male or a man; for God transcends human gender. Rather, these names imply *relationships* among the Persons of the Trinity and distinguish them as separate *Persons* who exist in a community of love. The names lead us to contemplate the *correct* relationships among the three Persons; they are clues to the inner life of the Trinity.

Gregory wrote: "While there are many other names by which the Deity is indicated in the historical books of the Bible, in the prophets, and in the law, our master Christ passes by all these and commits to us these titles as better able to bring us to the faith about the Self-Existent, declaring that it suffices for us to cling to the titles 'Father, Son, and Holy Spirit' in order to attain to the apprehension of him who is absolutely Existent" (*Against Eunomius*, Book 2).

Gregory states that it is with the terms "Father, Son, and Holy Spirit" that men can enter into the depths of God's life, somewhat equipped to understand the inner relationships and Persons of the Trinity.

DIVINE FATHERHOOD

Of particular interest in our own day is Gregory's explanation of the term "Father", which is under scrutiny by feminist theologians as a harmful metaphor that resulted from a patriarchal church structure and culture.

The name "Father", said Gregory, leads us to contemplate (1) a Being who is the source and cause of all and (2) the fact that this Being has a relationship with another person—one can only be "Father" if there is a child involved. Thus, the human term "Father" leads one naturally to think of another member of the Trinity, to contemplate more than is suggested by a term such as "Creator" or "Maker". By calling God "Father", Gregory notes, one understands that there exists with God a Child from all eternity, a second Person who rules with him, is equal and eternal with him.

"Father" also connotes the initiator of a generation, the one who begets life rather than conceiving it and bringing it to fruition in birth. This is the mode of existence, the way of origin and being, of the First Person of the Trinity. He acts in trinitarian life in a mode of existence akin to that of a father in the earthly realm. Before time, within the mystery of the Holy Trinity, God generated another Person, the Son, as human fathers generate seed.

Nowhere does Gregory suggest that this "Father" is a male creature: "It is clear that this metaphor contains a deeper meaning than the obvious one", he notes. The deeper meaning, is found in a passage of Paul to the Ephesians:

"For this reason I bow my knees before the Father, from whom every family (*patria*, fatherhood) in heaven and on earth receives its true name" (Eph 3:14–15). This passage implies that God is the one, true, divine Father, whose generative function human fathers imitate in a creaturely, imperfect way. When God generates a Child, the generation is eternal and transcends time and space, unlike human fathers, who imitate this generative function but are bound in time, space, and creaturely "passions," as Gregory notes (*Against Eunomius*, Book 4).

All the patristic writers insist that God is not male, but God possesses a generative characteristic, for which the best analogy in the human realm is that of a human father generating seed. Hence, the word "Father" for God is the human word most adequate to describe the First Person of the Holy Trinity, who possesses this unique characteristic.

The divine Father is as different from earthly fathers as the divine is from the human. Nevertheless, it is *fatherhood* and not *motherhood* which describes his mode of life, his relationship to the Second Person of the Trinity, and even his personal characteristics. The First Person of the Trinity does not just *act* like a father (though he sometimes acts like a mother!). Rather, he *possesses* divine fatherhood in a perfect way. That God's fatherhood transcends and is the perfection of human fatherhood is part of the meaning of Jesus' statement in Matthew 23:9: "And call no man your father on earth, for you have one Father, who is in heaven."

Clement of Alexandria, another fourth-century Christian teacher, expressed this idea most aptly: "God is himself love, and because of his love, he pursued us. [In the eternal generation of the Son] the ineffable *nature* of God is father; in his sympathy *with us* he is mother" (*How Will the Rich Be Saved?*).

SON OF THE FATHER

In his explanation of the term "Son", which is also a term often considered non-inclusive in our era, Gregory of Nyssa reiterates that this also is a precise theological term leading one to the inner relationships of the Godhead. It has primacy over other scriptural terms. He says:

"While the names which Scripture applies to the Only-begotten are many, we assert that none of the other names is closely connected with reference to him that begot him, for we do not employ the name 'Rock' or 'Resurrection' or 'Shepherd' or 'Light' or any of the rest, as we do the name 'Son of the Father', with a reference to the God of all. It is possible to make a twofold division of the signification of the divine names, as it were, by a scientific rule: for to one class belongs the indication of his lofty and unspeakable glory; the other class indicates the variety of providential dispensation" (*Answer to Eunomius' Second Book*).

All sorts of epithets for God are available to man through revelation—goodness, love, mother, fire. But none of these is exchangeable or comparable to the revelation of God as Father, Son, and Holy Spirit. These are the terms by which man enters trinitarian life to discover the unique Persons of the Trinity and their distinguishable marks.

The traditional trinitarian terms are precise theological terms, not easily exchangeable for any others. They lead us to the Persons of the Trinity, as well as defining relationships between them. To be unbegotten, begotten, and in procession are characteristics of the Persons of the Father, Son, and Holy Spirit. Paternity, generation, and procession are the unique marks of the respective Persons.

"MALE" THEOLOGY?

What about the feminist allegation that the traditional doxology is the product of a patriarchal structure, of a "male" theology? Did the patristic writers harbor animosity toward women or femininity? Did they use masculine terms for God, the source of all life, because they mistakenly thought that human fathers are the sole source of human life? Indeed, the opposite appears to be true.

First, some women did have opportunities to express their understanding of the Godhead. Macrina, elder sister of two of the greatest theologians of the fourth century, Basil the Great and the aforementioned Gregory of Nyssa, was referred to by her brothers as the "teacher". It was she who raised them in the Faith and instructed them in the theology of the Father, Son, and Holy Spirit. She defended these titles as revelations recorded in Scripture (*A Select Library of Nicene and Post-Nicene Fathers of the Christian Church.* second series, eds. Philip Schaff and Henry Wace. Vol. 5: *Gregory of Nyssa: Dogmatic Treatises,* etc. [Grand Rapids, Mich.: William B. Eerdmans, 1892], pp. 1–6).

Likewise, Nina, the evangelizer of the Georgians, converted that nation by her teaching of Jesus Christ and of the Holy Trinity—Father, Son, and Holy Spirit. She did so by her own will; she was not commissioned by the bishops (*Lives and Legends of Georgian Saints,* by David Marshall Long [Crestwood, N.Y.: SVS Press, 1956], pp. 13–39).

PRAISE FOR WOMEN

Second, the most accurate way to describe the Church Fathers' attitude toward women would not be animosity but ambivalence. One can indeed find passages in their writings deriding women for their weak wills and for leading the human race into sin (John Chrysostom writes that "the woman taught once and ruined all"). But one also finds passages extolling women for being of great character and teaching the gospel better than men. Gregory of Nazianzen, in writing of his parents, explains that his father's virtue was "the result of his wife's prayers and guidance, and it was from her that he learned his ideal of a good shepherd's life.... They [his parents] have been rightly assigned, each to either sex; he is the ornament of men, she of women, and not only the ornament but the pattern of virtue" (*Funeral Oration on His Sister Gorgonia*).

Jerome says his reader may laugh at him for so often "dwelling on the praises of mere women ..., [but] we judge of people's virtue not by their sex but by their character and hold those to be of the highest glory who have renounced both rank and wealth" (*Letter* 127, *To Principia*).

It must also be noted that in several instances the Church was much fairer toward women than the surrounding culture. Gregory of Nazianzen exemplified this by upbraiding the men of his flock in regard to a civil law which meted out strict punishment for wives committing adultery but disregarded husbands committing the same crime: "[Let me discuss] chastity, in respect of which I see that the majority of men are ill-disposed and that their laws are unequal and irregular. For what was the reason why they restrained the woman but indulged the man, and why a woman who practices evil against her husband's bed is an adulteress (and the legal penalties for this are very severe), but if a husband commits fornication against his wife, he has not account to give? I do not accept this legislation; I do not approve this custom. Those who made the law were men, and therefore the legislation is hard on women" (*On the Words of the Gospel*).

Fourth, it appears that it was not unknown to the leaders of the fourth-century Church that mothers as well as fathers contributed as sources to the making of a child. John Chrysostom wrote:

"A man leaving *them* that begat him, and from whom he was born, is knit to his wife. And then the one flesh is, father and mother, and the child from the substance *of the two* commingled. For indeed, *by the commingling of their seeds* the child is produced" (*Homily* 20, *On Ephesians* 5:31).

Yet, even with this knowledge of mothers and fathers both acting as "sources" in the life process, the Church insisted on using the exclusive term "Father" for God.

THE SPIRIT AND THE FEMININE

Perhaps even more interesting, patristic writers never excluded the ideas that women were made in the image of God or that human femininity had some relationship to God. In many texts, there appears the idea that women, with their femininity, are closely associated with the Person of the Holy Spirit and the Spirit's mode of life. In the patristic period, the Fathers compared the procession of the Holy Spirit from the Father with the "procession" of Eve from Adam.

Later, in the seventh century, Anastasius of Sinai wrote: "Eve, who proceeded from Adam, signifies the proceeding Person of the Holy Spirit. This is why God did not breathe in her the breath of life; she was already the type of the breathing and life of the Holy Spirit" (*On the Image and Likeness*). Especially in Syriac hymnody, the association between human femininity and the mode of existence of the Holy Spirit was stressed. Therefore, the "masculine" terms used in the trinitarian names are not the result of disdain for the feminine.

With this evidence, it is clear that the patristic writers were interested in preserving the scriptural terms of "Father, Son, and Holy Spirit" as revelations from God rather than reflections of patriarchal culture. This is evident from their frequent appeals to Scripture for the bases of their arguments.

PRECISE THEOLOGICAL TERMS

In view of this historical background, it appears the arguments supporting "non-exclusive" language changes for God are untenable — incompatible with Scripture, apostolic teachings, and Christian experience. Against the historical backdrop of Church life, the terms "Father, Son, and Holy Spirit" appear not as exchangeable metaphors, human imaginings, or pillars of a patriarchal culture, but rather as precise terms revealed by Jesus Christ through the Holy Spirit and preserved in the canon of Scripture.

The challenge to Christians today compares to the challenge to Christians in the fourth century; to preserve these names as gifts from God which give us clues to his inner life, for us as adopted children through his Son, Jesus Christ, our Lord.

IN DEFENSE OF GOD THE FATHER

Juli Loesch Wiley

When I was pregnant with my little son Benjamin, I liked to feel him elbowing around inside of me and to watch the front of my dress move as he executed his slow rolls and quick nudges. O God, "in whom we live and move and have our being"—is it not natural to think of God as a *Mother?*

I remember visiting my friend Elizabeth in the hospital after she had had a rather horrific caesarian delivery. The doctor, in making the low transverse incision, had sliced straight across the placenta. There was copious bleeding, and Elizabeth nearly died. Yet there she lay on the hospital bed, pale as a sheet, propped up on pillows as she had requested so she could nurse her newborn. "Take and eat. This is my body, broken for you." Is it not natural to think of *God* as a Mother?

I remember nursing my own baby and then lying on the floor and holding him up so he could toddle up and down the hills and valleys of the Mommy Mountains: my topographic self. I was the hand that held him, the voice that called him, the very ground under his feet. Is it not *natural* to think of God as a Mother?

I am a firm believer in God the Father, and yet I am one who has taken feminist challenges seriously. You have to take them seriously. You cannot just flick them away and say, "Well, they're flaky, they probably had unsatisfactory relationships with their fathers, they're probably lesbians", etc.

First of all, that sort of ad hominem argument is just not fair. We do not like it when they do it to us. And have we not all heard it before? They say we are rigid, that we probably have masochistic relationships with our husbands, that we are probably sexually repressed. And so forth. We do not like to be stereotyped because we know it is just a way to be dismissed without consideration. So let us not dismiss feminist challenges lightly.

Second, if we brush off feminist challenges, we miss a chance to develop a richer understanding of our own Catholic Faith. I believe that some of the re-imaging of God has been a response to a real need to acknowledge the image and likeness of God in women. And I believe that is legitimate. I also believe this vision of feminine holiness can be developed most beautifully and most authentically only within—and not outside of—a Bible-based Faith in a Bible-based Church—or rather, in *the* Bible Church, the Catholic Church.

Twenty years ago, when I was out of the Church, I was into the neo-pagan "womanspirit" scene, and then I spent eleven years as a lay associate of a convent where the prioress was busy revising Christianity along feminist lines. I went along with it for awhile. I read what everybody was reading and listened to what everyone was saying. Then at some point I turned around and came back to the catechism, back to the Creed, back to God the Father. I want to share here a few of the considerations that brought me back.

THE GODDESSES OF ANTIQUITY

Some of the critics of God as Father make much of the fact that all ancient peoples had goddesses: the Babylonians, Eleusinians, Egyptians, and Celts worshipped Birgit, Juno, Ceres, Diana, Minerva, Pallas Athene, Venus, Aphrodite, Isis, Ishtar, Astarte—the list goes on and on. Some take these to be archetypes representing different aspects of Everywoman's personality. Hence, we get from feminists the image of God as Immanent Mother.

As anyone can see, this view is not derived from the Bible. What some Christian feminists fail to see is that it cannot be added to or mixed with the biblical view. It is *not* an expansion or enrichment of the biblical view: it is *anti*biblical.

The Hebrew Scriptures, clear through, are a thousand-year polemic against their neighbors' myth systems. Adherence to the rival images of the other nations is plainly forbidden as idolatry.

What is the sin most frequently denounced by the Hebrew prophets? Idolatry. The prophets linked it closely with their second-most-denounced sin, the oppression of the poor and helpless. The prevalence of novel and popular myths is seen as being so dangerous to the community as to bring about its ethical, and then its physical, destruction.

A NEW IMAGE FOR THE TRUE GOD?

The worship of false gods is dangerous—very dangerous. But what about the idea that we can worship the God of Abraham, of Isaac, and of Jacob, the God who is, and was, and is to come—*the true God,* in other words—under the garb of different poetic imagery?

Every created thing is, in some way, a revelation of God; and so any image the artist or poet can come up with can have, in the very broadest sense of the word, "sacramental" significance—in the sense that it is an outward sign through which the Creator acts and communicates. There can be considerable freedom in symbolic language.

The Hebrew and Christian Scriptures abound with various titles and images for God. The titles include Lord, Wonderful Counselor, Sun of Justice, Prince of Peace. The images include animals and inanimate objects, natural things and things of human making. A rock. A shield. A fortress. A doorway. A mother bird. And metaphorically, God is seen as farmerlike, shepherdlike, soldierlike—and motherlike.

But all metaphors, evidently, are not equal. Lambs and calves may be equal; yet, while Christ can be the "Lamb" of God, we *never* call Him the "Golden Calf" or the "Sacred Cow". Why? Because serious confusion would arise, due to the other associations we have with calves and cows. So these terms are ruled out.

MALE AND FEMALE: IMAGE AND LIKENESS

Going back to our beginnings—Genesis—we find exactly one-third of a verse describing God's image as both male and female. Despite its brevity, it really is a crucial text: one that flashes like a kind of beacon light across seventy-two books of Scripture. Woman and man as co-image-bearers for God: that *is* Genesis. That is Plan A. That is the way it is supposed to be.

Genesis also shows feminine things being intimately connected with God. For instance, when Eve is called Adam's "suitable helper", it is not at all necessary to understand the word "helper" in an ancillary or inferior sense. The very same Hebrew word is applied to God Himself: "The Lord is my help and my salvation." God is the one who opens and closes the womb. God delights in pregnancies. In Isaiah, God longs to provide milk and comfort for His people.

Most touchingly, to me, God is described over and over as being full of *rachmones,* the Hebrew word that is usually translated "lovingkindness". Actually, it is derived from the root-word *rechem,* "a mother's womb". God loves us with *womb love.* Surely this is profoundly significant.

Yet never, in all seventy-two books of the Bible, is God ever called, personally and directly, "our Mother". Why? A Father with a womb hardly seems plausible. Hardly attractive. Hardly, with the present feminist agenda, *usable.* But there it is.

It is not that the idea of a mother God was not culturally available. It seems that, given the prominence of both priestesses and goddesses in all of Israel's neighbors—Canaanite, Hellenic, Mesopotamian, Persian, and Egyptian—the Judeo-Christian avoidance of "God the Mother" and insistence upon "God the Father" was not a matter of cultural conditioning at all. It went against the conditioning. It was countercultural. It is as if "God the Mother" imagery were specifically considered and rejected. Again, why?

I do not know. The reason could *not* be because God is a biological male. God is neither male nor female and infinitely beyond biology. Moreover, the reason could *not* be because God is uniquely the paradigm of masculine virtue: God is the Creator and source of *all* virtue, masculine and feminine.

Given that the image of a female God could be plausible, attractive, and useful—and that it was and is culturally available—and given that both the male and the female are created in the image and likeness of God, the complete absence of "God the Mother" as a form of address in the Bible has a truly striking and deliberate aspect. It cannot have been an oversight. Goddess devotion would have been expected. An exclusively masculine identity for the Godhead would have been odd, radical, counterintuitive, unexpected. What possible harm could come from goddess imagery?

Perhaps Father is in and Mother out for the same reason that "Lamb of God" is in but "Golden Calf" is out: because of our tendency to get jumbled and confused. Perhaps God, who is the source of all good things, chooses to limit Himself to Fatherhood, not for His greater glory but because we need to relate to Him that way.

The first and ultimately best reason for addressing God as Father is that this is how He asked to be addressed. If Cassius Clay has a right to be called Muhammad Ali; if Agnes Gouxha has a right to be called Mother Teresa; if your dark-skinned neighbor prefers to be called African-American and your coworker in a wheelchair wants to be described as "differently abled"; if a Welshman bristles at being called English and a woman insists on "woman" and not chick, dame, or girl—then respecting the requested form of address is a matter of courtesy at least, and ultimately an acknowledgment of the right to self-definition. We call God our Father because it would be plain rude not to do so.

But part of me wants to have a reason. Part of me wants to know "why". And I know of no authoritative voice in Sacred Scripture or in Sacred Tradition that tells me why. But I can hazard some guesses, drawing clues from my own grab-bag of symbolic and psychological notions. So, without claiming any authority on my own, let me offer four speculations as to why God might want to limit His relations with us to Fatherhood.

First, there is *sexual metaphor.* Maybe it is better for us to see God's creativity as a kind of masculine begetting rather than a kind of feminine conceiving. Second, there is the *emotional burden* of relating to a human mother and a divine mother at the same time. Third, there is the *benevolence of God.* Perhaps God chooses to relate to us as a Father because this is an area of acute and chronic need for us. Perhaps God knows that, on the average, we tend to run a fathering deficit. And fourth—and this is my favorite— there is what I will call the *humility of God:* perhaps God assumes a kind of masculine role relationally because he wants to crown all of us with the glory of the feminine.

SEXUAL METAPHOR

Let us look at the question of sexual metaphor. There is an item in biology I would like to lead off with in a tentative way. Procreation requires action that is conscious or deliberate on the part of the male but not on the part of the female. That is, a man can have intercourse with a female who is entirely nonactive—even unconscious or in a coma—and beget a child.

This is, admittedly, an extreme example, but it illustrates a fact that is not social or cultural but anatomical: the act that begets life is *always* active for the male but not necessarily for the female. In this sense (if in no other), the male initiates generation.

I have no general social theory of female passivity—God forbid. But in terms of choosing natural images—sheer metaphor—this may be relevant to the idea of God's coming, God's active giving— and, our openness, our "letting God", our patient bearing of what God has implanted. These ideas are common in Christian mysticism.

THE EMOTIONAL BURDEN OF MOTHERHOOD

With the same tentativeness, let us look at a second speculation: the emotional burden of relating to a human mother and a divine mother at the same time. This involves some psychological theory.

Psychologist Dorothy Dinnerstein interprets our prolonged human infancy as a time of strong emotions, physical helplessness, and pre-verbal frustration directed, almost always, at our mother or female caregiver. Dinnerstein shows that we all have deeply ambivalent relationships with mother figures. Because we depended on them absolutely, we raged against them with infant tears because they were so controlling of every sensate need: milk, touch, comfort.

As a mother of a yearling boy, I can testify from experience that rage—wild, screaming fury—is as much a part of his emotional repertoire as the smiles and giggles of nursling intimacy.

In her book *The Mermaid and the Minotaur,* Dinnerstein cites the work of many other infant psychologists—Anna Freud, Melanie Klein, and so forth—who describe how we go through stages of feeling "smothered" by our mothers, and by women generally. Human infants are both *much* more helpless, and *much* more emotionally sensitive, than, say, infant kittens or infant chimps. That means we build up an enormous reservoir of irrational resentment against these giant female figures who suckle us, and diaper us, and pick us up and put us down, because—unlike animal cubs—human infants feel the full emotional weight of their helplessness.

Dinnerstein emphasizes that the father, the male, is *not* the object of all this fervent need and howling resentment—not in the crucial pre-verbal months of unweaned infancy—because the man's role in the day-to-day nurturant care of tiny infants has been smaller—and in most cultures, *much* smaller.

One of Dr. Dinnerstein's main contentions—a theme found in much feminist psychology—is that being the focus of all these emotions is a burden that women should not have to carry alone. She argues that one of the main projects for human maturity is to distribute our strong emotions—our infant rage and infant bliss—more equally among men and women. Yet she doubts that this can actually be done on a wide scale. For 99 percent of the human race, it is still mothers and other women who tend tiny babies, and it is likely to remain so.

Then—still following this theory—we might still compensate for the power of all our original "Mothergods" by transferring those emotions onto a male figure in some other way.

I am suggesting—and, ironically, feminist psychoanalytic theory itself suggests—that at this point, the resurgence of God as *Mother* could be disastrous. All our impelling hopes and wild fears, our tearful petitions, our upwelling resentments, would still be heaped upon—who? *The Mother!* It is Mother's fault. It always was. How liberating.

Maybe one of the sane aspects of the old "improbable" biblical God is that He gives us, at last, a chance to climb into the womb and be born again, from the Father this time.

The theology of the Father gives us a masculine figure to love impossibly and struggle with like Jacob, a terrible Papa (not Mama) to reproach with Jeremiah-like accusations.

It frees us all from the awful weight of being under the mother, again. And it relieves our mothers—and all women—of the burden of being God Almighty, so to speak, again.

To sum up what I have said so far: God as Father makes sense as a sexual metaphor: God is active and creates something that is *not* a "part of Himself". God begets. Second, there is the emotional burden of being seen as akin to Almighty God, responsible for everything in the whole universe, so to speak. Virtually all human beings have already encountered an all-powerful woman: our mothers, as seen in our infant eyes. Perhaps it is better for us women, and for men, too, that men should bear the burden of divinity through identification with God the Father.

THE BENEVOLENCE OF GOD

There is a third reason why seeing God as Father might be a good thing, for our sakes. Perhaps fatherhood is an aspect of the benevolence of God because God sees that we have a particular need, not so much for a bolstered-up motherhood but for remedial fatherhood.

It is hard for some people to pray to God the Father because they had such a troubled relationship with their own fathers. Too many girls have suffered from abuse from their natural fathers; too many boys have felt the wounding pain of rejection or the slow starvation of emotional abandonment. The word "father", to these girls and boys, these men and women, suggests the man who abandoned them, who hurt them—or it may suggest flat nothing, a zero, an emptiness: the man who was not there. These feelings are often called back to life when the person tries to establish a relationship with God the Father.

I have heard Christian counselors wonder out loud whether these people would not have an easier time if they could just picture God as their Mother.

This is a real problem, and one that in some communities must seem overwhelming. In the United States today, one out of five children in the white community is born into a household without a father. In the Hispanic community, it is one out of three. In the black community, two out of three. In America's underclass, the adult male, when he is present at all, is all too often "present" as a parasite—or as a predator.

Nor is this a problem only for our society or for the waning decades of this century. The fact is that responsible fathering has always been harder to come by than responsible mothering. By its very nature, fathering seems a chancier, more inconstant, more *erratic* social role.

Why should that be? I would say it is biology.

The female, mothering role is strongly rooted in instincts and hormones. The first weeks after I had my baby, I was still as bound to him as before his cord was cut. When he cried, I could feel my milk spurt and my uterus contract. I was almost physically incapable of ignoring or resisting my crying newborn son.

I later learned that the breastfeeding hormones, oxytocin and prolactin, condition strong mothering responses both in humans and in other suckling mammals. So striking is the biochemical impetus toward protective and nurturant behavior that psychologists have discussed giving doses of lactation hormones to violence-prone criminals to mellow out their more aggressive emotions.

For this and many other reasons, the natural role for a mother in a family is fairly obvious. Mothers may not always *do* what they are supposed to do, but most mothers at least *know* what they are supposed to do.

The same cannot be said for fatherhood. To begin with, except under conditions of strict monogamy, the relationship between a particular man and a particular child is never a sure thing. Without blood tests and DNA analysis, paternity is hard to prove and easy to deny. Almost every child knows who his mother is; but, as folk wisdom has observed in a dozen different languages, it is a wise child who knows his father.

So being identified as a mother is inescapable once one has given birth, but paternity is socially constructed. Legal marriage and curbs on sexual activity are the fragile social inventions that create "legitimacy" and, by doing so, create fatherhood.

But what is the father supposed to do? The mother holds, warms, comforts, nourishes. The father—??

Again, just as the *identity* of father has to be socially constructed, the *role,* the behavior, has to be constructed, too. Does the father sit with the other men and discuss politics? Does he sit with the other men and drink? Does he teach his children about religion? Can he change a diaper? Does he know a lullaby?

Does the father control the paycheck? Does he hand it over to his wife? Does he honor his wife as an equal? Does he beat on her, or cheat on her? Does he carry a knife? Does he carry a rosary? Does he carry the statue of the saint on the big feast day? Is he a strong support for people weaker than himself?

When he gets middle-aged, can he dump his wife? Can he talk to his daughters? Does he teach his sons a trade? Does he take them into his business as partners? Is he gone on a whaling ship? Gone on a business trip? Gone to war? Does a father have to be present to his family, or can somebody else do what he does?

At all times and in all places, almost all single-parent families are mother-headed families. At all times and in all places, fatherhood is chancier. At all times and in all places, men need role models. I need role models, too, but even if I did not have any, I would still be a mother. *But without role models, almost no man will be a father.*

As long as we are a live-bearing, warm-blooded furry mammal species, motherhood will survive somehow. But the real thriving, the real flourishing of a family in all its members, depends *also* on a man, a father, who has a high view of his calling, an unshakable identity, and a sure grasp of his role.

I suspect that God chooses to relate to us as a Father because this is an area of acute and chronic need for us. Fatherhood needs remedial action. It needs repeated and constant emphasis. It always has—because without constant emphasis, fatherhood is all too prone to fade out, to slip away, and to disappear altogether.

He, God, has chosen to serve us by showing us Fatherhood. He has chosen to serve us the way we needed to be served.

THE HUMILITY OF GOD

There is a fourth reason, I think, that the Creator and Sovereign Master of the Universe, who is the source of male and female and yet is beyond male and female, has chosen to reveal Himself to us as a Father. I believe it has to do with his inconceivable humility.

Think, first of all, of the complete self-sufficiency of deity. God, who exists from all eternity as a Trinity of love beyond time and space, dwells in perfect bliss. Not because He needed anything, but out of sheer generosity, God created the universe out of nothing and sustains it in being by His powerful word. God knows all things, can do all things, can be all things.

But God does not choose to be the only will in the universe. He does not choose to do everything. God condescends to give some will, some independence, some ability to act, to the creatures that He made.

When we got ourselves lost by stupidly attempting to use our wills in opposition to His, He willed to save us.

The English woman mystic Julian of Norwich calls God a "courteous Lord", and there is an almost incredible courtesy in the *way* God wills to save us. God—to whom the whole universe is just "dust on the scales"—could overpower us all, seize and sway the wills of humankind with the tiniest fraction of His might. He could sweep us into ecstasies in which we would be quite out of our wits, beside ourselves, helpless before the irresistible power and beauty of God.

But He does not. Instead, veiling His power, He stands far

back—behind a thick door, so to speak—and, bowing low to the dust He created, He humbly asks, "Will you be mine? Will you?"

The galaxies go off like fireworks in silence, stars go supernova, charged particles dance—but all is mute. God waits. And waits. And out of the inarticulate cosmos, out of the spiraling universe, one voice is heard. A girl's voice. "I will. According to your will."

We are so lucky! Now the Savior could take flesh, salvation became possible, because someone was full of grace, graceful enough, to just do it. "Behold the handmaid of the Lord." Thank you, Mary.

Mary knew her dependence on God. But perhaps even more amazing is God's dependence on Mary. Although God could have been both "Father" and "Mother", He chose self-limitation. Self-sufficient, God chose to relinquish self-sufficiency. The Greek word *kenosis,* emptying, described the amazing truth that God is so powerful that He can even empty Himself of power. Jesus' *kenosis* was the emptying of his limitlessness into the limits of humanity. Perhaps we can say that the Creator's *kenosis* was the emptying of His creativity into the limits of paternity.

God as the Bridegroom chose to need the Bride. God as the Son chose to need the Mother.

If there is something Godlike in motherhood—and I strongly believe there is—then the wonder is that God did *not* say, "I'll be Father-Mother. I'll do it all myself." The *wonder* is that God's motherhood is entirely bestowed on us, in Mary.

C. S. Lewis says something to the effect that the whole of creation is feminine in relation to the Creator. If that is true, then Mary speaks for all Creation: she is the articulate member, the one who finally says, "I'm all yours." Then she is overshadowed by the Holy Spirit, just as the universe, which she represents, was overshadowed by that same Spirit in the beginning, on the first day of creation.

Some feminist theologians believe that women have been held back from full participation in the Christian mysteries. It would be closer to the truth to say, however, that it is *only* women who are admitted to the Christian mysteries. You see, any man who would participate must first become, symbolically, "woman". This is because, in traditional Christian terms, *all* souls are feminine.

Like Mary, all of us, men and women, are to hear the word of God and keep it. Like Mary, we are to let it take root in us and grow in us. Like Mary, we are to bear Christ within us. We are to bring Him to birth.

The prophets of Israel, the authors of the Epistles, the Fathers of the Church, the mystics, male and female, all through the, ages, agree on this. They see that God's choice image is that He is the Bridegroom: and Israel, and Mary, and the Church, and all of us, *men and women,* are the Bride.

So it is not that *we* need to search for *God* through a better, more egalitarian, more up-to-date feminist symbol system. The point is that *God* is searching for *us,* to raise us up from the dust, male and female, because He wants us to be His Bride.

APPENDICES

APPENDIX A

STATEMENT ON FEMINISM, LANGUAGE, AND LITURGY

Women for Faith and Family,
Forum of Major Superiors,
Consortium Perfectae Caritatis

Because we are Catholic women who accept and affirm all the teachings of the Catholic Church, not only as true propositions but as the norms of our thought and life;

Because we are aware of the influence within the Church and in society of alien ideologies which attack the fundamental assumptions of Christianity about human life and of the relationship of human beings with their Creator, and which effectively undermine the Catholic Church;

Because we understand our responsibility as Catholics and as women to witness to the truth which the Catholic Church teaches and our willing and free acceptance of her just and true authority vested in the Magisterium of the Church, particularly in Christ's vicar, the Pope, and Bishops in union with him, we believe it our duty to make the following statement:

1. In our time and culture, ideological feminism, which denies the fundamental psychic and spiritual distinctiveness of the sexes and which devalues motherhood and the nurturing role of women in the family and in society, is often misrepresented as

expressing the collective belief of women. As women, we are particularly concerned about the pervasive influence and the destructive effects on the Church, on families and on society of this "feminism".

2. As Catholics who have been formed, inspired and sustained by the Sacraments of the Church through participation in the liturgy, the Church's central action and principal means of transmission of the Catholic Faith, we are strongly aware of the power of symbol in human consciousness. We therefore deplore attempts to distort and transform language and liturgy, both of which make such potent symbolic impressions on the human mind, to conform to a particular contemporary ideological agenda at odds with Catholic belief and practice.

3. We reaffirm our belief in the divine origin of the Church and that the hierarchy of the Catholic Church, which is often criticized in our time as insufficiently egalitarian, was intentionally established by Christ, and that He selected the Apostles and Peter, among them, as head, giving them and their legitimate successors magisterial authority to guide His Church until He comes again.

4. We believe that Jesus Christ, the Word of God made man, was limited and restricted by His culture only in that which, apart from sin, limits man. But we also believe that He came in a time and to a people chosen by God. Thus, all that Jesus took up from His culture by His teaching or action is normative for every culture of every time and place. We reject the notion that Jesus Christ, God Incarnate, was limited or restricted in the fulfillment of the Mission entrusted to Him by the Father by the cultural context of His presence on Earth, His life as a Jew of the first third of the first century, or by any other factor.

5. Accordingly, we also reaffirm the constant teaching of the Catholic Church that ordained priesthood is not a "right" accorded to any member of the Church, but a state of life and a service to which, by Christ's will, only men, not women, may be called.

6. Following the teachings and example of Christ and the constant tradition of the Catholic Church, and mindful of its full significance, we consider it a privilege to call God "Our Father", a name which reflects not only the relationship between human beings and their Creator, but which also provides a powerful symbolic model for men of the steadfast love, faithfulness, justice, mercy, wisdom and objectivity which are ideal components of human fatherhood vital to women, to families and to the social order. Contemporary efforts to impute a "feminine" aspect to the Godhead, by retrojection of alien and anachronistic notions into the body of Sacred Scripture, by forcibly changing the language used to refer to God, by deliberate reversion to pagan notions of deity, or by any other means, we regard as dangerously misguided and perverse.

7. Therefore we reject all attempts to impose ideologically motivated innovations on the liturgy of the Church or changes in official lectionaries or sacramentaries or catechisms in the name of "justice" to women. We deplore the deliberate manipulation of liturgical actions, signs and symbols and the politicization of both liturgy and language which effectively impede both receiving and transmitting the Catholic faith and harm the unity of the Church.

8. For these reasons, we oppose the systematic elimination from Scripture translations, liturgical texts, hymns, homilies and general usage of "man" as a generic. The claim that the language is "sexist" and that such changes are required as a sensitive pastoral response to women collectively is false. We believe that the symbolic effect of mandating such changes in the language and practice of the Catholic Church is negative and confusing, effectively undermining the authority of the Church and her hierarchy.

9. We also oppose changing the constant practice of the Church in such liturgical matters as acolytes or "altar servers" and homilists, and repudiate the increasingly frequent practice of women saying parts of the Eucharistic Prayer with the priest or in his place or performing other liturgical functions reserved to ordained men.

10. We are grateful for the profound contribution of Pope John Paul II to our understanding of the meaning of human life and of the fundamental relationship of human beings with one another and with God through the many theological works he has given the Church during his pontificate, including his Apostolic Letter, *Mulieris Dignitatem,* which help to deepen our understanding of the centrality of the role of Christian women to the Church's evangelical mission. Constantly seeking the aid of the Holy Spirit, and in solidarity with the Pope, the Bishops in union with him, and with the universal Church, we pledge to respond to our Christian vocation with wisdom, with love and responsibility.

APPENDIX B

CRITERIA FOR THE EVALUATION OF INCLUSIVE LANGUAGE TRANSLATIONS OF SCRIPTURAL TEXTS PROPOSED FOR LITURGICAL USE

On November 15, 1990, during the plenary assembly of the National Conference of Catholic Bishops, the members approved the Criteria for the Evaluation of Inclusive Language Translations of Scriptural Texts Proposed for Liturgical Use. *These criteria, developed by the Joint Committee (Liturgy and Doctrine) on Inclusive Language over the past three years, are intended to assist bishops in evaluating the suitability of inclusive language translations of scriptural texts proposed for liturgical use. The text follows:*

INTRODUCTION: THE ORIGINS AND NATURE OF THE PROBLEM

1. Five historical developments have converged to present the Church in the United States today with an important and challenging pastoral concern. First, the introduction of the vernacular into the Church's worship has necessitated English translations of the liturgical books and of sacred scripture for use in the liturgy. Second, some segments of American culture have become increasingly sensitive to "exclusive language", i.e., language which seems to exclude the equality and dignity of each person regardless of race, gender, creed, age or ability.[1] Third, there has been a

---

[1] Cf. Bishop Members of the Pastoral Team, Canadian Conference of Catholic Bishops, *To Speak as a Christian Community* (Aug. 16, 1989), p. 2.

noticeable loss of the sense of grammatical gender in American usage of the English language. Fourth, English vocabulary itself has changed so that words which once referred to all human beings are increasingly taken as gender-specific and, consequently, exclusive. Fifth, impromptu efforts at inclusive language, while pleasing to some, have often offended others who expect a degree of theological precision and linguistic or aesthetic refinement in the public discourse of the liturgy. Some impromptu efforts may also have unwittingly undermined essentials of Catholic doctrine.

These current issues confront a fundamental conviction of the Church, namely, that the Word of God stands at the core of our faith as a basic theological reality to which all human efforts respond and by which they are judged.

2. The bishops of the United States wish to respond to this complex and sensitive issue of language in the English translation of the liturgical books of the Church in general and of sacred scripture in particular. New translations of scriptural passages used in the liturgy are being proposed periodically for their approval. Since the promulgation of the 1983 Code of Canon Law these translations must be approved by a conference of bishops or by the Apostolic See.[2] The question confronts the bishops: With regard to a concern for inclusive language, how do we distinguish a legitimate translation from one that is imprecise?

3. The recognition of this problem prompted the submission of a varium to the National Conference of Catholic Bishops requesting that the Bishops' Committee on the Liturgy and the Committee on Doctrine be directed jointly to formulate guidelines which would assist the bishops in making appropriate judgments on the inclusive language translations of biblical texts for liturgical use. These two committees established a Joint Committee on Inclusive Language, which prepared this text.

4. This document, while providing an answer to the question concerning translations of biblical texts for liturgical use, does not attempt to elaborate a complete set of criteria for inclusive lan-

[2] Code of Canon Law [hereafter CIC], 825.1.

guage in the liturgy in general, that is, for prayers, hymns, and preaching. These cognate areas will be treated only insofar as they overlap the particular issues being addressed here.

5. This document presents practical principles for the members of the National Conference of Catholic Bishops to exercise their canonical responsibility for approving translations of scripture proposed for liturgical use. However, just as this document does not deal with all cases of inclusive language in the liturgy, neither is it intended as a theology of translation. The teaching of *Dei Verbum* and the instructions of the Pontifical Biblical Commission prevail in matters of inspiration, inerrancy, and hermeneutics and their relationship with meaning, language, and the mind of the author. While there would be a value in producing a study summarizing these issues, it would distract from the immediate purpose of this document.

6. This document treats the problem indicated above in four parts: General Principles; Principles for Inclusive Language Lectionary Translations; Preparation of Texts for Use in the Lectionary; Special Questions, viz., naming God, the Trinity, Christ, and the Church.

PART ONE: GENERAL PRINCIPLES

7. There are two general principles for judging translations for liturgical use: the principle of fidelity to the Word of God and the principle of respect for the nature of the liturgical assembly. Individual questions, then, must be judged in light of the textual, grammatical, literary, artistic, and dogmatic requirements of the particular scriptural passage, and in light of the needs of the liturgical assembly. In cases of conflict or ambiguity, the principle of fidelity to the word of God retains its primacy.

I. Fidelity to the Word of God

The following considerations derive from the principle of fidelity to the Word of God.

8. The People of God have the right to hear the Word of God integrally proclaimed[3] in fidelity to the meaning of the inspired authors of the sacred text.

9. Biblical translations must always be faithful to the original language and internal truth of the inspired text. It is expected, therefore, that every concept in the original text will be translated within its context.

10. All biblical translations must respect doctrinal principles of revelation, inspiration, and biblical interpretation (hermeneutics), as well as the formal rhetoric intended by the author (e.g., Heb 2:5–18). They must be faithful to Catholic teaching regarding God and divine activity in the world and in human history as it unfolds. "Due attention must be paid both to the customary and characteristic patterns of perception, speech, and narrative which prevailed at the age of the sacred writer and to the conventions which the people of his time followed."[4]

II. The Nature of the Liturgical Assembly

The following considerations derive from the nature of the liturgical assembly.

11. Each and every Christian is called to, and indeed has a right to, full and active participation in worship. This was stated succinctly by the Second Vatican Council: "The Church earnestly desires that all the faithful be led to that full, conscious, and active participation in liturgical celebrations called for by the very nature of the liturgy. Such participation by the Christian people as 'a chosen race, a royal priesthood, a holy nation, God's own people' (1 Pet 2:9; see 2:4–5) is their right and duty by reason of their baptism."[5] An integral part of liturgical participation is hearing

[3] CIC 213.

[4] Second Vatican Ecumenical Council, Constitution on Divine Revelation *Dei Verbum*, no. 12.

[5] Second Vatican Ecumenical Council, Constitution on the Sacred Liturgy *Sacrosanctum Concilium*, no. 14. English translation is from *Documents on the Liturgy 1965–1979: Conciliar, Papal and Curial Texts* [hereafter DOL], (Collegeville, Minn.: The Liturgical Press, 1982), p. 1, no. 14.

the word of Christ "who speaks when the scriptures are proclaimed in the Church".[6] Full and active participation in the liturgy demands that the liturgical assembly recognize and accept the transcendent power of God's word.

12. According to the Church's tradition, biblical texts have many liturgical uses. Because their immediate purposes are somewhat different, texts translated for public proclamation in the liturgy may differ in some respects (cf. Part Two) from those translations which are meant solely for academic study, private reading, or *lectio divina.*

13. The language of biblical texts for liturgical use should be suitably and faithfully adapted for proclamation and should facilitate the full, conscious, and active participation of all members of the Church, women and men, in worship.

PART TWO: PRINCIPLES FOR
INCLUSIVE LANGUAGE
LECTIONARY TRANSLATIONS

14. The Word of God proclaimed to all nations is by nature inclusive, that is, addressed to all peoples, men and women. Consequently, every effort should be made to render the language of biblical translations as inclusively as a faithful translation of the text permits, especially when this concerns the People of God, Israel, and the Christian community.

15. When a biblical translation is meant for liturgical proclamation, it must also take into account those principles which apply to the public communication of the biblical meaning. Inclusive language is one of those principles, since the text is proclaimed in the Christian assembly to women and men who possess equal baptismal dignity and reflects the universal scope of the Church's call to evangelize.

16. The books of the Bible are the product of particular cultures, with their limitations as well as their strengths. Consequently not

[6] Ibid., no. 7.

everything in scripture will be in harmony with contemporary cultural concerns. The fundamental mystery of incarnational revelation requires the retention of those characteristics which reflect the cultural context within which the Word was first received.

17. Language which addresses and refers to the worshiping community ought not use words or phrases which deny the common dignity of all the baptized.

18. Words such as "men", "sons", "brothers", "brethren", "forefathers", "fraternity", and "brotherhood", which were once understood as inclusive generic terms, today are often understood as referring only to males. In addition, although certain uses of "he", "his", and "him" once were generic and included both men and women, in contemporary American usage these terms are often perceived to refer only to males. Their use has become ambiguous and is increasingly seen to exclude women. Therefore, these terms should not be used when the reference is meant to be generic, observing the requirements of n. 7 and n. 10.

19. Words such as "adam", "anthropos", and "homo" have often been translated in many English biblical and liturgical texts by the collective terms "man", and "family of man". Since in the original languages these words actually denote human beings rather than only males, English terms which are not gender-specific, such as "person", "people", "human family", and "humans", should be used in translating these words.

20. In narratives and parables the sex of individual persons should be retained. Sometimes, in the Synoptic tradition, the gospel writers select examples or metaphors from a specific gender. Persons of the other sex should not be added merely in a desire for balance. The original references of the narrative or images of the parable should be retained.

PART THREE: THE PREPARATION OF TEXTS FOR USE IN THE LECTIONARY

21. The liturgical adaptation of readings for use in the lectionary should be made in light of the norms of the Introduction to

the *Ordo Lectionum Missae* (1981). Incipits should present the context of the various pericopes. At times, transitions may need to be added when verses have been omitted from pericopes. Nouns may replace pronouns or be added to participial constructions for clarity in proclamation and aural comprehension. Translation should not expand upon the text, but the Church recognizes that in certain circumstances a particular text may be expanded to reflect adequately the intended meaning of the pericope.[7] In all cases, these adaptations must remain faithful to the intent of the original text.[8]

22. Inclusive language adaptations of lectionary texts must be made in light of exegetical and linguistic attention to the individual text within its proper context. Blanket substitutions are inappropriate.

23. Many biblical passages are inconsistent in grammatical person, that is, alternating between second person singular or plural ("you") and third person singular ("he"). In order to give such passages a more intelligible consistency, some biblical readings may be translated so as to use either the second person plural ("you") throughout or the third person plural ("they") throughout. Changes from the third person singular to the third person plural are allowed in individual cases where the sense of the original text is universal. It should be noted that, at times, either the sense or the poetic structure of a passage may require that the alternation be preserved in the translation.

24. Psalms and canticles have habitually been appropriated by the Church for use in the liturgy, not as readings for proclamation, but as the responsive prayer of the liturgical assembly. Accordingly, adaptations have justifiably been made, principally by the omission of verses which were judged to be inappropriate in a given culture or liturgical context. Thus, the liturgical books allow the

[7] Secretariat for Christian Unity (Commission for Religious Relations with Judaism), *Guidelines and Suggestions* for the application of no. 4 of the conciliar declaration *Nostra aetate,* Dec. 1, 1974 [AAS 67 (1975), 73–79].

[8] Sacred Congregation of Rites (Consilium), Instruction *Comme le Prevoit* on the translation of liturgical texts for celebrations with a congregation (Jan. 25, 1969) (DOL 123), nos. 30–32.

adaptation of psalm texts to encourage the full participation of the liturgical assembly.

PART FOUR: SPECIAL QUESTIONS

25. Several specific issues must be addressed in regard to the naming of God, the persons of the Trinity, and the Church, since changes in language can have important doctrinal and theological implications.

I. Naming God in Biblical Translations

26. Great care should be taken in translations of the names of God and in the use of pronouns referring to God. While it would be inappropriate to attribute gender to God as such, the revealed word of God consistently uses a masculine reference for God. It may sometimes be useful, however, to repeat the name of God, as used earlier in the text, rather than to use the masculine pronoun in every case. But care must be taken that the repetition not become tiresome.

27. The classic translation of the Tetragrammaton (YHWH) as "LORD" and the translation of Kyrios as "Lord" should be used in lectionaries.

28. Feminine imagery in the original language of the biblical texts should not be obscured or replaced by the use of masculine imagery in English translations, e.g., Wisdom literature.

II. Naming Christ in Biblical Translations

29. Christ is the center and focus of all scripture.[9] The New Testament has interpreted certain texts of the Old Testament in an explicitly christological fashion. Special care should be observed in the translation of these texts so that the christological meaning is not lost. Some examples include the Servant Songs of

[9] Cf. *Dei Verbum*, no. 16.

Isaiah 42 and 53, Psalms 2 and 110, and the Son of Man passage in Daniel 7.

III. Naming the Trinity in Biblical Translations

30. In fidelity to the inspired Word of God, the traditional biblical usage for naming the Persons of the Trinity as "Father", "Son", and "Holy Spirit" is to be retained. Similarly, in keeping with New Testament usage and the Church's tradition, the feminine pronoun is not to be used to refer to the Person of the Holy Spirit.

IV. Naming the Church in Biblical Translations

31. Normally the neuter third person singular or the third person plural pronoun is used when referring to the People of God, Israel, the Church, the Body of Christ, etc., unless their antecedents clearly are a masculine or feminine metaphor, for instance, the reference to the Church as the "Bride of Christ" or "Mother" (cf. Rev 12).

CONCLUSION

32. These criteria for judging the appropriateness of inclusive language translations of sacred scripture are presented while acknowledging that the English language is continually changing. Contemporary translations must reflect developments in American English grammar, syntax, usage, vocabulary, and style. The perceived need for a more inclusive language is part of this development. Such language must not distract hearers from prayer and God's revelation. It must manifest a sense of linguistic refinement. It should not draw attention to itself.

33. While English translations of the Bible have influenced the liturgical and devotional language of Christians, such translations have also shaped and formed the English language itself. This should be true today as it was in the age of the King James and

Douay-Rheims translations. Thus, the Church expects for its translations not only accuracy but facility and beauty of expression.

34. Principles of translation when applied to lectionary readings and psalm texts differ in certain respects from those applied to translations of the Bible destined for study or reading (see nos. 22–25 above). Thus, when submitting a new or revised translation of the Bible, an edition of the lectionary or a liturgical psalter for approval by the National Conference of Catholic Bishops, editors must supply a complete statement of the principles used in the preparation of the submitted text.

35. The authority to adapt the biblical text for use in the lectionary remains with the conference of bishops. These criteria for the evaluation of scripture translations proposed for use in the liturgy have been developed to assist the members of the National Conference of Catholic Bishops to exercise their responsibility so that all the People of God may be assisted in hearing God's Word and keeping it.

PRINCIPLES FOR
PREPARING NAB PERICOPES

The National Conference of Catholic Bishops, meeting in plenary assembly on November 11–15, 1990, approved the Principles for Preparing Pericopes from the New American Bible for Use in the Second Edition of the Lectionary for Mass. *These nine principles are designed solely to assist the Lectionary Subcommittee in preparing the biblical texts for inclusion in the* Lectionary for Mass *in conformity to the liturgical requirements of the* editio typica altera *of the* Ordo Lectionum Missae (1981). *The approved introduction and principles follow:*

NINE PRINCIPLES FOR PREPARING PERICOPES
FROM THE *NEW AMERICAN BIBLE*
FOR USE IN THE *LECTIONARY FOR MASS*

The following principles have been formulated to assist the Lectionary Subcommittee of the Committee on the Liturgy in the preparation of the pericopes from the *New American Bible with the Revised New Testament* which will be used in the second edition of the *Lectionary for Mass.* It is understood that these principles are to be applied with great care and that the adapted texts never alter the meaning of the biblical text.

Principle A: An incipit is supplied, expressing the context of the reading in accord with lectionary tradition.

Principle B: A pronoun is replaced by a noun for purposes of clarity or facility in public reading.

Principle C: A clause is put into the plural so as to be inclusive in language, without affecting the meaning of the clause.

Principle D: A clause is changed from the third person singular to the second person so as to be inclusive in language, only when it does not affect the meaning of the clause.

Principle E: The expression "the Jews" in the Fourth Gospel is translated as "the Jewish authorities" or "the Jewish religious leaders" or "the Jewish leaders" or the "Jewish people", etc., in accord with the *Guidelines on Religious Relations with the Jews* (December 1, 1974), Part II: Liturgy, of the Apostolic See's Council on Religious Relations with the Jews.

Principle F: The Greek word *adelphoi* is translated as "brothers and sisters" in a context which, in the judgment of Scripture scholars, includes women as well as men.

Principle G: In those instances where the meaning of the text would not be altered, a word which is exclusive in meaning is replaced by an inclusive word or words when the context includes women as well as men.

Principle H: Individuals are not described by their disability ("a paralytic", "a leper", etc.), but as a man (woman) who is paralyzed, a man (woman) with leprosy, etc.

Principle I: In occasional instances a word which is difficult to read publicly or to understand is replaced by a simpler or easier word, without affecting the meaning of the sentence.

COMMENTS ON NCCB'S 1990 CRITERIA

Helen Hull Hitchcock

The Criteria for Evaluation of Inclusive Language in the Liturgy raise serious questions of theology, history, liturgy, and the meaning of worship. The observations below are intended merely to highlight some of the most obvious problems, especially from the perspective of the pews.

1. The first paragraph of the Introduction of the Criteria lists several historical developments which caused the bishops of the Joint Committee (Liturgy and Doctrine) to concern themselves with issuing official guidelines governing use of feminist ("inclusive") language. The list includes the liturgical use of vernacular English and alleged changes in English usage. (These changes—by eliminating "gender" references—set the stage for re-formation of the Church's worship, retranslation of the Scripture, and reconstruction of the language of the liturgy. However, the Criteria do not mention that this program of reform conforms both to the analysis and the demands of feminist liturgists and theologians.)

The Committee alludes to the increasingly widespread practice of making unauthorized changes in the liturgy, "correcting" the words of Scripture and prayers to conform as much as possible to feminist sensibilities. But no mention is made here or elsewhere of the fact that if the English *translation* of the Latin text contains offensive "sexist" language, the Latin *original* must also be in need of revision. Neither did the authors of the Criteria comment on the effect on the liturgy—the prayer of the Church which must transcend time and space and cultures—if its language is to be subject to continual emendation and endless tinkering in order to render it palatable to the constantly changing whims and fashions of any particular culture or which prevail at any particular time.

2. The document neglects to emphasize adequately that liturgical language is (and must be) *secondary* to the central sacramental event—the revelation of Christ's sacrifice; and that the language of worship *must always* convey the whole truth of the Eucharist. The fundamental purpose of the liturgy in the Catholic Church is to make the meaning of the eucharistic sacrifice immediately accessible to those who are directly engaged in this worship. Liturgical language must make this meaning clear: it must not be used to *change* the meaning; it must not be used to *alter* core beliefs to make them more acceptable to those who reject them—even if they may be influential, well-educated and highly vocal.

3. The assertion that English usage has changed implies that this has been a normal, or organic and gradual change. This is simply untrue. Feminist usage does not represent the almost imperceptible composting of layer upon layer of a multitude of influences and other psychological and sociological factors which slowly build and enrich the fertile and complex soil of a language. Feminist usage has never been "grass-roots". It has been the invention and conscious objective of a small, relatively affluent minority. It has always been artificially imposed from the top.

4. There is not only no mandate from the pews for feminist usage—either in the secular world or in the Church—there is considerable confusion, resistance and resentment of this artificial and imposed usage—precisely *because* it is artificial and imposed. Ordinary people, in fact, often make jokes about "politically correct" speech; and even if they obediently say or sing the "corrected" words to prayers and hymns, the effect is disturbing, jarring. Worshippers more often feel manipulated and annoyed than uplifted and consoled when this happens—hardly a spiritual condition allowing maximum participation in the liturgy.

5. Arbitrary imposition of "correct" usage is particularly unfair to the poor, the uneducated, who are powerless to evaluate adequately the liturgical changes or their implications to the Faith. They are powerless, also, to defend their Faith from ideological invasion; although it is they who are, arguably, the most deeply affected by ideological manipulation, as well as most deeply distressed by a lack of authentic Catholic spirituality. (The "unedu-

cated" must now include fully two generations of young Catholics who have been deprived of comprehensive instruction in their religion, and are thus ill-equipped to evaluate any theological or liturgical innovation.)

6. The Criteria's implicit suggestion that feminist language is greatly desired by all or most *women* is false. Many women are reluctant, however, to make an issue of this with their parish priests, in part because they have been intimidated by feminist women who hold influential positions in the Church. In fact, it is women who *believe* as Catholics, and who reject feminist claims of "oppression" by the "patriarchy", who are usually ignored by Church professionals. Non-feminist women—including many scholars and professionals—are ridiculed by feminists. These women are the ones who are *truly* marginalized, having neither voice nor influence in theological and liturgical circles.

7. Forcing politicized and contrived usages on ordinary worshippers—even if those who mandate changes genuinely believe it is being done for the "people's own good", set up additional barriers to getting the Church's teaching to the people, rather than making it more effective and accessible.

8. "Sensitizing" people to feminist liturgical innovations, feminist usage (and "sensitizing" is the goal of consciousness-raising techniques) *actually* makes spontaneous expression of religious beliefs through prayer, song, and other healthy, unselfconscious pieties—a genuine sense of the sacred—recede farther and farther into the distance. This severely inhibits true worship.

9. Lacking a reliable source of spiritual nourishment in the Church's liturgies, ordinary believers will increasingly seek other forms of religious practice, other churches. Believers who are cut off from the True Vine by the incomprehensible convolutions of liturgical experts are beginning to seek elsewhere for the Truth to fill the spiritual vacuum. This is disastrous both for them and for the Church.

If this phenomenon is allowed to continue, public Catholic worship could become the sole province of the elite, the *cognoscenti,* the ideologically and theologically "correct" group—a group whose views have pervaded liturgical "reform" for the past thirty years.

10. The Criteria attempt to make a special category for the text of the Scripture and forms of address for God, perhaps in an effort to protect at least God and the Bible from feminist assault. However, in practice (as reformers know well) the distinctions between liturgical prayers, hymns, and Scripture easily become blurred. If only hymns which have been purged of all remnants of "patriarchy" are to be sung; if "non-sexist" language for the Church's liturgical prayers are all that remain, drawing some sort of magic margin around the Scripture will be both illogical and, ultimately, impossible.

The Criteria were undoubtedly intended as "damage control" by most bishops who voted to approve them in the brief time allowed for discussion and vote at the November 1990 meeting of the National Conference of Catholic Bishops. Some bishops may have hoped that approval of the Criteria would give them some control, some means of meliorating liturgical mutiny in their dioceses—a situation becoming widespread because of the unchecked actions of self-proclaimed liturgists operating on their own (or borrowed) authority to impose radical changes in the liturgy and liturgical language.

Even if it was not the bishops' intention, however, they have approved *in principle* the claims of the party of liturgical revision (1) that feminist ideologically "improved" usage is now to be the *lingua franca* of all English-speaking people; and (2) liturgical language in the Catholic Church should conform to feminist usage. In so doing, they have thereby undercut any objections they themselves may wish to raise—now or in the future—to any feminist "reforms". By accepting the Criteria's principles, the bishops have made it virtually impossible for any bishop to object to any feminist language translations of the liturgy or Scripture, or to halt any pro-feminist liturgical "innovation" whatsoever—even within his own diocese. Although perhaps unintentionally, through the approval of these Criteria, the authority of the bishops has been further eroded and yet another chunk of it given to advocates of sweeping theological and liturgical "reform".

August 1992

APPENDIX C

BIBLIOGRAPHY

I. Books and articles advocating
feminist language in Scripture and liturgy
with selected quotations

Aggeler, Maureen, R.S.C.J. *Mind Your Metaphors: A Critique of the Language in the Bishops' Pastoral Letters on the Role of Women.* New York: Paulist Press, 1991.

* Boadt, Lawrence, C.S.P. "Problems in the Translation of Scripture as Illustrated by ICEL's Project on the Liturgical Psalter". In *Shaping English Liturgy.,* edited by Peter C. Finn and James Schellman, pp. 405-29. Washington, D.C.: Pastoral Press, 1990 .

Boff, Leonardo, *The Maternal Face of God.* New York: Harper and Row, 1987.

Brown, Raymond, S.S. "Communicating the Divine and Human in Scripture". *Origins* 22, no. 1, (May 14, 1992): 1-9. (Keynote address to National Catholic Education Association. St. Louis, April 20, 1992.)

"In the American mainstream the lingua franca of religious belief is supplied by the Bible" (p. 4).... "Jesus phrased his teaching in the context of his own time and ... it requires translation to move to our times from the situation he addressed as a Jew of the early first century...." "Over and over again the caution must be kept in mind: Is this an issue that a Jew living in the first century would have spoken about? (God may well be concerned with the issue, but that may be through the agency of the Holy Spirit who did not become incarnate at a particular time or in a particular place)" (p. 6). "Women today are increasingly sensitive to the presence of a dominant male language, outlook and societal structure in the Bible—an outlook that affects the persuasiveness of the biblical texts that enter the discussion. When passages that women regard as offensive are read in the church lectionary, they are often hurried over [to] avert an outcry" (p. 8).

Buckley, Francis, S.J. "Inculturation and Orthodoxy: The Christian Message". *Origins* 21:249ff.

"We live in a land of secularism and pluralism. . . . Unless the [Gospel] message is presented in a 'language' the people can understand and appreciate, unless it is shown as clearly meeting their basic human needs and answering their deepest yearnings, it will appear alien and irrelevant, at best marginal to their lives."

Carr, Anne, "The Scholarship of Gender: Women's Studies and Religious Studies". In *Transforming Grace: Christian Tradition and Women's Experience,* pp. 63–94. San Francisco: Harper and Row, 1988.

Christ, Carol and Judith Plaskow, eds. *Womanspirit Rising.* New York: Harper and Row, 1979.

Collins, Mary, "Glorious Praise: The ICEL Liturgical Psalter". *Worship,* July 1992, pp. 290–310.

Daly, Mary. *Beyond God the Father.* Boston: Beacon Press, 1973.

Eakins, Barbara Westbrook and R. Gene Eakins. *Sex Differences in Human Communication.* Boston: Houghton Mifflin, 1978.

Farley, Margaret A. "Feminist Consciousness and the Interpretation of Scripture", *Feminist Interpretation of the Bible.* Philadelphia: Westminster Press, 1985.

Farley, Margaret A. "Feminist Theology and Bioethics". In *Feminist Theology: A Reader,* edited by Ann Loades, pp. 238–55. Louisville, Ky.: Westminster/John Knox, 1990.

"A methodological commitment to the primacy of women's experience as a source for theology and ethics yields . . . a feminist hermeneutical principle which functions in the selection and interpretation of all other sources. . . . In some [feminist theologies] it leads to the rejection of the authority of the Bible altogether; in others it allows the relativization of the authority of some texts; in still others, it leaves all texts standing as a part of an authoritative revelation, but renders their meaning transformed under a new feminist paradigm. The same is true for theological doctrines, historical events, and for other sources of theology and ethics" (p. 247).

Fiedler, Maureen, and Dolly Pomerleau. *Are Catholics Ready: An Exploration of the Views of 'Emerging Catholics' on Women in Ministry,* pp. 9–91. Mt. Rainier, Md.: 1978.

* Finn, Peter, and James Schellman, eds. *Shaping English Liturgy.* Washington, D.C.: Pastoral Press, 1990. (Cf. Boadt, Henderson, McManus.)

Fiorenza, Elisabeth Schüssler. "Feminist Theology as a Critical Theology of Liberation". In *Woman: New Dimensions,* edited by Walter J. Burghardt. New York: Paulist Press, 1977.

Fiorenza, Elisabeth Schüssler. *In Memory of Her: A Feminist Theological Reconstruction of Christian Origins.* New York: Crossroad, 1983.

"Hermeneutic of suspicion" applied to Scripture texts; demands that these "oppressive" texts be "demythologized as androcentric codifications of patriarchal power" that "cannot claim to be the revelatory Word of God" (p. 32).

Fiorenza, Elisabeth Schüssler. "The Power of the Word", *The Review of Books and Religion* 12, no. 6 (March 1984): 5.

Fiorenza, Elisabeth Schüssler. "Toward a Feminist Biblical Hermeneutics". In *Readings in Moral Theology,* No. 4, edited by Charles Curran and R. McCormick. New York: Paulist Press, 1984.

Fitzmyer, J. A. *Scripture and Christology,* pp. 8–10. New York: Paulist, 1978. " . . . Studies of Judaism . . . in the time of Jesus are clearly a preliminary and necessary condition for the full understanding of his personality."

Greeley, Andrew. *The Mary Myth: On the Femininity of God.* New York: Seabury, 1977.

* Henderson, Frank J. "ICEL and Inclusive Language". In *Shaping English Liturgy,* edited by Peter C. Finn and James Schellman, pp. 257–78. Washington, D.C.: Pastoral Press, 1990.

Kramarae, Choris. *Women and Men Speaking.* Rowley: Newbury House, 1981.

Lakoff, Robin. *Language and Woman's Place.* New York: Harper and Row, 1975.

McFague, Sallie. *Metaphorical Theology, Models of God in Religious Language.* Philadelphia: Fortress Press, 1982.

"[Religious language] becomes *idolatrous* because without a sense of awe, wonder, and mystery, we forget the inevitable distance between our words and the divine reality: metaphorical theology understands that images need not be traditional, literal. Christians are unwilling to substitute traditional images [fatherhood of God] because they see traditional metaphor as literally true" [p. 2], cited in Maura O'Neill, p. 36. [Cf. Ruether, *Sexism and God-Talk.*]

McManus, Frederick R., ed. *Thirty Years of Liturgical Renewal–Statements of the Bishops' Committee on the Liturgy.* Washington, D.C.: Secretariat, Bishops' Committee on the Liturgy, NCCB, July 1987.

* McManus, Frederick R. "ICEL: 1963–1965". In *Shaping English Liturgy,* edited by Peter C. Finn and James Schellman. Washington, D.C.: Pastoral Press, 1990.

Macquarrie, John, *God-Talk: An Examination of the Language and Logic of Theology.* New York: Harper and Row, 1967.

Marsili, Salvatore, O.S.B. "Liturgical Texts for Modern Man". In *The Crisis of Liturgical Reform. Concilium* 42 (1969): 49–70.

Mollenkott, Virginia. *The Divine Feminine: The Biblical Imagery of God as Female.* New York: Crossroad, 1984.

O'Neill, Maura. *Women Speaking, Women Listening: Women in Interreligious Dialogue.* New York: Orbis, 1990.

"The fact that Christian doctrine maintains the inexpressibility of God's nature is not sufficient justification to ignore the dangers of using sexist language. Language conjures up metaphors and images. Metaphors and images compose our conceptual framework that, in turn, influences our faith and values. Hence exclusive language for God has a great bearing on who and what Christians believe the Ultimate Reality to be, and, in the past, Christians have believed this Ultimate Reality to be male" (p. 36).

"Unless the male representatives of the monotheistic faiths were able to view the oppressive significance of the traditional male images of God (and not dismiss the issue as *merely* language), dialogue could not be fruitful. So far in most of the inter-religious dialogue among predominantly male participants, God has rarely if ever been referred to in gender inclusive language. Men have continually referred to God as 'He' without considering any of the philosophical and theological works [of feminists]" (p. 40).

Rae, Eleanor, and Bernice Marie-Daly. *Created in Her Image: Models of the Feminine Divine.* New York: Crossroad/Continuum, 1990.

Rakow, Lana F. "Rethinking Gender Research in Communication", *Journal of Communication* 36 (Autumn 1986): 23.

Ramshaw, Gail. *Letters for God's Name.* Minneapolis: Seabury, 1984. Excerpted in *Feminist Theology: A Reader.* Edited by Ann Loades, pp. 165–66. Louisville, Ky.: Westminster/John Knox Press, 1990.

"Q
"What if our God were Queen of heaven?
"If our God were Queen of heaven, we could burn incense to her and bake cakes for her, and our adoration would be acceptable.
"If our God were Queen of heaven, her crown would rest on hair long and curly and rainbowed, and we could grab on to that hair as we nursed and so be saved from falling. Her shining face, smooth and clear as light, would enliven the universe. And when we were poor, the Queen would take from her necklace flowing with pearls and opals and every coloured gem perhaps an amber to fill our needs. The resplendent gold of her majestic robe would be what we call the sun, and the sheen of her nightdress the moon. Her rule would reach to the deepest corners of the darkness; her beauty would rout the devils and her wisdom rear the world. Her royal blood would give us divinity.

Our being born again in God would be a nativity from the divine womb.... Our death would be, as with all babies, a going home to mother....

"Hebrew poetry and Christian metaphor have made our divine Sovereign only a king. But a king, say the fairy tales, requires a queen. The universe must be balanced. So the court was filled. The Queen is Mary, bearing the king's son and wedded to Christ the King.... And again, the Queen is the Church, which is sometimes a virgin, sometimes a whore, always the desired, the divine lover, married to God and reigning with God over all of creation....

"But it is all so many words, noises grunting out adoration, a cat purring affection, babble ill-informed and misdirected, and alphabet shouted out into the abyss, preceded by a prayer that the angels will shape it into a canticle of praise."

* Ramshaw, Gail. *Searching for Language.* Washington, D.C.: Pastoral Press, 1988.

Ramshaw-Schmidt, Gail. "The Gender of God". In *Feminist Theology— A Reader,* edited by Ann Loades, pp. 158–70. Louisville, Ky.: Westminster/John Knox Press, 1990.

Ramshaw-Schmidt, Gail. "An Inclusive Language Lectionary", *Worship* 58 (1984): 35.

* Ramshaw-Schmidt, Gail, and Gordon Lathrop, eds. *An Inclusive Language Lectionary.* Revised edition. 4 vols. Atlanta: John Knox Press, 1986.

Ricoeur, Paul. *The Rule of Metaphor.* Toronto: Univ. of Toronto Press, 1977.

Riley, Maria. *Transforming Feminism.* Kansas City: Sheed and Ward, 1989.

"For Catholic feminists who choose to remain within the faith tradition, the transformation of the church beyond patriarchy is the enduring agenda. Most of our writings and strategies have been aimed at revealing and transforming the patriarchy of the church as it takes shape in its all-male hierarchy, in its God-language and imagery, its sacramental life, its anthropology, its articulation of a male-defined theological, scriptural, and moral magisterial [teaching], and its subtle but all-pervasive misogyny" (xiii).

Ruether, Rosemary. "Feminism and Religious Faith: Renewal or New Creation?" *Religion and Intellectual Life* 9 (Winter 1986): 7–20.

Lists five questions on the agenda of religious feminism: "1) How can the elements of the religion be reinterpreted from a female perspective so that they help to make women subjects of their own history? 2) Can religion and spirituality function to enhance the liberationist transformation of history rather than the sacralization of male domination? 3) How can stories and symbols drawn from religious traditions be translated from their androcentric form into one defined by and for women? 4) Should we continue merely to translate from androcentric traditions or do we need to go beyond them and create new stories, new symbols, etc.? 5) Should women remain divided from each other and immured in androcentric traditions or should women unite across religious boundaries in some synthesis of the perspectives traditionally set against each other?"

Ruether, Rosemary. *Religion and Sexism.* New York: Simon and Schuster, 1974.

Ruether, Rosemary. *Sexism and God-Talk: Toward a Feminist Theology.* Boston: Beacon Press, 1983.

"The proscription of idolatry must . . . be extended to verbal pictures. When the word *Father* is taken literally to mean that God is male and not female, represented by males and not females, then this word becomes idolatrous" (p. 66). "Parent model for the divine has negative resonances. . . . It suggests a kind of permanent parent-child relationship to God. . . . Patriarchal theology uses the parent image for God to prolong spiritual infantilism as virtue and to make autonomy and assertion of free will a sin. Parenting in patriarchal society also becomes the way of enculturating us to the stereotypic male and female roles" p. 69.

Ruether, Rosemary. *Women-Church: Theology and Practice of Feminist Liturgical Communities.* San Francisco: Harper and Row, 1986.

Russell, Letty, ed. *Feminist Interpretation of the Bible.* Philadelphia: Westminster Press, 1985.

Russell, Letty, ed. *The Liberating Word: A Guide to Non-sexist Interpretation of the Bible.* Philadelphia: Westminster Press, 1975. See especially "Changing Language in the Church", pp. 82–98.

Saiving, Valerie. "The Human Situation: A Feminine View". In *Womanspirit Rising,* edited by Carol Christ and Judith Plaskow. New York: Harper and Row, 1979.

Schneiders, Sandra M. *Beyond Patching: Faith and Feminism in the Catholic Church.* New York: Paulist Press, 1991.

Schneiders, Sandra M. "Women and Power in the Church: A New Testament Reflection". *Proceedings of the Catholic Theological Society of America* 37 (June 10–13, 1982), 123–28.

Schneiders, Sandra M. *Women and the Word: The Gender of God in the New Testament and the Spirituality of Women.* New York: Paulist Press, 1986.

Showalter, Elaine, ed. *The New Feminist Criticism: Essays on Women, Literature and Theory.* New York: Pantheon, 1985.

Spretnak, Charlene, ed. *The Politics of Women's Spirituality.* Garden City, N.Y.: Anchor Press, 1982.

Starhawk (Miriam Simos). *The Spiral Dance: A Rebirth of the Ancient Religion of the Great Goddess.* San Francisco: Harper and Row, 1989.

Starhawk (Miriam Simos). *Truth or Dare: Encounters with Power, Authority, and Mystery.* San Francisco: Harper and Row, 1987.

"The Goddess, the Gods, the great powers, are the material world, are us. If they extend beyond us they do so like the sun's corona flaring beyond its core. No power is entirely separate from our own being. [Witchcraft opens] new eyes and sees that there is nothing to be saved *from,* no struggle of life *against* the universe, no God outside the world to be feared and obeyed, only the Goddess, the Mother, the turning spiral that whirls us in and out of existence" (p. 27).

Starhawk (Miriam Simos). "Witchcraft as Goddess Religion". In *The Politics of Women's Spirituality,* edited by Charlene Spretnak. Garden City, N.Y.: Anchor Press, 1982.

Tavard, George H. "Sexist Language in Theology?" In *Woman: New Dimensions,* edited by Walter Burghardt. New York: Paulist Press, 1977.

Thistlethwaite, Susan Brooks, "God Language and the Trinity". *EKU–UCC Newsletter* 5, no. 1 (Feb. 1984): 21.

Thorne, Barrie, Cheris Kramarae, and Nancy Henlye. *Language, Gender, and Society.* Rowley: Newbury House, 1983.

"Transforming Scripture, Transforming Ourselves: A Report on the Inclusive Language Project". *Priests for Equality News & Notes* (Spring, 1992).

"If one word can be used to describe the process of developing inclusive language readings, it is *transformational.* . . . What we are doing is developing ways to proclaim Sacred Scripture in a non-sexist and non-classist manner. . . . To do this, we change the forms of language that perpetuate sexist and classist concepts. What we are challenging are traditional ways of speaking about God. . . . This process begins with looking through the standard translations of Scripture for sexist and classist forms and attitudes. . . . Realizing that any translation is an interpretation, we do not limit ourselves to the standard translations, but also look at the other inclusive language texts and style forms in order to get a sense of how others have worked through the problems of sexism in the Scriptures. We go over each text *line by line* in order to ensure a faithful, non-sexist rendering in both content and style. . . . We do this by attending to the recent feminist scholarship in recovering the place of women in Scripture . . . " (pp. 1–2 [emphasis in original]).

Trible, Phyllis. "Feminist Hermeneutics and Biblical Studies". In *Feminist Theology: A Reader,* pp. 23–29. Louisville, Ky.: Westminster/John Knox, 1990.

"Born and bred in a land of patriarchy, the Bible abounds in male imagery and language. For centuries interpreters have explored and exploited this male language to articulate theology: to shape the contours and content of the Church, synagogue and academy. . . . " "As a critique of culture in light of misogyny, feminism is a prophetic movement, examining the status quo, pronouncing judgement and calling for repentence. In various ways this hermeneutical pursuit interacts with the Bible in its remoteness, complexity, diversity and contemporaneity to yield new understandings of both text and interpreter."

Trible, Phyllis. "God, Nature of in the Old Testament". In *Interpreter's Dictionary of the Bible.* Supplement. 1976, pp. 368–86.

Trible, Phyllis. "The Pilgrim Bible on a Feminist Journey". *The Auburn News* (Spring 1988).

Trible, Phyllis. *Texts of Terror: Literary Feminist Readings of Biblical Narratives.* Philadelphia: Fortress Press, 1984.

Trible, Phyllis. *God and the Rhetoric of Sexuality.* Philadelphia: Fortress Press, 1978.

Visser't Hooft, W. A. *The Fatherhood of God in an Age of Emancipation.* Geneva: World Council of Churches, 1982.

* Wren, Brian. *What Language Shall I Borrow"—God-Talk in Worship; a Male Response to Feminist Theology.* London: SCM; New York: Crossroad, 1989.

II. Style handbooks, manuals and dictionaries espousing "gender-neutral" language (Compiled by Germaine F. Murray, Ph.D.)

Allen, Pamela Payne, "Taking the Next Step in Inclusive Language". *The Christian Century* (April 23, 1986).

Baron, Dennis E. *Grammar and Gender.* New Haven, Conn.: Yale University Press, 1986.

Capek, Mary Ellen S. *A Woman's Thesaurus.* New York: Harper and Row, 1987.

Chopp, Rebecca S. *The Power to Speak: Feminism, Language, God.* New York: Crossroad, 1989.

Daly, Mary. *Websters' First New Intergalactic Wickedary of the English Language.* Boston: Beacon Press, 1987.

Dictionary of Cautionary Words and Phrases, compiled by the 1989 Multicultural Management Fellows of the University of Missouri Journalism School.

Dumond, Val. *The Elements of Nonsexist Usage: A Guide to Inclusive Spoken and Written English.* New York: Prentice Hall, 1990.

Dworkin, Andrea. *Our Blood: Prophecies and Discourses on Sexual Politics.* New York: Harper and Row, 1976.

Eichler, Margrit. *Nonsexist Research Methods.* Boston: Unwin Hyman, 1988.

Frank, Francine Harriet Wattman. *Language, Gender, and Professional Writing: Theoretical Approaches and Guidelines for Nonsexist Usage.* New York: Commission on the Status of Women in the Profession. Modern Language Association of America, 1989.

Frye, Marilyn. *The Politics of Reality: Essays in Feminist Theory.* Trumansburg, N.Y.: Crossing Press, 1983.

Goldfield, Bina. *The Efemcipated English Handbook.* New York: Westover Press, 1983.

Hardesty, Nancy. *Inclusive Language in the Church.* Atlanta: John Knox Press, 1987.

Kramarae, Cheris, and Paula A. Treichler. *A Feminist Dictionary.* Boston: Pandora Press, 1985.

Lennert, Midge, and Norma Wilson. *A Woman's New World Dictionary.* Lomita, Calif.: 51% Publications, 1973.

* Maggio, Rosalie, *The Dictionary of Bias-Free Usage: A Guide to Nondiscriminatory Language.* Phoenix, Ariz.: Oryx Press, 1991.

Mairs, Nancy. "Who Are You?" In *The Norton Reader.* Arthur Eastman, et al. 8th ed. New York: W. W. Norton, 1992.

* Miller, Casey, and Kate Swift. *The Handbook of Nonsexist Writing.* New York: Harper and Row, 1988.

* Miller, Casey, and Kate Swift. "What about New Human Pronouns?" *Current* 138:43–49.

Miller, Casey, and Kate Swift. "Who's in Charge of the English Language?" In *The Norton Reader.* Arthur Eastman, et al. 8th ed., pp. 363–69. New York: W. W. Norton, 1992.

Mitchell, Felicia. "Including Women at Emory & Henry College: Evolution of an Inclusive Language Policy". *Women's Studies Quarterly* (Spring 1990).

Neaman, Judith S., and Carole G. Silver. *Kind Words.* New York: Avon Books, 1991.

Random House Webster's College Dictionary. New York: Random House, 1991.

   [incorporates feminist-coinages, e.g., 'wimmin']

Rosenau, Pauline Marie. *Post-Modernism and the Social Sciences.* Princeton, N.J.: Princeton University Press, 1991. [Pamphlet required for Princeton graduate students.]

Spender, Dale. *Man Made Language.* London: Routledge and Kagan Paul, 1985.

   Feminist linguistic theory influential in subsequent Critical Studies and Literature Studies.

Spender, Dale. *Women of Ideas and What Men Have Done to Them.* London: Routledge and Kegan Paul, 1982.

Three Rivers, Amoja. *Cultural Etiquette: A Guide for the Well-Intentioned.* Indian Valley, Va.: Market Wimmin, 1990.

Women and Language in Transition. ed. Joyce Penfield. Albany, N.Y.: State University of New York Press, 1987.

* Items marked with an asterisk are listed as "resources" in Bishop Edward D. Head's *Guidelines for Inclusive Language: Diocese of Buffalo* (July 26, 1992).

INDEX

"Abba and Jesus' Relation to God" (J. Fitzmyer), 172

abortion, lv, 39; and abstraction, 13–14; and the body, 15; and Church, xxvn, li, 36; and feminism, 35, 48, 257, 258n, 259, 260; and Jesus, 269

Abraham, 27, 40, 121

abstraction, 5–11, 12, 13, 20, 23, 62; and the body, 13–16

Adam, xxii, 238; and Christ, 190–91; and Eve, 305, 310; and "man", 143, 190, 332

Adelphi College, 294

adelphoi, 294, 338

adoption: and God as Father, 166–69, 219–20, 222

Advisory Committee (ICEL), xxxix, xl, xlii

Aelfric, 111

Aelfric's *Grammar,* 230

Aelfric's *Lives of the Saints,* 231

Agatha, St., 231

Aggeler, Sr. Maureen, R.S.C.J., xxvn, 343

Albright, William, 159

Alfred's Bede, 110

Ali, Muhammad, 311

"Alternatives to Sexist Usage", 19

American Bible Society, xlv, 82, 90

Anastasius of Sinai, 305

Anat, 159

Andrewes, Bishop Lancelot, 143

aner, 99, 100, 160n, 279

Anglican Church, l–li, 20, 213–16, 255n

anthropos, 99–101, 102–3, 109, 279, 332

anti-Catholicism, 40–41

anti-semitism, xxxix, 40, 137, 290

Aorchengota, 231

Apostolic See, xxxiiin, 255n, 338; and feminism, xlvi, 179, 255–56; guidelines of, xxxiv, lii, and ICEL, 263, 270; and Scripture translations, xxxvin, 179–80, 328

Aquinas, St. Thomas, 200

Arianism, 263, 298

Arnobius, 220

Ashtoreth, 217

Association of Catholic Colleges and Universities, xl

International Commission on
English in the Liturgy
(*continued*)
feminism, xxvi, xxviii–
xxix, xlvii, 255; and inclusive language, xxix, xxxv–
xxxvii, xxxviii–xlii, xlvii,
lii, 97, 251n; incompetence
of, 262, 263, 270; and life in
womb, 269; and liturgy,
xxxiiin, xlvii, 254, 262;
misleading expressions of,
266–70; mistranslations by,
263–66; "Preface for
Thanksgiving", 253, 262;
and racist language, 253,
262; and retranslation of
Missal, xxxv–xlviii
International Consultation on
English Texts (ICET), xxxii
Irenaeus, St., 183, 185, 212, 213,
266
Isaac, 27
Isaiah, 218
Ishtar, 308
Isis, 308
Israel, 44, 154, 197, 331; adopted
by Father, 166–67, 168–69,
219; cultures surrounding
ancient, 155–60, 163, 165,
168; and the Father, 218–19;
as feminine, 18, 319, 335. *See
also* Jews; Judaism
Italian language, 63, 72, 74,
144, 285

Jacob, 27, 314

Jagger, Alison, 285–86
James, St., 259
James I (king of England) and
IV (king of Scotland), 231
Jean-Nesmy, Dom Claude, 181
Jeremiah, 163–64, 314
Jerome, St., 105, 184, 186, 304
Jerusalem Bible, xxxiv, 82, 83,
90; French, 84, 85, 87;
German, 84; and "man", 97,
102–4, 106–7; New, xxxvi,
97, 99, 100, 102–4, 106–7;
samples from, 84–85, 87
Jesuit School of Theology
(GTU), xxvi
Jesus Christ, lviii, 40, 51, 206,
264, 266; and Adam, 190–
91; calls God Father, 154–55,
187–89, 210–11, 220, 221–23;
as Child, liv, 293–94; and
Church, 181, 204, 324, 340;
and culture, 88, 324; and
Father, 151, 153, 187–89,
219, 220, 264–65, 301;
feminine imagery for, 244–
45; and feminism, 37, 199,
257, 295; and hell, 87–88;
as Human One, 100, 121,
293–94; Incarnation of, 221,
268–70, 318–19; knowing
God through, 88, 200, 204,
223, 227; as Lamb of God,
309, 311; and "man", 144,
190–91; names for, 302, 329,
334–35; and names of
Trinity, 299–300, 306;
nature of, 245, 297–99; and

Jesus Christ (*continued*)
our Father, 90, 210, 223,
228; and Peter, 83–87, 324;
in psalms, 179, 181–88, 189–
92, 334–35; and revelation,
67, 88, 197, 204, 205–6, 227;
and Scripture, 10, 82, 90,
189, 209–10, 334; as Son of
Man, 100, 109; in various
heresies, 213, 298, 299. *See
also* God; Trinity; Son
Jews, 155–60, 163, 165, 168,
337–38. *See also* anti-
Semitism; Israel; Judaism
John Paul II, Pope, 18, 152–
53, 244–45, 283, 284, 325;
Love and Responsibility, 284;
Mulieris dignitatem, 152–53,
325
John, St., 219
Joint Committee on Inclusive
Language (NCCB), 327,
328, 339
Jonah, 164
Jones, Rev. Alexander,
xxxivn
Joseph, St., 221, 276
Judaism, li, liii, 38, 44, 214, 290,
291; and fatherhood of God,
166–69; and gender of
God, 155–65, 218. *See also*
anti-Semitism, Hebrew
language; Israel; Jews
Judas, 183
Julian of Norwich, 317
Juno, 308
Jurist, xl

justice, liii, 48, 120, 238; and
feminism, xxiv, 35, 48, 196,
325
Justin, St., 266

Kant, Immanuel, 201n
Kenny, Anthony, xxxivn
Kett, Joseph, 120, 274
Kimmel, Rev. Alvin, Jr., 1n,
139–40, 216–17
Kimmey, Rev. Jimmye, 140, 142
King James Version Bible, 58,
62, 81, 231, 290, 335–36
King, Martin Luther, Jr., 141
Klein, Melanie, 313
Kollontai, Alexandra, 260n
Kramarae, Cheris, 97
Krisman, Fr. Ronald F., xln
Kyrios, 334

Lakoff, Robin, 127, 128
language, xxviii, lvii, 45–47,
63, 145, 330; and abstraction,
5–16, 20, 23, 62; artificial
changes to, xlix–l, 127n,
133, 335; biblical, 205, 209–
11, 254–55; Chinese, 280; and
Church, l, 12–16, 56; and
control, 17–20, 134–37; and
culture, xlix–l, 126, 129, 275,
280, 327; descriptions of, 3–
4, 28, 52–53, 58, 69, 95–96,
122; and determinism, 30;
Eskimo, 124, 126; French,
63, 70–71, 125, 144; German,
32, 87; Greek, 87, 99, 100,
109, 129, 279–80; Hebrew,